A New America

An awakened future on our horizon

80 July 2005
To David Isaacs & Juanita Brown

For a global awakening!

from Tislu Alex

America is a society whose strength
is based in part
on the hopes and aspirations that
arise from a longing for enlightenment
and compassion.

…What choices will Americans
make to tap this enormous potential?

How to Read This Book

THIS BOOK CAN BE APPROACHED IN SEVERAL DIFFERENT WAYS:

A. The usual method: cover to cover.

B. Begin with a **Part Overview,** which provides an encapsulated view of that portion of the book.

C. Read Part Four first to familiarize yourself with the research upon which this book is based.

A detailed **TABLE OF CONTENTS** is provided with chapter and section headings. This provides an immediate overview of the tapestry of *A New America.*

A FEW KEY CONCEPTS: Describes several significant concepts introduced in the book that will allow you to more easily grasp the detailed discussions found throughout.

Each **CHAPTER FACEPLATE** features an appropriately thought-provoking quote and a brief detailing of the chapter's key concepts. Turn the page for the Chapter At A Glance.

Each **CHAPTER AT A GLANCE** serves as a handy checklist of the chapter sections. Once into the chapter, you'll find various elements that relate directly to the contents, from graphics to quotes to director's comments.

D. Open to any **chapter**, which begins with a short synopsis of the key concepts of that chapter, followed by a **Chapter At A Glance** on the next page that lists the chapter sections.

E. At any point, refer to **Key Concepts**, which describe significant concepts important to the understanding of the discussions in this book.

There are **SIX PARTS** to *A New America*. The face plate of each Part highlights a portion of the cover graphic representing possible stages in the evolution in humanity.

Each **PART OVERVIEW** provides a synopsis of the salient points of that Part and a sense of the range and depth of content discussed. Turn the page and you'll find the first chapter in that Part.

A wide spectrum of **QUOTES** are found throughout providing background from context to commentary to supportive analysis.

Many illustrative, full-color **GRAPHICS** are used to provide conceptual validity.

APPENDICES are available at the end of the book if you desire in-depth information on several topics. A complete listing of appendices can be found in the Table of Contents.

Table of Contents

PART ONE

Elements of Hope

PART TWO

Social &
Political Change

PART THREE

Strategic Initiatives of Connection & Movement

PART FOUR

A New Look at the American Electorate

PART FIVE
Epilogue

PART SIX
Appendices

Acknowledgements

First and foremost, Tish and I want to acknowledge the important contributions made by Dr. John J. Hudy. We are very grateful for John's enthusiasm and commitment to the research effort and the endless analytical exploration and discussions that used his talents and experience. John's involvement covered roughly three years as we delved into various insights and ideas and tested them through statistical and commonsense analysis. His statistical experience and insight were invaluable to the development of the research data and its meaning overall. We will always appreciate the frequent and stimulating discussions and reflections on humanity we had as we explored the implications and applications of this work. We wound around many byways of human consciousness and values, sometimes humorously, sometimes with great consternation, yet always with optimism for the future. The spring of 2004, Dr. Hudy passed on to another plane of existence. Thank you John for your being, and may you continue to grow and evolve in your spirit.

We especially want to thank David Christel, friend and editor, whose support and involvement over a two-year period was so essential in bringing this work to a skillful and thoughtful completion. His depth of social and spiritual awareness and experience enabled him to grasp the scope and depth of this project, as well as see its tremendous potentials on many levels.

Our thanks and deepest appreciation for the patience and fortitude of our graphic designer, Suzanne Haddon. Her technical and artistic abilities, as well as philosophical attunement, were so important in completing the complex color and design work needed to make the best presentation of the rich complexity of material this book presents to a wide variety of readers.

A member of the original team of research professionals, John Hetherington was able to step in to complete some of the analysis and data interpretation that halted upon John Hudy's passing. Many, many "thank you's" to John Hetherington for his enthusiasm and grasp of the social implications of this project.

Our many thanks to ND Koster, our indefatigable proof reader, for his attention to so many details and his goodwill and support.

Lastly, we wish to acknowledge our friend and agent Bill Gladstone for believing in this project, and everyone else who contributed in one way or another.

Thank you!

THIS BOOK IS DEDICATED

TO EVERYONE WHO IS

AN AGENT OF HIGHER PURPOSE

AND POSITIVE CHANGE...

AND TO EVERYONE WHO HAS EVER

WONDERED ABOUT THEIR

OWN TRUE NATURE.

Prologue

We are all members of a very interesting social biology, living on an incredibly beautiful planet, and we have been blessed with an innate capacity to consciously evolve in all facets of our individual and collective being. True, most people are not awakened to these possibilities and appear to be focused on an "old game" that feeds a devolving spiral.

While much progress has been made, humanity has yet to recognize its members have more in common with one another than differences between races, religions, or nationalities. The "old game" uses these differences to manipulate people to become self-reinforcing. Hence, a "new game" is needed that will encourage people to realize their tremendous potential and the possibility of living in a state of grace.

The key is in making the choice to create something *new* that serves our extraordinary future potential. The alternative is to risk "going down with the ship" by remaining in the confines of an "old game" – one that is rapidly falling apart and endangering everyone's future.

This book includes key elements for political, social, economic, and cultural changes that can facilitate a global awakening. It can be used as a guide, providing basic and advanced insights into how it could be possible for individuals and human society to make a massive shift into a more enlightened society – together.

Alex Kochkin and Tish Van Camp, Directors

Introduction

Dear Reader,

This is really about *all* of humanity. *A New America: An Awakened Future on Our Horizon* offers new research and new insight into U.S. society, the most diverse country in the world. This material demonstrates practical pathways in our personal and social psyche directly leading to a better way of living for all human beings. It is a story based on a remarkable national research study conducted at the turn of the millennium. It is also a story based on many years' experience with philanthropy, business, technologies, social/political activism, and spiritual awakening.

We have written this for *anyone* who cares and wants to make a positive difference – as well as for those people who are in positions of leadership and greater influence to make immediate use of this material. Our motivation in conducting formal research of this scope was to determine the extent to which we could identify and articulate a greater unity within diversity throughout society. We are excited that this research project succeeded beyond measure.

In this story there are ultimately no simple good guys or bad guys. Instead, we offer "discernment with compassion" to bridge the illusory gulf between people. "Illusory," you say, "aren't these very 'real' differences at the root of conflict and suffering?" Yes… and no. Consider that your consciousness is an aspect of a greater consciousness. This is a non-physical counterpart to the idea that your physical body is really composed of "star-stuff" and that your body's chemical make-up is remarkably similar to the surface of the Earth. It is in this light that our perceived differences can be seen as micro-cosmic variations of the greater whole macrocosm of creation.

Perhaps our differences are simply one way the vast sea of creative consciousness can better understand its cosmic self and the potential of creation. Perhaps human society, as a collection of "micro-wholes" comprising a "macro-whole," got a little too caught up in its own individual "beingness" – as individuals and as a species. This has been the basis for justifying individual gain at the expense of another – and for humans to justify their domination over nature at the expense of the planetary ecosystem.

So how to find solutions to this situation? Any *genuine* solutions will require us to be honestly *open* to the possibility that there could be a higher common denominator – and then *to act* upon this awareness by *welcoming it* as it becomes more *visible* in our daily lives. As a basic process, this has within it the potential to facilitate a growing capacity for positive change – a growing capacity that has the potential to rapidly overcome what may appear at times to be a hopeless situation.

In this book, we explain new strategies that can bridge our individual and collective *"uniquenesses"* so often mistaken as irreconcilable *differences*. In so doing, the tremendous spirit and energy of an awakening population can be harnessed for the good of all. Through this we can create new social processes, structures, and institutions whose purpose is to help further our evolution as human beings in a positive way. This is emerging in the world now and is a focus of The Global Interchange.

A New America: An Awakened Future on Our Horizon helps people recognize that they have the innate capacity to intend and to choose new ways of being for themselves and for all. This book shows how there are other choices than the narrow ones placed daily before us by our dominant social institutions. The material contained in this book shows how and where there is a greater unity within our extraordinary diversity at a basic social and individual level.

Moreover, we are all at heart, first and foremost, spiritual beings who happen to be having human experiences. Once this is grasped by more people and made part of our daily lives, we will find to our surprise how fast and how enjoyable positive, conscious evolutionary change can be!

We each have the innate gifts to be a part of birthing a new world free of conflict and domination.

A New America is not only about Americans, it is about everyone and concerns all humanity.

Please do not mistake our intent and think that we are saying that the U.S. represents the world and that as the U.S. goes, so should the world. We are not being so American-centric. What we are saying is that there is an overriding universality among all people, regardless of nationality, race, or religious identification. We are saying that every person on this planet holds much the same higher aspirations as one another – and that these are not reflected or expressed in our social institutions. By higher aspiration, we mean the innate drive to gain deeper meaning and connection with life and creation as a whole. This has nothing to do with baser strivings for material gain. That the U.S. is made up of one of the most diverse populations on the planet makes it easier for it to serve as a microcosm for many others.

As an economic, political, cultural and military superpower that has gained much from its dominance, the U.S. has a unique responsibility to the world. We also have a unique opportunity to evolve into a true participatory democracy and to re-energize the concept of civil spirituality from which to guide our values, ethics, and actions. It is in this light that national-level research in this book can be applied. (Future research can include other countries, as well as more in-depth work in the U.S.)

Most importantly, to us and to the greater value of this material, this is about humanity – all of humanity.

Lastly, some readers may wonder if we are or have been members of or heavily influenced by a particular spiritual or religious tradition or teacher. No, not really, but having grown up in the U.S. (a predominately Christian society) and attended church as children, we came into a world dominated by western Christianity. Nevertheless, we have always paid attention to what has inspired us from our own experiences and from those of many others. Each of us has, in our own way, always sought to realize "greater truth" than what passes for ordinary reality. We have come to recognize and honor the potential every individual has to fully realize a higher consciousness beyond what passes for the ordinary individual self. In so doing, anyone can know their true self and personal connection to greater levels of cosmic awareness and consciousness of the sacred – something for which humanity has invented many names.

In service and friendship,

Alex Kochkin and Tish Van Camp, Directors
Fund For Global Awakening and The Global Interchange

"In our ways, spiritual consciousness is the highest form of politics.

We must live in harmony with the natural world and recognize that excessive exploitation can only lead to our own destruction.

We cannot trade the welfare of our future generations for profit.

…We are instructed to carry love for one another, and to show great respect for all beings of the earth.

…Our energy is the combined will of all people with the spirit of the natural world, to be of one body, one heart, and one mind."

– Chief Leon Shenandoah
Fire Keeper of the Central Fire
for the Haudenosaunee (Iroquois) Confederacy

Food for Thought, or What if…?

…there was a widespread social movement that places the awakening of our hearts in the forefront of every person, community, and nation as a gift for all humanity? What if it could involve nearly everyone, regardless of beliefs and social class and be supported at the highest levels of government and social and cultural leadership? What if this movement had a significant grassroots presence in communities throughout the world and resonated with people's highest aspirations and values in alignment with their higher heart consciousness? Imagine how such a presence could lead to a rapid and beautiful transformation in consciousness and institutions. Imagine, if you will, Decade of the Heart.

…there was an Internet portal entirely dedicated to personal and global transformation for a more compassionate and caring world? What if it was not commercially oriented, and offered a wide range of news and information, interactive discussion services, e-mail, as well as comprehensive Internet access? What if such a service also helped support and sustain local and global initiatives and gave people powerful reasons to be involved more personally in creating a better world at whatever local or global level they could? What if such a service could help establish new social economic patterns for media communications, charitable giving, finance, and positive future innovations? Imagine, if you will, The Global Interchange.

…people the world over began waking up in the morning with a greater sense of clarity, vitality, and purpose? What if, in waking up, people became more intimately aware of their higher consciousness, a higher conscious that is unique to everyone and at the same time, something we are all part of? What if people began to see themselves as spiritual beings having a human experience – a grand context for all that humanity has come to be? Imagine, if you will, seeing the world with new eyes and with a new found intelligence: discernment with compassion.

A Few Key Concepts

Throughout these discussions, frequent reference is made to broad terms and concepts that require understanding in a contemporary context, chief among them the old and new social paradigms (or world views), positive future, global awakening, future-present, civil spirituality, and discernment with compassion.

OLD PARADIGM refers to the tendency in human society to dominate and exploit nature, and to dominate and compete as individuals, cultures, or nations with one another. In social organizations, this orientation takes the form of the command-and-control style of management, and objectification in science – the artificial separation of object and subject. Individuation or individual identity is sought through conflict. This model is rooted in the perception of scarcity and fear for survival. It takes conflict and scarcity as a natural state of being, and division, separation, and control as its goals.

NEW PARADIGM represents the emergent tendency in human society to cooperate with one another, whether as individuals, cultures, or nations, and to live and work with, rather than against, nature. This model focuses on awareness of the whole in human, physical, and spiritual terms and on new frontiers of consciousness. In social organizations, this orientation takes the form of cooperation. Self-awareness is understood in the context of the whole. This model is rooted in the perception of abundance, and in science through the widening understanding of the interconnectivity of natural phenomena. Wholistic and integrative, this model assumes compassion, balance, and interconnectivity as a way of being and incorporates unity within diversity, universal compassion, and healing as its goals.

POSITIVE FUTURE is a general term referring to transformational outcomes of the evolution of human consciousness through the generating of new societal structures and processes that bridge polarities. It honors universal interconnectivity, and enables individuals and nations to achieve deeper connections with a higher wisdom. Inherent in this term is the hope that humankind can and will move beyond the constraints of the "old paradigm," and the long history of social, cultural, political, and religious conflict to fulfill a higher human destiny – a global spiritual and social awakening.

GLOBAL AWAKENING means individuals and communities becoming aware of and embracing their authentic nature – one of interconnectedness, service, nurturance, and spirituality, as we express extraordinary dimensions of our larger being. It is remembering who we truly are as we seek ways of developing global-scale processes and structures specifically designed to assist the fullest expression of social and spiritual awakening. Global awakening also encompasses an appreciation and acceptance of the diverse qualities and uniqueness of all humanity's contributions, and how individual and community actions have global impact.

FUTURE-PRESENT refers to the influence of placing our attention on that of our higher nature calling to us from our horizon of being. This becomes, in effect, an attractor helping us navigate in the present in accord with a new paradigm of being while we decouple from old paradigm structures and beliefs that do not serve our conscious evolution.

CIVIL SPIRITUALITY describes a global atmosphere wherein society openly acknowledges the universal interconnection of all people, creation, and consciousness. New ethics would emerge to guide thought and action for the highest good of all. There would be no place for any individual or society to dominate another, or for humanity to be in conflict with nature. People would be free to explore their fundamental nature as spiritual beings without that experience being based on suffering. This new civil spirituality would spread universal love and mutual regard among all people. It is within such a larger context that the world's religions could find coherence around ancient truths that have been obscured for too long. The potential for this would be far-reaching, as it would liberate enormous amounts of human energy for creation of a positive future, rather than fighting over the present.

DISCERNMENT WITH COMPASSION represents an ever-evolving broadness of mind that combines the use of free-will and innate intelligence to resolve specifics within the context of an integral whole. It emphasizes the interconnectedness of a greater "oneness" that we all share as sentient beings in a larger cosmos of creation.

PART ONE

Elements of Hope

PART ONE:
Elements of Hope

Within each of us reside the seeds of our highest and most sincere aspirations for a more positive future, one encompassing not only immediate family and community, but all humankind and beyond. Today it is abundantly clear that Americans, as well as all humanity, are at a major crossroads. Many are seeking answers and the ways and means for creating a world of consideration, authenticity, accountability, and connection on more intrinsic levels. The question is: Are we ready to step upon the path of an ascending spiral of conscious evolution based on the core spiritual values and beliefs of compassion, cooperation, and the interconnectedness of all life? We believe it to be possible and achievable.

A New America: An Awakened Future on Our Horizon is based partly upon an extensive, three-year formal research study and partly on intuitive insight and personal experience. The research, called *In Our Own Words 2000*, is of a quality seldom seen. It set out to explore the social and spiritual consciousness of Americans and to examine scientific evidence for a greater unity within our diversity. This landmark study, conducted by an accomplished, professional research team, reveals that within our vast diversity, there is greater consensus of accord than we may realize or find evident in mass culture at present.

One value derived from research of this caliber is that it provides a representative picture of society upon which very real strategies and actions can be based. The research shows the extent to which a diverse population has underlying it a strong sense of connection and goodness. It encompasses personal connection to one another, creation, nature, and with the cosmos and higher consciousness. It expresses a desire to help others, support nations helping nations, and to make a difference in the world. It relates to beliefs in the sacred interconnectedness of all life, a widely encompassing spirituality going beyond traditional religious practices, and belief in a global awakening of humankind to a higher consciousness.

Unlike the bulk of opinion polling and typical survey research, *A New America* detects and explains deeper drivers of our behavior, both conscious and unconscious. A unique analysis of the 2000 U.S. election is also offered, further demonstrating these points by examining differences in voting patterns.

Major new typologies of Americans are disclosed that will help bridge our differences with a set of core values and beliefs not commonly known or acknowledged. One of these typologies is The 8 American Types. It offers a context in which individuals and society can better understand themselves, and shows a coherent set of overlapping patterns offering practical ways in which to bridge our society as a whole.

A New America offers hope for the future by offering a roadmap through which "discernment with compassion" can guide our actions to create a positive future. As we re-examine values and beliefs that have often been implicit in our way of life, these initial study findings address the heart of global conflict. Recognizing a universal context of the interconnection of all life and consciousness can allow humankind to become wiser stewards of ourselves as a species and for this planet as a whole.

In this material, we make a case for the social basis of a "culture of wisdom," which currently lies close enough to the surface of our personal and group awareness that it could be quickly brought forth in response to both a new type of leadership and a new type of social movement.

We need only *choose* a new future for ourselves.

CHAPTER 1

Light at the End of the Tunnel

*"We are not human beings having a spiritual experience,
but rather spiritual beings having a human experience."*

– Pierre Teilhard de Chardin

The spectrum of human endeavors is as astonishing and far-reaching as the exceptional diversity of human consciousness and depth of expression. Our global history is testament to extraordinary achievements, as well as painful shortcomings. In spite of and because of the peaks and valleys of our shared human drama, we have now arrived at a decisive crossroads. The basis for a positive future lies before us – we have but to choose this for ourselves and then to act on this impulse. We have the potential; do we have the awareness that will carry us forward toward realizing our highest aspirations now, as a planetary human society?

There are so many people today who are seeking ways to use spiritual consciousness to make their lives better, as well as the lives of others. There are also many people who have little idea how this can change their lives for the better, yet nevertheless recognize spirituality as important to them.

What will it take?

Chapter 1 At A Glance

Light at the End of the Tunnel

- Basis for a Positive Future
- Where We're At
- A New Way

The New Social-Spiritual Landscape

A New America is a seminal work demonstrating, through landmark research, our potential to evolve to a new level of consciousness – one that will allow us to realize our highest aspirations of interconnectedness, integrity, reconciliation, and ethical responsibility. Through a new perspective of "discernment with compassion," we can create new structures, processes, and initiatives beyond our current paradigms that hold the potential to move humanity toward a more positive future on a personal level and at a global scale.

In times of great uncertainty, individuals and entire societies can temporarily forget who they are as sentient beings – a part of something much greater than their own selves – whether as individuals or as nations. America is a diverse society, with the potential to show the world new ways of being that transcend conflict and retribution. Much has been accomplished in little more than two centuries of nationhood. Much remains to be done, however. What choices will Americans make to tap such enormous potential?

There must be a new social movement of people in which is found a new common ground and language based on mutual interconnection and regard for one another and the ecosystem. A new civil spirituality must be encouraged that transcends religious differences. New types of political and social leaders must be encouraged who are fundamentally aligned with this. Young people need to be given an equal place from which to express their highest aspirations and find fertile ground for growth. This will be the beginning of a new epoch for humanity wherein a culture of wisdom and generosity replaces a culture of conflict and domination that only benefits the few. Once this is more widely expressed, it will find fertile ground among all people.

A greater positive context already exists throughout all aspects of American society and culture. It flows from a tremendous reservoir of core values and aspirations countless numbers of Americans share in common. We will see, as A New America continues to explore these commonalities, greater levels of connection that exist rather than alienation. And through discernment with compassion, we can appeal to a deeper wisdom residing in each of our hearts and higher minds to find a way that appeals to the collective higher nature of the human race.

Basis for a Positive Future

In times of crisis and necessity, extraordinary solutions are called for. We are now living in such a period. Only by recognizing a *greater positive context* in which we can truly embrace everyone, will we reach beyond suffering and conflict and usher in a new era in which war, conflict, and adversity can eventually become anachronisms.

This greater positive context has been expressed in diverse ways by many people over many centuries, and increasingly so, over the past decade. It is like a message from our higher, future selves trying to be heard. It speaks of a greater whole, the interconnectedness of all life, or an innate spirituality that is shared by all, even though it may not be immediately recognized. This context offers everyone a foundation from which to forgive and reconcile perceived or manifest tribulations and suffering that humanity has inflicted upon itself and this planet out of fear and ignorance.

Let's take a quick look at a few indicators from the *In Our Own Words 2000 (IOOW-2000)* research that show widespread identification among American households with "positive future paradigm" values and beliefs:

Connection and Involvement

- 93% agreed that it is important to teach our children to feel connected to the earth, people and all life, and 69% "strongly agreed."
- 80% acknowledged that the earth as a whole is a living system, and 50% "strongly agreed."
- 91% "would like to be involved more personally in creating a better world at whatever local or global level" they can and 54% of all respondents "strongly agreed."

Tolerance

- 86% believed that we don't all have to agree to have a successful community.
- 68% believed we should be tolerant of all lifestyles and groups even if we don't like what they do.

From me to you...
A Culture of Wisdom

Personally

Each of us will receive the bounties of a global cooperative synergy continually striving to elevate the support structures and resources that can provide each of us pathways toward our own self-realization, interconnectedness, and greater levels of consciousness.

The Greater Community

The life of any community is expressed through the creativity and energy of its people. When given the means, its residents can develop community infrastructures and initiatives based on an upward spiral of reciprocity, capacity, and an endowment toward a more positive future.

Spirituality

- 55% said they had experienced a sense of the sacred in everything around them and had perceived everything as spiritually connected.

- 95% said they believe in God or a higher spiritual consciousness, and 85% "strongly agreed."

- 83% agreed that whether we recognize it or not, we all just want to connect to God or a higher spiritual consciousness, and 49% "strongly agreed."

- 96% believed it is important that we attend to our own spiritual growth, and 71% "strongly agreed."

- 86% felt a need to experience spiritual growth.

- 33% agreed that they feel their spiritual needs are not currently being met.

- 61% say that religion and spirituality are not the same.

Technology

- Only 46% were optimistic that technology will help foster trust by increasing communication.

- Only 37% believed that technology will take care of the environmental problems we face today.

Leadership ethics and values

- 82% preferred that politicians hold the *same* moral and ethical values as they do.

- 64% preferred that politicians hold *higher* moral and ethical values than they do.

- 85% believed that the more information we have at our fingertips, the better our lives will be.

These indicators offer an inkling of the tremendous reservoir of core values and aspirations countless numbers of Americans share in common. *These extraordinary findings clearly validate the intimation that within our vast diversity as a society and a culture, we are fundamentally interconnected to a degree previously unacknowledged.* With this new perspective, the ramifications and possibilities are heartening as we appraise our current situations in the myriad arenas impacting our daily lives.

Open acknowledgement of our core values and higher aspirations can allow humanity to be more compassionate toward itself as it seeks to create something positive for its future. With a greater awareness of these fundamental principles, we can resolutely choose to end harmful, old practices and create something new, something that serves and nourishes our future selves, and something that will also serve us in the present.

Where We're At

We may be at the threshold of nothing short of a profound change in the evolution of human consciousness, and the creation of new societal structures and processes to facilitate a social and spiritual awakening beyond anything previously experienced in history. (Although this book focuses on data from the U.S., much of what is put forth has broad implications for all of humanity. Future research will include other countries.)

There is the potential for a positive future society *in the present* that promotes social and spiritual awakening by employing *discernment with compassion* to innovate positive change. By working together, we can create a vital and practical bridge between our present situation that will lead to realizing our higher aspirations as human beings. Yet, our political, economic, and social institutions continue to actively support and passively accept a paradigm based on conflict and domination favoring those who hold power over these institutions. Their power is based on separation, fear, and domination.

- How can we overcome thousands of years of conflict and transcend our species' past and present behavior that arises from humanity's limited perspective based on fear and survival, and which is focused on gaining dominance over one another and over nature?

- How can we move beyond the self-imposed constraints of the individual self, communities and cultures, religions, nationalism, and other manifestations and projections of our collective ego-personalities that has led to a long history of cultural, political, and religious conflict?

- How can we appeal to a deeper wisdom residing in each of our hearts and higher minds and find a way that appeals to the collective higher nature of the human race?

"Through wise discernment and resolve, we can, as individuals, reach deep within our being to connect with and express our higher aspirations for ourselves and within our network of interrelated communities for the uplifting of the entire global community."

Humankind is at a crossroads:

- One path leads to an ascending spiral of conscious evolution based on core spiritual values and beliefs of compassion, cooperation, and the interconnectedness of all life.

- Another path leads to a descending spiral of de-evolution fed by the old patterns of fear, conflict, and domination.

"In examining the benevolent traditions of America's minorities, we have identified some common elements that can be used to affirm and advance the connectedness of humanity. Not only do they provide the basis for a new American creed, but they also point to civic values and habits shared in common with America's majority. They remind us that America as a civil community is still a multicultural experiment."

– James A. Joseph, from
Remaking America, On A New American Creed

Has it ever been clearer than at the present time that we cannot afford *not* to? We believe the answer may be as simple as the need to embrace it is urgent.

A New Way

As we seek new ways of conducting ourselves as individuals and as a society, new solutions cannot be created through attacking old structures and processes. Human history and culture were shaped by these old structures and norms as various societies evolved to serve the interests of personal and collective survival, and emergence from the feudalism of industrial commerce. It serves little good to complain and fight these old structures that helped to get us where we are today. Of course, where great harm is occurring, discernment may dictate appropriate interventions.

A much greater power exists based on the power of compassion, universal love, and cooperation. It is time for that power to now assert itself more visibly. This is a vast untapped reservoir of universal awareness that will give rise to new structures and processes specifically focused on creating a positive and sustainable future – not just in the U.S., but globally as well.

Greater numbers of people than ever before are rediscovering the imperative of honoring the Earth and our natural environment, identifying with spirituality and spiritual values, and taking a responsible view of our future on this planet. A major change is already underway.

What we are focused on in this material has a great deal to do with listening to, identifying with, and acting upon the higher or deeper aspirations we all share, in order to bring more people together around the highest common denominators possible in any given circumstance.

"In times of great uncertainty, individuals and nations can forget that, as sentient beings, we are all part of something much greater than our own selves."

– *IOOW-2000* Research Executive Briefing

As our consciousness continues to outreach the ability of our old social structures to serve our future interests *in the present*, there will be increasing situations where what is new and emerging will be at odds with old paradigms. Until new structures dedicated to serving a positive future are in place, short-term circumstances may necessitate adapting what is worth adapting of our existing social, political, and economic structures. Such actions would be taken in the context of facilitating our transition to a positive future – so that we not waste energy trying to repair what can no longer be repaired.

This book presents ways to help make our positive future present in the here and now.

"America is a society whose strength is based in part on the hopes and aspirations that arise from a longing for compassion and enlightenment."

– *IOOW-2000* Research Executive Briefing

CHAPTER 2
Fundamentals of Connection

"Only by recognizing a greater positive context in which we can truly embrace everyone will we reach beyond suffering and conflict."

As we seek to embrace the whole of humanity, we must look to create a more enlightened future *now* from our current position in the present. We believe it is our higher potential that is most on our "*event horizon.*" It is as if it is *asking* to be acknowledged and welcomed – our positive future becoming present – our "*future-present.*" If only we could recognize it better so as to welcome it into our lives.

It is this future-present perspective that enlivens the ideals of our deeper connections, our desire to serve others for a greater good, and an intrinsic spirituality encompassing all of humankind. Like an enormous attractor on the horizon, the influence of our future selves in the here-and-now is just now becoming apparent. With it comes a new source of encouragement and hope that enables all humanity to choose to participate in the creation of a more evolved and spiritually mature global society.

Spirituality is a very large context that helps us embrace our diverse connection with one another. With spiritual awareness comes a greater capacity to take in the entirety of all that is and all that has been, and to then take responsibility for creating our future. It begins one person at a time reaching beyond his or her customary perceptions to recognize the depth and breadth of our interconnectedness, to embrace the concept of *discernment with compassion,* and to encourage the larger diversity enhancing and expanding us as individuals, societies, and as nations. We need only to allow this for ourselves.

"...a big part of the evolutionary process has to do with the cultivation of the all-important capacity to discriminate – to see things more clearly....that being able to see clearly what those relationships are doesn't necessarily imply a negative judgment, but is simply the expression of clear discrimination. If one aspires to have a liberated relationship to the human experience, then one has to be able to see things clearly in order to know how to make the right choices, how to respond in the most appropriate way in any given circumstance."

– Andrew Cohen
What Is Enlightenment? Fall/Winter 2002-2003

We Have the Potential – Do We Have the Awareness?

Americans have the potential to show the world new ways of being that transcend conflict and retribution, despite our major shortcomings. We have accomplished much as a nation in providing for basic rights, developing technology, meeting material needs, and providing an extraordinary creative environment. At the same time, we face major economic problems, serious social class disparities, significant erosion of democratic rights, and major health and nutritional problems, to name just a few examples. What choices will Americans make to tap such enormous potential? *One choice is to work consciously and resolutely to create a positive, compassionate and enlightened future in the present, and to demonstrate new ways in which human society can evolve.*

The question is: If people are not well connected to their inner being or willing or able to expand beyond the comfort of their perceptions, how can they connect with others and contribute in a positive way to human society?

Essentially, what we are talking about is a comprehensive spiritual awareness, one going beyond any individual religion or belief, and is more closely associated with "awakening" to a higher consciousness and a more integral and encompassing view of the interconnectedness of life.

This shift in consciousness toward a global social and spiritual awakening has the potential to heal generations of conflict and suffering and create a new way of life for everyone, everywhere.

Connection and Alienation

When one feels excluded from or unconnected due to a lack of commonalities, or disenfranchised because of perceived "otherness," then the options most people feel are to withdraw, become resentful, and develop an opposing polarity as a means of emotional and physical survival. Another word for this would be alienation.

A New America presents valuable research and insight that demonstrates ways humanity can find within its collective heart the courage to recognize and embrace not only a greater truth, but a greater good, and in so doing, end old patterns of separation and conflict. This recognition can also help all humanity forgive and reconcile its differences that have led to tragic conflict for generations and blocked our ability to access a higher potential to grow beyond the narrow confines we may have set for ourselves as individuals and as a species. Recognizing the universal interconnection of all life and consciousness can allow humankind to become wise stewards of ourselves as a species and of this planet as a whole.

In discovering The 8 American Types, we found three statistical indices directly relating to disconnectedness from self, others, nature, or a greater consciousness: *Connection, Service,* and *Spirituality.* These three qualities and other qualities are reflected in our choice of naming one of The 8 American Types "Disengaged from Social Concerns," which includes a concentration of individuals who feel a lack of community with others, a weak connection to self, and a tendency to focus on material issues. (Further insight into the role that "disconnection" plays will be seen later in this material as we delve into the research typologies and discuss strategies for a positive future.)

Disconnection from self and from larger aspects of being makes it possible for those people most influenced by disconnection to function as a type of "social ballast." The basic *inertia* of "social ballast" naturally favors those in positions of power who stand to benefit most by maintaining the status quo, as long as the material conditions of society do not fall too far. Discussed in greater detail in Chapter 6, this concept of social ballast represents people who lack the fundamental capacity to connect with anything new.

What, then, will provide a means of connection for those who feel disengaged or alienated from themselves or society? Part of the answer will come from engaging others who may share this sense of alienation but who are also motivated by a desire to create a more evolved community.

Our Deeper Wisdom

Humanity is at a crossroads. How can we appeal to a deeper wisdom that resides in each of our hearts and minds? Are we truly ready to tap into the reservoir of universal values and aspirations that can give rise to new structures and processes specifically focused on creating a positive and sustainable future?

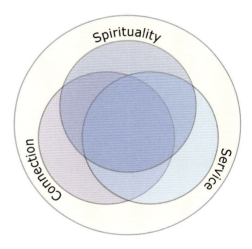

In the diagram above, the beige shaded region outside the three circles includes roughly 16% of the population that fell outside the three basic elements of connection, service, and spirituality.

It is these who exhibit the strongest *disconnection* from self or society or a larger picture. (The other 84% readily identified with any one or combination of these three basic elements.)

Discernment with Compassion

DISCERNMENT WITH COMPASSION

An ever-evolving broadness of mind combining the use of free-will and innate intelligence to resolve specifics within the context of an integral whole that emphasizes the interconnectedness of a greater "oneness" we all share as sentient beings in a larger cosmos of creation.

Discernment *with compassion* is a relatively new vision with ancient roots. It asks each of us to allow a more expansive perspective to come into play in order to remember and reestablish our interconnectedness, to acknowledge that what happens to another ramifies each of us in myriad ways. Our world has seen too many examples of the outcome of selfish thinking and actions. We have evolved technologically to the point of completely annihilating every species on Earth with the push of a single button that would launch an irreversible destructive cascade effect. Conversely, our need to step back and recognize the crossroads at which we stand has become just as critical an imperative.

Extreme circumstances, such as natural disasters, war, and near-death experiences, can stimulate new openings for people to connect with their innate freedom to choose greatness over smallness. Greatness of being is our potential and promise. But it is as though we have fallen into a deep sleep of endless distractions and cannot find the clarity or energy or will to awaken long enough to remember this promise of greatness.

Therefore it seems fitting that it often takes extreme situations to shake us from this state of seeming helplessness.

Could it be that to learn to consciously reach for our potential greatness of being, humanity has been unconsciously involved in a game of brinkmanship, going from one set of extreme situations of conflict and dangers to another? Perhaps these extreme situations help to mirror our best and worst as a way to present clear choices to people as we begin to reach for choices that represent a positive future in the present.

Choice is the operative word.

"...being 'non-judgmental' under all circumstances...one ends up tying oneself in knots trying to cultivate a dubious kind of compassion that often goes against all common sense."

– Andrew Cohen
What is Enlightenment? Fall/Winter 2002-2003

Choice...

It *implies* freedom and *provides* freedom at the same time. True freedom, though, entails responsibility: the ability to allow another their space to make choices no matter the consequences, but to also provide information and support to make *wise* decisions. In order to provide that kind of fluid context, discernment with compassion is of vital necessity.

In today's world, a polarity of black and white (or "my way is the right way") has insinuated itself into many communities and cultures as a means of survival. An aura of self-righteousness without flexibility permeates many of the conflicts we see challenging humanity, which includes blame and retribution, and entrenchment into mythic dogmas. Instead, what conscious choices can be made to bring about an environment of balance, integrity, respect, and compassion?

Compassion is founded on awareness of our interconnectedness with one another, our natural environment, and the cosmos. It recognizes our interconnectedness as a species, as part of a greater sea of consciousness, as one heart beating as many. It recognizes that this commonality is greater than our perceived differences. This interconnection is felt with our heart, mind, spirit, and body. To act from this awareness is our next step, but this requires the right use of will.

The conundrum is that we are not *sufficiently* aware of our innate will that naturally favors wisdom over ignorance. It also informs us that ultimately we have *no one to blame,* not even ourselves. By kindling the recognition of our deeper connections, compassion informs us that we need not blame ourselves to the point of self-destruction. Thus, humanity can reconcile and heal its differences, real or perceived. We can choose wisdom over ignorance, greatness over smallness, if we only will ourselves to that choice.

Today, more people than ever before are seeking and finding ways to connect with and use their innate free-will to choose a positive future *before* dangerous and traumatic circumstances force new choices upon us. What will it take for various human societies to make collective choices – out of free-will – that serve a positive future instead of a devolving one? This is where a new type of discernment is needed to satisfactorily

"If one aspires to a liberated relationship to the human experience, one has to be able to see things clearly in order to know how to make the right choices, how to respond in the most appropriate way in any given circumstance."

– Andrew Cohen
What is Enlightenment? Fall/Winter 2002-2003

address the needs of the individual, as well as the whole of humanity and the planet. This new discernment will be used to create new ways of living – new patterns – and not to simply attack whatever is perceived to be wrong, as we so often do.

New Patterns

Too many of the movements for social, economic, or environmental justice emphasize attacking undesirable structures and values rather than creating new ones that can serve a positive future. This all points to the need to create new social, economic, and political structures and processes, and to modify what we can of our existing ones to serve us in the present for our future as a species. This in turn points to the need for a type of discernment that chooses to look for and encourage the emergence of our new selves. This is a different approach than righteous judgment that seeks blame and retribution.

"Choosing out of higher motivation is really about thought or consciousness determining form, instead of tacitly allowing existing forms to determine out consciousness and thoughts."

"…for people who are engaged in the spiritual dimension of life, there is a tremendous fear, often to the point of becoming a superstition, of any conclusion about anything that could possibly be seen as being other than – accepting of all stances."

Humanity has lived and died and learned through physical and psychological pain and suffering to such an extent that our schools cruelly teach young people that this pattern is a natural part of "human nature." Because our underlying and overarching connection with one another is obscured by much of human culture, blame and retribution help to perpetuate trans-generational warfare.

What if our natural state is to evolve beyond this type of learning by negative experience? A child can quickly learn that it is not desirable to put his or her hand in a hot flame. It only takes one example to grasp this and create a new and supportive pattern. Can humanity not learn that it is not desirable – nor is it necessary – to repeat learning patterns based on conflict and pain? Humanity can acquire a new pattern for learning based on enriching principles of cooperation, joy, awe, and expanding awareness of possibilities that have always been there for the asking.

Collective and individual denial lead to circumstances that will most likely devolve into endless conflict over domination. Instead, we can choose to evolve into cooperation and a positive future fully dedicated to our evolution as individuals and as a species. This latter path can move us toward *conscious* participation in the vast cosmos of creation – fully awake and fully participating. Such discernment may be the greatest expression and greatest use of our free-will as we discover just how much more we can be.

Discernment with compassion allows us to love ourselves enough to learn to see our various crises as the "birth pains" of something new. Our planet is a vast source for the creation of life. We are on the verge of evolving ourselves into a new species, emerging from a planetary mother. This is not so different from the relationship between a mother and the child she is bearing. The ills of our society are due to the "natural" strain of our own development as a species that is barely awake enough to know what our possibilities are. However, just as a birth process has a term for its delivery, so does humanity as a species.

We are on the verge of something wonderful before us, if only we learn to recognize it and encourage it.

"Humanity is at the threshold of nothing short of a profound change in the evolution of consciousness: the possibility of creating new societal structures and processes to facilitate a social spiritual awaking beyond anything previously experienced in history."

CHAPTER 3

A New Look at Americans

"Fourscore and seven years ago our fathers brought forth on this continent, a new nation, conceived in Liberty, and dedicated to the proposition that all men are created equal."

– Abraham Lincoln

The *In Our Own Words 2000* research demonstrates a growing shift in core American attitudes, beliefs and values toward a more integral way of life, a shift that has profound implications for all facets of our society. Our current social structures and institutions do not reflect these values, as they were developed to maintain a course based more on old paradigm, conflict-based history rather than a new, cooperation-based paradigm for a positive future.

Two quadrant models were developed to help identify and compare these different paradigmatic worldviews. They describe differences and commonalities among Americans, which show greater connection than may be apparent among the many diverse tendencies in American society. Overall, they provide a "roadmap" to a positive future and through extensive statistical analyses, The 8 American Types were discovered, dramatically providing scientific evidence of unity within our diversity.

Moving "Out of the Box"

The *IOOW-2000* study was first intended as a tool purely for exploration of social consciousness. Once enough data was collected, extensive analysis and review was conducted with a particular focus on the extent to which a shift in consciousness is occurring. Next, we asked ourselves what we could do with these remarkable findings that would be of benefit to others. The result is the first study quantifying, defining, and demonstrating a strategic and powerful direction along which people can move "out of the box" toward their higher aspirations. What we discovered is a set of unique typological patterns that present – never-before-published – scientific evidence for a greater unity within our diversity.

Americans may appear generally optimistic in their philosophy about the future with 79% expressing confidence that no matter what happens in the future, humankind will adapt to it. It is also worth noting that 55% of the respondents believe most children are not worried about their future. (A question phrased this way also encourages respondents to project their own concerns.)

In contrast, 70% believe that humanity is headed for serious problems in the next several years and that the three major threats to the future of the world are disease epidemics, terrorism, and world war.

Only 17% believe science will eventually be able to explain everything, and only 37% believe that during the next ten years technological breakthroughs will take care of the environmental problems facing us today.

What we do not share, however, is a clear sense of what the future could bring us as a society. In asking Americans three "large scope" questions about our future during the next ten years, the *IOOW-2000* research discovered some basic patterns. These were partly based on three questions that asked whether life will go on pretty much the same, whether people are concerned that humanity is headed for serious problems, or whether a social or spiritual awakening will make the world a better place.

Deeper questions arose when looking at responses to various combinations of these questions. We will explore more of "future outlook" in Chapter Seven in the context of change.

In the sections that follow, we will take a look at some core traits and values of the U.S. population, and present some unique typological patterns.

While surveys based on simple demographics and opinions can reflect some basic trends and differences in our society, they also fail to detect and explain the deeper drivers of our conscious and unconscious behaviors.

The *IOOW-2000* research shows wide difference between different *types* of individuals in terms of their future outlook, worldview, and basic values and beliefs. It also provides evidence for different levels of personal and collective alienation: disconnection from self, society, and higher consciousness. We are also able to see at the same time a way out of what could be a downward spiral from which there may be no recovery. And that is evident when we focus on what does connect people personally and collectively to inner self, society, and higher consciousness. Therein is the proverbial light at the end of the tunnel. The key has to do with people being more aware of their innate free-will to make higher choices for themselves, future generations, and the planet.

Conflicts often arise when people believe they are too different from one another to find common ground. The *IOOW-2000* typologies identify positive commonalities among groups that can be used to help stimulate positive social change and greater awareness of innate spirituality on a societal scale. The typologies also provide a valuable conceptual map showing greater connection than may be apparent among the many diverse tendencies in American society. Through extensive statistical and graphical analyses, conceptual maps were produced to show both differences and commonalities among Americans. This in turn provides strategic support for the development of new social, cultural, and political initiatives for positive change.

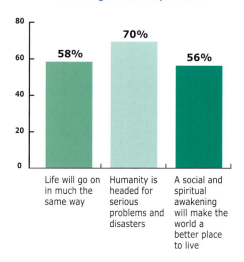

"DURING THE NEXT TEN YEARS..."

Percentage of all respondents

(bar chart: 58% – Life will go on in much the same way; 70% – Humanity is headed for serious problems and disasters; 56% – A social and spiritual awakening will make the world a better place to live)

The *IOOW-2000* Research

The statistical research data is based on over 210 questions, including over 30 demographic and geographic variables plus key media and political questions, affording a surprising look at American views on politics, leadership, business, ethics, and spirituality – and their important relationship to individuals, society, and the common good. (A complete listing the *IOOW-2000* survey questions is found in the Appendix.)

GENERAL QUADRANT MODEL

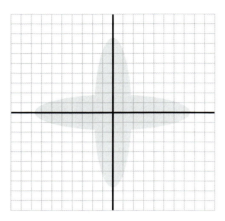

This model compares scales and indexes to one another, or to individual items. The quadrants also lend themselves to displaying data in a visually intuitive manner.

Introducing Two Simple Quadrant Models of U.S. Society

To develop new strategies effectively bridging differences between people, we must look at core values and beliefs and the patterns their combinations create in American society. The *IOOW-2000* research produced the following dimensions used to create general quadrant-style models that provide a solid overview of society, and aid in identifying and comparing different worldviews (paradigms) in society as measured by various scales or indexes.

These models compare scales and indexes to one another, or to individual items. The quadrants also lend themselves to displaying data in a visually intuitive manner. In this context, two x-y quadrant models are introduced:

- Positive Future – Cooperative Integrative (PFCI) scale

by

- Social Material Stress (SMS) scale

…and a variation

- Positive Future – Cooperative Integrative (PFCI) scale

by

- Social Traditional - Religious Conservative (STRC) index

The first quadrant model employs the *Positive Future – Cooperative Integrative* (PFCI) scale as its vertical axis. In general, the PFCI scale measures people's sense of connection to society and life, forgiveness, openness to diversity, and identification with social and spiritual awakening.

A second axis called the *Social Material Stress* (SMS) scale measures people's sense of disconnection from society, concerns with getting by day to day, reporting of emotional problems, and a generally pessimistic view of the future.

(One goal for *A New America* was to identify a model illustrating societal factors that relate to recent voting habits. As it turned out, this second scale

(SMS) had an added benefit of maximizing the statistical differentiation between those who were likely to vote, from those who were not.)

Conceptually, as well as statistically, it makes sense that "social material stress" would have a strong relationship with voting habits.

Since much attention is given to conservative values and traditionalism, a supplementary index was developed from the *IOOW-2000* data called the *Social Traditional - Religious Conservative* (STRC) index to examine the broader implications of social, traditional, religious, and conservative beliefs and values.

In general, the STRC index measures people's identification with old values and habits with which they are comfortable, conservative and Republican political inclinations, low tolerance for diversity, support for the death penalty, and high attendance of religious meetings.

When combined with the PFCI scale, this index provides useful insight into ways people's traditional and conservative outlooks interact with an outlook more associated with a connection to society, life in general, and a broader spiritual worldview.

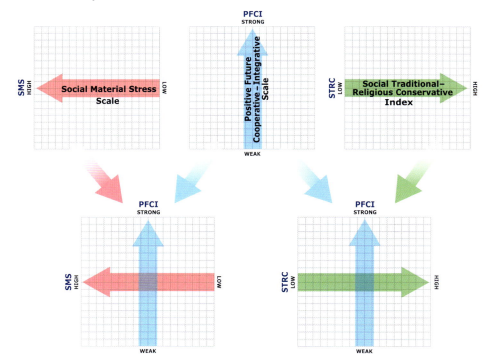

"POSITIVE FUTURE – COOPERATIVE INTEGRATIVE" SCALE

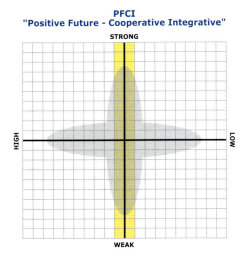

The PFCI scale measures people's sense of connection to society and life, forgiveness, openness to diversity, and identification with social and spiritual awakening.

The "Positive Future – Cooperative Integrative" Scale

The 10 items listed below constitute the PFCI scale measuring people's sense of connection to society and life, forgiveness, openness to diversity, and identification with social and spiritual awakening. This scale measures a trait existing (to a greater or lesser extent) within all Americans.

Items in the PFCI scale:

1. Our Earth is a unique kind of living organism and as a whole system is fundamentally alive.

2. I believe that helping those in need is one of the most important things nations can do within the global community.

3. Underneath it all, we're all connected as one.

4. There is a global awakening to higher consciousness taking place these days.

5. If we could forgive and reconcile all our past hurts and conflicts, we could all accomplish so much more.

6. Over the next 10 years, social and spiritual awakening will make the world a better place to live.

7. Have you ever experienced a sense of the sacred in everything around you or perceived everything as being spiritually connected together as one?

8. It is important to teach our children to feel a connection to the Earth, people, and all life.

9. Interacting with other cultures broadens our horizons.

10. Whether I am aware of it or not, I believe that God or a higher spiritual consciousness is present everywhere.

The "Social Material Stress" Scale

The ten items below constitute the SMS scale measuring people's sense of disconnection from society, concerns with getting by day-to-day, reporting of emotional problems, and a generally pessimistic view of the future. This scale measures a trait existing (to a greater or lesser extent) within all Americans.

Items in the SMS scale:

1. I often feel lonely and cut off from those around me.

2. I feel judged by most others around me.

3. I sometimes think of moving elsewhere because I feel that I don't belong where I am.

4. My main goal in life is to make a lot of money.

5. Most people cannot be trusted.

6. I am concerned that humanity is headed for serious problems and disasters in the next 10 years.

7. All I want out of life is getting by day-to-day.

8. One of the most important achievements in life is to acquire a higher standard of living.

9. Thinking about your overall emotional life, are you currently experiencing any serious problems with your emotional relations?

10. At any point in the past four weeks, have you felt so sad and unhappy that nothing could cheer you up?

Now let's see what happens when these are combined to create a simple model or map of society that separates into five zones or types: one for each quarter or corner and a fifth in the middle area that straddles the other four.

"SOCIAL MATERIAL STRESS" SCALE

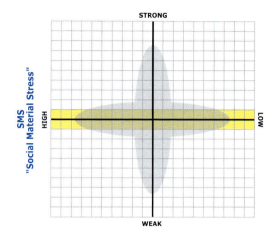

The SMS scale measures people's sense of disconnection from society, concerns with getting by day-to-day, reporting emotional problems, and a generally pessimistic view of the future.

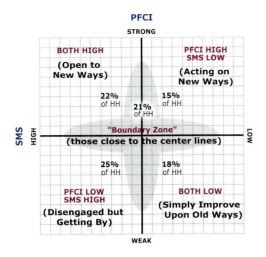

PFCI

STRONG

BOTH HIGH (Open to New Ways)	PFCI HIGH SMS LOW (Acting on New Ways)
22% of HH	15% of HH

21% of HH

SMS HIGH / LOW

"Boundary Zone" (those close to the center lines)

25% of HH	18% of HH
PFCI LOW SMS HIGH (Disengaged but Getting By)	BOTH LOW (Simply Improve Upon Old Ways)

WEAK

High PFCI/Low SMS ("Acting on New Ways")

- (15% of households) identify with a more positive and integrated future, and they do not feel social material stress.

Both High ("Open to New Ways")

- (22% of households) identify with a more positive and integrated future, and they strongly feel social material stress.

"Boundary Zone" (those close to the center lines)

- (21% of households) are very close to the boundary between two or more quadrants and, as such, cannot be reliably identified as belonging to one single quadrant.

Low PFCI/High SMS ("Disengaged but Getting By")

- (25% of households) do not identify with a more positive and integrated future, and they strongly feel social material stress.

Both Low ("Simply Improve Upon Old Ways")

- (18% of households) do not identify with either of these two lines of measurement.

Differences and Commonalities – the PFCI-SMS Quadrant Map

Through extensive analyses, various conceptual maps were produced to show both differences and commonalities among Americans. One of these maps can also be considered a typology consisting of five major zones: the four corners or quadrants plus a middle region. This quadrant model was created by overlaying the two statistically reliable scales (PFCI and SMS), each of which constitutes a continuum connecting everyone to some extent. To summarize these scales:

- The PFCI scale measures values and beliefs concerning the earth as a whole living system, global awakening to higher consciousness, and interconnectedness of people and life.

- The SMS scale measures values and beliefs concerning money and material well being, emotional stress, and lack of community and connection.

Combined, these scales can be used to define a quadrant model, which has some very interesting characteristics and some very consistent patterns in terms of beliefs, values, voting, and life patterns.

Overall, Americans who fall into the two right-side quadrants (low SMS) are more politically engaged, and do not report feeling much social and material stress. Those who fall into the two left-side quadrants (high SMS) are less politically engaged and do report feeling social and material stress. More non-whites than whites came in on the high side of the SMS scale and very little difference between gender.

Americans who fall into the two upper quadrants (high PFCI) strongly identify with a more positive and cooperative future. Those who fall into the two lower quadrants (low PFCI) do not identify much with a positive and cooperative future. A much larger portion of women and non-whites placed higher on the PFCI scale.

There are also those Americans who fall very close to one or more of the boundaries between the four quadrants in the model. These respondents (who are +/- 5% from any boundary, and who could arguably fit either side of the boundaries due to limits in statistical reliability) make up a fifth group, which we call "Boundary-Zone."

In later chapters, as we discuss voting and politics, the PFCI-SMS model is heavily used in analyzing voting due to its statistical and content value. The concept of social material stress is also valuable in understanding what may motivate people more.

LOW PFCI/LOW SMS ("Simply Improve Upon Old Ways"):

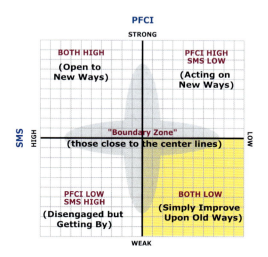

- Americans who do not report feeling social or material stress and who do not strongly identify with a more positive and cooperative future, are what we call "Both Low."

- Only 28% agree that a global awakening to higher consciousness is taking place, and only 26% believe that social and spiritual awakening could make the world a better place to live.

- On an index measuring spirituality, this group scored the lowest of all (only 20% strong spirituality). They were also least likely to want to be more personally involved in making the world a better place (38% strongly agree).

- This group, which makes up 18% of the U.S. population, is most likely to vote and to choose a candidate (70%). Without regard for voting likelihood, 18% didn't want any candidate and 21% wanted some other candidate than those listed as running for president. Of those most likely to vote in this group, 49% preferred Bush followed by 24% wanting someone other than the main list of candidates.

- The overall pattern of results suggests that this group identifies more with the "status quo," and thus seeks to maintain our current socio-political systems and processes, with a few improvements.

- They also least agreed (44%) with the statement, "What goes around comes around is how things really work." This suggests that Americans in this quadrant seem to least believe that whatever they have "planted" along the way in life will not necessarily be "harvested" later on.

- The makeup of this segment tends to include more whites and men than non-whites and women.

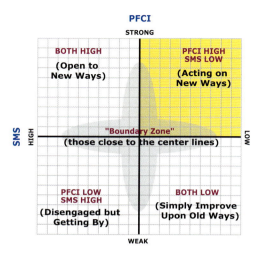

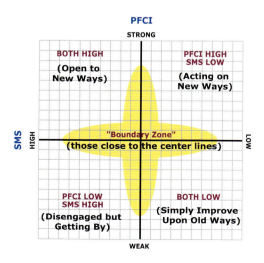

LOW SMS/HIGH PFCI ("Acting on New Ways"):

- Americans who are not experiencing social or material stress and who strongly identify with a more positive and cooperative future, are what we call "High PFCI/Low SMS."

- A full 81% agree that global awakening to higher consciousness is taking place, and 85% believe that social and spiritual awakening could make the world a better place to live.

- On an index measuring spirituality, this group scored the highest of all (85% strong spirituality). They were also most likely to want to be more personally involved in making the world a better place (69% strongly agreed).

- This group, which makes up 15% of the U.S. population, is also very likely to vote and to choose a candidate (68%). Without regard for voting likelihood, 25% didn't want any candidate and 7% wanted some other candidate than those listed as running for president. Of those most likely to vote in this group, 33% preferred Gore, followed by 30% for Bush, 27% for McCain.

- This overall pattern of results suggests that this group is very interested in bringing about a more positive and cooperative future, and would likely be open to using some of our current socio-political systems and processes as means to get there.

- More than half (59%) also agreed that, "What goes around comes around is how things really work."

- The makeup of this segment tends to include more women than men but shows no difference in race/ethnicity.

BOUNDARY ZONE (Those close to the center lines):

- Americans who score near the crossover points of two (or more) quadrants fall into a "Boundary-zone."

- Only half (50%) agree that global awakening to higher consciousness is taking place, and only half (48%) believe that social and spiritual awakening could make the world a better place to live.

- On an index measuring spirituality, this group scored moderate (only 46% strong spirituality). They were also moderately likely to want to be more personally involved in making the world a better place (55% strongly agree).

- This group, which makes up 21 % of the U.S. population, is about average in likelihood to vote and to choose a candidate (57 %) – as well as their preference for candidate. Therefore no one choice stood out for those in the middle or boundary zone.

- This overall pattern of results suggests that this group is "middle of the road" – while they feel some social and material stress, and somewhat identify with a more positive and cooperative future, they do not appear to be any more strongly invested in change than they are in the status quo.

- More than half (59 %) also agree that, "What goes around comes around is how things really work."

- The makeup of this segment shows no difference in composition by gender or race/ethnicity.

HIGH SMS/LOW PFCI ("Disengaged but Getting By"):

- Americans who are experiencing social or material stress and who do not identify with a more positive and cooperative future, are what we call "High SMS/Low PFCI."

- Less than half (41 %) agree that global awakening is taking place, and only 41 % believe that global awakening could make the world a better place to live.

- On an index measuring spirituality, this group scored low (only 34 % strong spirituality). They were also not very likely to want to be more personally involved in making the world a better place (44 % strongly agree).

- This group – the largest of all – makes up 25 % of the U.S. population, is somewhat below the average of all respondents in terms of their likelihood to vote and to choose a candidate (51 %), as well as in their candidate preference. Therefore, no one choice stood out for those in the middle or boundary zone.

- This overall pattern of results suggests that this group is not very interested in bringing about a more positive and cooperative future, and acts as a sort of "social inertial ballast" favoring the status quo in our socio-political system.

- Many (70 %) also agree with the statement, "What goes around comes around is how things really work."

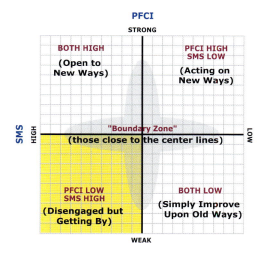

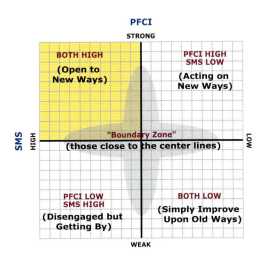

- The makeup of this segment shows no difference in gender or race/ethnicity.

HIGH SMS/HIGH PFCI ("Open to New Ways"):

- Americans who are experiencing social or material stress and who strongly identify with a more positive and cooperative future, are what we call "Both High."

- This group most agrees (89%) that global awakening is taking place, and most believe (88%) that global awakening could make the world a better place to live.

- On an index measuring spirituality, this group scored high (80% strong spirituality). They were also very likely to want to be more personally involved in making the world a better place (66% strongly agree).

- This group, which makes up 22% of the U.S. population, ranked lowest in their likelihood to vote and to choose a candidate (37%). While 25% tended to support Gore, when adjusted for voting likelihood, was only marginally in favor of Gore over other choices.

- This overall pattern of results suggests that this group is very interested in bringing about a more positive and cooperative future, but who would not be open to using some of our current socio-political systems and processes as a means to get there.

- More than any other group, (82%) they also agree with the statement, *"What goes around comes around is how things really work."* Americans in this quadrant seem to most believe that whatever they have "planted" along the way in life, will be "harvested" later on.

- Compared to the other PFCI-SMS quadrants, this segment tends to include more non-whites and women.

The mass media and our culture, especially with regard to politics and personal values, have loosely encouraged people to think of themselves as either tending to be liberal or conservative. Whether we like this artificial distinction that makes it easy for people to be manipulated by others, or not, it is in our culture. Its historical roots have been increasingly blurred and at times deliberately obscured. Therefore in any simple model of American society, it is essential to look at this as well.

So now let's take a look at a model that shifts the focus of our quadrant to Traditional, Conservative, and Religious factors.

"Established norms are historically based, – based on the past. They're not based on the "now" – and they're certainly not based on future-present. They are based on past and past-present. Consider the whole of humanity referencing its past as a way to guide itself into the future. It is a wonder that there has been any progress at all."

ON A PERSONAL NOTE:

Given our highly materialistic society, "social and/or material stress" affects your sense of relative freedom to explore new horizons or to feel comfortable staying with and defending whatever has worked for you in the past.

The higher you are on the PFCI scale, the stronger you will identify with a wholistic and spiritual worldview. The more you are to the left of the SMS scale, the more guarded you are with feelings of material or psychological stress and alienation. If it wasn't for the demands of material or social stress in life, most of the people who place in the upper left quadrant would probably be found in the upper right quadrant and perhaps our society would be that much closer to its ideals.

SMS factors are definitely related to motivation and behavior. Often, in a materially focused society such as America, the options available to someone are limited by availability of material resources and thus heavily affect one's outlook in life. Nevertheless, as we will see later in this book, the values and beliefs people have can help them overcome social material stress and persist in trying new ways and ideas. If you are in the upper right quadrant, it is likely that you are concerned about the condition of humanity and the planet, and will be more in a position to act upon this calling. If you are in the lower right quadrant, chances are your success by traditional, material standards seems satisfying enough. Without a counter influence of PFCI factors, why change anything?

If you are in the lower left quadrant, chances are good that life has not always seemed to be quite right, with the stresses of daily life and material limitations of having relatively less social economic advantage than that enjoyed by people on the right half of the grid. This has made it sometimes difficult to connect with others in a positive and meaningful way.

Clearly, "having it all" isn't what "it" is all about.

The "Social Traditional - Religious Conservative" Index

The fourteen items below constitute the STRC index measuring people's identification with old values and habits with which they are comfortable in their daily lives, conservative and Republican political inclinations, low tolerance for diversity, support for the death penalty, and high attendance of religious meetings. This index measures a trait existing (to a greater or lesser extent) within all Americans.

Items in the STRC index:

1. There is basically only one correct way to live.

2. I want a world where people live by traditional values.

3. We should be tolerant of all lifestyles and groups even if we don't like what they do.

4. My community is too diverse in its beliefs.

5. Maintaining law and order is the most important issue today.

6. Do you attend church services or other meetings of a religious organization?

7. Which of the following best describes how frequently you attend services or meetings at this church or religious organization?

8. Political party affiliation: Democrat / Republican ("Other" recoded as missing).

9. Which of the following describes your political ideology: conservative to liberal scale?

10. Children and youth are allowed too much freedom these days.

11. Family values are the basis for a successful society.

12. To what extent do you support having a death penalty in any state of the U.S.?

13. I believe that traditional religious literature tells the truth.

14. I follow the teachings of a specific spiritual or religious leader.

One notable difference between the SMS and STRC measures is that the SMS scale is focused mainly on descriptions of a person's reality and the

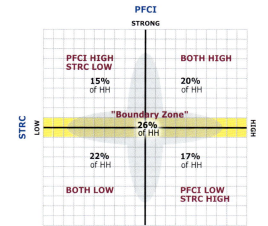

THE "SOCIAL TRADITIONAL-RELIGIOUS CONSERVATIVE" INDEX

High PFCI/Low STRC

- 15% of households identify with a more positive and integrated future, and tend to not identify with traditional, conservative, or religious values.

Both High

- 20% of households identify with a more positive and integrated future, and they identify with traditional, conservative, or religious values.

"Boundary Zone" (those close to the center lines)

- 26% of households are very close to the boundary between two or more quadrants and, as such, cannot be reliably identified as belonging to one single quadrant.

Low PFCI/High STRC

- 17% of households do not identify with a more positive and integrated future, and they do identify with social traditional conservative or religious values.

Both Low

- 22% of households do not identify very strongly with either of these two lines of measurement.

STRC index is focused mainly on values and beliefs that shape a person's reality. This index showed no appreciable differences when it came to gender or race/ethnicity.

We will revisit the PFCI-STRC and other models further on in more detail. To provide a greater level of detail and give more life to these very broad models of society, we can combine these with a more detailed representation of our society: The 8 American Types. To help introduce the 8 Types, we begin this next section with their basic building blocks, the "Three Core Traits."

"As we will soon see, there are types of people who represent natural bridges between these various quadrants. Using shared values and beliefs to unite and overcome differences can potentially unify upwards of 84% of the adult population around socially and spiritually enlightened strategies and themes. This is truly practical information, available to anyone who is motivated by a desire to serve society and the earth in creating a more positive and awakened society."

"In Letters from an American Farmer, Hector St. John de Crèvecoeur, a Frenchmen who came to America in 1759, described an American, 'this new man,' as 'one who leaves behind all ancient prejudices and manners to become a new person who acts upon new principles…. Here,' he said, 'individuals of all races are melted into a new race of man." (In its time, Crèvecoeur's book was a best-seller in Europe.)

– from James A. Joseph, *Remaking America*

CHAPTER 4

The 8 American Types

"A practical demonstration of "unity within diversity – the discovery of The 8 American Types showed a coherent set of overlapping patterns offering practical ways to bridge our entire society."

Conflicts arise when people are made to believe they are too different from one another to find common ground. One of the most important uses of the *In Our Own Words 2000* typology is that it identifies positive commonalities among people, which can be used to help stimulate positive social change and greater awareness of innate spirituality on a societal scale.

When the entire 8 Types are overlaid on the PFCI quadrant maps, a remarkably rich picture emerges: We are not as distant from each other in our beliefs and aspirations as we might believe. It is just a matter of discovering ways to bridge our diversity to create a more positive forward movement uplifting all of humanity. Whether one is characterized as "Disengaged from Social Concerns" or "Working for a New Life of Wholeness," each of the 8 Types is an integral part of the whole and when combined, we are much greater than the sum of our parts.

THREE CORE TRAITS

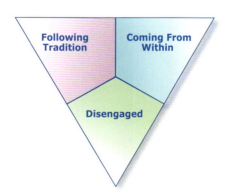

Three Core Traits

To understand how The 8 American Types were discovered, it is helpful to start with its three major building blocks. A "trait" is a personal characteristic that is relatively persistent and stable across people, places, and time. Traits determine (to a fairly predictable extent) an individual's potential behavior. A "typology system" exemplifies an image, impression, or model of a certain set of shared tendencies and is simply a way to measure multiple traits, and determine to what extent they exist (singly or in combination) within the population at large.

The *IOOW-2000* typology system is a statistically reliable and valid means of categorizing and differentiating various subgroups of the U.S. population, each having different combinations of traits. After conducting extensive factor analyses and internal consistency (Cronbach's Alpha) analyses, three core traits emerged from the *IOOW-2000* data. These traits are measured by reliable multi-item scales and reflect the following orientations for individuals:

- **Disengaged** – feel a lack of community with others and connection to self, and tend to be focused on material issues.

- **Coming From Within** – are more identified with community, the interconnectedness of life and spirituality, and tend to have a more positive outlook on life.

- **Following Tradition** – tend to follow a specific religious teaching, feel there is only one correct way to live, and see God or higher consciousness as something separate from themselves.

Those having the "Coming From Within" and the "Following Tradition" traits share much more in common of their core values than either may realize, including spirituality. However, in our current society, it seems as if their "reality languages" are often "foreign" to one another.

Each of these core traits represents a continuum, present to some extent, for everyone. (While being essentially independent statistical constructs, a small overlap of 4.4% was observed between the "Coming From Within" and "Following Tradition" traits.) Each of these Three Core Traits can by themselves make up a "pure" type in the population, or they can exist in combination to make up other "blended/combined" types.

A person's type is determined by the number of traits in which he or she scores above average compared to all other respondents in the sample (i.e., higher than the norm-referenced 50th percentile). As such, an individual may have anywhere from zero (all three traits scoring below 50%) to three (all three traits scoring above 50%) predominant traits that comprise his or her type.

Three core traits by themselves provide some general insight into people's basic value system, but are too general to portray society in a useful manner. The PFCI-SMS quadrant model essentially gives us four major types of value orientation, but they are still too general to see enough detail. However, by themselves, the 8 Types provide rich enough detail and when combined with the PFCI models, offer a powerful map of society and individuals.

To help see the connection between the Three Core Traits and the 8 Types, the following table shows the composition of the 8 Types with the Three Core Traits, and the percentage that they are found in the population at large:

IOOW-2000 THREE CORE TRAITS	IOOW-2000 THE 8 AMERICAN TYPES	PERCENTAGE OF ALL HOUSEHOLDS
1 TRAIT OF 3 SCORES HIGH	3 "CORE" TYPES	38.2%
2 TRAITS OF 3 SCORE HIGH	3 "COMBINED" TYPES	31.0%
ALL 3 TRAITS SCORE HIGH	1 "COMBINED" TYPE	16.4%
NONE OF THE TRAITS SCORE HIGH	1 "LEAST EXPRESSED" TYPE	14.4%

(If you want to see the actual questions and scoring used in defining the 8 Types, you can jump ahead to Chapter Five: "What Type Am I?"

How can we bridge the best of traditional values and focus on inner growth with our higher aspirations? How to engage the disengaged? Before we attempt to answer this, we first must look a little closer at the make-up of our society. The discovery of The 8 American Types showed a coherent set of overlapping patterns offering practical ways to bridge our entire society.

What is a Trait?

A "trait" is a personal characteristic that is relatively persistent and stable across people, places, and time. Traits determine (to a fairly predictable extent) an individual's potential behavior.

What is a Typology?

A "typology" is an analysis of human social groups. It exemplifies an image, impression, or model of a certain set of shared tendencies. Each social group in a typology has unique qualities that are stable, inherent, and essentially defining characteristics as opposed to superficial, impermanent ones. The use of the term "types" then becomes shorthand for variations within a typology.

The qualities encapsulated by a type are found within all people. Some people are very close to two or three types, as we will see in Chapter 5's self-scoring exercises.

Note: The psychometric standards and processes for developing a trait-based typology system are beyond the scope of this book.

Overview of The 8 American Types

An important contribution of the *IOOW-2000* research program is the creation of a new typology of attitudes, values, and behaviors offering a context in which individuals and society can better understand themselves. The 8 American Types emerged from further analysis of the Three Core Traits, which were too general when described by themselves. The typology was developed using univariate and multivariate statistical approaches and multiple indicators, and tested for replicability throughout.

In analyzing the *IOOW-2000* research data, many conceptual possibilities were tested, eventually yielding eight different types of Americans within the U.S. population over 18 years of age. These types are all based on statistically reliable scales using 30 key variables drawn from the entire set of over 210 items. The items that did not constitute final typology scales were then used to provide a more enriched portrayal of Americans in the year 2000 by comparing how the different types responded to them.

Of these eight types, three correspond to the Three Core Traits introduced previously. Together, these three account for 38.2 % of the U.S. adult population. (It is important to keep in mind that our use of the word "core" does not in any way denote importance or ranking over combination types.)

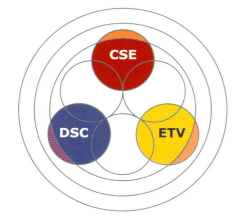

- One basic type, **Embracing Traditional Values** (ETV), represents 12.1 % of households embracing a strong sense of traditional values and ethics, and identifying with a so-called American heartland worldview. For these individuals, applying oneself to established norms has provided a good life.

- Another basic type, **Disengaged from Social Concerns** (DSC), represents 14.2 % of households, tends to not be connected with social concerns, and has not experienced the promise of material and personal well being.

- The third basic type, **Connecting through Self-Exploration** (CSE), represents 11.9 % of households and tends to be internally oriented and focused on exploring facets of themselves to gain greater awareness. They also have a high identification with non-traditional forms of spiritual expression.

While these three basic types reveal striking differences, not all of the American population has a type comprised of just *one* predominant trait of the Three Core Traits. Three basic types by themselves simply cannot adequately reflect the diversity comprising American society.

Further analysis demonstrated combinations of five other types of Americans (types comprised of different *combinations* of scores on the Three Core Traits). A person who scored high on two of these basic traits was identified as one of the following "combined" types. Together, these three "combined" types account for 32.9% of U.S. households.

- The first of these combination types, **Cautious and Conservative** (CC), represents 10.0% of households and tends to be a combination of traditionally conservative values and beliefs with a sense of disconnectedness from society.

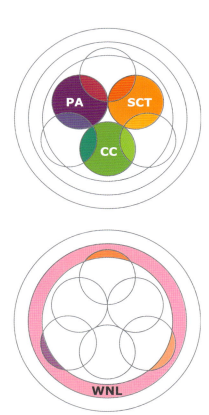

- Another combination type, **Persisting against Adversity** (PA), represents 9.4% of households and may not have an easy life but does identify with new paradigm values while making a go of getting by in life.

- A third combination type, **Seeking Community Transformation** (SCT), represents 11.6% of households and includes those individuals who have achieved social-economic success and who are focused more on service and new paradigm values. They are likely to be very involved in positive change, and are comprised of a majority of women.

In addition to combinations of two traits, there is a type blending qualities of all Three Core Traits:

- **Working for a New Life of Wholeness** (WNL), represents 16.4% of households. These people identify with new paradigm values but due to social and economic situations, may be more focused on material well being for themselves and their families. This last combination group also includes an unusually large percentage of people who have recently made America their home.

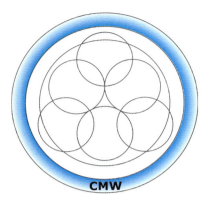

Lastly, there was a distinct type that did not include strong expression of any of the Three Core Traits and so appears as an outer ring, not touching or intersecting any of the other seven types. In naming the types, we could not help but give this one the following title:

- The **Centered in a Material World** (CMW) type represents 14.4% of households, seems to be less involved in society as a whole, and tends to be more concerned with ways relating to furthering a successful relationship with materialistic culture and ideas that do not threaten their primary interests.

In naming each of these types, we tried to keep the name short (two to four words) and sufficiently distinct and descriptive of each one's key qualities.

There are significant portions of the U.S. population identifying with values and beliefs not yet obvious at a national level of leadership or popular culture. Nevertheless, these individuals collectively place a high value on spirituality, service to others, and on the interconnectedness of all life. Even among people who identify more strongly with material success, there is an awareness and interest in these matters. *Lastly, and of great importance to people concerned with positive social change, there is only a very small portion of the population that seems highly constricted and inflexible in their worldview.*

Later on we will show ways of bringing forward the vast majority of society for social, cultural, and political change.

Examples of Diversity and Commonality

On the following pages, we have selected graphics that show similarities and differences between the 8 Types taken from the *IOOW-2000* research. A very brief explanation is included for each.

THE 8 AMERICAN TYPES

Percentage of U.S. Households

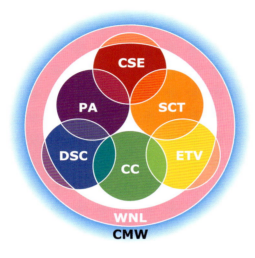

■ 14.4% (CMW) Centered in a Material World

■ 14.2% (DSC) Disengaged from Social Concerns

■ 12.1% (ETV) Embracing Traditional Values

■ 10.0% (CC) Cautious and Conservative

■ 11.9% (CSE) Connecting through Self-Exploration

■ 9.4% (PA) Persisting through Adversity

■ 11.6% (SCT) Seeking Community Transformation

■ 16.4% (WNL) Working for a New Life of Wholeness

INCOME AND EDUCATION

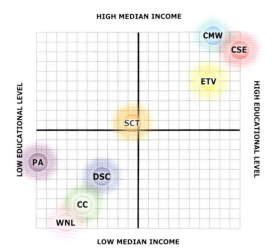

HIGH MEDIAN INCOME

LOW EDUCATIONAL LEVEL

HIGH EDUCATIONAL LEVEL

LOW MEDIAN INCOME

CMW
CSE
ETV
SCT
PA
DSC
CC
WNL

MEDIAN AGE

Years by each type

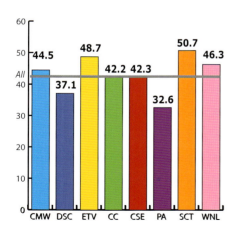

44.5 · 37.1 · 48.7 · 42.2 · 42.3 · 32.6 · 50.7 · 46.3

All

CMW DSC ETV CC CSE PA SCT WNL

Common Demographics and The 8 American Types

INCOME AND EDUCATION

Starting with the upper left graph on this page, we see a very interesting distribution of the 8 Types by income and education. (Income and education were never considered in defining the 8 Types.) Those types in the upper right quadrant of this grid have highest education and highest household income while those in the lower left have lowest income and education.

AGE

Age was never a factor in defining the 8 Types. Generational differences are in evidence here. The PA type and DSC are much more likely to include younger generations than are the SCT and ETV types.

GENDER

Here we see the composition of each of the 8 types by men and women. (The U.S. Census reports a ratio of 48.3% male to 51.7% female for those 18 years and older.) The SCT and CSE have a dramatically higher percentage of women over men than the other types.

RACE/ETHNICITY

The *IOOW-2000* didn't collect enough data to analyze all major racial/ethnic types therefore only white and non-white is shown here. PA and WNL types are most likely to include non-whites while CMW and ETV are least likely to.

GENDER

Percentage within each type

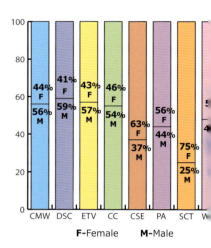

CMW DSC ETV CC CSE PA SCT

F-Female   **M**-Male

RACE/ETHNICITY

Percentage within each type

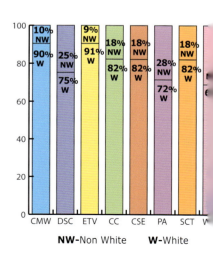

CMW DSC ETV CC CSE PA SCT

NW-Non White   **W-**White

DIVERSITY AND TOLERANCE
Percentage within each type

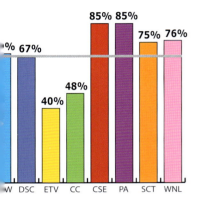

EARTH AS LIVING ORGANISM
Percentage within each type

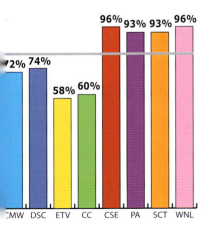

The 8 Types by Selected Questions

DIVERSITY AND TOLERANCE

Overall, 68% of all respondents believe that *"we should be tolerant of all lifestyles and groups even if we don't like what they do."* Here we see major differences across the 8 Types in this question with those in the ETV and CC types least in agreement with this statement and those in the CSE and PA types most in agreement. Several other questions were asked that also bear on diversity, tolerance and forgiveness.

EARTH AS LIVING ORGANISM

One indicator of a wholistic perspective and a capacity to embrace diversity is the extent to which one agrees or not whether our Earth is *"a unique kind of living organism and as a whole is fundamentally alive."* Those in the ETV and CC types least agreed with this while those in the CSE, PA, SCT, and WNL types most agreed.

SENSE OF SACRED AND FORGIVENESS

In the first bar chart to the upper right, the distribution of responses to a question that asked about having *"experienced a sense of the sacred in everything around them,"* we see that the DSC and CMW types are on opposite ends of the spectrum from WNL and SCT. Below this graph, the 8 Types are compared against the having experience a sense of the sacred and the extent to they reported expressing forgiveness to others. In the lower left are those least likely to identify with either of these factors. In the upper right are those who most identified with these.

EXPERIENCED SENSE OF SACRED
Percentage within each type

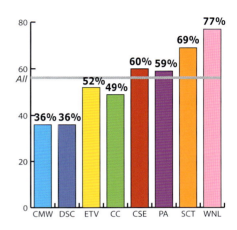

EXPERIENCED SENSE OF SACRED AND OFFER FORGIVENESS

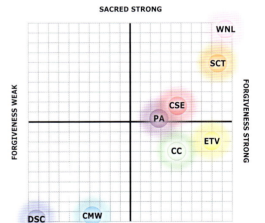

47

CONNECTION TO GOD OR HIGHER CONSCIOUSNESS

GOD OR HIGHER CONSCIOUSNESS SEPARATE FROM ME

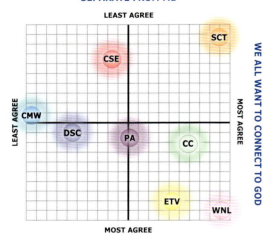

STRONGLY WANTING TO BE INVOLVED IN CREATING A BETTER WORLD

Percentage within each type

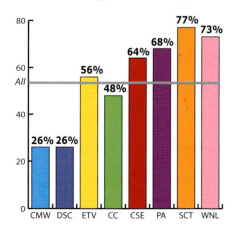

The 8 Types by Selected Questions

CONNECTION TO GOD OR HIGHER CONSCIOUSNESS

These are two of several questions that focused on aspects of spirituality: *"Whether we recognize it or not, we all just want to connect to God or a higher spiritual consciousness"* and *"God or a higher spiritual consciousness is something separate from me."* Here we see the 8 Types compared to the combination of these two questions. Those types in the right half of graph most agree we all want this connection, but have two different perspectives as to whether or not it is something that already is a part of them.

WANTING TO BE INVOLVED

"Wanting to be involved more personally in creating a better world at whatever local or global I can" is not something everyone may agree with. Here we see a very large difference between the CMW and DSC types and SCT, PA, and WNL in terms of strong agreement.

SPIRITUALITY INDEX

This is described in detail in Chapter 8. To briefly introduce this important index, it is made up of factors that do not include attending religious services. Once again, we see significant differences between the 8 Types with those of the CMW and DSC types scoring lowest on this composite measure, while those in the SCT and WNL types scoring highest.

ACKNOWLEDGEMENT OF SPIRITUAL NEEDS

*"I feel my spiritual needs are **not** currently being met"* was a question that brought a surprising answer, especially from those types least inclined toward matters of spirituality. Here we see, for example, that a significant portion of the DSC type shares this concern. Herein lies one avenue of possible bridging some of the seeming gulfs in our society.

SPIRITUALITY INDEX

Mean score by type

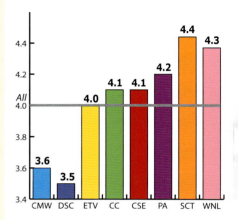

SPIRITUAL NEEDS NOT BEING ME

Percentage within each type

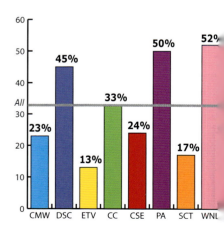

SUPPORT FOR AWAKENED BUSINESSES

Percentage within each type

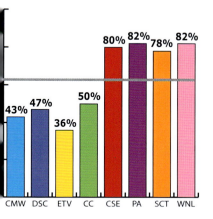

CONCERN THAT HUMANITY IS HEADED FOR DISASTER

Percentage within each type

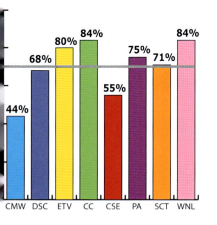

The 8 Types by Selected Questions

FOR AWAKENED BUSINESSES

62% of all respondents agreed that: *"Assuming the products and services were what I wanted, I would prefer to purchase them from businesses that solidly supported global awakening."* CSE, PA, SCT, and WNL types were in strongest agreement.

CONCERN ABOUT THE FUTURE

70% of all respondents agreed they were *"concerned that humanity is headed for serious problems and disasters in the next ten years."* The WNL type registered the greatest level of concern. It is this type that also embraced optimistic perspectives on our future.

HEALTH ISSUES

Various questions were asked to address health, physical trauma, and emotional stress. The graph in the upper right shows large differences between how the 8 Types reported experiencing serious health problems. CMW, ETV, and CSE types report the lowest levels of problems.

SOCIAL AND SPIRITUAL AWAKENING

Overall, 57% of all respondents agreed that: *"Over the next 10 years, social and spiritual awaking will make the world a better place to live."* Here we see how each of the 8 Types responded. SCT and WNL showed the strongest in agreement. While CWM and DSC had the weakest agreement, there still were a small percent who were in strong agreement.

PHYSICAL OR EMOTIONAL PROBLEMS

Percentage within each type

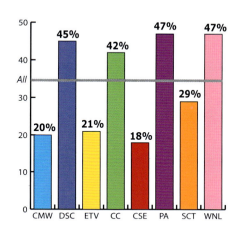

SOCIAL AND SPIRITUAL AWAKENING WILL MAKE WORLD A BETTER PLACE

Percentage within each type

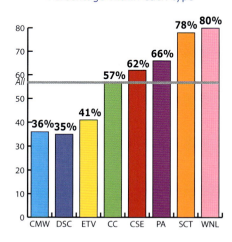

Embracing Traditional Values (ETV)

This is a fairly conservative group of people who are living the traditional ideal of the "American dream." They are materially successful, believe strongly in God, go to church, and feel that family is important. They are highly likely to vote, are conservative, tend to vote Republican, and are one of two types most likely to support the death penalty. This group fits the general STRC profile of "social traditional - religious conservative."

Spirituality for these people involves following the teaching of a specific spiritual or religious teacher, practicing prayer or meditation regularly, or believing that traditional religious literature tells the literal truth. As such, established religious institutions help this group maintain what works for them.

Further Descriptions of The 8 American Types

To provide you with a better feel for the qualities distinguishing these eight gradations of American society, we have selected highlights from the *IOOW-2000* research to create a thumbnail sketch of each:

Embracing Traditional Values (EVT)

Social Beliefs and Perspectives on Life

- Interested in personal involvement in creating a better world
- Not as important that nations should help others in need in the global community
- Less likely to see people as caring
- Household volunteers time for causes and donates generously, particularly to religious/spiritual organizations
- Feels connected to local community
- Less likely to express tolerance and embrace diversity, yet recognizes value of forgiveness
- Would like to see the world with fresh eyes of a child
- Less likely to see all connected as one
- Does not necessarily see goodness as prevailing

Spirituality and Global Awakening

- Likely to pray or meditate frequently
- Less likely to identify with global awakening
- God or higher consciousness separate from self, yet recognizes God or higher consciousness is present everywhere
- Less likely to see the Earth as a living whole system
- Feels need for spiritual growth

Religion

- Attends services more often than most
- Likely to follow specific teacher or teachings
- More likely to be a member of an older religious institution, probably Protestant
- Most likely to have changed religion at some point
- Believes their religious literature is literal truth

Health and Stress

- Likely to have participated in self-help groups
- Less likely to have used tobacco
- Less likely to use alcohol
- Probably never used marijuana
- Uses nutritional supplements, homeopathy, or naturopathy
- Not having serious health problems
- Not likely a risk taker

Lifestyle and Media

- Watches less television than the average
- Probably watches national/international news
- Likes to watch dramas such as Emergency Room or Touched by an Angel
- Agrees there are too many dark themes on television
- Uses Internet more than the average
- Likes to read a good book and uses reading for personal growth
- More likely to prefer magazines such as Home and Garden or Sports/Leisure publications
- Likes personal outdoor activities such as running or walking, hiking, golf, fishing, gardening
- Likely to listen to radio more, preferring call-in talk shows, sports, and gospel-religious stations
- Less likely to travel outside the U.S.
- Their movie-going preferences are typical, except they might like action adventure themes more at times

Embracing Traditional Values (ETV) (Continued)

This type is less likely not to believe a global awakening is taking place, nor that it will make the world a better place. They are also skeptical of technology, and generally experience good health and well being.

EVT has the most noticeable concentration of baby boomers and are least likely to include Gen-X or Gen-Y (18-36) individuals. The median age for this group is 48.7 years, the median annual income is $51,001. The majority (75%) are married, and over half (57%) are male. On average, this group has completed four years of college. They are one of two types most likely to be white/Caucasian.

This type constitutes 12.1% of U.S. households.

Disengaged from Social Concerns (DSC)

This is a group of politically moderate, socially reserved individuals whose general outlook on life is somewhat negative. Compared to other types, they tend to be disinterested in volunteering at either a local or international level. This type is least comfortable in reaching out to others. They are less likely to vote and consider themselves moderate with no outstanding party affiliations. This group does not fit the general STRC profile of "social traditional - religious conservative."

This group most believes that their spiritual needs are not being met and have a higher incidence of depression and non-family violence. They generally do not believe a global awakening is taking place, nor that it will eventually make the world a better place.

Disengaged From Social Concerns (DSC)

Social Beliefs and Perspectives on Life

- Not as interested in personal involvement in creating a better world
- Not as important that nations should help others in need in the global community
- Least likely to see people as caring or trustworthy
- Not likely to volunteer time or donate to causes
- Doesn't feel as connected to local community and may want to move elsewhere
- Less likely to express tolerance and forgiveness or embrace diversity
- Not as likely to relate to seeing the world with fresh eyes of a child
- Less likely to see all connected as one
- Does not necessarily see goodness as prevailing
- Likely to want to "just get by" and make money

Spirituality and Global Awakening

- Not as likely to pray or meditate frequently
- Less likely to identify with global awakening
- God or higher consciousness separate from self and does not feel God or higher consciousness is present everywhere
- Less likely to see the Earth as living whole system
- Spiritual needs not being met

Religion

- Not likely to attend services or follow a religious teacher
- More likely to not be affiliated with any religion
- Does not believe that religious literature is literal truth

Health and Stress

- Experiences depression or other emotional problems but not having serious physical health problems
- Less likely to use self-help groups or nutritional supplements
- Likely to have used marijuana
- Less likely to take risks

Lifestyle and Media

- Less likely to use self-help groups or nutritional supplements
- Television use is about average
- Likes to watch sports and comedy shows such as The Simpsons, Friends
- More likely to have Internet access at home but is average in usage level
- Less likely to read books
- More likely to prefer automotive, fashion, sports magazines such as Sports Illustrated
- Likes outdoor team sports
- Likely to listen to radio more, preferring country, hard rock, rhythm & blues, easy listening, and news
- Their movie-going preferences include comedy, action adventure, and westerns

Disengaged from Social Concerns (DSC) (Continued)

While they recognize a need for spiritual growth, they are not likely to participate in personal growth activities, and are less spiritually inclined than other types.

DSC, like the PA type, has a noticeable concentration of both Gen-X and Gen-Y (18-36) individuals and are least likely to include members of the older, pre-boomer generation. The majority of this group is male (59%) and many are single (38%). The median age is 37.1, the median annual income is $41,654. On average, this group has completed high school and some college.

This type constitutes 14.2% of U.S. households.

Connecting through Self-Exploration (CSE)

The self is the doorway to connection for this group. Spirituality for these people involves connecting to God or a higher spiritual consciousness through oneself; they believe it is important to teach our children to feel connected to the Earth, people, and all life, and that we are all just looking to be loved and accepted as human beings. CSEs are highly likely to vote and tend to be independent of the main parties, as well as liberal in their orientation.

They are extremely interested in personal growth activities and seek a wide range of conventional and unconventional means to achieve personal growth.

The predominately female (63%) group believes in a sacred connection to all aspects of their lives. They tend to believe a global social and spiritual awakening will eventually make the world a better place.

Connecting through Self-Exploration (CSE)

Social Beliefs and Perspectives on Life

- Interested in personal involvement in creating a better world
- Important that nations should help others in need in the global community
- Likely to see people are generally caring and trustworthy
- Household volunteers time for causes and donates particularly to arts and cultural, educational, environmental, and political causes
- Likes having their beliefs challenged
- Feels connected to local community
- More likely to express tolerance and embrace diversity
- Likely to see all connected as one
- Sees goodness as prevailing

Spirituality and Global Awakening

- Not as likely to pray or meditate frequently
- Not as likely to see global awakening occurring now but does see it making a difference in ten years
- God or higher consciousness is not separate from self but is present everywhere
- Likely to see the Earth as living whole system
- Has experienced sense of sacred in everything
- More likely to have experienced something of non-ordinary reality

Religion

- More likely to have Jewish, Middle Eastern, Asian, or Catholic religious affiliation
- Does not believe religious literature is literal truth
- Does not follow specific teacher or teachings

Health and Stress

- Physical and emotional health is likely to be good
- Used self-help groups
- Likely to have used marijuana
- More likely to take risks

Lifestyle and Media

- Television use tends to be lower
- Likes to watch games shows, news, drama, comedy, news. Programs include Friends, ER.
- Most frequent Internet user of all the types
- Feels more information is better
- More likely to spend time in nature
- Likely to read books
- More likely to prefer magazines on arts and entertainment, social science, health & fitness, National Geographic
- Likes personal activities such as swimming/diving, running/walking, gym workouts as well as outdoor social activities
- Not as likely to listen to radio; prefers classical music, jazz, news, and public radio
- More likely to have attended New Age events
- Most likely to have traveled outside the U.S.
- Movie-going preferences include comedy

Connecting through Self-Exploration (CSE) (Continued)

This group tends to be altruistic, have a positive outlook on life, and to be least likely to suffer health problems.

Over half (53%) are married, and have the fewest number of children in the household. CSE includes a small but noticeable portion of younger generations. The median age is 42.3, the median annual income is $54,039. On average, this group has completed four years of college.

This type constitutes 11.9% of U.S. households.

Cautious and Conservative (CC)

This is a group of people who strongly believe in God and subscribe to fundamental religious values. In this sense, they are very similar to the "Embracing Traditional Values" (ETV) type. Another characteristic of this group is feeling somewhat distanced from others. They are less ready than other types to freely reach out to others who have a different spiritual outlook.

The Cautious and Conservative type has no distinct political party affiliation but they do identify themselves as predominately as conservative and have an average voting likelihood. Along with the ETV type, DSC is likely to support the death penalty.

This group does not want to have its thinking or beliefs challenged. They also have conservative social and political values, and tend to be less open to or trusting of others. This group fits the general STRC profile of "social traditional - religious conservative."

Cautious and Conservative (CC)

Social Beliefs and Perspectives on Life

- Less interested in personal involvement in creating a better world
- Less important that nations should help others in need in the global community
- Not likely to see people as generally caring or trustworthy
- Donates money to religious/spiritual organizations
- Feels less connected to local community
- Less likely to express tolerance or forgiveness or embrace diversity
- Not as likely to relate to seeing the world with fresh eyes of a child
- Less likely to see all connected as one
- Does not see goodness as prevailing
- Likely to want to "just get by" and make money

Spirituality and Global Awakening

- Likely to pray or meditate frequently
- More likely to see global awakening occurring now but not likely to see it making a difference in ten years
- God or higher consciousness is separate from self yet is present everywhere
- Not likely to see the Earth as living whole system
- Does not have sense of sacred in everything
- Feels need for spiritual growth

Religion

- Attends services more often than most
- Identifies with newer Christian religious organizations
- Most likely to believe religious literature is literal truth

Health and Stress

- More likely to have serious physical and emotional health issues
- Has used physical body work such as chiropractors
- Not as likely to have used marijuana, tobacco, alcohol
- Used faith or energy healing
- Not likely to take risks

Lifestyle and Media

- Television use tends to be average
- Watches news, drama such as Touched by an Angel, or lighter fair (Friends, The Simpsons)
- Agrees there are too many dark themes on TV
- More frequent Internet user with less access than other types, but does not necessarily feel more information is better
- Less likely to spend time reading books; does read for personal growth, however.
- More likely to read lifestyle, science, and nature magazines
- Likes outdoor social activities such as team sports and is more likely to go camping/hunting
- Not as likely to listen to radio; prefers gospel/religious stations
- Would like to live with less technology
- Less likely to have traveled outside the U.S.
- Movie-going preferences favor comedy, drama, and sci-fi

Cautious and Conservative (CC) (Continued)

This group somewhat believes a global awakening is taking place, not necessarily that it will make the world a better place in ten years. They are least likely to feel the need for personal spiritual growth, and most believe there is only one correct way to live.

Just under half (47%) of this group is married. CC, like the CMW type, has not outstanding generational component. The median age is 42.2, the median annual income is $38,265, and slightly over half (55%) are male.

Similar to the "Persisting through Adversity" (PA) group, the CC group tends to have completed fewer years of formal education than other types.

This type constitutes 10.0% of U.S. households.

Persisting through Adversity (PA)

This group has a strong positive outlook and believes in connecting to God through the self. They tend to look within themselves for spiritual direction and sustenance. This group feels (more than any other type) that we should each attend to our own spiritual growth, and that we need to become more conscious of and connected to all aspects of ourselves.

This type is one of three most likely to oppose having a death penalty. They are less likely to vote, tend to be independent of the main political parties, and have a somewhat liberal orientation.

Even though this group reported experiencing more feelings of distance from others and has experienced the most personal and family trauma, as well as problems in general, they value personal growth and expressing their creativity.

Persisting through Adversity (PA)

Social Beliefs and Perspectives on Life

- Interested in personal involvement in creating a better world
- Important that nations should help others in need in the global community
- Likely to see people as generally caring but less trustworthy
- Not strong on volunteering or donating, but do give to environmental causes and hungry/needy
- Likely to want to "just get by" and make money
- Likes having their beliefs challenged
- Feels less connected to local community
- More likely to express tolerance and forgiveness and embrace diversity
- Likely to see all connected as one
- Sees goodness as prevailing

Spirituality and Global Awakening

- Not as likely to pray or meditate frequently
- Somewhat more likely to see global awakening occurring now but does see it making a difference in ten years
- God or higher consciousness is separate from self but is present everywhere
- Likely to see the Earth as a living whole system
- Has experienced sense of sacred in everything
- More likely to have experienced something of non-ordinary reality

Religion

- Has no strong religious affiliation, but somewhat more likely to be Middle Eastern/Asian affiliation
- Does not believe religious literature is literal truth
- Does not follow specific teacher or teachings

Health and Stress

- Likely to have emotional/depression problems
- Has used professional counseling/therapy
- Likely to use energy/faith healing, naturopathy, homeopathy
- Likely to have used marijuana
- Most likely to have used alcohol and tobacco
- More likely to take risks

Lifestyle and Media

- Television use tends to be higher
- Likes to watch comedy, reality TV, drama, and shows like Friends and ER
- Low Internet user yet feels more information is better
- Likely to read books
- More likely to spend time in nature
- Enjoys quiet contemplation
- More likely to prefer magazines like People, as well as ones on music, family/kids, sports & leisure, fashion
- Likes team sports and dancing
- Likely to listen to radio; prefers soft and hard rock, country, oldies
- More likely to have attended New Age events
- Movie-going preferences include drama, romance, horror, and thrillers

Persisting through Adversity (PA) (Continued)

This group somewhat believes a global awakening is taking place, and that it will make the world a better place. They are tolerant and interested in making a difference and are most likely to try alternative health care, as well as to use marijuana and alcohol. It may be that this group is trying to break through cultural or social limitations.

This group has the largest number of children per household. PA, like the DSC type, has a noticeable concentration of both Gen-X and Gen-Y (18-36) individuals and are least likely to include members of the older, pre boomer generations. The median age is 32.6, 56% are female, 40% are single, and the median annual income is $42,142. In addition, this group tends to have completed fewer years of formal education than other types. Along with the WNL, a PA type is more than likely to be non-white in race or ethnicity.

This type constitutes 9.4% of U.S. households.

Seeking Community Transformation (SCT)

This group embraces a combination of two different spiritual outlooks. They tend to exercise their spirituality in traditional ways and to look within themselves for spiritual direction and sustenance. Compared to the "Working for a New Life of Wholeness" (WNL) type, this group makes less of a distinction between God or a higher spiritual consciousness and themselves.

This type is one of three most likely to oppose having a death penalty. They are slightly above average in voting likelihood, tend to be average in preference to political parties, and are more likely to consider themselves as conservative Democrats. They also tend to fit the profile of social traditional - religious conservative while at the same time embracing a wholistic positive future perspective.

Seeking Community Transformation (SCT)

Social Beliefs and Perspectives on Life

- Interested in personal involvement in creating a better world
- Important that nations should help others in need in the global community
- Likely to see people are generally caring and trustworthy
- Strong on volunteering, average level of donating, likely to give to religious or spiritual organizations, health/medicine, and hungry/needy
- Feels connected to local community
- More likely to express tolerance and forgiveness and embrace diversity
- Would like to see the world with fresh eyes of a child
- Likely to see all connected as one
- Sees goodness as prevailing

Spirituality and Global Awakening

- Likely to pray or meditate frequently
- Likely to see global awakening occurring now and sees it making a difference in ten years
- God or higher consciousness is not separate from self and is present everywhere
- Likely to see the Earth as a living whole system
- Most likely to have experienced sense of sacred in everything
- Sees need for spiritual growth
- More likely to have experienced something of non-ordinary reality

Religion

- Slightly more likely to be Catholic or other older Christian religion
- Likely to believe religious literature is literal truth
- Likely to attend services
- Likely to follow specific teacher or teachings

Health and Stress

- Somewhat likely to have physical health problems
- Less likely to have emotional problems
- Has used self-help groups
- Likely to use energy/faith healing, naturopathy, homeopathy, nutritional supplements
- Has used physical body work such as chiropractors
- Not likely to have used marijuana or tobacco or alcohol
- Less likely to take risks

Lifestyle and Media

- Television use tends to be higher
- Likes to watch news, game shows, drama such as Touched by an Angel and ER
- Agrees there are too many dark themes on TV
- Lower Internet user yet feels more information is better
- Likely to read books
- More likely to spend time in nature
- Enjoys quiet contemplation
- More likely to prefer magazines like Readers Digest, Good Housekeeping, Better Homes and Gardens, family/kids, and other lifestyle type publications
- Likes indoor personal and social activities such as swimming, dancing, bowling, as well as running/walking exercise
- Not as likely to listen to radio; no distinctive preferences in programming
- Movie-going preferences include drama, musicals, romances/love stories

Seeking Community Transformation (SCT) (Continued)

Connection with others and unity with all of life are also dominant qualities of this type. They are most interested in making a difference and most likely to give to charity.

Like the WNL type, they strongly believe a global awakening is taking place, and that it will eventually make the world a better place. This group is optimistic and compassionate, and wants to be more personally involved in creating a better world.

Over half of this group is married (57%) and the overwhelming majority is female (75%). SCT, like the WNL type, has the most noticeable concentration of pre-boomers and are least likely to include Gen-X or Gen-Y individuals. The median age is 50.7, the median annual income is $46,661. In addition, this group tends to have completed high school plus some college.

This type constitutes 11.6% of U.S. households.

Working for a New Life of Wholeness (WNL)

While working hard to establish a strong material foundation for themselves and their families, this group may not have ready access to new avenues for personal growth. While they tend to rely on traditional forms of expressing spirituality, they also acknowledge an internal spiritual connection. However, unlike the "Seeking Community Transformation" (SCT) group, they make a distinction between themselves and God or a higher consciousness, holding these as separate from each other. This may reflect a less integral approach to spirituality and life.

This type is one of three most likely to oppose having a death penalty. They are slightly above average in voting likelihood, tend to be average in preference to political parties, and are more likely to consider themselves liberal Democrats, yet they also have a conservative orientation. Like the SCT type, they tend to fit the profile of social traditional - religious conservative, while at the same time embracing a wholistic positive future perspective.

Working for a New Life of Wholeness (WNL)

Social Beliefs and Perspectives on Life

- Interested in personal involvement in creating a better world
- Important that nations should help others in need in the global community
- Likely to see people as generally caring but not as trustworthy
- Not as strong on volunteering or donating level, but likely to give to children's causes
- Feels connected to local community
- More likely to express tolerance and forgiveness and embrace diversity
- Would like to see the world with fresh eyes of a child
- Likely to see all connected as one
- Sees goodness as prevailing
- Likely to want to "just get by" and make money

Spirituality and Global Awakening

- Likely to pray or meditate frequently
- Likely to see global awakening occurring now and sees it making a difference in ten years
- God or higher consciousness is separate from self yet is present everywhere
- Likely to see the Earth as living whole system
- Has experienced sense of sacred in everything
- Spiritual needs not being met
- Sees need for spiritual growth
- More likely to have experienced something of non-ordinary reality

Religion

- Somewhat likely to be Catholic or a newer Christian religion
- Likely to believe religious literature is literal truth
- Likely to attend services
- Likely to follow specific teacher or teachings

Health and Stress

- Likely to have emotional and most likely to have physical health problems
- Likely to use nutritional supplements
- Has used physical body work such as chiropractors
- Not likely to have used marijuana or alcohol
- More likely to take risks

Lifestyle and Media

- Television use tends to be higher
- Likes to watch news, drama, soap operas, Touched by an Angel, Who Wants to Be a Millionaire
- Agrees there are too many dark themes on TV
- Lowest level of Internet use yet feels more information is better
- Would like to live with less technology
- Enjoys quiet contemplation
- More likely to read magazines on home and garden, lifestyles, family/kids, arts and entertainment such as Ebony or Women's Day
- Likes indoor personal activities as well as fishing and team sports
- While not as likely to listen to radio; likes soft rock, easy listening, news, and gospel/religious programs; no distinctive preferences in programming
- Movie-going preferences include romance and love stories

Working for a New Life of Wholeness (WNL) (Continued)

They also tend to feel somewhat isolated and distant from others. Nevertheless, this group (which is least likely to have been born in the U.S.) embraces a global perspective allowing them to acknowledge the importance of spirituality in their lives. They also embrace traditional values, which may provide additional social permission to embrace spirituality.

This group, like the SCT group, is most likely to believe a global awakening is taking place and that it will make the world a better place.

Less than half (43%) of this group is married. WNL, like the SCT type, has the most noticeable concentration of pre-boomers and are least likely to include Gen-X or Gen-Y individuals. The median age is 46.3, 52% are female, and the median annual income is $35,424. This group, on average, has completed a high school education.

In addition to the PA type, WNL is also most likely to be non-white in race or ethnicity.

This type constitutes 16.4% of U.S. households.

Centered in a Material World (CMW)

This type is the most materially successful of all the types. Like those who are described as "Disengaged from Social Concerns" (DSC), this type is not as concerned with their spiritual growth, nor in expressing spirituality in any form.

While this group does not seem socially distanced from others, they are unlikely to want to be personally involved in creating a better world, and are unlikely to think that nations should help those in need. It may be that the material world, as it is, is just fine for those materially oriented.

They are about average in voting likelihood, tend to not affiliate with any one political party, and have a liberal orientation.

Centered in a Material World (CMW)

Social Beliefs and Perspectives on Life

- Not as interested in personal involvement in creating a better world
- Not as important that nations should help others in need in the global community
- Less likely to see people are generally caring yet generally think others are trustworthy
- Not as strong on volunteering, but likely to donate to arts and cultural causes
- Not as connected to local community
- Less likely to express tolerance and not strong on forgiveness
- Not as interested in having their beliefs challenged
- Not likely to relate to seeing the world with fresh eyes of a child
- Less likely to see all connected as one
- Less likely to see goodness prevailing

Spirituality and Global Awakening

- Less likely to pray or meditate frequently
- Not likely to identify with global awakening
- Somewhat less likely to see God or higher consciousness as separate from self, yet somewhat less likely to see it as present everywhere
- Not likely to see the Earth as living whole system

Religion

- No religious affiliations
- Not likely to believe religious literature is literal truth
- Not likely to attend services
- Not likely to follow specific teacher or teachings

Health and Stress

- Not likely to have emotional or physical health problems
- Likely to have used marijuana or tobacco and uses alcohol
- Less likely to take risks

Lifestyle and Media

- Television use tends to be low
- Likes to watch news, dramas like ER, and shows such as Friends, Frasier
- Very high Internet use yet doesn't necessarily feel more information is better
- Not as likely to enjoy reading books
- More likely to prefer magazines on food/wine and news, such as Time or Newsweek
- Likes outdoor personal activities such as running/walking, hiking/ climbing
- Likely to listen to radio; preferring call-in talk shows, oldies, soft rock
- Movie-going preferences include sci-fi, children/family themes, musicals, romance, and love stories

Centered in a Material World (CMW) (Continued)

Of this group, just under half (47%) are married. CMW, like the CC type, has no outstanding generational component. The median age is 44.5, 56% are male, and the median annual income is $55,897. This group tends to have completed high school and some college. In addition to the ETV type, CMWs are also most likely to be white/Caucasian.

This group constitutes 14.4% of U.S. households.

THE 8 AMERICAN TYPES

Percentage of U.S. Households

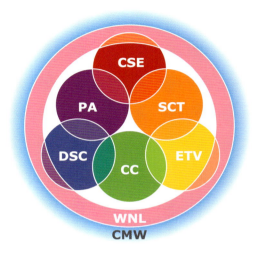

■ 14.4% (CMW) Centered in a Material World

■ 14.2% (DSC) Disengaged from Social Concerns

■ 12.1% (ETV) Embracing Traditional Values

■ 10.0% (CC) Cautious and Conservative

■ 11.9% (CSE) Connecting through Self-Exploration

■ 9.4% (PA) Persisting through Adversity

■ 11.6% (SCT) Seeking Community Transformation

■ 16.4% (WNL) Working for a New Life of Wholeness

The 8 Types and the PFCI-SMS-STRC Quadrant Models

By overlaying the 8 Types on the PFCI-SMS model, more detailed information becomes available to us.

The PFCI scale works well, neatly dividing the SCT, WNL, CSE, and PA types (those who most endorse broad spiritual connection and cooperation) from the CC, ETV, DSC, and CMW types (those who least endorse broad connection and cooperation).

The SMS scale also works well. The four types with the lowest annual income (CC, DSC, PA, and WNL) are most focused on money, while those with the highest annual incomes (CSE, SCT, CMW, ETV) are the least focused on money. The four types (DSC, CC, PA, WNL) who report the highest incidence of physical and emotional problems are also the most distressed.

In this simple placement of the five divisions of the PFCI-SMS types with the 8 Types, we can start to see the possibilities for bridging and connection based on shared values and beliefs. One of the most evident commonalities is shared PFCI values and beliefs by the four types found in the upper half. When we shift our attention to the STRC version in the second graphic, we see where traditional values and beliefs represent a commonality on the right half of the quadrant and the lack of traditionalism on the left offers yet another type of commonality.

It would not be an over-simplification to point out at this stage that the possibility becomes visible of PFCI values anchoring one major set of commonalities among four of the types and that shared traditional values on the right can provide a basis to unite two more. The lack of traditional beliefs by those people found on the left-hand portion of the grid provides an opening for them to connect with new, non-traditional values and beliefs. Later on, we shall see more of how this could potentially bring together 84% of Americans for a positive future.

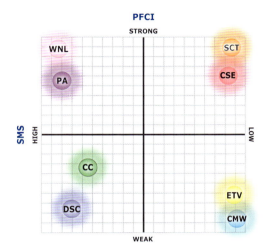

PFCI-SMS

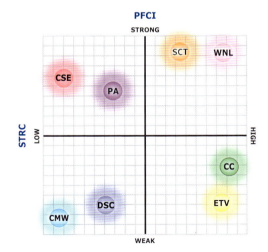

PFCI-STRC

THE 8 TYPES AND THE SMS SCALE

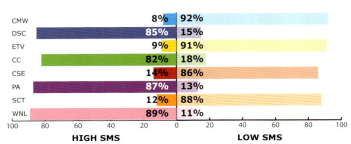

	HIGH SMS	LOW SMS
CMW	8%	92%
DSC	85%	15%
ETV	9%	91%
CC	82%	18%
CSE	14%	86%
PA	87%	13%
SCT	12%	88%
WNL	89%	11%

THE 8 TYPES AND THE STRC INDEX

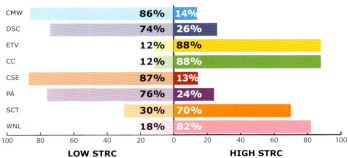

	LOW STRC	HIGH STRC
CMW	86%	14%
DSC	74%	26%
ETV	12%	88%
CC	12%	88%
CSE	87%	13%
PA	76%	24%
SCT	30%	70%
WNL	18%	82%

THE 8 TYPES AND THE PFCI SCALE

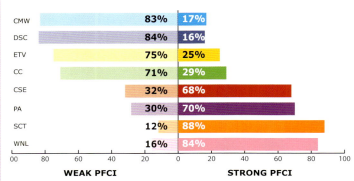

	WEAK PFCI	STRONG PFCI
CMW	83%	17%
DSC	84%	16%
ETV	75%	25%
CC	71%	29%
CSE	32%	68%
PA	30%	70%
SCT	12%	88%
WNL	16%	84%

To help further see the relationship of the 8 Types to each of the three quadrant axes, we show the average strength for each of the 8 Types by each of the main three measurements – SMS, STRC, and PFCI – that make up the grid quadrants. Each graph is split to show the percentage of each of the 8 Types scores below and above the median or these three measurements.

For example, in the first graph 92% of CMW scores in the lower median of the SMS scale and 8% of the CMW scores in the upper median. In the next graph, we see that 86% of the CMW scores in the lower median of the STRC index and 14% of CMW scores in the upper half. In the last graph, 83% of CMW scores in the lower median of PFCI and 17% in the upper median. Given what we can infer about CMWs, this is consistent with their profile of relatively little difficulty with material life, and low identification with social traditional - religious conservative values, as well the PFCI scale.

In presenting these simplified schematics, we have omitted the true distribution of population. On the following page, a set of scatterplot graphs show the existence of shared commonalities and the possibility of certain types of people acting as natural bridges to neighboring types.

In addition, we have darkened a small area within each of the zones. This marks the approximate position of the "center of gravity" or greatest density of population for each of the 8 Types.

These individual graphs are very important in that they show that portions of each type cross the PFCI quadrant boundaries – in effect, these people are potential bridges between groups.

Since two different grid scaling measures were used for graphical convenience, there are obvious differences in the placement of each of the 8 Types on these PFCI-SMS and STRC quadrants. For the discerning reader who is interested in a truer positioning, we recommend relying on the shaded scatterplot graphics that follow on the next pages.

SEEKING COMMUNITY TRANSFORMATION

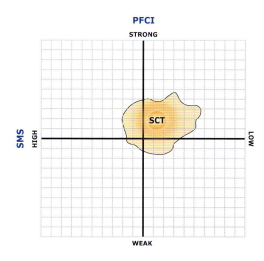

CONNECTING THROUGH SELF-EXPLORATION

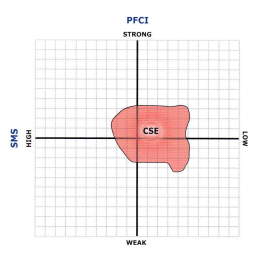

PFCI-SMS and the 8 Types

SCT and CSE: The left two types are relatively consistent homogenous groups strongly attracted to positive future values, and do not have high social or material stress. CSE has many similarities to the SCT group, but it has slightly more of its population in the lower right area of the quadrant than the SCTs.

WORKING FOR A NEW LIFE OF WHOLENESS

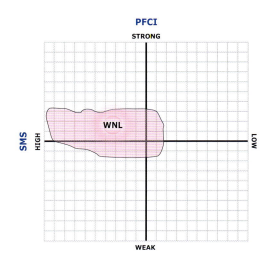

PERSISTING AGAINST ADVERSITY

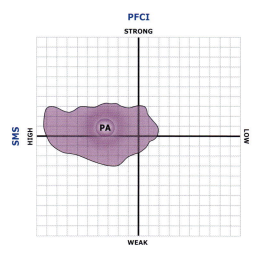

WNL and PA: These groups are attracted to positive future values and beliefs but are also strongly influenced by the pull of social and material stress.

PFCI-SMS and the 8 Types (continued)

CC: The CC group has relatively high social and material stress and, as a whole, is moderately attracted to positive future values and beliefs.

DSC: The DSC group does not have a very strong attraction to positive future values and beliefs, and experiences social or material stress.

CMW: The CMW group is not strongly attracted to positive future values and beliefs, and experiences relatively little social or material stress.

ETV: The ETV group has similarities to the CMW group, but has more of its members experiencing social material stress than the CMW group.

CAUTIOUS AND CONSERVATIVE

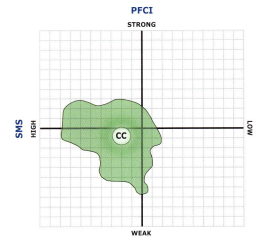

DISENGAGED FROM SOCIAL CONCERNS

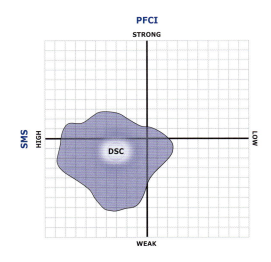

CENTERED IN A MATERIAL WORLD

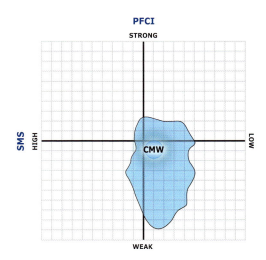

EMBRACING TRADITIONAL VALUES

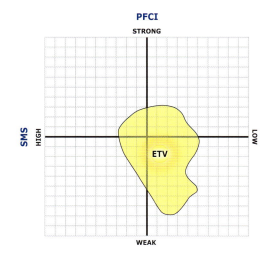

While some of the shaded regions of the 8 Types may seem to occupy similar areas to one another, they are each very distinct groups.

The overlaying of all 8 Types together on the PFCI-SMS quadrant dramatically illustrates their relationship to one another, as well as to the overall map of society and the range of the 8 Types. One of the most striking things about this is its demonstration of commonalities within a diverse American population.

Hopefully these explanations and illustrations of the combination the 8 American Types with the PFCI quadrant maps have provided visible insight of the existence of a greater unity within our diversity throughout society. This is a far cry from superficial labeling of people as "young urban professional" or "male/female age 35 to 45," etc.

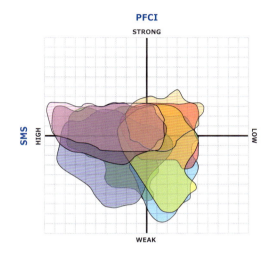

Traits and Types – Deeper than Surface Appearance

Simple demographic analyses used in the majority of survey research often raise more questions than they answer because typical population demographics divide, separate, and segregate. Adding together more bits and pieces of superficial demographic data, the more different "slices" one is left with. Attempting to attempt to integrate these back into a cohesive whole usually fails to provide useful meaning. It's like trying to get the "big picture" from a jumbled pile of "little pieces."

Traditionally, demographic data are usually easy to obtain, which leads to misleadingly easy analysis. However, this approach reflects more of what is "outside" or "on the surface" (e.g., gender, ethnicity, party affiliation, income, education, age, geography, etc.) rather than what is "deep inside" (e.g., core values and beliefs that affect behavior). For example: knowing that someone is a "white female under 30" does not tell us nearly as much as knowing that this person may believe strongly in traditional values, feels there is only one correct way to live, and may believe that traditional spiritual literature tells the literal truth.

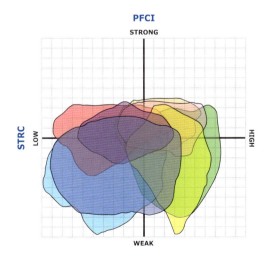

This raises some important questions:

- What core values and beliefs do voters and non-voters have beyond simple demographics?

- To what extent are these core values shared by all Americans, not just those who are politically disenfranchised?

- How can these core values be used to identify and create new political and social strategies for a positive future – ones that will be meaningful to those individuals who may not feel enfranchised into U.S. society in terms of voting or other forms of participation?

Typological research provides a solid basis for identifying sections of society, as well as unique individuals who best bridge the most positive elements and build suitable public communication and actionable strategies around these. This has many applications in developing leadership and societal involvement in innovative strategies and campaigns.

People have their likes and dislikes. When we look at core traits, spirituality and general outlook, some basic interactions come into play with each of the 8 Types embracing a range of these dynamics.

- Some people are more driven by attachment or attraction to the past or the current norm – either because they fear change in general or because they fear what they do not like.

- There are those who are more driven by their attraction or aspiration to the new and are working toward this. Some people have a great enough conflict between these that they are temporarily "cancelled out" and seem very disconnected or alienated.

- There are people who are driven more by rejection of what they do not like and have not found a new attractor to move toward.

- There are those who seek to actively oppose what they fear or dislike, setting up a "negative" dynamic that couples them to what they oppose, as much as a more positive attractor draws them to something new.

These points have serious implications and are addressed later in Part Three under the context of meaningful strategies for a positive future. These strategies are intended to express that which is presently not being given voice, and to provide a directional vector for movement into a more positive future.

In this next set of graphs, we see a truer picture of the relationship of The 8 American Types to the more generalized quadrant road map of PFCI-STRC. In each of the shaded regions, there is a darker portion around the type label. This marks the approximate "center of gravity" for each of the 8 Types.

"And so we are literally an eccentric people, our emotional life is disorganized, our passions are out-of-kilter. Those who call themselves radical float helplessly upon a stream amidst the wreckage of old creeds and abortive new ones, and they are inclined to mistake the motion which carries them for their own will. Those who make no pretensions to much theory are twisted about by fashions, 'crazes,' at the mercy of milliners and dressmakers, theatrical producers, advertising campaigns and the premeditated gossip of the newspapers."

– Walter Lippmann, *Drift and Mastery: An Attempt to Diagnose the Current Unrest* (Ch. 2: A Big World and Little Men)

**CONNECTING THROUGH
SELF-EXPLORATION**

PFCI-STRC and the 8 Types

CSE and PA: These two groups are relatively similar, are strongly attracted to positive future values, and are not strong on Social Traditional - Religious Conservative values and beliefs.

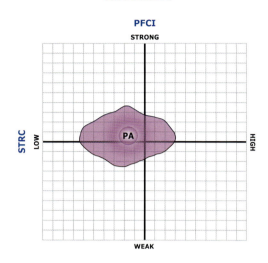

**PERSISTING AGAINST
ADVERSITY**

**SEEKING COMMUNITY
TRANSFORMATION**

SCT and WNL

These groups are also strongly attracted to positive future values and beliefs. In addition, they identify strongly with Social Traditional - Religious Conservative factors.

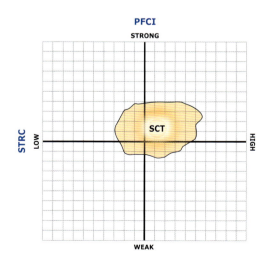

**WORKING FOR A NEW LIFE
OF WHOLENESS**

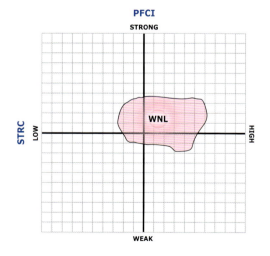

CAUTIOUS
AND CONSERVATIVE

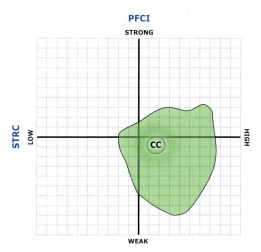

EMBRACING
TRADITIONAL VALUES

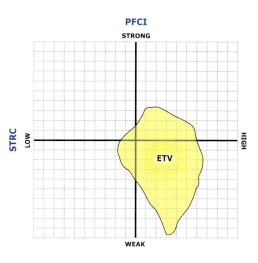

PFCI–STRC and the 8 Types (continued)

CC and ETV: These two groups have much in common. They both tend to be low on the PFCI scale and strongly identify with Social Traditional - Religious Conservative values.

DISENGAGED
FROM SOCIAL CONCERNS

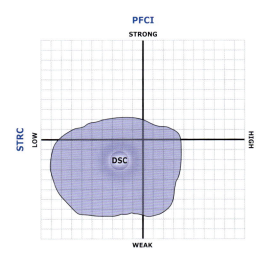

CENTERED IN
A MATERIAL WORLD

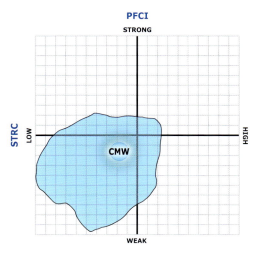

DSC and CMW: These groups are not strongly attracted to positive future values and beliefs, and do not identify much with the traditional conservative factors of the STRC index.

Powers of Magnification

• Looking at a single variable, such as age or income, voting, or religious connection, it is fairly easy to see how difficult it can be to find relevant information. Looking at one or several questions by themselves can tell us very little about a person.

• Combining a few individual items such as gender, age, and voting tells us a little more, but also quickly becomes limiting as it is too general and leads to superficial labeling of people.

• Combining many items into a mathematical measurement scale or index can help identify and screen for more complex factors.

• Combing two such scales or indexes can lead to more coherent maps, such as the PFCI quadrants. But even these need to be made more discerning. This can be achieved by overlaying individual items such as gender, voting, religious practice, etc. on this map. However, there are times when a little more resolution or magnification is needed.

• The 8 Types essentially provide twice the detail of the PFCI models and can be used to compare many other individual factors.

• Further detail is seen by combining the 8 Types with the PFCI types.

• Within these, it is also possible to select individual items for an even closer look.

• Obviously, at some point, it is possible to look too closely and not see anything relevant because there is not enough information at too fine a level of detail to see a relevant median pattern and context.

We have now looked at two quadrant typologies: one oriented around the PFCI quadrant model, another based on the 8 Types, and in combination with one another. When we use this to look at specific details of lifestyle, voting, media, future outlook, age, gender and other data, the result is analogous to having a powerful microscope that allows us to change lenses or zoom in and out as permitted by the data.

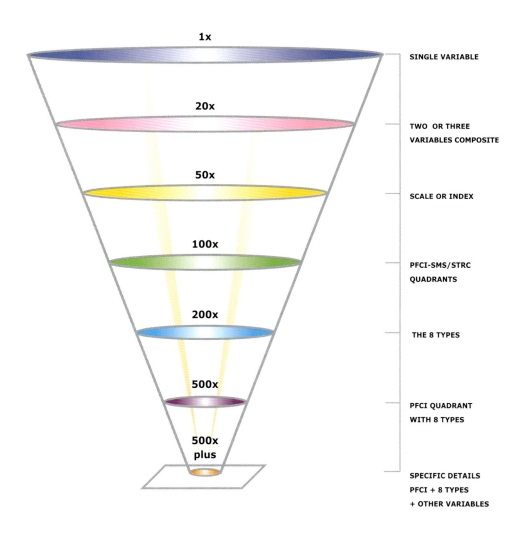

1x — SINGLE VARIABLE

20x — TWO OR THREE VARIABLES COMPOSITE

50x — SCALE OR INDEX

100x — PFCI-SMS/STRC QUADRANTS

200x — THE 8 TYPES

500x — PFCI QUADRANT WITH 8 TYPES

500x plus — SPECIFIC DETAILS PFCI + 8 TYPES + OTHER VARIABLES

One of the major contributions of *A New America* is that it can help orient leaders in our society to the totality of the values and belief systems within which we all operate. By showing where there are commonalities of values and aspirations, new cooperative and integrative approaches can be developed to effectively transform basic organizational relationships and, eventually, the community of communities that comprise the sum total of any given business or social enterprise. The typologies we've discovered can also be used to help monitor change and provide new, predictive tools bridging professed interests to and with behaviors.

As we apply these values – and beliefs-based typology models to the U.S. elections and social and political strategies – ways to bridge these seemingly disparate groups will become more evident. In this way, meaningful strategies can be developed that help elevate and unify so the whole of American society can truly be much greater than the sum of its parts.

CHAPTER 5

What Type Am I Closest To?

"…the IOOW-2000 research scientifically corroborates the concept that we have much more in common than we may think, and that by exploring these points of commonality, we can then move toward a more compassionate and future-present perspective as a species."

This chapter gives everyone the opportunity to see where they most closely fit in the three major typological systems presented so far: The two PFCI quadrants and The 8 American Types models. To make this process easy, we assembled simple self-scoring questionnaires that take only minutes to complete. Ask your friends to try these as well. These questionnaires can also be found on our website.

First, see where you place on the more generalized PFCI quadrants relative to the Social Traditional - Religious Conservative Social index or the Material Stress scale. This will give you a rough idea of the roadmap we have developed from a more personal perspective. If you score with in a point or two of another type, then it means you are likely a good bridge with the next closest type. If you can identify exactly which questions your score could most easily change, this can give you some interesting personal insights.

You can continue on to see which of The 8 American Types you are closest to. Then combine the PFCI quadrant map with the 8 Types. This is like "zooming in" for more detail.

Have fun with these!

The PFCI-STRC Quadrant Map and How to Use the Question Tables

- There are two separate tables. The first one corresponds with the vertical **PFCI** axis on the quadrant. The second table corresponds to the horizontal **STRC** axis.

- Read each question and circle the number that best approximates how strongly you identify with that item. Do not analyze these, as there are no right or wrong answers! Go with your first impression.

- Add up your ratings at the bottom of each table.

- Then circle the ONE letter at the bottom of each table that corresponds to your total score.

- After you have completed the **STRC** table, use the letter matrix on the page following to find where you place on the **PFCI-STRC** map.

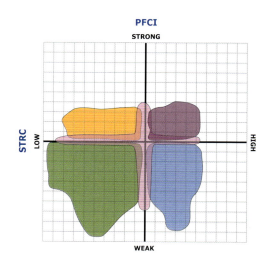

POSITIVE FUTURE – COOPERATIVE INTEGRATIVE (PFCI) SCALE		
1 = Strongly Disagree 2 = Somewhat Disagree 3 = Neither 4 = Somewhat Agree 5 = Strongly Agree		
1. Our earth is a unique kind of living organism and as a whole system is fundamentally alive.		1 2 3 4 5
2. I believe that helping those in need is one of the most important things nations can do within the global community.		1 2 3 4 5
3. Underneath it all, we're all connected as one.		1 2 3 4 5
4. There is a global awakening to higher consciousness taking place these days.		1 2 3 4 5
5. If we could forgive and reconcile all our past hurts and conflicts, we could all accomplish so much more.		1 2 3 4 5
6. Interacting with other cultures broadens our horizons.		1 2 3 4 5
7. Over the next 10 years, social and spiritual awakening will make the world a better place to live.		1 2 3 4 5
8. Have you ever experienced a sense of the sacred in everything around you or perceived everything as being spiritually connected together as one?		1=No 2=Yes
9. It is important to teach our children to feel a connection to the earth, people, and all life.		1 2 3 4 5
10. Whether I am aware of it or not, I believe that god or a higher spiritual consciousness is present everywhere.		1 2 3 4 5
ADD UP YOUR RATINGS FOR THESE QUESTIONS. TOTAL =		
If your TOTAL is EQUAL to or LESS than 38, circle "A" If your TOTAL is EQUAL to 39 or 40, circle "B" If your TOTAL is Equal or GREATER than 41, circle "C"	A B C	

SOCIAL TRADITIONAL – RELIGIOUS CONSERVATIVE (STRC) INDEX

1 = Strongly Disagree **2 = Somewhat Disagree** **3 = Neither** **4 = Somewhat Agree** **5 = Strongly Agree**

1.	There is basically only one correct way to live.	1 2 3 4 5
2.	I want a world where people live by traditional values.	1 2 3 4 5
3.	My community is too diverse in its beliefs.	1 2 3 4 5
4.	Maintaining law and order is the most important issue today.	1 2 3 4 5
5.	Do you attend church services or other meetings of a religious organization?	1=No 2=Yes
6.	I believe that traditional religious literature tells the truth.	1 2 3 4 5
7.	I follow the teachings of a specific spiritual or religious leader.	1 2 3 4 5
8.	Children and youth are allowed too much freedom these days.	1 2 3 4 5
9.	Family values are the basis for a successful society.	1 2 3 4 5
10.	To what extent do you support having a death penalty in any state of the U.S.?	1 2 3 4 5
11.	We should be tolerant of all lifestyles and groups even if we don't like what they do.	Strongly Disagree 5 Somewhat Disagree 4 Neither 3 Somewhat Agree 2 Strongly Agree 1
12.	Democrat / Republican / Other	Democrat 1 Republican 2 Other 0
13.	Which of the following describes your political ideology?	Conservative 3 Moderate 2 Liberal 1
14.	Which of the following best describes how frequently you attend services or meetings of a religious organization?	More than once a week 7 Usually every week 6 2-3 times a month 5 Once a month 4 Less than once a month 3 Hardly ever 2 First time 1

ADD UP YOUR RATINGS FOR THESE QUESTIONS.   **TOTAL =**

If your TOTAL is EQUAL to or LESS than 34, circle "D" If your TOTAL is EQUAL to 35 or 36, circle "E" If your TOTAL is Equal or GREATER than 37, circle "F"	D	E	F

TABLE		POSITIVE FUTURE – COOPERATIVE INTEGRATIVE (PFCI) SCALE BY SOCIAL TRADITIONAL – RELIGIOUS CONSERVATIVE (STRC) INDEX	
PFCI	STRC		
A	D	Low PFCI/Low STRC	Lower right
C	D	High PFCI/Low STRC	Upper right
B	E	Boundary Zone	Middle region
A	E	Boundary Zone	Middle region
C	E	Boundary Zone	Middle region
B	D	Boundary Zone	Middle region
B	F	Boundary Zone	Middle region
A	F	Low PFCI/High STRC	Lower left
C	F	High PFCI/High STRC	Upper left

You will find yourself in one of these four quadrants, or perhaps in the boundary zone, perhaps traditional and at the same time strongly aligned with positive future or integral values. Whom do you know with whom you get along who might be very different in their placement? How do you connect with that person? Who do they connect with? Imagine someone who might score very low on the PFCI scale, how might you connect with them?

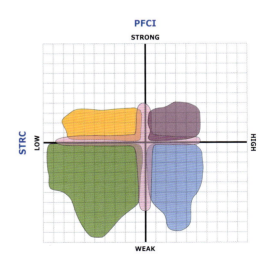

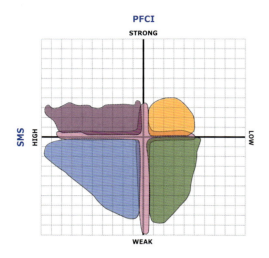

The PFCI-SMS Quadrant Map

- One additional variation to the PFCI model is provided that corresponds to the SMS horizontal axis.

- Read each question and circle the number that best approximates how strongly you identify with that item. Don't analyze these, as there are no right or wrong answers! Go with your first impression.

- Add up your ratings at the bottom of the table.

- Then circle the ONE letter at the bottom of each table corresponding to your total score.

- After you have completed the **SMS** table, use the letter matrix on the page following and the letter score from the **PFCI** table on page 81 to find where you place on the **PFCI-SMS** map.

SOCIAL MATERIAL STRESS (SMS) SCALE			
1 = Strongly Disagree 2 = Somewhat Disagree 3 = Neither 4 = Somewhat Agree 5 = Strongly Agree			
1. Most people cannot be trusted.	1 2 3 4 5		
2. I often feel lonely and cut off from those around me.	1 2 3 4 5		
3. I feel judged by most others around me.	1 2 3 4 5		
4. I sometimes think of moving elsewhere because I feel that I don't belong where I am.	1 2 3 4 5		
5. I am concerned that humanity is headed for serious problems and disasters in the next 10 years.	1 = No 2 = Yes		
6. My main goal in life is to make a lot of money.	1 2 3 4 5		
7. All I want out of life is getting by day-to-day.	1 2 3 4 5		
8. One of the most important achievements in life is to acquire a higher standard of living.	1 2 3 4 5		
9. Thinking about your overall emotional life, are you currently experiencing any serious problems with your emotional relations?	1 = No 2 = Yes		
10. At any point in the past four weeks, have you felt so sad and unhappy that nothing could cheer you up?	1 = No 2 = Yes		
ADD UP YOUR RATINGS FOR THESE QUESTIONS. TOTAL =			
If your TOTAL is EQUAL to or LESS than 20, circle "D" **If your TOTAL is EQUAL to 21 or 22, circle "E"** **If your TOTAL is Equal or GREATER than 23, circle "F"**	D	E	F

TABLE		POSITIVE FUTURE – COOPERATIVE INTEGRATIVE (PFCI) SCALE BY SOCIAL MATERIAL STRESS (SMS) SCALE	
PFCI	**SMS**		
A	D	**Low PFCI/Low SMS**	Lower right
C	D	**High PFCI/Low SMS**	Upper right
B	E	**Boundary Zone**	Middle region
A	E	**Boundary Zone**	Middle region
C	E	**Boundary Zone**	Middle region
B	D	**Boundary Zone**	Middle region
B	F	**Boundary Zone**	Middle region
A	F	**Low PFCI/High SMS**	Lower left
C	F	**High PFCI/High SMS**	Upper left

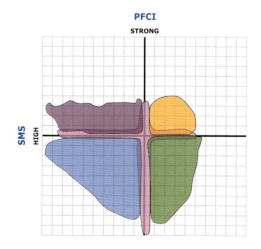

PFCI
STRONG

SMS
HIGH

Whether or not you find yourself in the same zone on this grid as you did on the previous PFCI-STRC exercise, these two quadrant maps are very different from one another. The only thing they share in common is the PFCI vertical axis. How might stress affect your outlook on life? Voting tendencies? How might PFCI values be used to bridge differences in perceived or experienced social or material stress in your life? How might this make a difference in our communities or nationally?

Let's take a closer look with stronger magnification provided by the 8 Types instead of the four basic patterns provided by these quadrant models.

The 8 American Types and How to Use the Question Tables

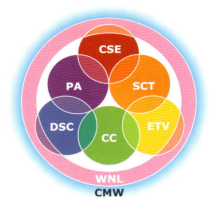

- There are three separate tables, each corresponding to a primary or core trait. Read each question and circle the number that best approximates how strongly you identify with that item. Don't analyze these, as there are no right or wrong answers! Go with your first impression.

- Add up your ratings at the bottom of each table.

- Circle the ONE letter at the bottom of each table corresponding to your total score.

- Use the letter matrix on the page following the last table to find which type you are closest to.

- If your score for any one table is within one point of changing your letter code on any or all of the tables, you can go back and see which of The 8 American Types that new letter code combination could also become.

GROUP ONE – THE 8 AMERICAN TYPES					
1 = Strongly Disagree 2 = Somewhat Disagree 3 = Neither 4 = Somewhat Agree 5 = Strongly Agree					
1. I believe in God or a higher spiritual consciousness.	1	2	3	4	5
2. I practice meditation or prayer regularly.	1	2	3	4	5
3. I follow the teachings of a specific spiritual or religious teacher.	1	2	3	4	5
4. Whether we recognize it or not, we all just want to connect to God or a higher spiritual consciousness.	1	2	3	4	5
5. Have you ever been directly aware of or personally influenced by the presence of God or a higher spiritual consciousness?	1=No			2=Yes	
6. I believe that traditional religious literature tells the literal truth.	1	2	3	4	5
7. Going to church, synagogue, or mosque gives me the opportunity to make and maintain social contacts.	1	2	3	4	5
8. There is basically only one correct way to live.	1	2	3	4	5
9. I believe that every person has a purpose in life.	1	2	3	4	5
ADD UP YOUR RATINGS FOR THESE QUESTIONS. TOTAL =					
If your TOTAL is GREATER than 34, circle "A" **If your TOTAL is EQUAL to or LESS than 34, circle "B"**	A			B	

GROUP TWO – THE 8 AMERICAN TYPES					
1 = Strongly Disagree 2 = Somewhat Disagree 3 = Neither 4 = Somewhat Agree 5 = Strongly Agree					
1. Underneath it all, we're all connected as one.	1	2	3	4	5
2. It is important to teach our children to feel a connection to the earth, people, and all life.	1	2	3	4	5
3. I believe that most people are genuinely caring.	1	2	3	4	5
4. The best way to connect to God or a higher spirituality is through yourself.	1	2	3	4	5
5. One of the most important things in my life is expressing my own creativity.	1	2	3	4	5
6. The bottom line is that we are all just looking to be loved and accepted as human beings.	1	2	3	4	5
7. I believe that helping those in need is one of the most important things nations can do within the global community.	1	2	3	4	5
8. I believe that good eventually prevails.	1	2	3	4	5
9. We all need to become more conscious of and connected to all aspects of our own selves.	1	2	3	4	5
10. Our earth is a unique kind of living organism and as a whole system is fundamentally alive.	1	2	3	4	5
11. Everyone should look at life as a glass half full rather than half empty.	1	2	3	4	5
12. I would like to be involved more personally in creating a better world at whatever local or global level I can.	1	2	3	4	5
13. I offer forgiveness to those who do me wrong.	1	2	3	4	5
ADD UP YOUR RATINGS FOR THESE QUESTIONS. TOTAL =					
If your TOTAL is GREATER than 56, circle "C" **If your TOTAL is EQUAL to or LESS than 56, circle "D"**			C		D

GROUP THREE – THE 8 AMERICAN TYPES					
1 = Strongly Disagree 2 = Somewhat Disagree 3 = Neither 4 = Somewhat Agree 5 = Strongly Agree					
1. Most people cannot be trusted.	1	2	3	4	5
2. I feel judged by most others around me.	1	2	3	4	5
3. My community is too diverse in its beliefs.	1	2	3	4	5
4. All I want out of life is getting by day-to-day.	1	2	3	4	5
5. I often feel lonely and cut off from those around me.	1	2	3	4	5
6. I sometimes think of moving elsewhere because I feel that I don't belong where I am.	1	2	3	4	5
7. People don't seem to connect to each other these days.	1	2	3	4	5
8. My main goal in life is to make a lot of money.	1	2	3	4	5
ADD UP YOUR RATINGS FOR THESE QUESTIONS. TOTAL =					
If your TOTAL is GREATER than 22, circle "E" If your TOTAL is EQUAL to or LESS than 22, circle "F"				E	F

Find Your Type

If your score, for example, from Group One was a "B"; your score from Group Two was a "C"; and your score from Group Three was an "F," finding "B-C-F" in the table below points to the type CSE (Connecting through Self-Exploration).

GROUP NUMBER			THE 8 AMERICAN TYPES	
ONE	TWO	THREE		
A	D	F	"ETV"	Embracing Traditional Values
B	C	F	"CSE"	Connecting through Self-Exploration
B	D	E	"DSC"	Disengaged from Social Concerns
A	C	F	"SCT"	Seeking Community Transformation
B	C	E	"PA"	Persisting through Adversity
A	D	E	"CC"	Cautious and Conservative
A	C	E	"WNL"	Working for a New Life of Wholeness
B	D	F	"CMW"	Centered in a Material World

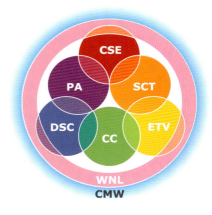

If your score in Group Two was a "57" (right on the edge), then your score could easily have been "B-D-F," which would mean that you also were close to "Centered in a Material World" (CMW). As we will see in later chapters on social and political strategies, these crossover qualities can lend themselves to bridging the diversity within our society.

In the preceding chapter, we have provided a descriptive profile of each of the 8 Types. How do these fit with your sense of self? Keep in mind that none of these is definitive or restrictive. Any type can develop or move into any of the other types, as their values and beliefs may change.

The 8 American Types and the PFCI-STRC Quadrants

Let's see how the 8 Types provide a more detailed understanding of the PFCI quadrants. The darker colored circle within each of the colored areas shows the approximate "center of gravity" or concentration of those people who most closely fit one of the 8 Types relative to the quadrant they are in. The shaded area shows the extent to which any one type is present across the entire map grid.

Interpreting the 8 Types in combination with a quadrant map

EXAMPLE:

In the first diagram, the **CSE** type is centered mostly in the **upper left** quadrant where there is a relatively low identification with Social Traditional - Religious Conservative values *and* a relatively high identification with Positive Future - Cooperative Integrative values.

CONNECTING THROUGH SELF-EXPLORATION

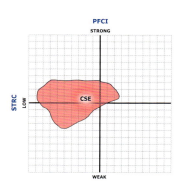

SEEKING COMMUNITY TRANSFORMATION

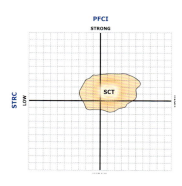

WORKING FOR A NEW LIFE OF WHOLENESS

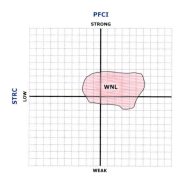

PERSISTING AGAINST ADVERSITY

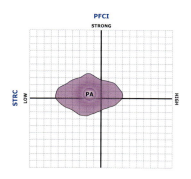

CAUTIOUS AND CONSERVATIVE

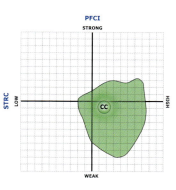

DISENGAGED FROM SOCIAL CONCERNS

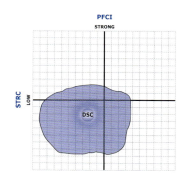

CENTERED IN A MATERIAL WORLD

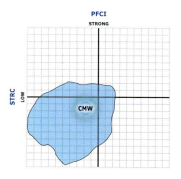

EMBRACING TRADITIONAL VALUES

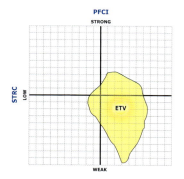

The 8 American Types and the PFCI-SMS Quadrants

Let's switch our "PFCI lenses" for a slightly different colored version, the PFCI-SMS quadrant. Here we can see the effect of Social Material Stress for each of the 8 Types.

Interpreting the 8 Types in combination with a quadrant map

EXAMPLE:
In the first diagram, the **CSE** type is centered mostly in the **upper right** quadrant where there is a relatively low identification with Social Material Stress *and* a relatively high identification with Positive Future - Cooperative Integrative values.

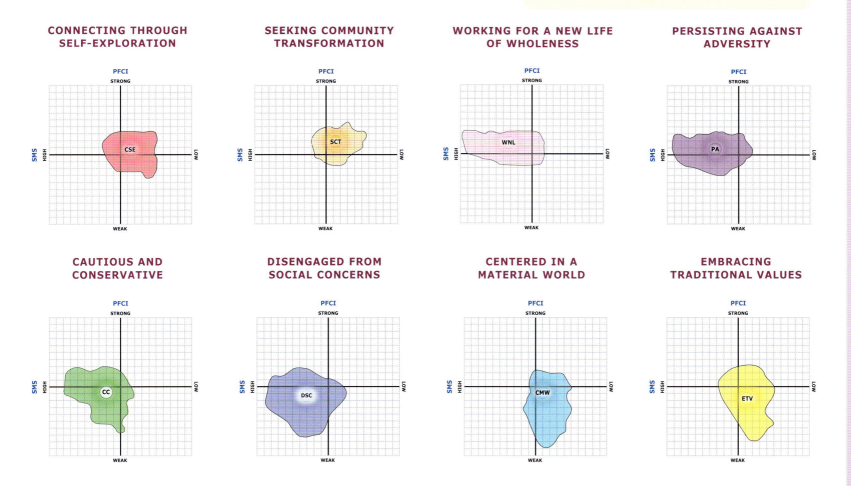

CONNECTING THROUGH SELF-EXPLORATION

SEEKING COMMUNITY TRANSFORMATION

WORKING FOR A NEW LIFE OF WHOLENESS

PERSISTING AGAINST ADVERSITY

CAUTIOUS AND CONSERVATIVE

DISENGAGED FROM SOCIAL CONCERNS

CENTERED IN A MATERIAL WORLD

EMBRACING TRADITIONAL VALUES

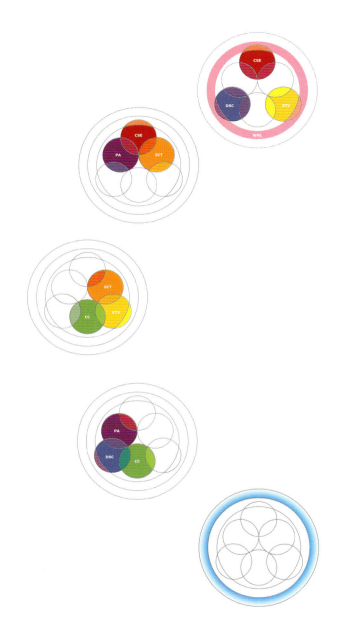

Some Help with Interpretation

By now you have seen ways that each of the 8 Types can be very close to another. Even types that don't have a graphically obvious connection (like the CMW and CSE types) can share similar typological space. Using these two types as an example, we can see how they share a similar socio-economic standing and are open to spirituality and discovering greater meaning to their lives (although perhaps in different ways). The possibility exists for a CMW to look to a CSE for connection in this regard. What we are seeing demonstrates ways people can be similar and yet seem so different.

In scoring yourself, it is easy to see how slight changes in beliefs and values can shift a CSE to CMW and vice versa, for example.

Overlaying these on a PFCI-SMS or STRC quadrant map more clearly shows certain relationships between these types and suggests ways of connecting more of the "whole tapestry" of society. What you are seeing is the coincidence of similar values and beliefs against a more generalized context as another example of unity within diversity.

Though we've clearly delineated the 8 Types and you've had a chance to determine what type you might be, we know that in society all 8 Types interact and move among each other unaware of the beliefs and values of many of the people surrounding them. How then do we intermingle socially and culturally while maintaining our sense of self and focusing on the things that matter to us? What brings us together through commonality, camaraderie, or even opposition as we express ourselves through our various types?

Even though we consider our beliefs and values fundamental to our being, we exist in a vast matrix of fluid consciousness that enables us to continually find that which we can consider touchstones or connection points with those we would ordinarily regard as too different from ourselves.

One of the major points of *A New America* is that the *IOOW-2000* research scientifically corroborates the concept that we have much more in common than we may think, and that by exploring these points of commonality, we can then move toward a more compassionate and future-present perspective as a species.

A Vignette

A much-beloved, world-renowned religious and spiritual leader is the central attraction at a fundraiser held near San Jose, California, the heart of Silicon Valley and Stanford University. In general, it is also a center of financial, technological, scientific, and academic excellence.

- People like the CSE type would attend simply because the speaker represents a safe and familiar form of expression very close to the way they would like to carry themselves in the world. They can also afford to donate to this cause.

- For likely different reasons, CMW people would attend, perhaps as a way to get closer to spirituality, something they think could be important to them, and to support a worthy cause; it would be the "right thing to do." This group can also afford to attend and donate.

- SCTs would go because they are involved in changing the world into a better place and appreciate the value of the speaker's message. They would also feel comfortable with the mix of people attending.

- People who are ETV would most likely not attend as they feel the speaker's religious-spiritual background is too different from their own. They would rather donate to their church.

- Few of the DSC type would attend as they don't believe much in religion nor do they identify much with spirituality. Additionally, the admission cost might be too high.

- Of the WNL, most of this particular type wouldn't attend simply because they are less likely to be on the mailing list. They also tend to be more traditionally oriented in their approach to religion and might be concerned about a conflict with their religious practice. It wouldn't stop them from admiring this world leader and some might go to the large public event.

- PAs wouldn't attend mostly because it's a fundraiser in an expensive locale. However, if there were a large public event with free or low admission, they would be interested in going.

- Lastly, those of the CC type wouldn't be likely to attend, as they prefer that which is familiar to them and prefer not to be exposed to an alternative spiritual tradition.

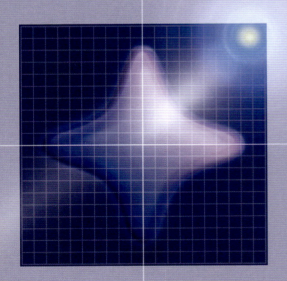

PART TWO

Social & Political
Change

PART TWO:
Social & Political Change

Genereal strategies are outlined in this section addressing both social and political initiatives. These general strategies are both *independent* of one another, yet clearly *connected* as one without the other would create an imbalance that could derail a positive future agenda for society.

The "social strategy" put forth lays a framework that, from the start, unites people who are already taking initiative or leadership in creating an awakened society with many more who already resonate with this. It also unites both the religious and the secular in a consciousness of the heart and in so doing energizes people to rise to the occasion of social and spiritual awakening. This social strategy, called Decade of the Heart, offers the possibility of diverse practical and social expressions of our highest aspirations. Its proposed initial campaign is guided by the understanding that forgiveness and reconciliation are a portal to global awakening, freeing us to connect with our higher selves.

The "political strategy" emphasizes the values, actions, and integrity of leadership for those holding or seeking office, and in leading social-political action campaigns. The strategies do not center upon any one party or the formation of a "positive future" third party for its own sake, but rather on ways to connect people, regardless of party affiliation, who are willing to stand for a positive future with integrity and resolve. (This does not mean however that a new party embracing spiritually aligned, positive future values and positions is undesirable. On the contrary, a new party standing for an awakened world could play a valuable and influential role, as long as voters or party members are not forced to choose along party lines.)

Both approaches – social and political – focus on movement toward a more positive future, seeking to find the commonalities within our multitude of socio-economic groupings and alignments. "Bridges" are then identified that can bring seemingly disparate individuals, associations and organizations together, organized around a new and more inclusive paradigm: integrating the greater whole through connection, service, and spirituality.

We begin first by offering a backdrop to the current national and world stage and a look at some future outlook indicators. Ultimately, real change is about using our precious gift to consciously choose.

Do we choose an enlightened life or death by disconnectedness and denial…or worse?

CHAPTER 6
Conditions for Change

"Choosing out of higher motivation is really about thought or consciousness determining form, instead of tacitly allowing existing forms to determine our consciousness and thoughts."

A simple framing of the conditions for widespread social change typically includes three elements:

- Old structures and processes developed to serve the old ways become increasingly unable to meet current needs.

- Society as a whole becomes increasingly unwilling to be governed in the old way, in terms of social custom, as well as law.

- New leadership, structures, and processes emerge representing a viable alternative.

Even if current news headlines are only showing the "tip of the iceberg," recent events involving many levels of government and business demonstrate the existence of serious structural problems in both these sectors. The 2000 election saw a nearly split-even difference among U.S. voters. More importantly, it showed continued discouragement by potential voters in the candidates put forward. Additionally, voter participation remained very low with those not voting representing a passive "vote" of low confidence in the U.S. political system and process. What may be showing publicly, in terms of a breakdown within the power circles at the highest levels of business and government, barely scratches the surface of deeper and murkier matters affecting everyone's well being.

A new kind of "third element," devoted to helping give birth to a new society, is only now starting to appear. It is not based on partisan politics. It is based fundamentally on a *consciousness shift*.

What *Will* It Take?

On one hand, we could list all the likely types of initiatives, movements, policies, organizations and such. But let's not, as it fundamentally is not about policies and regulations but rather consciousness and choosing to use our innate free-will in accord with the interconnectedness of all life and our higher aspirations as spiritual beings. This is something that really cannot be taken away. It can be obscured, it can be temporarily set aside by preferring to "go along for the ride," but it cannot be taken away. Near the end of the third of the Matrix movies, the hero is asked by the "villain" why he persists in trying to break through the Matrix to another reality, to which he answers: "Because I choose to."

When you start to list all the myriad contributing factors, it is not hard to see why it is so challenging to engage more people in imagining and creating a positive future. (Add to this list as you like: *poor quality of education, nutritional factors that deaden the senses and mind, too much bad television, too much loud and angry music, too much soft and dead "musak," constant lies by government, omission and lies in the news media, conspiracies within conspiracies, drug companies pushing mood controlling drugs, toxic air, water, living and working environment, too long a work week, not enough employment, too many cell phones, nuclear war, terrorism (governmental and private), global warming, energy crises, election rigging, et cetera, et cetera.)* The list is endless and it leads to a sense of profound discouragement over the future – as defined and based on past-present behavior.

In a society such as the U.S., organizational structures and processes are very complex and national-level decision makers are generally inaccessible and rarely accountable to the public. It is easy to become discouraged and to feel powerless to create a positive future, even if you have an idea of how to change things. Overlay endless consumerism and mass media distractions, and it can at times look as though too many people prefer to live in a nether world that mixes fear of the future with denial and a sense of futility. Add to this the recent advent of sweeping military police powers at local and national levels, and an atmosphere of intimidation exists that limits free public expression of opinions and concerns that otherwise could challenge people to look "outside of the box."

What is "the box"? Taken as a whole, our society (and most of humanity for that matter) has succeeded in wrapping itself tighter and tighter in the layers of a self-imposed prison with freedom *seemingly* not in sight. Indeed, there are those who *seemingly* "operate" the prison, also known as "the powers that be," but even they are trapped in the very system by which they seem to benefit.

Those who think they are warden-managers of this world will facilitate endless distractions to keep people from waking up to this simple truth and keep people working to maintain the privilege and power of these warden-managers. One day it is entertainment and another day it is "economic growth." Yet another day it may be an "oil crisis" or another political election cycle that offers barely distinguishable choices to people. When these options start running thin, there is always the trump card of a major war or global threat.

Think about it: rich or poor, powerful or not, most everyone wonders at some time or another what higher meaning there may be to life and beingness. Many will wonder if there is something more that is expansive and nourishing.

There is a quiet sort of revolution taking place in the minds and hearts of people, no matter what they may think they believe in. This quiet change is in the very cells of people. It is a like a primal urge to evolve or fade away. The intense interest these days in matters of the heart and spirituality are good indicators of this. Naturally, there will be a counter current from those people seeking to control the minds and hearts of people in this all-important arena. Their preferred method is to evoke fear and conflict. These people legitimize their position based on rigid dogma and present people with deliberately false options from which to choose.

The power of the awakened hearts and minds however is much greater and ultimately cannot be so easily controlled. The near omnipresence of beliefs and values – such as a sense of the sacred in all creation, belief in higher consciousness, and recognition of the importance of spirituality – is beginning evidence of this.

In one of his lectures, Adam Smith said:

"…In all commercial countries the division of labor is infinite, and everyone's thoughts are employed about one particular thing…. The minds of men are contracted, and rendered incapable of elevation. Education is despised, or at least neglected, and heroic spirit is utterly extinguished."

– Adam Smith is generally considered one of the first architects and intellectuals to promote the rising power of capitalism. His landmark book *An Inquiry into the Nature and Cause of the Wealth of Nations* was published in 1776, the same year as the American Declaration of Independence

"The wealth of a nation is derived from the love generated by the people of that nation."

– from Ken Carey, *Vision – A Personal Call to Create a New World*

"The power of our own higher consciousness "stepping in" cannot be dismissed, especially if it is part of a natural "fail safe" mechanism intended to intervene if too many people fail to engage their personality-based free-will to choose a more evolved and compassionate existence for themselves."

Europeans who landed here discovered that the indigenous people – populating much of the Great Lakes, Eastern Canada, New England, and Central Mid-western States – had a constitution and laws based on spiritual and democratic principles already centuries old, and directly applicable to the European's interest in founding a new society in the "New World."

However, as it turns out, it was so sophisticated that the medieval/early-industrial mind of the European arriving on the shores of the "New World" could not reconcile key differences, such as women's equality and laws prohibiting chattel slavery. Nevertheless, the Iroquois Confederation was an important model for the founding of the United States.

– *IOOW-2000* Research Notes

The question everyone has before them right now is: "How many more genocides, wars, ecosystem failures and horrific events, before people say, 'Enough is enough,' and truly mean it?"

This is not unlike a domestic violence situation when one person chooses to walk out and begin creating a new life for him or herself – or when the perpetrator comes to a truly profound realization and ends the violence. This is not unlike someone addicted to drugs, like alcohol, waking up one day to the realization that they have done something so awful that they know they desperately need help to stop their destructive behavior. For humanity as a whole, perhaps it will be a natural disaster of epic proportions that brings everyone out of their collective sleep – or perhaps something of human design.

There's nothing better than a *really big context* to help people put things into a new perspective for themselves.

Instead of disaster, perhaps something more extraordinary and sublime will happen. Perhaps more and more people will literally wake up to a sense of a different reality and realization of themselves as spiritual beings. Perhaps many will wonder how it was possible we have existed for so long, and with such a deep and potentially devastating level of *non-awareness* of a greater field of being we are all a part of. The power of our own higher consciousness "stepping in" cannot be dismissed, especially if it is part of a natural "fail safe" mechanism intended to intervene if too many people fail to engage their personality-based free-will to choose a more evolved and compassionate existence for themselves. This is like having a high-level program running in the background of our biologically based self, ready in the event of an imminent system failure.

How far will humanity "go along for the ride" by remaining asleep to our innate ability to choose a better and more evolved way of being?

First, A Little Historical Background

To begin, one assumption of the old paradigm and (currently dominant reality) is that we are the product of our past. Considering the influence of centuries of fear and conflict-based behaviors, reinforced by social-cultural institutions, this is not good news. It certainly is a restrictive and self-limiting worldview that assures infrequent new and innovative structures and paradigms of any depth or substance to ever emerge for society. The old paradigm also teaches us that we are separate from one another and from a higher consciousness. This further inculcates the old model, that what really matters is pragmatism and what is materially accomplished (output of goods and services). American society is rooted in individualism and has now evolved into the survival and gain of the individual with little consideration for anything or anyone else. This gets projected to the family unit versus the world, and the U.S. versus the world.

In this state of relative self-centeredness, fear and competition to survive predominates – and blame, shame, and power issues heavily influence our personal and collective behavior. These psychological factors also make it relatively easy for society as a whole to be generally manipulated by those people who have a big-picture perspective and the power to mold behavior and opinion to suit their private goals at the expense of humanity.

The U.S. is a unique society in the modern era – one that was founded upon principles based on civil spirituality and democracy. At the same time, it was also founded on fear and violence rooted in the cruel life of seventeenth century Europe, which was applied to the extermination of the indigenous American population and created a subclass of indentured servitude of their own people. This pattern extended forward in the brutal enslavement of a racially different people who, for 200 years, were systematically kidnapped from their communities and transported in chains across the oceans and forced to produce vast wealth for a small class of American landowners and emerging industrialists.

Since their inception, commercial corporations gained rights and powers far beyond that of any living citizenry. From before the early days of the East India Company and the related network corporations that were

"…When Alexis de Tocqueville wrote about the uniqueness of the American society half a century after the founders had pledged to form a more perfect union, he thought he had stumbled onto the unifying element: civic participation. He mused about everyone "taking an active part in the government of society." But several centuries later, Robert Bellah, lamenting the decline of civic participation, warned of the threat of a democracy without citizens."

– from James A. Joseph, Remaking America,

America is an example to the world, not for superficial government policy, but for the blending of races and peoples that occurs daily on her street corners, in her marketplaces, in her schools, churches and factories. In the United States, people from historically antagonistic nations have come together to live, work, play, and raise their children together. To the degree that they have learned respect and cooperation, America has prospered.

– from Ken Carey, Vision - *A Personal Call to Create a New World*

Hallmarks of fascist and proto-fascist regimes:

- Powerful and continuing expressions of nationalism.
- Disdain for the importance of human rights.
- Identification of enemies/scapegoats as a unifying cause.
- The supremacy of the military/avid militarism.
- Rampant sexism.
- A controlled mass media.
- Obsession with national security.
- Religion and ruling elite tied together.
- Power of corporations protected.
- Power of labor suppressed or eliminated.
- Disdain and suppression of intellectuals and the arts.
- Obsession with crime and punishment.
- Rampant cronyism and corruption.
- Fraudulent elections.

    – from Laurence W. Britt, *Free Inquiry Magazine,* Volume 23, Number 2. (See Appendix for a more complete summary)

connected with its global growth, corporations of all sorts were organized primarily to accumulate and concentrate more and more wealth in the hands of their owners and other investors. No morality or code of ethics was required. Often, groups of companies used the economic and the military power of government to further their private economic and geo-political ambitions. Today, with few exceptions, a relatively small number of incredibly vast global corporations control the majority of all human material supply, and also influence – and at times outright control – the office of state power to the detriment of the health of the public, the environment, and democracy itself.

Many of the financial and commercial forces that occupied the upper rungs of economic and political influence in the United States were intimately involved in financing opposing sides in World War I and later provided pivotal support for the rise of what quickly became known as the Nazi party under the leadership of Adolph Hitler. These corporations and descendants of these individuals are still in positions of high influence and power today.

From the end of World War II to present, millions of people have died directly at the hands of U.S. military power used specifically to consolidate global domination. In the name of American empire, entire countries have been laid to ruin and countless tens of millions of people left to suffer.

Generations of Americans have been systematically lied to about the deeds done in our country's name and today, we continue to be presented with false choices that deliberately obscure truth in order to keep people from choosing intelligently and from their hearts. Over the years, generation after generation has found itself increasingly trapped in an endlessly flexible reality matrix that encourages each generation to maintain its own state of imprisonment.

High Costs to Society and the Individual

American society has an enormous shadow side to it. Our material and social progress comes at a substantial price that has never been properly acknowledged. This pattern is now being carried forward and further amplified by powerful interests who have at their disposal extreme cultural, economic, and military power with which to project their global agendas.

One way of summarizing the situation would be to say that American society throughout its history neglected the principles of a universal spirituality and gradually became imprisoned in a personal and collective self-centeredness that worships material progress at the expense of those principles aligned with higher consciousness – the very principles that are most needed today for the general uplifting of all humanity.

*We may not have forever to turn things around for the better, but it is **not** too late to choose and act on behalf of positive and life-affirming change.*

There were those people who, from the earliest decades of the first colonies through to this day, sought to establish their own communities. They were created to explore and experience a more universal spirituality and social order than what was proffered by the various churches and their doctrines, and the limitations of the commodity-based social relations in the main population centers.

The level of disconnection from self, society, the Earth, and higher consciousness manifests in an endlessly dissatisfying culture and economy of consumerism and physical pleasure. The extent of this disconnection leads to profound levels of self-destructive and violent behavior: school shootings, domestic violence, sexual abuse of children, widespread use of drugs to mask the causes of physical and psychological pain, and so on. Simple self-denial and the calculated manipulation of the populace has led to the loss of democratic rights, militarization of the national economy, and a widespread level of fear and outright malaise.

The U.S. has the makings of a society ruled by fear and violence, a situation made easier through denial and a state-of-siege mentality fostered by the central government. We incarcerate over 2.1 million people in jails and

"In the early 1930s, some of America's wealthiest industrialists and bankers plotted to overthrow the government of President Franklin D. Roosevelt (FDR) and replace it with a fascist dictatorship. In 1933, the year Hitler took control of Germany, some of Wall Street's top financiers sent representatives to recruit the recently-retired General Butler into a fascist coup d'etat to overthrow FDR. Butler played along in order to find out who was behind the scheme and then, in 1934, he testified under oath before the MacCormack-Dickstein House Committee that was examining Nazi propaganda in the United States. Butler named names and exposed the key fascist plotters. He also identified a high-powered, business organization, the American Liberty League, as the "super-organization" behind the plan for an American coup. In fact, many megacorporations whose roots are firmly planted in the fascism of the 1930s, now dominate the globalized marketplace."

– April 2004, *Press for Conversion!* (Issue #53), Coalition to Oppose the Arms Trade (COAT)

"The people are always brought to the bidding of the leaders. That is easy. All you have to do is tell them they are being attacked and denounce the peacemakers for lack of patriotism and exposing the country to damage. It works the same in any country."

– Nazi Reich Marshall Hermann Goering at the Nuremberg Trials

"At the start of 2005, the U.S. House of Representatives passed a new rule that permits a small number of lawmakers to control the U.S. Congress in the event a natural or man-made calamity keeps a normal quorum from attending Congress. Any lawmaker unable to attend the session would no longer be counted as a congressman."

– Boston Herald January 9, 2005

prisons and have the largest number of people jailed of any country in the world. We have one of the highest incidences of violent crimes of any country in the world. There are grotesque disparities in the distribution of wealth and an intensified rate of concentration of wealth in the hands of an elite class of people. This elite class uses as a buffer a larger social strata of "wanna-be's" who receive very high incomes through salary, stock options, and other privileges.

As of this writing in 2004, 36 million people (12.5% of the U.S. population) fall below the official poverty level of $18,660 annual income – with simple correction, this number may be closer to 38 million, and in reality, far greater when factoring in nutrition, health, and the influence on the next generations. Over 45 million Americans are without health insurance. This exacerbates a toxic level of social division within the U.S. and between nations. In 2004, over 300 billionaires were personally identified in the U.S. (One cannot help wonder how many more there are who are not so identifiable.) In 2004 there were an estimated 70,000 people worldwide with personal assets estimated over USD 30 million, 30,000 of whom are headquartered in the U.S. and Canada. While a significant portion of this personal wealth is due to inflated market values, most is directly attributable to the systematic extraction and concentration of wealth in the hands of a very few.

As of this writing, democracy itself is under threat in the U.S. through a state-of-siege mentality being engineered by forces using the offices of government and the mass media. We are witnessing the systematic destruction of democratic rights through the introduction of electronic voting systems designed to permit hidden vote rigging and systematic attacks on freedom of speech. Additionally, journalism and mass media, rather than being a voice of truth and accountability, are subordinated to hidden private agendas. Add to this an escalating global environmental crisis, what message does this situation give us, and especially to humanity's young? At a level of personal and collective identity, how can people feel very good about anything, including themselves?

We are now living in a period in which government, mass media, and various hidden forces work closely to cloud people's minds and cynically undermine what remains of what was to be an extraordinary and noble experiment in democracy and civil spirituality.

Free-Will, Choice, and Power

Most of human history has demonstrated behavior based on perceived scarcity, conflict, and fear to an extent verging on addiction. What we have seen is an endless drama in which humanity has set up situations of extreme conflict – between light and dark, haves and have-nots, powerful and powerless – like a game of perpetual brinkmanship with itself and its planetary environment. Survival mechanisms have transformed into domination-accumulation-gratification mechanisms based on human foibles, but made to appear as progress, achievement, and evolutionary advancement of the species. Meanwhile, disastrous results are being reported as to our destructive impact on everything from human interactions to the decimation of cultures and environmental collapse.

Where is the turning point when people reach that place where they finally decide, "enough is enough," and then act on new imperatives for positive change? (Domestic violence works this way, with two people unable to reconcile themselves internally or with one another. This dynamic feeds international or civil wars that can last for many years, even spanning generations when projected across societies and nations.)

Have we become too psychologically accustomed to operating from an illusion of the separate, individual self? One can see this every day, particularly among discouraged young people who may question the assumptions of our society, but have no sense of how things could be substantially different in a positive way. What we now see in dress, behaviors, and other expressions is the unfocused angst tied to identity confusion, unresolved socio-cultural turmoil, and lack of security and hope for a future that seems worth investing in. Young people are only mirroring back what they are picking up from their families and society as a whole. This culturally reinforced sense of isolation keeps us from living in a more awakened way that further encourages emergence of a higher state of awareness and being for all, regardless of what generation one is a part of.

Our society generally informs us that we have the freedom to choose foods, styles of dress, jobs, schools, to marry or not, to vote or not, etc. Each of these choices includes a consequence or outcome. For some, material possessions, wealth, and the advantages of career advancement

A "Higher Power"

"Lack of power, that was our dilemma. We had to find a power by which we could live, and it had to be a Power greater than ourselves. We look upon this world of warring individuals, warring theological systems, and inexplicable calamity, with deep skepticism. In other moments, we found ourselves enchanted by a starlit night, 'Who then made all this?' There was a feeling of awe and wonder, but it was fleeting and soon lost."

Personal and Social Healing

"One of the hallmarks of this non-sectarian organization that pioneered a level of personal and social healing in a modern context, has to do with its emphasis on reconciling the 'personality self' to a greater self of 'higher power.' In doing so, a greater context representing a greater whole is available to anyone for healing and insight."

"The terms 'spiritual experience' and 'spiritual awakening'…show that the personality change sufficient to bring about recovery…has manifested itself among us in many forms."

– Excerpts from *Alcoholics Anonymous* (1939)

> *"We hold these truths to be self-evident that all men are created equal, that they are endowed by their Creator with certain inalienable rights, among these are life, liberty, and the pursuit of happiness, that to secure these rights governments are instituted among men."*
>
> – Thomas Jefferson, President of the United States 1801-1809 and co-author of the U.S. Constitution and Declaration of Independence

> *"The size of the lie is a definite factor in causing it to be believed, for the vast masses of a nation are in the depths of their hearts more easily deceived than they are consciously and intentionally bad. The primitive simplicity of their minds renders them a more easy prey to a big lie than a small one, for they themselves often tell little lies, but would be ashamed to tell big lies."*
>
> – Adolph Hitler

> *"If the American people were ever presented with an honest and truthful disclosure of the real and terrible human, environmental, economic, and cultural costs that our national "wealth" bases itself on, the majority of people would want no part of it and would immediately seek compassionate alternatives."*

with absolutely no consideration of a larger/higher perspective and the impact on others have become addictions.

Consequently, choices at this level do not involve very much of our higher or larger self. If we do not know any better than believing that the only game is what is presented through social-political norms – if we don't know any better than to continue making limited choices, then how can society as a whole change how it functions? Too often the result is a cynical, self-defeating, "can't change the system" attitude where positive "future-present" choices are obscured and dismissed as impractical or impossible. This culturally reinforced sense of isolation keeps us from living in a more awakened way that further encourages emergence of a higher state of awareness and being for all, regardless of what generation we are a part of.

It is time to change "the game" and the very rules describing "the game." It is time for the emerging new paradigm to become more evident for people to see, to compare, and to experience a fundamental difference for themselves. This will encourage more people to choose a positive future rather than a paradigm that continues to devolve into chaos.

Our current norms are not based on the immediate-now and they're not based on future-present. At best they are past-present. Yet throughout history, there have always been forward-looking people whose concerns and intentions are for the highest good of all. No matter what their personal circumstances, there are people operating from a level of timeless freedom that is perhaps difficult for many of us to imagine.

Currently, more and more people identify with forward-looking, positive values and beliefs *and the positive belief systems they are embodying are increasingly "out of sync" with established norms*. This can lead to a collective breakthrough in which large numbers of people create a new future and a greater level of freedom they can barely imagine at first.

Communicating this potential and facilitating people to act on these higher principles is of paramount importance now.

As this is communicated effectively, people will need help exercising their prerogative to choose in accordance with their higher self instead of their separate self. As more people come forward and participate from the context of their larger self-perspective, this process will gather speed and so will its rate of acceleration.

What if people were to re-discover the true power of their free-will? When people feel powerless, they withdraw into a deeper sense of separation and helplessness. Connecting with the heart and higher self provides insight into new solutions and offers a new type of hope based in certitude and intention for a positive future. Knowing and using our innate power to set intentions and make choices leads to advanced democracy and more mature planetary citizenship. (Strategies leading to greater connection, awareness, and action are addressed in subsequent chapters.)

Choosing out of higher motivation is really about thought or consciousness determining form, instead of tacitly allowing existing forms to determine consciousness. This is not about changing limited, old paradigm forms and expecting them to serve entirely new purposes. This is more like reaching into the well of one's own spirit, of one's own higher self, to help a new future self emerge into the present. This is what can create a positive future that works for everyone. To do this requires new ways of thinking, as well as of being. It is essential to our well being that we be aware of this.

Language and our use of it plays an important role in social or group consciousness. It can help in discerning the right choices.

"From the beginning, two obvious choices are offered to mankind. One is leading to a bright future if the desires of the Great Spirit are honored. ...the other would eventually lead to the destruction of this world as we know it. This destruction has happened several times before and for similar reasons."

– from Robert Boissiere *Meditations with The Hopi: A Centering Book*

"Could there be an evolutionary summit toward which evolution has been building since time began? Could there be a hidden purpose to Creation?"

"If we are to continue our evolutionary journey, it is imperative that we now make some equally prodigious leaps in our ability to transform our minds. We must wake up and develop the wisdom that will allow us to use our new powers for our own good and for the good of all. This is the challenge of out times."

– from Peter Russell, *Waking Up In Time*

"There are many of us scattered across the face of the Earth with a mysterious sense of the future and a profound attraction for the evolution of ourselves and our world. We are a future oriented family of humanity who sense within ourselves the birth of the Universal human.

...We can destroy our world. With the same powers – spiritual, social, and scientific – we can evolve our world.

Our mission is to serve as catalysts for a planetary awakening in our lifetime, to take a nonviolent path to the next stage of our evolution."

– from Barbara Marx Hubbard,
The Revelation - Our Crisis is a Birth

A Glimmer of Light in the Tunnel

Today, a quiet movement is underway to embrace a new paradigm for a positive future. It has very diverse roots – at times seemingly at odds with one another – as much as being at odds with established norms and structures. Some of these roots date back many centuries. It was not until the founding of America that new soil became available in which to grow and evolve a new society in the modern world, as the New World became known. *America still has tremendous potential to be a great light for the world. We need only choose this path for ourselves.*

Against a backdrop of a decaying paradigm, a vibrant and new paradigm is taking shape in human consciousness. *Thought precedes form. As we think and feel in our hearts, so we shall be.* The time is at hand for people to wake up to their true nature and create new patterns that nourish and enrich people's souls and future evolution, and thus bring an end to suffering of all kinds.

Fortunately, there have been those courageous people, regardless of their age and historical context, who maintained their integrity, sought truth and accountability, and pushed the boundaries of consciousness. Why? Because they chose to understand and realize humanity's true potential and destiny.

In the decade of the 1960s there was an ongoing threat of nuclear holocaust; the descendants of those enslaved a century earlier were being beaten and killed in U.S. cities and the countryside by brutal racists while law enforcement did little or nothing to intervene; and the president of the U.S. was assassinated under suspicious circumstances that have never been truthfully acknowledged. Continuing through the 1970s U.S.-centered political and economic interests systematically manipulated governments and leaders of other countries and thwarted democratic movements throughout the world. This included the assassination of elected leaders and the open and covert use of U.S. military and economic power.

In this time, there also emerged a powerful wave in many countries where social and cultural rebellion of young people questioned the "establishment" and traditional personal beliefs and behaviors. This period encompassed an extraordinary movement for racial and gender civil rights and it further promoted values of equality and connection. Awareness of the impact of human population on the natural ecosystem grew as did the awareness of pollution and a permanent environmental movement developed. In this same period, the horrible impact of the protracted war by the U.S. against the people of Southeast Asia made a powerful imprint on everyone all over the world, and a permanent peace movement arose. During this period ideas of social and economic cooperation and community were experimented with as were consciousness-altering drugs. Soon, humanity took the first steps toward materially moving beyond terrestrial limitations by extending our reach to the moon and beyond the solar system.

During this period, many people, especially the younger generations, began to disconnect from the dominant paradigm – personified by their parents, and governmental and business leaders – and sought new paths to greater self-awareness and community. New forms of spirituality emerged. Some referenced early roots that preceded the Judeo-Christian religions and encouraged people to seek direct communion with God, higher consciousness, or with the consciousness of nature, and higher consciousness in general. A renaissance of interest in ancient society, spirituality, and consciousness has emerged over recent decades, aided by a growing number of books and the Internet.

The overall effects of this can be seen in the *IOOW-2000* data and the factors that transcend and connect what otherwise might be separate divisions of our society. As we move further into social values and discussion of new strategies, we will be making these factors more plain.

Within all these new patterns that developed through recent decades, a host of issues – concerning war, peace, women, young people, sexuality, race, ethnicity and the ecosystem – became part our larger social awareness, as well as highly charged. Differences over these "issues" became heavily enmeshed with intense polarities based on "us" versus "them" beliefs; policy-oriented approaches versus mass-action; political left versus right versus center, and now, religion versus spirituality versus the non-religious.

Today, we find there are myriad organizations, each with admirable and

"Beliefs deal with how you construct, perceive, and otherwise interact with reality. Values pertain more to the criteria by which you discern and make choices."

– IOOW-2000

"One must first of all fight an enormous mass of foolish prejudices which put material and spiritual life irreconcilably against each other ... One must be able to take up all, to combine all, to synthesize all."

– The Mother (Mirra Alfassa)

"The green wave itself is the product of a hierarchical developmental unfolding from traditional to modern to postmodern, so when the green meme condemns all hierarchies, it's basically condemning the very process that produced its own higher position."

"To put it simply: boomeritis is pluralism infected with narcissism. It's the very high truths of pluralism completely corrupted and derailed by an ego that uses them to entrench itself firmly in a place where it can never be challenged because there is no objective truth that can get rid of it."

– Ken Wilber, *What Is Enlightenment?*
Fall/Winter 2002-2003

important goals, but most of them behave as if their issue or business focus is the most important. They compete for funding among the same populations and take a one-sided approach to the problems they identify, rather than a systemic approach. Consequently, there is no coordinated or coherent strategy among most of these organizations and leading individuals. The result appears as an idealistic or contentious assault on all fronts against what appears to be superior forces of the power elite, their corporations, and the governments and officials who they control.

What has yet to emerge from all this is a *coherent social movement of high enough consciousness* that could offer a *large enough context* in which to *resolve the differences* and problems that have loomed so large to so many.

Those of the baby boomer generation are now "of age" to make a profound difference. They, coupled with the older generation, can engage and involve newer generations for a positive, more evolved future – right now. Events and dynamics that are currently in motion will not wait.

So Why Haven't Things Changed for the Better, Sooner?

If so many people identify with the positive future values and beliefs that we introduced in Part One of this book, why have things seemingly not changed very much? Part of the answer has to do with the qualities of active social involvement.

- Many of those people who identified with this emerging new paradigm *dissociated* themselves from traditional materialist culture and power.

- A significant percentage of individuals who supported positive future beliefs *withdrew* from the electoral process.

- Add to this, the *force of habit* of old ways rooted in the section of society acting as an *inertial ballast* favoring established norms.

- There has not yet developed a visible leadership or material presence for a *positive future movement*, largely due to its relative newness, compared to its well-established counterparts.

- Out of necessity for being early pioneers, leading individuals representing a new paradigm based on spiritual or integral values of compassion and service tend to function *more individually than they do cooperatively.*

- Consequently, there has been *too little impetus to work together* to gather the necessary material resources needed to elevate a coherent message for all to hear and upon which to act.

This pattern however, is beginning to change – partly out of necessity, as well as that of individuals choosing to know truth.

Perhaps there has been an innate "governor" that we have not been much aware of, much like an attractor from our future, calling to us. This call is like a homing beacon guiding us to our higher selves and higher nature. It seeks to graduate ourselves from "adolescence" as a species to a more "mature" position that co-creates a positive future out of a greater awareness of interconnectedness with one another and our natural environment. We are speaking of a fundamental spirituality so vital that it has *always* been there, waiting for us to connect and access its fundamental wisdom and higher guidance.

"Wait," you may say. "What if you do not think spirituality or connection of all life is important. Or more so, what about those people whose ideaframe is contrary to much that we have been putting forward?" All right, let's first take a brief look at research-based indicators of a part of our society we have termed "inertial ballast."

"Social Inertial Ballast," Disconnection, and Disengagement

Two small but distinct groups were identified through the *IOOW-2000* research that, combined, constitute a significant minority (21.5%) of our population. They tend to act disproportionately as "inertial ballast" and are often used as a convenient excuse to hold everyone back.

One group, estimated to be 8.2% of the U.S., are generally constricted and very conservative in their worldview, as well as being generally disengaged from self and society. Their future outlook is very pessimistic, they vote, and do so along conservative political lines. They tend to go to religious services more than once a week. They also tend to be older

"Under extreme circumstances, such as a disaster, the best and worst in people can quickly emerge. Some people will help others to cope and maintain what is familiar, others will create something new to replace what no longer serves, and a small number will take advantage of the circumstances to take all they can for themselves."

"Even the traditional Golden Rule of 'Do unto others as you would have them do unto you' is not a part of our society's daily life, having been supplanted by another rule, 'Get away with what you can.' "

"As people strive to bring social, environmental, and financial capital into a more positive and meaningful relationship for society and our environment, all our relationships at all levels can be brought into a coherent harmony with one another."

Estimating Social Inertial Ballast

Using the *IOOW-2000* data, one way to identify this group within the population is to examine some of the qualities of those people who simply don't have any positive identification on the *IOOW-2000* indexes measuring Connection, Service, and Spirituality (see Chapter 11 for more information). The assumption is that they include a large concentration of highly disengaged individuals.

Another method would be to examine those 8.2% who fall into a category of people who scored high on Social Material Stress scale, high on the Social Traditional - Religious Conservative index, and low on the Positive Future – Cooperative Integrative scale. The assumption here is that when you have very little by way of positive or integrative factors to balance a stressful daily life and socially conservative values, you get another type of disengaged person.

Future research should include specific measures to address this level of outlying disaffection and disengagement in society with measures that could lead to help re-connect them in a healing and useful manner.

Summary profiles of these two groups are presented at the end of this section.

than the general population and are more likely to be men. They are, however, somewhat more aware of their need for spiritual growth. Of the 8 Types, Cautious and Conservative (CC) predominates here with a secondary component of Disengaged from Social Concerns (DSC).

Another group that functions as "inertial ballast" represents 16.2% of the population. This second group is noticeably not as constricted in perspective or conservatively oriented, but is more disengaged from self and society. They too, are more likely to be men (but not to the extent as the 8.2% group first described). This group is also younger than the overall population, mostly Gen-X, and single. They are not as likely to be very religious in terms of attending services, their future outlook is not as pessimistic, and they are not as likely to vote. Of the 8 Types, Disengaged from Social Concerns (DSC) predominates here with a secondary component of Cautious and Conservative (CC).

There is very little overlap between these two groups (only 2.9%) and combined, these two groups constitute 21.5% of the general population. Education and income are not significant factors in either of these two groups. Rather, what is key are their values and beliefs.

As "inertial ballast," these groups tend to function as a net energy drain by opposing positive innovations in a generally unconscious manner, usually passively, sometimes dynamically.

How often have people asked relevant questions or said things in the presence of individuals of this type that differed from established norms, only to have them put down with cynical remarks, thus stifling any meaningful discussion? This happens in countless situations from family meal times to workplace situations across the country. This dynamic is also fueled by news and entertainment mass media. They do this by denying copy space or airtime to investigate the truth, by purposeful misinformation, by crude rhetoric of on-air personalities, by promoting column space for cynical commentaries, and by endlessly promoting "dark" themes under the guise of "entertainment." People and organizations that are part of the social ballast dynamic are basically afraid of anything that hints of challenging their perceived world, whether it be in terms of their ideaframe, social or material privilege, or other belief systems that help them define their identity.

Such disaffected individuals might be more readily manipulated with superficial palliatives to support extreme conservative or reactionary positions. Here we wish to distinguish those who are disaffected and disconnected from those who are deliberately involved in deceiving society as to their true aims of power.

In the absence of truly innovative and courageous leadership, this inertial ballast factor in our society further makes it difficult for positive social innovations to become widely adopted by mainstream society. People *do* want to hear of a new perspective, people *are tired* of the old game, but without a coherent and substantial "stage" to speak from, most people will continue *not* to hear what is new and good, as it is drowned out (or met with silence) by the mainstream outlets for news and information.

Thus, powerful new strategies leading to the creation of new structures paralleling established ones are most invaluable at this time. Eventually, almost everyone will "see the light" although for some, the process may take longer.

Two Estimates of "Inertial Ballast" in Society: The 8.2% Group

The **"8.2% Group"** includes those who scored *high* on the Social Material Stress scale, *high* on the Social Traditional - Religious Conservative index, and *low* on the Positive Future – Cooperative Integrative scale. They constitute 8.2% of all respondents.

- 63% are male.
- Tend to be slightly older (mean age is 47.9 versus 45.7 for all, and median age is 45 versus 43 for all respondents), however generational make-up is typical of that for the U.S. overall.
- 47% are in the Cautious and Conservative (CC) type, compared to 10% for all respondents.
- 25% are in the Disengaged from Social Concerns (DSC) type, compared to 14% for the overall population.
- Voting likelihood about on par with everyone else.

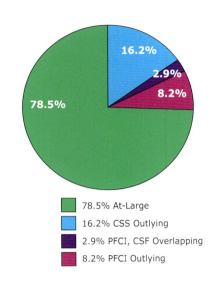

ESTIMATES OF "INERTIAL BALLAST"

- 78.5% At-Large
- 16.2% CSS Outlying
- 2.9% PFCI, CSF Overlapping
- 8.2% PFCI Outlying

The Narrow Worldview
"For people concerned with positive
social change, there is only a very small
portion of the population that seems
highly constricted and inflexible in their
worldview."

- Generally, 52% preferred Bush for president in the 2000 election and 65% of those most likely to vote chose Bush.

- 72% identify with conservative political views.

- Score high on the religious index and 32% tend to attend some sort of services more than once a week.

- 82% support the death penalty, compared to an average of 58.5% across all respondents.

- 59% did not agree with being tolerant of others and 36% strongly disagreed with being tolerant.

- Very pessimistic future outlook: 38% see only problems and disasters; 19% see either the same or problems and disasters.

- 25% disagree that the Earth is basically a unique kind of living organism; 12% are neutral.

- 48% do not think there is a global awakening taking place.

- 52% do not think that a global awakening will make the world a better place in 10 years.

- Only 38% report experiencing a sense of sacred in everything, compared to 56% for all respondents.

- Higher than average in feeling a need to experience spiritual growth.

- Tend to be almost on a par with – but slightly below – the rest of the population in terms of income and education.

- They are more likely to have Internet access at home but not on the job and their Internet usage is typical for the US overall.

Two Estimates of "Inertial Ballast" in Society: The 16.2% Group

The **"16.2% Group"** are those who simply don't have any positive identification on the *IOOW-2000* indexes measuring Connection, Service, and Spirituality. They constitute 16.2% of all respondents.

- 59% are male.

- May be slightly younger (mean age is 41.7 compared to 45.7 for all respondents).

- 42% are Gen-X and Gen-Y age groups, compared to 34% for all respondents; 30% are Gen-X, compared to 25% for all respondents.

- 33% are likely to be single, never married compared to 24% for all respondents.

- 78% score high on the Social Material Stress scale, compared to 42% for all respondents.

- 60% score low on the Social Traditional - Religious Conservative index, compared to 40% for all respondents.

- 48% are in the Disengaged from Social Concerns (DSC) type, compared to 14% for all respondents.

- Marginally less likely to vote: (51% likely to vote compared to 55% for general population).

- Choice of candidate in 2000 election was very similar to that of the general population of respondents.

- Score low on the religious index and 44.6% tend not to attend religious services.

- More likely to support a death penalty with 68% in support, compared to 58.5% overall.

- While 59% did agree with being tolerant of others, 21% nonetheless strongly disagreed with being tolerant.

- Pessimistic future outlook: 28% see only problems and disasters; 21% see either the same or problems and disasters; and 15% see things staying much the same.

- Slightly less likely to agree that the Earth is basically a unique kind of living organism and slightly more likely to disagree with this.

- 53% do not think there is a global awakening taking place.

- 59% do not think that a global awakening will make the world a better place in 10 years.

- Only 34% report a sense of sacred in everything, compared to 55% for all respondents.

- Less interested in being involved in creating a better world: 78% agreeing with this compared to 91% for the general population.

- Tend to be almost on a par with the rest of the population in terms of income and education.

- Internet access at home or work is on par with everyone else; however their Internet usage is high compared to the rest of the population.

- Less likely to feel their spiritual needs are not being met and lower than average in feeling a need to experience spiritual growth.

A simple comparison of overall key value and belief indicators show these groups are not that far from each other in a number of important areas. However, these two groups do appear to differ somewhat in terms of age, voting likelihood, candidate preference, social material stress, religious involvement, and global awakening.

While both groups have high concentrations of the Disengaged from Social Concerns (DSC) type and Cautious and Conservative (CC) type, the DSC type predominates in the 16.2 % group while the CC type predominates in the 8.2 % group.

Those people who most fit the "inertial ballast" profile do not have a set of positive values with which to balance the stress and challenges of daily life – with virtually no positive scoring on the Positive Future - Cooperative Integrative scale (PFCI). For example, we find in the 8 Types those who also share in a high Social Material Stress (SMS) score, yet who have a high PFCI value score and less constricted worldview. These would include Persisting against Adversity (PA) and the Working for a New Life of Wholeness (WNL) types. In contrast, there are those types – Cautious and Conservative (CC) and Disengaged from Social Concerns (DSC) – who also scored high on the SMS scale, but low on PFCI.

Meaningful bridging between these groups would likely meet with the best success first with the 16.2 % group in addressing their need for non-threatening connection, the possibility for spiritual growth in a non-doctrinaire manner, and creative, innovative projects in which to engage with others that also have some broader social benefit.

It is a matter of helping not only these people, but all 8 Types, to see beyond that which we find different or exclusive about each other.

One valuable aspect of this data is to show an unmistakable overlap of our core values and beliefs. The reactive position of "me/us versus them" becomes moderated by recognition of something more inclusive and inspiring of humankind's greater being.

Roots of Disconnection within Society

Today, we have a few typically simple but obvious dynamics showing ways behavior is intimately associated with how our society structures and conducts itself. Seemingly locked into an endless tug-of-war with one another, there are those who tend to be "conservative" in wanting to maintain an old way of life that may be increasingly impossible to maintain; and those who prefer to rebel or fight against the old ways, seeking to dismantle the old.

These people, together, constitute a small portion of the overall population.

To those people who are understandably angry at all the things that seem so wrong and are angry with those people who are in positions of power, we ask that you consider a different approach that embraces both discernment and compassion. It is vital to set aside one's anger so as to be able to see other possibilities. This is vital in reaching the hearts and minds of the greater majority of people who are ready to hear a new message for a new society that is based on connection, service, and spirituality.

There is already resident among most people a potential power of the heart-centered mind to seek and create a new positive future, and that does not seek confrontation or conflict. This leads to healing without glossing over real problems, and yet embodies a high level of discernment. *People are ready to be involved in creating a positive future based on new principles.* Now the question before us is how best to engage them?

Values and beliefs, and the behaviors that arise from them, influence and impact our personal or family relations, our geographic or virtual communities, national society, and the entire world.

If the collective reality in which you live and operate does not allow enough space for those higher beliefs and aspirations that are important to you, you will eventually disengage from that reality. It is not unlike the simple example of voting and what it represents. Clearly half of

Close to the surface:

What the *IOOW-2000* research indicates is that a positive and awakened future has its immediate basis in the fact that there is already a great deal of positive energy close to the surface of our society, quietly growing, waiting to be recognized and encouraged forth. To bring this to the forefront of our personal and collective life, effectively, takes a new type of leadership and new institutions of all kinds.

"A great deal has been accomplished in providing for basic rights, developing technology, and meeting material needs in little more than two centuries of nationhood. The question before us is: What will we do with this? Will we use what we have for the benefit of humanity or not?"

– IOOW-2000

121

"I see in the near future a crisis approaching that unnerves me and causes me to tremble for the safety of my country. As a result of the war, corporations have been enthroned, and an era of corruption in high places will follow, and the money power of the country will endeavor to prolong its reign by working upon the prejudices of the people until all wealth is aggregated in a few hands and the Republic is destroyed. I feel at this moment more anxiety for the safety of my country than ever before, even in the midst of war."

– President Abraham Lincoln in a letter to Colonel William F. Elkins

"Fascism should more properly be called corporatism, since it is the merger of state and corporate power."

– Benito Mussolini, totalitarian leader and Prime Minister of Italy from 1922-1943

Americans disengaged from voting. Why? It is not that people do not care anymore, for clearly people do care. They are generally discouraged with a system in which there are too few meaningful choices for them – and it is business as usual for powerful interests that dominate policy and law for private benefit.

If your beliefs and aspirations are not met among friends, co-workers or others with whom you are in close personal contact, then there is the basis for disengagement as well. Over time, what develops is a split or compartmentalization of the way you live. By day, you are one way with co-workers. Away from work, you act differently, talk about things differently, and generally find other ways to live that hopefully can nourish or sustain you. Add to this the overall isolation that individuals and families experience, regardless of their circumstances, and a slowly unfolding calamity becomes apparent.

- Our educational and political systems and our general culture do very little to encourage people to connect with their potential to create a positive future. Substituted instead are shallowness of thought and goals of personal gain. These are the antithesis of creating ways that lead to new structures and processes serving our future and future-present selves. Everything references the past and historical trends, and is designed to reinforce and maintain values and beliefs that arose from the early medieval period and political-economic structures and processes developed to serve the interests of the ascendant power of commerce and capitalism.

- Most of our modern institutions (and socially acknowledged values and beliefs) evolved from earlier periods of scarcity, survival, and fear. The resulting paradigm, in which the few dominate the many and also try to dominate nature, has produced short-term material rewards, and now jeopardizes everyone's survival.

From all of this, it is easy to see how very powerful interests, familiar with the reins of social, economic and political power can project their agendas and *appear* to receive support from the general population to implement such agendas.

Some people might say we have forgotten the role of institutions in society: that they are here to serve us. However, the question really is: "What is it that our institutions are to serve?" They were a natural outgrowth of the evolution of a new commerce-based society that emerged from pre-medieval and medieval society. Taxes, armies, labor enforcement, etc., have all been priorities of state apparatus and specific individuals for centuries. Concern for human needs and social benefit came much later. The ecology of the planet has only in recent decades been seriously considered. How then could anyone expect social, political, and economic structures – whose very natures are based on maintaining the concentration and accumulation of private wealth – to serve the emergence of a more evolved society based on spirituality and the interconnectedness of life? Clearly new principles and structures are in order.

As such, our current institutional "organisms" may be incapable of change and need to be allowed to serve out their useful life while new ones are created that serve a more positive future. (This is yet another example of change without conflict.)

Presently, our forms of social organization are dominated by an old paradigm and are clearly at odds with what is new and emerging. What is needed are new structures and processes dedicated to serving the emergence of a positive future. However, we must ultimately and deliberately evolve new ways of governing ourselves as our consciousness continues to outreach the ability of our old social structures to serve.

If our definition of "what we need to serve a new way of being" emphasizes our higher potential and encourages growing into more highly evolved and spiritually aware individuals and a species, then our social and political institutions must be very different than what we currently employ. This latter point is relatively new and requires new social, cultural, and institutional constructs, as it is based on an entirely different set of assumptions and intentions.

Fundamentally, we need to focus on creating new structures and processes, representing our "future-present," that are aligned with a higher awareness of the interconnectedness of all life, and structures and processes based on discernment with compassion and principles that are in accord with this awareness.

From Barbarism to High Democracy

The early development of "rule by law," to bring civil order to an essentially savage human society, was preliminary to creating a future, enlightened society. Such a society would be self-governing, self-referencing, and self-empowering replacing rule by law with "rule by custom." This is one of a number of yet-unrealized ideals of the founding of American democracy, as well as of many ancient societies.

"Rule by custom" implies that compulsory laws and their enforcement are no longer necessary in a sufficiently mature society. Rule by custom does not mean rule by tradition. Rule by custom dynamically changes as society evolves.

This ideal would be an experience beyond what one person, one vote could ever achieve. Practically, this could be seen as a more highly evolved form of "consensus" building – not an artificial consensus of 100%, but rather agreement representing a group sense that has the capacity to embrace diversity and difference, yet not have internal contradictions that give rise to conflict.

Déjà Vu: A Century of Conflict For Global Domination

A more detailed examination of the events and issues around the early 20th century in the U.S. and Europe, shows remarkable parallels to what is presently unfolding in our present world of the early 21st century. Then, as now, U.S. elected leaders and governmental leaders were afraid to debate substantive issues or to disclose to the American public the real dynamics surrounding global conflicts and the implications of world war. Partly, they were afraid of being labeled "unpatriotic."

The domestic economy was headed into a period of serious economic instability and decline. The war and conflicts in Europe were really over control of Europe and intense competition over control of the colonial-imperial empires of the major European powers. Through all this, the U.S. was the home base for a small group of individuals who formed the core of powerful financial and oil interests that sought to gain a major share of the international oil economy, the basis for nearly all modern industrial and military expansion of the century. A military draft was instituted as the powerful U.S. interests prepared to involve Americans directly in a world war.

Today these historical political-economic interests are overlaid onto the centuries-old conflicts known as the "Crusades" in which European "Christendom" and the Muslim world were engaged in a thousand-year war in the Middle East. (A region with an even more ancient history of conflict.)

The implications of the confluence of a modern oil economy, political-economic control, and the Christian-Muslim conflicts having roots dating back many centuries B.C. offer a noteworthy highlight to past and present conflicts.

– *IOOW-2000* Research Notes

From Disconnection to Differentiation

Today, two realities are apparent:

- One has its origins preceding the European medieval period developed from fear and a survival-based drive to "master" the material world. It favored a paradigm based on domination and separation from our basic connection as spiritual beings.

- The other has multiple origins developed from practical concerns over the well being of our natural and social-cultural environment. It includes the profound impulse to grasp the deeper meaning of existence and basic purpose of being, as individuals and as a species.

Parallels to these can be seen everywhere in human society. There are the "less developed countries" in the world whose leadership is more interested in dominating the people of their own regions and exploiting natural resources and less interested in creating an exemplary society based on compassion and a shared abundance. Likewise, there are those individuals *at all socio-economic levels* of society who are primarily concerned with achieving material success or domination through any available means.

Over the recent century, there have been two common responses to systemic failures. One is the military domination of existing forces of political, economic, and social control such as the totalitarian movements that swept through the Eastern and Western world. Another has been the uprising, often violent, of those most socially and politically excluded who have the least to lose and most to gain. Both shared a common element of desiring to acquire greater material well being. Neither can succeed without placing, foremost, the fundamental spiritual perspective of a common connection and the well being of all.

These dynamics permeate every facet of human society. Since they have been the dominant paradigm, the current structures and values of human society reflect this and have the force of habit in their favor. Nevertheless, there is growing daily evidence of dissatisfaction with the prevailing values, structures, and processes that our society uses to govern itself.

Globalization Is…

Globalization of information, political-economy, culture, and environmental concerns begins to force the issue of "one world" and "one humanity" to the forefront everywhere. The question is not over globalization, since it exists and cannot be undone. The questions are more, "What is humanity to intend for itself?" and "What is to be acted upon?"

- The commodification of every person and natural resource for endless material growth and expansion, and likely reinforced by increased use of political and military power?

OR

- Will we reach for something new that calls to us from all our hearts and souls – a higher potential to grow beyond the narrow confines we may have set for ourselves as individuals and as a species?

The "event horizon" is now upon us and it needs to be acknowledged. It is our future becoming our present, the "future-present" enlivening the ideals of our deeper connections, our desire to serve others for a greater good, and an intrinsic spirituality encompassing all of humankind. Again, we must deliberately evolve new ways of conducting ourselves as our consciousness continues to outreach the ability of our old social structures to serve our future interests in the present.

What all people in all nations must now be asking themselves is what we can do individually and collectively as members of the human species to contribute toward the entire species' positive evolution for the highest good of all concerned.

Before getting into how things could be turned around, this is a good point at which to present some of the research findings concerning how people feel about the future. (As you consider these points, please keep in mind that these questions from the *IOOW-2000* research survey were asked at the end of 1999 and the start of 2000.)

The Recent History of Globalization

- **1870-1917** Often referred to as the First Era of Globalization; fueled by colonial expansion and industrialization, creating cheaper transportation, faster communication technologies and the integration of markets.

- **1917-1945** The end of the "First Era," as signaled by the beginning of World War I, the Russian Revolution and the Great Depression, halting the integration of the world's economy through World War II.

- **1945-1989** The Cold War divides the world into spheres of influence, fostering increasingly integrated economies within the spheres, but keeping these markets separate from each other.

- **1989-Today** The beginning of the "Second Era of Globalization," featuring the technological revolution, and the end of the Cold War, integrated economies, greater technology, and faster communication resulting in the present era of unprecedented economic growth.

– U.S. Council on Foundations Board Briefing: Globalization, June 2002

CHAPTER 7
Future Outlook

"Perhaps humanity planned for itself a solution – its own awakening into higher consciousness – to address human suffering from the deepest resources of our souls, united through spirit and purpose."

W hen discussing anything about the future, one can easily be dismayed at the amount of chaos and upset in the world and determine that the future of humanity is rather bleak. Likewise, one can also see that there are many who are very interested in making changes – from personal to collective agendas – to help create something more uplifting and sustaining. One would think that everyone would want to move in the direction of a more positive future, but when considering the enormity of the challenges with which we're faced, one might just as well throw their hands up in despair and figure it's not worth the effort as nothing can be done.

It may help to take a step back and look at some general positive and negative indicators of future concerns.

Chapter 7 At A Glance

Future Outlook

- Optimistic
- Pessimistic
- Comparison of The 8 American Types and Their Future Outlook
- A New Roadmap – Identifying Bridges

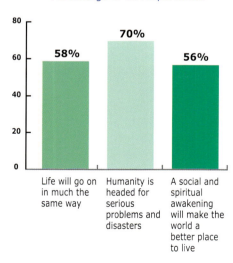

"DURING THE NEXT TEN YEARS..."

Percentage of all respondents

The *IOOW-2000* research specifically included several questions concerning future outlook in general and specifically over 10 years.

Of these, there were three questions in particular that framed a general perspective of what people thought the next ten years might bring:

- "A social and spiritual awakening to higher consciousness will make the world a better place to live."
- "Humanity is headed for serious problems and disasters."
- "Life will go on in much the same way as it always has, but with small or minor improvements."

Examples of other questions that were asked included:

- "During the next 10 years, technological breakthroughs will take care of the environmental problems taking place today."
- "No matter what happens in the future, we will adapt to it."
- "Most children are not worried about their future."

People who scored high on the Positive Future – Cooperative Integrative (PFCI) scale share the following future outlook in that they tend to agree:

- "Over the next 10 years, social and spiritual awakening will make the world a better place to live."
- "No matter what happens in the future, we will adapt to it."

This suggests some good values-based common ground.

Americans who scored high on the Social Material Stress (SMS) scale share the following future outlook in that they tend to agree:

- "Science will eventually be able to explain everything."
- "I am concerned that humanity is headed for serious problems and disasters in the next 10 years."
- "I believe that most children are not worried about their future."

This suggests that those experiencing social material stress may feel that even though humanity faces serious trouble in the next decade, "science" may be the means to help deliver us from the environmental problems we have created on this planet.

By combining these three basic future-oriented questions, some patterns are seen that can be roughly summarized into seven main categories:

Optimistic:

- Things will carry on about the same; we will be headed toward serious problems and disasters, but global awakening will eventually make a huge positive difference.

- Serious problems and disasters but a global awakening will occur.

- Things carrying on about the same and an eventual global awakening will make the world a better place to live.

Pessimistic:

- Just serious problems and disasters.

- Things carrying on about the same with serious problems and disasters ahead.

- Things carrying on about the same with small improvements (denial?).

Unsure:

- A catch-all for the balance of all other possible combinations.

Optimistic

Those who are the youngest (Gen-X and Gen-Y age) tend to be the most optimistic in that they embrace a perspective of serious problems or sameness with only small improvement with that of a global awakening eventually having a significant positive impact. Those in the oldest age group (pre-boomers) embraced all three: things continuing along as they have been, serious problems and disasters, and that a global awakening will occur. (One way of interpreting this would be to infer some measure of insight based on life experience: *"If things continue on as they have been, humanity will face disastrous consequences and will eventually (need to) experience a global awakening to a higher consciousness than that which predominates now."*)

In looking at the 8 American Types, those of the SCT (Seeking Community Transformation) type identified with all the optimistic combinations and not the pessimistic ones. Those of the WNL (Working for a New Life

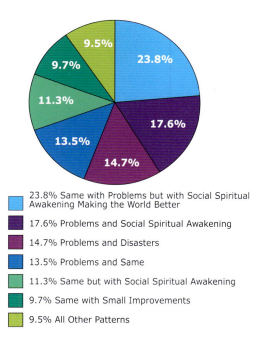

DURING THE NEXT TEN YEARS...

9.5%
9.7%
11.3%
13.5%
14.7%
17.6%
23.8%

23.8% Same with Problems but with Social Spiritual Awakening Making the World Better

17.6% Problems and Social Spiritual Awakening

14.7% Problems and Disasters

13.5% Problems and Same

11.3% Same but with Social Spiritual Awakening

9.7% Same with Small Improvements

9.5% All Other Patterns

Is it optimism or denial to think things can continue on as they have been?

A few readers might be wondering why we included the "same with small improvements" category under pessimism. Considering how human affairs and environmental concerns looked at the turn of the millennium and the heightened political, military, economic and environmental tensions the world is currently facing, we would counter by asking how is it optimistic to believe that things will simply move along the "same as always" (with small improvements)?

The 8 Types and Future Outlook Circa 2000

CMW:

Things will continue as they have been

DSC and CC:

Sees serious problems and disasters ahead

ETV:

See serious problems and disasters but also sees things could continue as they have been

CSE and PA:

Things continuing as they have been and social and spiritual awakening will make the world a better place

SCT:

Serious problems but also sees things could continue as they have been. In addition sees social and spiritual awakening will make the world a better place

WNL:

Embraces all three perspective: Problems, sameness, and global awakening.

of Wholeness), PA (Persisting against Adversity), and CSE (Connecting through Self-Exploration) types also embraced optimistic combinations and not pessimistic ones. There were also many in the CSE who fell into the indistinct category of "all other." These four types also share a common belief that, no matter what happens in the future, we will adapt.

Curiously, those of the WNL type, beyond all other types, have faith that technology can help take care of the environmental problems we face. Why this could be *might* have to do with a lack of basic familiarity with the serious extent of the environmental problems humanity is facing, and perhaps a basically optimistic faith in things turning out okay after all. If we are at all correct in this, it means that *there remains a great need for basic environmental education ~ something that perhaps those who are most focused on finding solutions to environmental problems may be taking for granted.*

Pessimistic

Baby boomers registered most pessimistic, seeing things continuing along as they have been or with serious problems and disasters ahead.

People of the "Embracing Traditional Values" (ETV) type held the most pessimistic perspective, closely followed by those of the "Disengaged from Social Concerns" (DSC) type. Of all the 8 Types, the "Centered in a Material World" (CMW) saw things mostly continuing the same, with minor improvements. They also shared the distinction with the ETV and CSE groups of falling into the indistinct "all other" category that includes the balance of the 27 variations of responses to these three questions.

Interestingly, those in the "Cautious and Conservative" (CC) group were somewhat split between the completely pessimistic perspective of problems and disasters ahead and a global awakening being possible. This represents one possible bridge to reach out to CC types who generally tend to be low on the PFCI scale.

Those of the CC and ETV types share a common *lack of confidence* in the ability of people to adapt in the future, no matter what happens.

Only 37% of all respondents agreed that technology breakthroughs can correct our current environmental problems. Of all the 8 Types, the CMW might be expected to have the greatest faith in technology. However they show the least faith in technology to solve our current problems. In addition the CC, DSC, and ETV types are least likely to have faith in technology. Perhaps it is because the CMW's know it well, given their situation, and the CC, DSC, and ETV groups are either too traditional in their beliefs or otherwise unaware that things simply cannot continue as they have, which means that something has to give in a major way.

WE WILL ADAPT TO WHATEVER HAPPENS

Percentage within each type

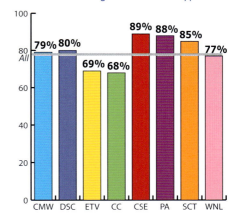

On the average, 79% of all respondents agreed that *"No matter what happens in the future, we will adapt to it."* CC, ETV were the least optimistic about this and CSE, PA and SCT were the most optimistic.

TECHNOLOGY AND ENVIRONMENT

Percentage within each type

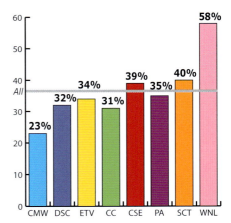

Here we see the 8 Types' responses to whether technology will take care of the environmental problems we are facing. WNL is most optimistic about this prospect and CMW is least. On the average, only 37% of all respondents agreed that *"During the next ten years, technological breakthroughs will take care of the environmental problems facing us today."*

131

Comparison of The 8 American Types and Their Future Outlook

The following provide a more graphical analysis of some of the points that have just been covered: Here we can see the 8 Types' responses to whether technology will take care of the environmental problems we are facing and the extent to which humanity may eventually adapt, no matter what happens.

SERIOUS CONCERNS ABOUT THE FUTURE

Precentage within each type

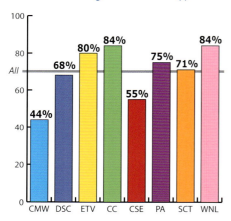

LIFE WILL GO ON IN MUCH THE SAME WAY

Precentage within each type

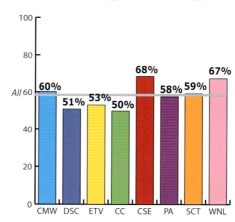

SOCIAL AND SPIRITUAL AWAKENING

Precentage within each type

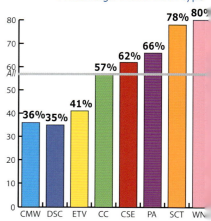

"Humanity is headed for serious problems and disasters."

Those people in the ETV, CC, and WNL groups most identified with this choice, while those in the CSE and CMW groups least agreed with this. Those in the CSE and CMW tend to be more affluent, educated, and score low on the social material stress scale.

"Life will go on in much the same way as it always has, but with small or minor improvements."

Those people who fall into the CSE and WNL groups most closely identify with this mid-case, slightly hopeful scenario. Those CC and DSC types, both sharing a strong element of disconnection and SMS factors, least identify with this statement

"A social and spiritual awakening to higher consciousness will make the world a better place to live."

Those people in the CSE, PA, SCT, and WNL groups most identify with this, whereas those in the CMW, DSC, and ETV groups identify the least with this.

DOMINATION MODEL:

High degree of violence and fear

Ranking of male half of humanity over female half

Authoritarian social structures; hierarchies of domination

Myths and stories idealize domination and violence, and present them as normal

PARTNERSHIP MODEL:

Mutual trust and low degree of fear and social violence

Equal valuing of males and females

Generally egalitarian social structure; hierarchies of actualization

Myths and stories honor partnership and present it as normal.

– from Riane Eisler, *The Power of Partnership*

A New Roadmap – Identifying Bridges

How can a democratic society that appears to be so unaware of its magnificent potential wisely discern difficult choices and address the complexities presented by a massive globalization of trade, culture, information, etc.?

To begin to answer this, basic principles need to be widely articulated, discussed, and culturally and socially supported in ways that would encourage ordinary people and leaders to make good choices for themselves, their communities, humanity, and for this planet that sustains us.

What model for global ethics, values, and beliefs can help humanity move toward embracing an emerging social, cultural, and spiritual synthesis? What will be the new core values propelling and attracting our world?

The very founding of America is practically and philosophically based on a pressing desire to create a new society based on spiritual and democratic principles. Its very founding is a convergence of profound spiritual traditions spanning time and space, and originating from all parts of the world representing millennia of spiritual progress. The spiritual concepts and traditions intersecting with the origin of America bring together ancient Eastern and Western beliefs and with Native American beliefs and traditions. This is fundamental and primary.

However, where we now stand is with a strong orientation to materialism and pragmatism – the early promise of rich land outside of town and the opportunity to develop commercial wealth – the paradigm that has brought us to our current crossroads. The illustrative graphic symbolizing our potential trajectory as a species provides not only insight but hope, as we look to reinvent and reorganize ourselves toward a greater sphere of consciousness. It is but a matter of making a decision to be "Where we could be now if we so choose."

The 8 American Types add invaluable depth and insight to the purpose of identifying bridges uniquely centered to how people currently act and behave. This research is one way to acknowledge, honor, and bridge the new to the old. Because of the nature of the research items, the *IOOW-*

2000 is unique in that it not only asks what the individual may profess to, it asks with what she or he identifies.

In the next chapter, *A New America* develops the concept of spirituality as a means of establishing a foundational basis for bridging and transcending the current polarities of our culture. Spirituality is fundamental and central to positive, future social and political strategies.

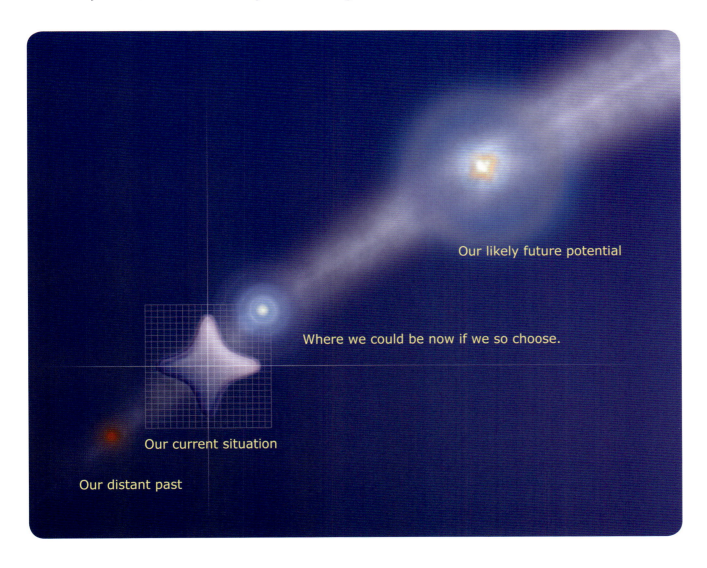

Our likely future potential

Where we could be now if we so choose.

Our current situation

Our distant past

CHAPTER 8

Spirituality – A Grand Context and Unifying Field

"Right before us, there are infinite compelling reasons to choose and act differently. There is an enormously compelling and attractive force that is the voice of our higher reason, higher self, and heart of hearts. All we need do is pause long enough to listen."

What if American society were to encourage the fullest expression of a higher common denominator – one that was grounded in principles of discernment with compassion and regard for the well being of all people and the planet?

Most Americans (73 %) report being directly aware of or individually influenced by the presence of God or a higher consciousness, and 84 % of people attending church services or religious meetings report having been directly aware of or personally influenced by the presence of God or a higher spiritual consciousness. Even those people, who may not have a place in their lives for spirituality, acknowledge their need for spiritual growth.

Whatever way you look at it, enormous numbers of people are open to, actively seeking, and otherwise acknowledging spirituality and its importance in their lives. Perhaps this will provide humanity with the inspiration and impetus to change the nature of their existence – and for the better. Connection with the sacred in all life and with our own higher selves and higher consciousness is the key ingredient to informing our actions. In this way, it is possible for people to discern truth from non-truth.

The vast majority of people, if given the opportunity, *do* want to make a positive difference in the world.

Yet, a gross disparity exists between the deeper aspirations of people and the capacity of our social and political institutions to assist in bringing forth a more enlightened and benevolent society. Projected internationally, this disparity places the American people in a position of both being envied for their material well-being and vilified for the world's problems. Even more ominous is *the enormity of the gulf between what beliefs and values are most important to the overwhelming majority of Americans* on the one hand, and on the other hand, *the actual behavior of America's leaders both internally and globally.*

Americans may have achieved much materially, but now the challenge is how to use our knowledge and wealth for the benefit of *all* humanity and our planet. In such a beneficent context, the artificial polarities of social class, race, gender, political parties, and religious and non-religious could not thrive. Guided by higher aspirations of our hearts and higher consciousness, we can then know what actions to take. The alternative is continued polarization and chaos.

With such enormous numbers of Americans – voters and non-voters – identifying with and aspiring to be more spiritually evolved and involved in positive ways, it is important to recognize that our dominant social and political institutions do not reflect this higher calling. Therefore, what if "walking this talk" became the first priority as individuals and as a country?

Under conditions of extreme urgency, people commonly find ways to move beyond being focused on themselves to helping others. Right now, between impending military, ecological, political and economic crises, we have ample urgency to motivate people to at least know what they *do not want* to occur. But, *in the absence of a clear sense of what we do want, a form of inertial paralysis can set in.*

On the other hand, there are infinite compelling positive reasons to choose and act differently in new ways. These "reasons" emanate from an enormously compelling and attractive force that is the voice of our higher reason, higher self, and heart of hearts. Taken together, this provides a more profound context for appreciating the interconnectedness of creation and of all life on this planet – one of unity within diversity.

A Context of Unity within Diversity

The results of various analyses from the *IOOW-2000* research survey show that there are significant portions of the U.S. population identifying with values and beliefs not yet obvious at a national level of leadership or popular culture. Nevertheless, these individuals collectively place a high value on spirituality, service to others, and on the interconnectedness of all life. Even among those people who identify more strongly with material success, there is awareness and interest in these matters.

"Unity within diversity" is a way of providing a greater context or container for all the uniqueness of individuals and their ideas. It is an important theme common to spiritual wisdom throughout the world.

- Unity refers to a greater connection we all share that transcends the immediate personal or material situation. This points to a basic unifying field present within and between our perceived diversity, or our personal or collective expression of diversity.

- Spirituality broadly acknowledges levels of consciousness and existence beyond the individual and collective personalities we all get to "wear" for our sojourn in a physical body, and reaches beyond individual or religious differences.

It is through the context of unity within diversity that differences need not lead to conflict, but can exist harmoniously and appreciatively. Such an overarching context can also inform strategies and actions to create a positive future. As these strategies unfold, they will naturally increase people's awareness and expression of a larger context, one that has the capacity to unify increasing numbers of people around common action for the common good.

It is the personal belief of the authors of this book that God and Higher Consciousness are *not* separate from our individual self, rather we see this as a continuum of consciousness in which awareness operating at one end of the "spectrum" may perceive itself as separate from the other end of the "spectrum" simply out of self-limiting beliefs. In many cases, the personality self can feel profoundly alone and unconnected to a larger field of consciousness. Psychologically and spiritually, this has profound

Elements of a "Self-evident" Spirituality

- Universal Connection
- Tolerance and Reconciliation
- Service
- Spirituality

It is worthwhile to note that the people who believe "traditional religious literature tells the literal truth," are evenly divided, nearly 50-50, on whether they are separate or not from a higher consciousness.

Of those people who do *not* believe that the traditional religious literature tells the "literal truth," 55% do not believe they are separate from God or higher consciousness, 9% are neutral, and 36% believe they are separate.

implications for each person, as well as for humanity. The impulse to connect with a greater meaning and field of consciousness is one of the innate "directives" everyone has built into their internal "software."

Given humanity's ability to instantly communicate and propagate ideas globally, this can be amplified for the greatest good. Conversely, for those focused on "differences within diversity," personal and global conflict can also be amplified.

This is an important focus of *A New America:* How can we find a new way to be, to do things, to be on this planet, to be with one another? The research themes highlighted in the adjoining sidebar on "self-evident spirituality" are evidence of a social basis for a new charter for America, as well as all humanity.

A Self-Evident Spirituality

These points are taken from the *IOOW-2000* research as examples of a self-evident underlying spirituality.

Universal Connection

- Belief that "What goes around comes around" (and thus do no harm) helps provide a basis for people to recognize another facet of our mutual "interconnectedness."
- Our earth is a unique kind of living organism, and as a whole system is fundamentally alive.
- Underneath it all, we're all connected as one.

Tolerance and Reconciliation

- Interacting with others broadens our horizons.
- To have a successful community, we do not all have to agree.
- Tolerance of lifestyles and groups is essential in a society composed of such diversity.
- Forgiveness and reconciliation help us all accomplish much more.
- We are all looking to be loved and accepted as human beings.

Service

- To be more personally involved in creating a better world. Helping those in need is one of the most important things nations can do within the global community.

Spirituality

- We need to be more conscious of and connected to all aspects of our own selves.
- Whether we recognize it or not, we all want to connect to God or a higher spiritual consciousness.
- Importance of and need for spiritual growth.
- Social and spiritual awakening can make the world a better place in which to live.
- Experience a sense of sacred in everything or see everything as spiritually connected.

EXPERIENCED SENSE OF THE SACRED

Percentage within each type

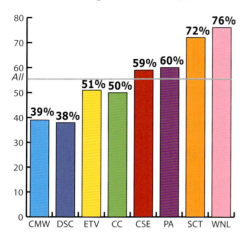

Overall, 55% of all respondents reported having *"experienced a sense of the sacred in everything around them."* This graph highlights dramatic differences in awareness between the 8 Types on significant indicator of spirituality.

"Spirituality I take to be concerned with those qualities of the human spirit – such as love and compassion, patience, tolerance, forgiveness, contentment, a sense of responsibility, a sense of harmony – which brings happiness to both self and others."

– His Holiness, The Dalai Lama

A Sense of the Sacred

In its exploration of the connection between spirituality and consciousness, the *IOOW-2000* research study found that most Americans (73%) report being directly aware of or individually influenced by the presence of God or a higher consciousness. More than half (55%) say they have *"experienced a sense of the sacred in everything around them or perceived everything as being spiritually connected."*

Data from *IOOW-2000* and other studies show that roughly half of all Americans report having had at least one type of non-ordinary state of consciousness such as near-death experiences, out-of-body experiences, awareness of other presences not ordinarily visible, precognition, and other related experiences. These experiences can lead people to seek a greater spiritual awareness, and for people seeking greater spiritual awareness, experiences of non-ordinary states of consciousness can occur.

The first question that the *IOOW-2000* study asked of everyone was the extent of their agreement with a basic concept: *"Our Earth is a unique kind of living organism and as a whole system is fundamentally alive."* After a few decades of being exposed to ecological issues, it is not too surprising that, overall, 81% answered in the affirmative.

What is surprising is that there remain such differences in our society on this point – as disclosed by closer examination under the "lens" of the 8 Types. Additionally, there are striking differences within each of the 8 Types in terms of the strength of their agreement. This perspective elicited the strongest and unequivocally positive response among the CSE type, as 76% were strongly in agreement. They were closely followed by strong positive responses among the PA, SCT and WNL types.

Those who most strongly disagreed with this perspective were those in the CC and ETV types, with followed by CMW. A notable portion of the ETV group weighed as neutral. The DSC type came in as neutral to somewhat positive on this. While one might consider this an important "given" in modern society, it clearly goes "against the grain" in terms of certain core values and beliefs. Nevertheless, even among those types where there is overall disagreement with this concept, a substantial portion did agree to some extent. So here we see, in this concept of Earth as a living system, another example of bridging between types through those individuals who do share certain values and beliefs that are "outside the box" of their predominate type.

Both of these factors (sense of sacred and earth as living organism) imply a sense of wholism or integratedness that is essentially spiritual but not religious, per se.

Nearly half of everyone interviewed (48%) expressed a positive relationship between these two important concepts. More so, fully one third of those people who did not express feeling a sense of the sacred in everything or everything being spiritually connected, did agree with the concept of Earth as a unique kind of whole system and living organism. Twenty or thirty years ago this would have been considered a quirky question by most. Once again, we can see the basis for a positive future. Now the challenge is to make this one of humanity's first orders of business. Why shouldn't America lead the way?

The *IOOW-2000* research study also offers new insight on the relationship between attendance at church services or religious meetings and the experience of God or a sense of the sacred. For example:

- 84% of respondents who attend church services or religious meetings report having been directly aware of or personally influenced by the presence of God or a higher spiritual consciousness.

- 47% percent of respondents who do not attend church services or meetings report the same experience.

- 60% of those who attend church services or religious meetings report experiencing a sense of the sacred in everything around them.

- 44% of those who do not attend report experiencing a sense of the sacred in everything around them.

These findings provide a fresh perspective on how Americans experience spirituality, independent of religious institutions. The sense of the sacred, recognition of the presence of divinity, and general feeling of spiritual connection or oneness, is not exclusive to membership and practice of a religion. This gives further support to the thesis that religion does

EARTH IS A UNIQUE KIND OF LIVING ORGANISM AND AS A WHOLE SYSTEM IS FUNDAMENTALLY ALIVE

Percentage within each type

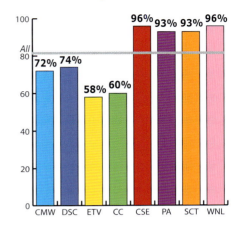

The 8 Types and their expressed agreement with this concept.

EARTH IS WHOLE LIVING SYSTEM PLUS EXPERIENCE OF SACRED IN EVERYTHING

Percentage within each type

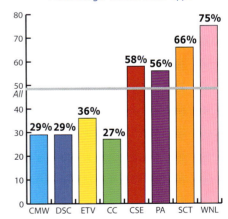

This graph shows both of these factors in combination for each of the 8 Types. These are important value and belief statements that form a foundational component for humanity in creating a new way of life for itself.

An Early "Patriot Act"

Religious institutions have historically sought control over humanity's consciousness and "soul." Any spiritual practice that was not in accord with the official edicts of whatever religious institution was dominant in society would often be met with harsh or murderous punishment. This is a shadow that has been associated with religious institutions for several thousand years.

During the most recent millennium, the Catholic Church instituted the Inquisition during which anyone who was considered a threat to the Church was accused of heresy or witchcraft. This usually meant imprisonment and torture by the Inquisition to extract "confessions" and get people to recant. Those who did not would often find themselves slaughtered and entombed in a mass grave or executed, often by being burned alive in public. This went on for several hundred years from the 1200s through to the early 1800s. In 1908 the "Holy Inquisition" was recast as the "Holy Office."

The power of the Church as a global "transnational state" unto itself was extraordinary and included its own military force. Coupled with the power of the nation-state, this represented a nearly ultimate authority, often dictating the actions of monarchs and heads of state.

not have the same meaning as spirituality and that religious institutions cannot control the "market" or the "supply" of spirituality – it is free for the asking.

The findings of the *IOOW-2000* study support the idea that organized religion is but only one pathway for people to explore or express their innate spirituality. *If anything were to come close to spiritual expression requiring no institution or doctrine, it would be the feeling of sacredness and feeling of connection with creation. These are important value and belief statements that form a foundational component for humanity in creating a new way of life for itself.*

It is time to look at religion and spirituality. Is religion the same as spirituality? Is spirituality a larger context for higher consciousness and is religion a form of spiritual expression for some people?

Church, Religion, State, and Society

What is religion? While there are many definitions, it is instructive to note that its root etymology means "to tie back" and its archaic use meant "scrupulous conformity." Religion is the formal organization of individuals around specific scriptural writings of accepted people in positions of authority. Such writings usually proscribe how to connect with God, as well as provide details of daily life conduct and rules for governance of society. *As much as religions have claimed to have answers to the big questions of life and consciousness, religions have historically exercised extreme control over people's thoughts and lives for the benefit of powerful elites.*

Regardless of the size or historical roots, most religions have a few features in common with one another: Namely adherence to a single teacher or set of teachings, as interpreted by others and handed down to subsequent generations who in turn put their own "spin" to it. These teachings nearly always prescribe very specific ways for people to connect to a supreme creator being. Most religions – old and new – developed various branches, often winding up in intense conflict with one another over various interpretations and contemporary "spin."

Nearly all religions institutionalize a social and theocratic hierarchy that determines who is in and who is out, and what the current spin should be on their brand of supreme creator worship.

Naturally, religions develop their own social-cultural patterns and usually have a community presence centered around their geographically local buildings and hierarchy. Those people who are particularly enthused about their brand of worship may proselytize their version to others in the hope of gaining converts.

As religions gained more converts, sometimes due to their ability to deliver "human services," a social base permitted the manipulation of political-economic power by the religious hierarchy. During the start of the Crusades and the Inquisition, there were two politically powerful Christian centers: the eastern headquarters in Constantinople and the western one in Rome. In later centuries, the Church of England would challenge the Catholic Church in Rome and vice versa. Religious institutions – and political and economic power elites – have throughout history found commonality in their respective drive for control and domination over society.

With our current system, political-economic power is based largely on the ability of religious hierarchy to deliver votes for the politician whose agenda best fits their own. Usually, this implies that their politician also espouses compatible values, but is not always a pre-requisite. According to a July 1, 2002 issue of Time magazine, "36% of those people polled who also supported Israel" (against the Arabs/Palestinians) did so "because they believe biblical prophecies that Jews must control Israel before Christ will come again." From a political and military perspective, this directly translates to support for accelerated military involvement by the U.S. on behalf of the conservative Israeli interests that are fixated on absolute control of "Jewish" territory at the expense of the Palestinian and other Arab people in the region.

What is often overlooked in the public discourse over this belief is that this same "end-time" prophecy calls for two-thirds of the Jews to die and the remaining third are required to embrace Jesus as the Messiah or face damnation. (Historically, the Jewish "end-time" prophecy from the middle of the first millennium addressed the longing for release of a people who had suffered devastating attacks by the Babylonian empire. Similarly, the

The American religious inquisition:

Based in Salem, Massachusetts, from the early 1600s through to 1702 when it was officially outlawed, a local inquisition was set up by the Puritans following English law, which made witchcraft a capital crime. Torture and execution, including being burned alive in public, were instituted by their religious leaders.

The Apocalypse

Lifting of the veil of mystery and revelation of future events, particularly with regard to dramatic changes to ordinary reality and spiritual consciousness. Influenced by the Biblical Revelation of St. John.

Armageddon

According to the Bible's Book of Revelations, this refers to the ultimate battle between good and evil, marked with great destruction and the death of much of humanity on Earth.

The first democratic colony:

Rhode Island was founded in 1635 by Roger Williams. Church and state were separated and complete religious freedom was granted to everyone. This was also where the first Jewish synagogue in the U.S. was founded.

Early Roots of the Middle East World Conflict

Islam from the 7th century onwards, sought to control people and their beliefs in the "Holy Land" by force. A letter, alleging atrocities committed against Christians on pilgrimage to and from Jerusalem, provided a convenient opportunity for Pope Urban II to launch the First Crusade in 1096. Its purpose was multifold: Partly to distract numerous warring forces within various European provincial families with a "holy" military campaign. (This, along with various edicts that included days during which war was not allowed (!) was intended to calm down the endless civil wars that threatened all of Europe.)

Secondly, it was to further strengthen the power of the Church over all "Christendom" and the Byzantine Empire (Christian), which, headquartered in Constantinople, had expanded to such an extent that it was in conflict with the indigenous population (non-Christian). Finally, the Pope promoted the Crusades as a way to take control of the Holy Lands from the "barbarian" Turks (non-Christian, primarily Muslim).

The Crusades intended to crush any political or religious challenges to the authority of the Church. The army of the First Crusade slaughtered both Muslims and Jews as they made their way to Jerusalem. The people who made up this army were not simply involved in military conquest. This was a "holy act of devotion" and a way of doing penance and earning "forgiveness." Several more "Crusades" were launched over the next two centuries.

In the industrial and modern era, this long history of religious-based war was overlaid onto the drive for economic and political empire by European, and later, American-based interests. It continues to this very day, and is still focused in the Middle East, where there has been nearly continuous war for the last thousand years.

Biblical Book of Daniel also addresses many of these prophecies.)

These "end-time" beliefs coincide, perhaps too neatly, with the geopolitical ambitions of key influencers of state policy, key architects of strategy and policy, and of certain power brokers operating outside of public scrutiny. If the ongoing battle in the Middle East region over control of oil, water, geography, and more is supported by religious leaders, then it would seem that the Crusades never ended, they only took a brief respite, and that the dominant trend today is leading closer to a nuclear exchange and possibly a third world war.

A currently popular book series appeals to more than just Evangelicals. It offers up to readers a deliberately skewed perspective of world history, current political affairs, and apocalyptic prophesy. What this feeds into is a deliberately constructed political-military "play book" and agenda for people to follow and support. The result is a small but tightly focused portion of collective consciousness and opinion that is willing to bring on cataclysmic military conflict, to help fulfill and expedite their version of Biblical prophesy just so they can experience Heaven as soon as possible.

It is important to note that not all Evangelicals support the deliberate acceleration of so-called "end-times" prophecies and would prefer people seek connection with God and Christ in a more personal, peaceful manner that encourages forgiveness and reconciliation and not destructive conflicts.

From a different angle, there is more in common than many people would admit between adherents to religious fundamentalist views of the Apocalypse and the Rapture – and many New Age spirituality trends. Both are concerned with the transformation of humanity to a more spiritualized and less physically focused state of being. Both are concerned with people connecting with Christ in hearts and minds. Both seek to learn and channel spiritual energies for the purpose of physical and emotional healing of people. Both are very oriented to future prophecy and divinely inspired communication between the spiritually attuned human beings and non-physical higher consciousness.

THE CHRISTIAN CHURCH:

The political power of Rome was primarily concerned with social and political order, and set about creating an official church whose primary function was to protect its central political power by maintaining social order. This laid the basis for the organizing of the Church of Rome.

By the mid-third century AD, there were about 200 variations of the story of Jesus, his teachings, and those of his disciples. Over 200 representatives met as the Council of Nicaea in June of 325 AD to decide which version of Jesus's life would be most palatable to the representatives as official "party line," which they could then present to the masses.

Hardly a very spiritual gathering, there were so many violent fights and corruption that Emperor Constantine, who was presiding over this gathering, sent in the army to maintain order among the delegates. This gathering took place over a period of two or three months and yielded "mixed results" to such an extent that a second such gathering was declared in 785 AD, wherein a number of decisions from the first council were renounced. (There were 7 councils altogether from between 325 AD and 785 AD, of which Nicaea II was the final "authoritative" council representing true consensus.

Following the Council of Nicaea meeting, it was also decided that no competing religions in the "Christian world" would be tolerated. Anything not officially sanctioned was outlawed: adherents were either persecuted, permanently banished, or put to death. (One remote region where the banished were sent was know as Pagi – thus the origins of the word "pagan.")

To build membership in the church, additional incentives were used to encourage new adherents (many of whom were slaves) including clothes and direct payments. In exchange for their membership, slaves were freed. In this way, large numbers of people were "converted" and massive public "baptisms" of thousands of people at a time were performed by church officials.

Religious holidays were declared that deliberately coincided with ancient solar and other events, and the intentional embellishment and fabrication of the official story of Jesus commenced.

ISLAM

Around the year 600, a merchant named Muhammad claimed that the angel Gabriel told him on Mt. Hira that both the Hebrew and Christian Bibles' view of God was correct, that there is only one God. Over a period of years, Muhammad conveyed what he said he experienced as clairaudient and clairvoyant visions from the angel Gabriel to his scribe and thus emerged the Qur´ān or Islamic bible.

Muhammad declared himself to be the messenger of God/Allah and proceeded to found a new religion. He and his followers sought to win converts and moved from defending themselves from others who attacked their right to speak and preach, to directly attacking opposing populations and imposing their beliefs on others. In time, these conflicts grew to military-scale warfare, which eventually led to an Islamic empire.

A central tenet of Islam is that there is only one God and all creation is derived from Him. Therefore, all humans should live in a corresponding unity (community) – interpreted by Islamic fundamentalists to mean under "Islamic Law." (Christian fundamentalists have their own versions of religious "law" that they think everyone should live under.)

"Summing up in the broadest possible way the characteristics of the religious life, as we have found them, it includes the following beliefs:

That the visible world is part of a more spiritual universe from which it draws it chief significance;

'That union or harmonious relation with that higher universe is our true end;

That prayer or inner communion with the spirit thereof – be that spirit 'God' or 'law' – is a process wherein work is really done, and spiritual energy flows in and produces effects, psychological or material, within the phenomenal world."

– James, William. 1958. *The Varieties of Religious Experience.* New York: The New American Library of World Literature, Inc.

"Beneath the surface there has been a steady realignment within each of the religious constituencies. ...Today, Evangelical Protestants, Mainline Protestants, and Catholics each have three distinct factions: traditionalists, who are characterized by a high level of orthodox belief, attend church very regularly, and are eager to preserve traditional beliefs and practices in a changing world; modernists, who subscribe to heterodox beliefs, attend church less frequently and are eager to adopt modern beliefs and adapt practices to changing conditions; and centrists, who fall between those two groups."

– John Green, Ph.D., *The American Religious Landscape*

Note: For added perspective, please see Appendix for excerpts from a research article written by John Green, Ph.D., Director: Bliss Institute, University of Akron titled "The American Religious Landscape and the 2004 Presidential Vote: Increased Polarization." The article was published by The Pew Forum on Religion and Public Life.

What may be the most profound difference in interpretation and application of ancient and contemporary prophecies is that the narrow fundamentalist approach actually encourages natural and human mass destruction as a way to solve all worldly problems – let Heaven sort it out through a day of "divine judgment." Perhaps all the major religions have been going at it just a little "off-track"?

A more enlightened approach encourages people to play a conscious and deliberate role in taking responsibility for their world using love and compassion, as well as discernment and directly seeking spiritual connection with higher consciousness. This would be in contrast to relying on religious hierarchies and heavily edited scriptures that are roughly two thousand years old, scripted to support specific agendas, and represent nearly two thousand years of bloodshed.

Cornering the Market on Spirituality

Historically, most of the world's religious institutions have tried in their own ways to "corner the market" on spirituality and morality – usually under the guise of "saving" (or controlling) people's souls. When coupled with powerful political-economic agendas and the power of the state, it has made for nearly 2,000 years of warfare, right up to the present day.

Religious institutions have either separated themselves from the meaning and term of "spirituality" as a concept allowing too much liberal interpretation – or they have sought to "monopolize" spirituality by declaring themselves to be the only true connection to God and higher consciousness.

It was only by social custom and the power of traditional religious institutions that people considered religion the accepted expression of spirituality. In this way, they came to be loosely equated. In the forming of the United States of America, it was not the founders' intention to keep spirituality separate from civil society and governance. In prohibiting government from interfering in religious expression and religious institutions, the founders helped assure the freedom of religious expression. Yet today, the question of whether religion and spirituality are the same is not settled in American society.

A Partnership Voice at the Core of All World Religions

"At the core of the major faiths – Hindu, Buddhist, Muslim, Hebrew, Christian, Confucian – are the partnership values of sensitivity, empathy, caring, and nonviolence. These are the spiritual values many of us are striving to reclaim. These are the values that support the relationships we yearn for. They are the values we can use to develop a partnership spirituality that infuses our day-to-day lives with empathy, caring, and responsibility – a spirituality focused on joy, life and love rather than pain, death, and hate."

"A spirituality that tells us to accept things as they are, to unquestioningly obey "higher authorities" – including punitive, angry deities – is not the spirituality of the great religious visionaries of history. Isaiah and Jesus, Gautama and Hildegard of Bingen did not ask us to tolerate injustice and cruelty. They tried to change things – Jesus stopped the stoning of a woman and Hildegard stood up to a pope."

– from Riane Eisler,
The Power of Partnership

Based on gross generalization, in January 2004, the highest authority on Islamic law in Egypt ruled that since yoga was one of the ways to practice Hinduism, it was therefore anti-Islamic and a sin for Muslims to practice yoga.

– Fatwa issued by
Grand mufti Ali Gomoa of Egypt

Dangerous Dogma or Spiritual Wisdom?

Today, leading religious fundamentalists – *among all the major religions* – who advocate religious "end-time" scenarios are *not* inspired or informed by a spirituality based in higher consciousness and wisdom. Rather, they are operating from a murky and dangerous agenda that applies quotations conveniently excerpted from their favorite religious texts to the politics and economics of global hegemony. Their appeal to people is based on fear, ignorance, and superstition. The wavelength they operate on is one of anger and hatred for anything they cannot control. They rely on traditionalism and polarity to keep people from considering that a new paradigm and spiritual experience could be possible.

Regardless of whether they are of religious or non-religious choosing, there are also those people who operate on a wavelength of love and compassion. Their words and actions are informed from their spiritual higher selves. This perspective does not seek to polarize based on "us versus them" but rather to establish a new position, a higher ground that elevates people, helping them to shift out of the old, conflict-based paradigm in which they find themselves trapped.

At this crisis point in human history, there is not the time to debate who did what or to whom at any point along an increasingly obscured religious time line. Any religion that uses the excuse of "divine guidance" to subjugate and slaughter people cannot be very close to higher consciousness, whether it is called God, Yawah, Krishna, Allah, or some other name.

America has been, and still is, one of the most spiritually oriented *and* religious of all countries in the world. Yet at the same time, it is a country that denies its own spirituality and spiritual heritage through tacit and deliberate silence on this matter. How can we realize a higher purpose under such circumstances? One of the goals of this book is to bring to light core values, attitudes, and beliefs that have long been implicit in our way of life.

Whether religion is an expression of spirituality or spirituality is an expression of religion, cannot be the issue. Though there are large numbers of people who do not identify strongly with any specific religion or religious institution, does this not mean they can embrace spiritual awareness or apply spiritual principles in their life?

Under present circumstances, a small minority of strident individuals with a religious-fundamentalist perspective and a dangerous global political agenda, have found ways to exert enough leverage to influence national and international policies. This leverage goes far beyond the question of prayer in public schools and abortion rights, and has direct bearing on global policy. It even goes beyond the Christian-Muslim-Hebrew conflicts. As long as institutionalized religion continues to be equated with spirituality, fundamentalist doctrines will continue to hold the vast majority of people "hostage" and the social dialogue kept to self-perpetuating confines.

Over the past few years, most religions and religious organizations – both older more established organizations and some of the newer ones, such as Evangelicals and born-again Christians – have seen the emergence of two tendencies. One is a new tendency embracing values and beliefs leading to honoring the sacred connection of all life, planetary stewardship, tolerance, forgiveness, compassion, peaceful solutions to conflict, and a desire to find transcendence beyond theology and scripture.

A counter tendency embraces values and beliefs supporting the projection of strong military and economic power, revenge and retribution, the domination and exploitation of nature by humankind, and the identifying of "moral" sanctions for behaviors emulating those found in the Bible and other religious dissertations. Both tendencies find passages in their respective scriptures to support their beliefs and practices.

If, as our research suggests, there are enormous numbers of people who mostly identify with new paradigm values and beliefs, yet are socially identified more with a traditional social-culture, then they need to be exposed to a meaningful and coherent message with which they can resonate in a positive way. Such as a message cannot primarily emphasize opposition – otherwise people cannot be expected to move forward in becoming involved. People of all backgrounds are waiting to hear something new that makes sense.

Religious versus Non-Religious?

Today, we find that the majority of people in the world subscribe to one religion or another. Among the many people non-religious people who are more attracted to rational, empirical approach of "facts and knowledge" of the material world, there is a bias against religions and religious institutions. Given the violent history of Western Christianity, this bias is all the more understandable. However, too many progressive-minded people, who prefer their secularism, tend to dismiss those who subscribe to Christian, born-again, or evangelical movements as hopelessly backwards or reactionary. Even more unfortunate is equating spirituality with religion and in rejecting traditional religion, rejecting spirituality as well.

In reality, most religious institutions reflect the differences in society as a whole. Thus the large traditional "moderate" religious institutions have their internal differences as well. Nearly all religious and spiritual institutions, old and new, have constituents who strongly support new paradigm values and concepts. Given the extent to which these perspectives are present throughout society, how could it be otherwise?

A simple indicator of what typically means "religiousness" to most people would be the index of the five items listed to the right. Religiousness, as defined by this index, is shown to be much higher in older generations than younger ones, and just about in the middle for baby boomers. However (and this is a big however) when we look at spirituality, the sense of sacred, and a host of other non-traditional religious concepts that are clearly spiritual concepts, we see no difference among age groups. This strongly suggests that traditional religion has less and less appeal to younger generations while interest in spirituality remains strong. (Also,

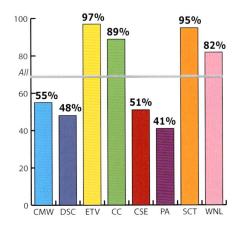

ATTEND RELIGIOUS SERVICES

Percentage within each type

Do You Attend Church Services or Other Meetings of a Religious Organization?

A traditional indicator of religiousness used in many research studies provides a false "read" in predicting social behavior. For example, an average of 70% of all respondents reported attending religious services. Just because you attend services doesn't mean that you share the same social values and beliefs.

When examining this social indicator through the "lens" of the 8 Types, we see, as this graph shows, that four of the 8 Types are strong on attending services, and four are not. Furthermore two of the four that are strong on attending services have very different perspectives relative to spirituality and positive future values – ETV and CC tend to be more conservative overall than SCT or WNL.

RELIGIOUSNESS INDEX

Percentage scoring in upper median

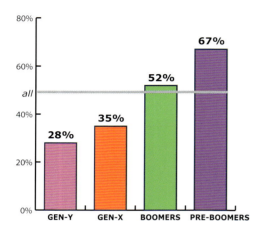

among the youngest age group, Gen-Y, and compared to all other age groups, there is the strongest sentiment that religion and spirituality are not the same.) In the graphs shown here, Side-by-side comparison by age generations suggest younger people are making a distinction between traditional religiousness and spirituality.

When we learn to hear with our hearts and higher minds, it is possible to "see" beyond the superficiality of form – and the politically and historically obscured doctrines of so many religions.

SPIRITUALITY INDEX

Percentage scoring in upper median

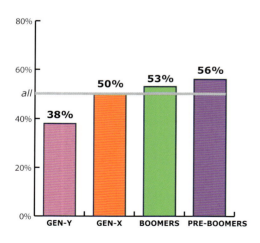

A Simple Religiousness Index

The higher you rate yourself in terms of agreement or frequency, the higher your score on this index.

- I practice meditation of prayer regularly.

- I follow the teaching of a specific spiritual or religious teacher.

- I attend church services or other meetings of a religious organization often.

- I have attended such services or meetings for a long time.

- Going to church, synagogue, or mosque gives me the opportunity to meet and maintain social contacts.

– IOOW-2000 Research

Religion and Spirituality

There is still too little dialogue in common between the various religions and even less between non-religious and religious people. Too often those involved in inter-religious conferences may naturally focus on the value or role of religion per se. For those people who are decidedly non-religious, in the sense that they may not identify with any religious order or doctrine, there is little commonality. What is needed is for people to see and appreciate the passion of anyone who is devoted to communion with God – however they may practice it, as long as their practice does not harm others.

The *IOOW-2000* research shows there are enormous numbers of people who identify with new paradigm values and beliefs, yet are socially identified with a more traditional society and culture. If they can be exposed to a meaningful and coherent message resonating with them in a truthful and positive way, then greater numbers of people can become involved in many new ways.

However, those people most advocating new paradigm perspectives at present lack a coherent message and strategy. Even more so, they lack a common language and means to communicate and engage large numbers of people.

Individuals who most identify with the creation of a new paradigm for culture and society – based on universal interconnectedness, planetary stewardship, compassion, and an enlightened society – must also strive their utmost not to fall into the very trap of criticizing those with traditional or conservative values and beliefs. Such polarization, whether it be over political parties, social policy or religious pre-eminence, only serves to harden respective positions.

Today, the question of religion and spirituality being the same is markedly blurred, both among those who are more involved in their religious practices and among those least involved. There are significant differences in perception as to whether religion and spirituality are the same.

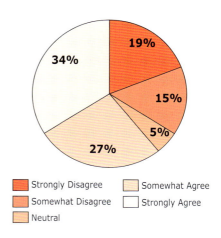

SPIRITUALITY AND RELIGION NOT THE SAME

Percent of all respondents

Legend:
- Strongly Disagree
- Somewhat Disagree
- Neutral
- Somewhat Agree
- Strongly Agree

Overall, 61 % of all respondents agreed that *"religion and spirituality are not the same thing."*

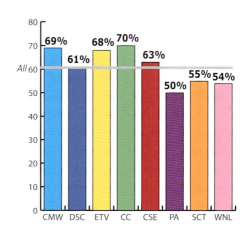

SPIRITUALITY AND RELIGION NOT THE SAME

Percentage within each type

CMW 69%, DSC 61%, ETV 68%, CC 70%, CSE 63%, PA 50%, SCT 55%, WNL 54%

Religion and Spirituality

We ask that religion take its rightful place as simply a *form of spiritual expression*. Whether a person chooses to follow a religious doctrine or religious leader – or not to – has little bearing on the degree to which they are spiritually aware.

Linking or otherwise equating religion and spirituality for whatever purpose, provides various factions the opportunity to exclude the role of spirituality in informing and guiding our society. The U.S. Constitution provided for the State to not interfere with religious expression. There is no law or legal principle that defines separation of "Church and State."

Thus, by equating spirituality with religion, spirituality is effectively excluded from public discourse and gets lost in false debates – as has been forced upon the public over separation of church and state.

"…unite in responsible cooperative action to bring the wisdom and values of our religions, spiritual expressions and indigenous traditions to bear on the economic, environmental, political and social challenges facing our Earth community."

*– from United Religions Initiative Charter
(In 2000, representatives of most of the world's religions and spiritual traditions gathered to sign the Charter for the United Religions Initiative.*

Whether you express spirituality in traditionally structured ways or not, there is much more we share in common: a strong identification with compassion and service, God, or higher consciousness; Earth as a living and conscious organism; and a sense of sacred connection of all life and higher consciousness.

- 83% agreed that whether we recognize it or not, we all just want to connect to God or a higher spiritual consciousness and 49% strongly agreed.
- 43% believed that "God or a higher spiritual consciousness is separate from me."
- 51% said that it is not separate.
- 86% agreed that they feel the need to experience spiritual growth in their life.
- 81% acknowledged that the earth as a whole is a living system and 50% strongly agreed.
- 55% said they had experienced a sense of the sacred in everything around them and had perceived everything as spiritually connected. Of those 55%, nearly half (48%) said they had experienced this more than a few times.
- 61% say that religion and spirituality are not the same.

Comparing similarities among the 8 Types, we find that even though there are various religious affiliations, there are four types sharing a stronger than average belief that "whether they recognize it or not, people really want to connect to God or higher spiritual consciousness": Connection through Self-Exploration (CSE), Embracing Traditional Values (ETV), Cautious and Conservative (CC) and Working for a New Life of Wholeness (WNL).

Spirituality: A Bridge Beyond Social and Religious Differences

For many of us, escape from the exigencies of the "daily grind," whether it's about work or family and other responsibilities, is a prime motivator. The stimulation of escapism eventually begins to fade, though, and we're left with trying to find some greater motivator to inspire or simply prod us along on our journey. "What meaning and purpose is there to our lives?" is one of the primary questions of our incredibly busy post-industrial era, something the baby boomers are contemplating in a big way. This particular question is causing plenty of angst with this group and their successors, the "Gen-X" and "Gen-Y" population cohorts. It calls into question the previous paradigms of family, work, progress, politics, ethics, spirituality, community, environment, and the values and beliefs they instilled. The central conundrum to all of this comes down to a matter of identity and purpose: "Who am I and what am I here for?" These days, not an easy question to answer.

Our major cultural and social institutions, though, do not support this quest. Spirituality does, however. It embraces all aspects of daily life, our higher self, our connection to creation, and the infinite.

A sense of the sacred in one's environment is only one of several key indicators of our relationship to spirituality, independent of religious identification.

Data from the *IOOW-2000* research and various other research studies show that over 90% of Americans believe in God or a higher spiritual consciousness. Most Americans (78%) claim to practice meditation or prayer, and almost two-thirds (64%) say they follow the teachings of a specific spiritual or religious teacher. Many (70%) attend church services or other meetings of a religious organization. For more than two-thirds of Americans (67%), going to church, synagogue, or mosque gives them the opportunity to make and maintain social contacts. As measured on the *IOOW-2000* Spirituality Index, spirituality is something nearly equally shared between whites and non-whites.

It is naive to believe that religion and spirituality are the same to the extent that any religion encourages individuals to seek their own direct

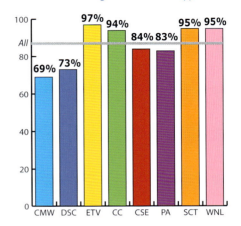

NEED TO EXPERIENCE SPIRITUAL GROWTH
Percentage within each type

While overall, everyone acknowledges they *"feel the need in their life to experience spiritual growth,"* important differences can be seen between the 8 Types.

Nevertheless, what is most important is that even among those who appear to be less spiritually oriented, there is a strong acknowledgement of the importance of spiritual growth that speaks volumes.

"Religious right" in the U.S.:

From various recent research studies, the closest approximation of a "religious right" would be somewhere near 15% of the U.S. In contrast, there is a nearly equal proportion of the U.S. that approximates its "polar opposite."

SPIRITUALITY INDEX
Mean score by type

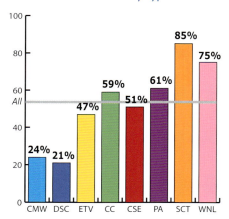

Comparison of The 8 American Types on the Spirituality Index

Two had the highest scores:

- Seeking Community Transformation (SCT)

- Working for a New Life of Wholeness (WNL)

Four had moderate scores:

- Persisting through Adversity (PA)

- Cautious and Conservative (CC)

- Embracing Traditional Values (ETV)

- Connecting through Self-Exploration (CSE)

Two scored lowest:

- Centered in the Material World (CMW)

- Disengaged from Social Concerns (DSC)

connection to God and higher consciousness, religion serves an important *spiritual* purpose. However, too many religions and religious institutions encourage blind belief in religious texts that have been edited and re-edited by elite religious-political authorities – their primary mission very often being social and political control. In contrast are the people who have avoided the control of religious elites as they seek their own connection to God, to realize spiritual knowledge and wisdom, and to seek direct experience of the divine. One does not have to be *religious* to be *spiritually* focused.

Spirituality is a subject many people shy away from discussing – it is both a pervasive, cosmic concept that many recognize at some level in their life, and at the same time, it is an intimately personal subject closely held and cherished, to be shared with but a few, if at all. Yet, as the *IOOW-2000* study demonstrates, vast numbers of people have a longing for a world that can embrace all within a greater unity of being. Many are now beginning to experience a spiritual awareness that goes beyond any individual religion or individual belief. People who may not have paid much attention to spirituality in their lives clearly recognize its importance to their own development.

This newly awakened recognition of the universal interconnection of all life allows that humanity can forgive and reconcile its differences within its diversity, and that it has the capacity to take in the entirety of all that is, all that has been, and to take responsibility for creating its future.

The Spirituality Index: Where Are You?

The *IOOW-2000* study team also created an index of spirituality based on analyses of eight questions. Two types (SCT and WNL) scored highest on this index. One type includes those most concerned with positive change in the world and creating a more integral society. The other type includes those more likely to be new to the U.S. and who are working to create a new life of wholeness for themselves and their families. The two types scoring lowest (CMW and DSC) are those who identify with a material outlook on life and those who are disengaged from social concerns.

The Spirituality Index

The more you agree with each or all of these statements, the more strongly you place on the *IOOW-2000* spirituality index.

- We all want to experience inner peace.
- There is a global awakening to higher consciousness taking place these days.
- For me, forgiveness feels like letting go of an uncomfortable burden.
- If we could forgive and reconcile all our past hurts and conflicts, we could all accomplish so much more.
- Over the next 10 years, social and spiritual awakening will make the world a better place to live.
- I believe that it is possible to see the world around me with the freshness of a child's eyes.
- The things I own aren't all that important to me.
- Whether I am aware of it or not, I believe that God or a higher spiritual consciousness is present everywhere.

"In what is widely regarded as the most vibrantly "religious" civil society on earth, many have been left out. Modern American society has equated spirituality with religion, and, as a growing proportion of the population has not embraced traditional religious institutions, spirituality seems to have lost its place in civil society. Compounding this situation are the schisms among the many faiths that have a long history in America and the reduction in modern culture of nearly all relationships to commodity exchange."

– *IOOW-2000* Briefing

"Spirituality I take to be concerned with those qualities of the human spirit – such as love and compassion, patience, tolerance, forgiveness, contentment, a sense of responsibility, a sense of harmony – which brings happiness to both self and others."

– His Holiness, The Dalai Lama
Ethics for the New Millennium

SPIRITUALITY IN THE WORKPLACE

"The spiritual revival in the workplace reflects, in part, a broader religious reawakening in America, which remains one of the world's most observant nations. (Depending on how the question is asked, as many as 95% of Americans say they believe in God; in much of Western Europe, the figure is closer to 50%). The Princeton Religious Research Index, which has tracked the strength of organized religion in America since World War II, reports a sharp increase in religious beliefs and practices since the mid-1990s. When the Gallup Poll asked Americans in 1999 if they felt a need to experience spiritual growth, 78% said yes, up from 20% in 1994; nearly half said they'd had occasion to talk about their faith in the workplace in the past 24 hours.

"Sales of Bibles and prayer books, inspirational volumes, and books about philosophy and Eastern religions are growing faster than any other category, with the market expanding from $1.69 billion to about $2.24 billion in the past five years, according to the Book Industry Study Group. Literally hundreds of those titles address spirituality at work, from Christian, Jewish, Buddhist, and nondenominational perspectives."

– From July 16, 2001 FORTUNE magazine, *"God and Business"* by Marc Gunther

Forgiveness and Reconciliation

Forgiveness is a key to opening our hearts and tapping into our higher nature and vast potential. While over 90% of Americans agree with the statement: *"If we could forgive and reconcile all our hurts and conflicts, we could all accomplish so much more,"* we have not created a culture that supports this process.

Forgiveness, and reconciliation and all that it implies, is a theme that has rarely been addressed in modern culture. It is one of the cornerstones of Decade Of The Heart (see Chapter 12 for more information), a campaign guided by the understanding that forgiveness is a portal to global awakening. By freeing us to connect with our higher selves, forgiveness opens us to broader conflict resolution in contemporary human society.

Forgiveness, somewhat like the sense of sacred connection, is not related to traditional or non-traditional spiritual expression. These are all aspects of a greater unity of diversity, a greater oneness. If we are all ultimately connected in such profound ways, shouldn't we forgive ourselves? Humanity could benefit immensely by declaring a universal forgiveness for itself, as a basically immature species that has developed dangerous implements for destruction. What if humanity forgave itself for all that has come before and embrace a reconciliation to address the problems that most need addressing? Can Moslims and Christians and Jews forgive each other, as well as themselves? Can whites and blacks forgive each other – as well as themselves – for slavery and racism and all that has wrought? Can humanity forgive itself for bringing itself, as a whole, to the brink of environmental and military catastrophe? Can Americans and those who suffered at the hands of the American empire forgive one another? Can Americans forgive themselves for their part in preferring to live in denial and comfort? ...

It is vitally important that we not focus on our past and the disparities and differences that have so often divided us as individuals and communities and cultures, but focus instead on our higher heartfelt aspirations which can serve as a positive attractor that moves us toward a positive future.

Yes, even today it is possible to have differences without conflict. Where they do occur, spiritual principles of forgiveness and reconciliation can

SENSE OF THE SACRED IN EVERYTHING AND OFFERING FORGIVENESS

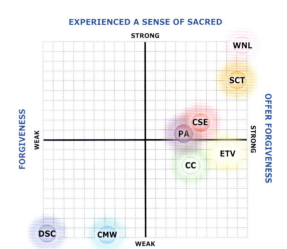

Here we can see a dramatic relationship in combining these two factors for comparison with the 8 Types: *"I offer forgiveness to those who do me wrong." ...and "Experienced a sense of the sacred in everything or perceive everything as being spiritually connected."*

be applied to create more space and time to allow for diversity and cooperation, and to find a larger context for unity.

Acknowledgement, forgiveness,and reconciliation can and must be done for all our sakes, for the sake of the planet, for the sake of future generations, and for the sake of our souls and spiritual upliftment?

Imagine for a moment if

forgiveness was easy:

If anger lasted only an instant –

What would it feel like?

Would there be more joy?

Would there be more dignity?

Would there be more tenderness?

Could it be that simple?

Imagine…

– from the Decade of the Heart media campaign,
Messages: Awakening the Heart of Humanity

FORGIVENESS

*Forgiveness is found in the heart
of a golden mountain*

It is the color of vibrant blue

It is a circle inside of you

Once spread with anger

Now whole again

*You'll have a certain glimmer about
you once you forgive*

And when people see that glimmer

they will know that you

Have a forgiving heart

If the world never forgave

All would be trapped

Inside of a dark, damp cave

Forever angry

Forever alone

Forgiveness is life

– by Stephen Readley, Grade 6

WONDER

I am the star of wonder

your light in the dark,

your mission far away,

getting brighter as you get better.

I am the dolphin in the sea,

I sing, I dance for joy.

*I am the dragon that takes you away to your
future, our future, everyone's future.*

*No more life, no more outside wonder, unless
you let me lead you, lead you in a song of
simpleness,*

a song of nature,

let me lead you.

I am the rainbow bird that sings you a song,

that sings of happiness and celebration.

– Catherine Janes, Grade 6

"Congress shall make no law respecting an establishment of religion, or prohibiting the free exercise thereof; or abridging the freedom of speech, or of the press; or the right of the people peaceably to assemble, and to petition the Government for a redress of grievances."

– Amendment to the U.S. Constitution, Article I

"Civil Spirituality"

A global atmosphere wherein society openly acknowledges the universal interconnection of all people, creation, and consciousness. New ethics would emerge to guide thought and actions for the highest good of all. There would be no place for any individual or society to dominate another – or for humanity to be in conflict with nature. People would be free to explore their fundamental nature as spiritual beings without that experience being based on suffering. This new civil spirituality would spread universal love and mutual regard among all people.

It is within such a larger context that the world's religions could find coherence around ancient truths that have been obscured for too long. The potential for this would be far-reaching, as it would liberate enormous amounts of human energy for creation of a positive future, rather than fighting over the present.

Unifying Potential of a "Civil" Spirituality

This is an important time for humanity, perhaps a most pivotal one. More people than ever before are identifying with spiritually aligned and integral choices for themselves and the planet.

How can humankind overcome thousands of years of conflict and heal itself? We believe the answer is as deceptively simple as the need to embrace it is urgent. As greater numbers of people rediscover the imperative of honoring the Earth, identifying with spirituality, and taking a responsible view of our future on this planet, a change has already been taking place in people's consciousness.

Data from the *IOOW-2000* research and various other research studies show that over 90% of Americans believe in God or a higher spiritual consciousness. This is in dramatic contrast to some countries or local regions where only a minority may hold this belief. Most Americans (78%) claim to practice meditation or prayer, and almost two thirds (64%) say they follow the teachings of a specific spiritual or religious teacher. Most (70%) attend church services or other meetings of a religious organization. For more than two-thirds of Americans (67%), going to church, synagogue, or mosque gives them the opportunity to make and maintain social contacts.

Research shows that the number of Christians in America fell from 86% in 1990 to 77% in 2001 as more people identified with alternative faiths or organizations. However, the U.S. is still one of the most spiritual, "faith-oriented" populations in the world, and overwhelmingly Christian.

More important is the fact that over 90% of U.S. households "believe in God or higher spiritual consciousness" and that 83% agree that "whether we recognize it or not, we all just want to connect to God or a higher spiritual consciousness." Research also shows that *the sense of a sacred interconnectedness is not related to whether a person identifies with organized religion or a religious practice.*

Those people who most relate to this also report having experienced a sense of the sacred in everything around them or see everything as spiritually connected.

It is this acknowledgment – of the sacred and the powerful aspirations of people to seek connection to higher consciousness and divinity – that already transcends the doctrines of the world's religious institutions. It is in this that we can see the basis for a spiritually open and aware society.

In our view, neither any one religion nor all religions taken as a whole – are the same as spirituality, but rather they are only *one form of expression out of many* that people may use to be reminded of their relationship to higher consciousness and creation. Ultimately, each one of us has a personal and direct connection to God or higher consciousness, regardless of what belief system our personality may clothe itself in at the moment.

It is this drive to connect to higher consciousness and the vastness of creation that is fundamental to all humanity.

For *spirituality* to be explored and experienced on the widest possible scale, it needs to be released from being confined to "official" religions. Indeed, given the consistent historical experiences of religious institutions using state power to further their own institutional agendas, separation of religion and state power continue to be essential, just as there needs to be separation of commercial corporate power from public governance. Given the tenor of these times we are in, laws about separation of church and state are meaningless when the central government and other key arms of state power are heavily influenced by and often controlled by religious zealots who turn state power to the furtherance of their ideological and institutional agendas.

Despite this, spirituality cannot be denied an active and vital role in civil society. All people should be allowed – indeed encouraged – to seek guidance from higher consciousness in whatever ways are best suited for their own unique situation. Humanity most desperately needs an inspired vision for itself if it is to thrive and advance beyond its current state of development. Eventually, most everyone will discover paths that are effective for themselves.

Such an outpouring of spiritual expression, linked with service to humanity and planetary stewardship, would create a powerful tide of goodwill toward all and new social, economic, and political structures

"…the great movements of the last hundred years and more – democracy, liberalism, socialism – have all failed to deliver the universal benefits they were supposed to provide, despite many wonderful ideas. A revolution is called for. …What I propose is a spiritual revolution."

– His Holiness, The Dalai Lama, *Ethics for the New Millennium*

"America is a society whose strength is based in part on the hopes and aspirations that arise from a longing for enlightenment and compassion."

"Studying the history behind the founding of the U.S. reveals an awareness and intention that far outreached the medieval mind in terms of society, political order, spirituality, and the relationship of human settlement with nature."

– *IOOW-2000* Research Notes

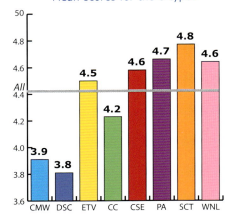

WANT TO BE INVOLVED IN CREATING A BETTER WORLD

Mean scores for the 8 types

The 8 Types Most Wanting to be Involved in Creating a Better World

In descending order of strongest agreement:

Seeking Community Transformation (SCT)

Working for a New Life of Wholeness (WNL)

Persisting against Adversity (PA),

Connecting through Self-Exploration (CSE)

Embracing Traditional Values (ETV)

would naturally emerge to replace what does not serve humanity's positive future. We can choose this for ourselves. Those who might oppose its emergence would only be doing so out of fear for their own personal power and control over others, something that would eventually become widely apparent.

People want to see a better world and participate in it. Forgiveness, universal connection, service, and spirituality can liberate unlimited social and material capital to make the world a place to love and be loved.

Wanting Involvement in Creating a Better World

Ninety-one percent of U.S. households agreed with the statement: *"I would like to be involved more personally in creating a better world at whatever local or global level I can."* Even more importantly, 53 % *strongly* agreed. (That 10 % didn't identify with this relates strongly to social and personal disconnection.)

Those most *strongly* identifying with wanting to be involved with positive change were the SCT, PA, WNL, and CSE types. This is essentially about *service*, which is a powerful connecting bridge between the ETV and others, especially with those in the SCT and CSE groups. Those in the DSC group had the least interest in being involved.

The value of this question is further reinforced by its consistency with many other analyses from the *IOOW-2000* data. (For those who may ask, when we examined the separate concepts of donating money and volunteering time, it was found that these factors were generally too low of a common denominator to provide enough insight into people's beliefs and behavior.)

In this last set of graphics, we see striking differences within our simple quadrant model that maps the U.S. population based on two important indicators:

- The Positive Future – Cooperative Integrative (PFCI) scale on the vertical

and

- The Social Traditional - Religious Conservative (STRC) index on the horizontal.

These all illustrate how spirituality and personal involvement in shaping a new future could be important bridges between major portions of the population. Involvement in helping others comes naturally to many people, but without a higher vision of the future, personal involvement can too often seem like a losing proposition in the face of the seemingly insurmountable problems of the world today. Involvement in creating a better world is a strong connecting bridge between people who tend to be more traditional and conservative (ETV) and those who are less traditional (CSE). In looking more deeply into the 8 Types, we see other points of connection that are not evident in these highly simplified models.

Humanity's social, political, and economic problems cannot be solved by the same type of thinking that led to these problems in the first place.

A social and spiritual awakening – a change not only in the way we think, but in the way we feel – will help us to build a more positive future. Once awakening changes our habitual ways of *thinking* and *feeling,* no mere plan, law, or institution could possibly motivate us to work together in the way that *social and spiritual awakening* can.

WANTING TO BE INVOLVED

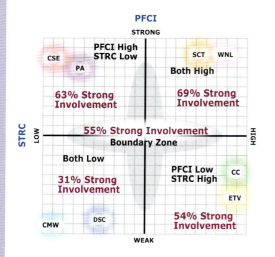

PFCI
STRONG

PFCI High
STRC Low
CSE
PA
SCT   WNL

Both High

63% Strong
Involvement

69% Strong
Involvement

STRC   LOW   HIGH

55% Strong Involvement
Boundary Zone

Both Low

PFCI Low
STRC High   CC

31% Strong
Involvement

ETV

CMW   DSC

54% Strong
Involvement

WEAK

While wanting to be involved in
creating a better world is highest
in the upper half of the PFCI-STRC
map, those types in the middle and
lower right also show this is a basis
for connection and positive actions.

SENSE OF SACRED

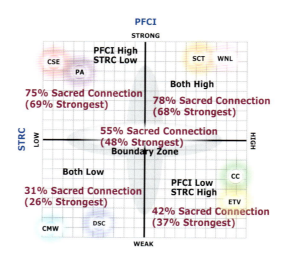

PFCI
STRONG

PFCI High
STRC Low
CSE
PA
SCT   WNL

Both High

75% Sacred Connection
(69% Strongest)

78% Sacred Connection
(68% Strongest)

STRC   LOW   HIGH

55% Sacred Connection
(48% Strongest)
Boundary Zone

Both Low   CC

PFCI Low
STRC High

31% Sacred Connection
(26% Strongest)

ETV

CMW   DSC

42% Sacred Connection
(37% Strongest)

WEAK

Although experiencing a sense of
sacred connection is found most
in the two upper quadrants, it is
most strongly present in the upper
left quadrant where the PFCI scale
is highest and identification with
the STRC index is lowest. It is least
present in the lower half, especially
in the lower right where the STRC
influence is high but PFCI influence
is weak. (The level of strongest
positive response is marked in
parentheses.)

SPIRITUALITY

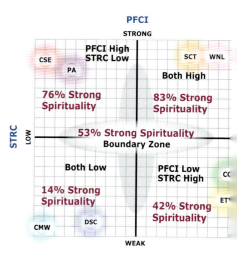

PFCI
STRONG

PFCI High
STRC Low
CSE
PA
SCT   WNL

Both High

76% Strong
Spirituality

83% Strong
Spirituality

STRC   LOW

53% Strong Spirituality
Boundary Zone

Both Low

PFCI Low
STRC High   CC

14% Strong
Spirituality

ETV

CMW   DSC

42% Strong
Spirituality

WEAK

The Spirituality Index registers
highest in both upper quadrants
of the PFCI-STRC model and it is
the strongest in the upper right
where identification is also high
with the STRC index. Here we see
the potential for non-religious
spirituality to connect at least
four of the 8 Types. Shared social-
traditional values provide a natural
connection between the SCT type
and those of the ETV type who
place higher on the PFCI scale.

Social and Spiritual Awakening

Global awakening has the potential to foster an extraordinary feeling of togetherness, a sense of joy in our being, and creating together a new future of our own making. The concept of "awakening" – socially and spiritually – represents a very large context embracing our diverse connection with one another, a wide-reaching spirituality, and the value of service to one another and the planet.

"Global awakening" is a general term and concept that has not, until very recently, come into much use. It is noteworthy that today there are more religious and spiritual groups beginning to use the expression "awakening" to refer to Heaven, God, Creator, or other terminology to describe a state of personal and collective connection to higher consciousness.

The term and concept of "waking up" or "awakening" is something that consistently evokes positive ideas and feelings having a relevancy crossing religious and non-religious beliefs. It also crosses voting and non-voting tendencies in ways suggesting it could be of great importance.

The *IOOW-2000* research provides overwhelming evidence of a nascent spirituality among Americans, one that bridges perceived differences between those who identify with traditional religion and those who do not. Even among those types who express the least concern with spirituality, a need for spiritual growth is widely acknowledged.

In our research, two phrases in two different questions were used to broadly reference this: "social and spiritual awakening" and "awakening to higher consciousness." (These questions were located in different sections of the survey and were deliberately not defined thus allowing each respondent to freely interpret them any way they liked.)

Overall, 57% of Americans agreed that, "there is a global awakening to higher consciousness taking place these days" and 56% of Americans agreed that, "over the next 10 years, social and spiritual awakening will make the world a better place to live." While the percentages reported are nearly the same, these are two distinct sets of perceptions sharing some commonality. Women and non-whites are much more likely than to strongly identify with both global awakening questions (however, at

GLOBAL AWAKENING

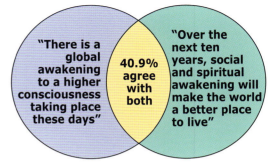

While nearly the same percentage of Americans acknowledge global awakening, some see it occurring now, yet are unsure it will make a future difference in the world in ten years.

Others believe it could make the world better in the future but are not aware it is taking place now.

Nevertheless, 41% believe it is taking place and see it making the world a better place.

– *IOOW-2000* Research

"TAKING PLACE NOW"

MOST AGREE

LEAST AGREE ← → MOST AGREE

"IN TEN YEARS"

LEAST AGREE

Types most wanting global awakening:

At the top of the vertical axis is the highest agreement with the statement that a global awakening is taking place now, and at the far right of the horizontal axis is the highest agreement that a global awakening will make the world better in ten years.

Comparing the 8 Types to both questions, we see, in the upper right, that the WNL and SCT types are most in alignment with both of these statements, and in the lower left, that the DSC and CMW types are least in agreement with these two statements.

While the CSE type is moderately in agreement with the future ten years statement, we see their overall level of agreement with the global awakening now statement to be on par with the ETV type, who as we see, is not very sure that a global awakening will make that big a difference in ten years.

moderate levels of agreement, this difference is less pronounced).

First, people who are aware of a change in consciousness taking place now also see it making a world of difference in 10 years (41%).

Secondly, there are people who are aware of a change in consciousness taking place now but may be concerned it is too little, too late and thus uncertain about its effect in 10 years. Lastly, there are those people who are not aware of a consciousness change taking place now, but are hopeful that it will be enough to make a difference in 10 years.

When looking at the *combined* responses to both of these items for everyone, we find the following breakout:

- 41% of Americans *agreed* that global awakening is taking place, and *agreed* that over the next 10 years, it will make the world a better place to live.

- 11% *disagreed* that global awakening is taking place, but *agreed* it would make the world a better place to live.

- 18% *disagreed* that global awakening is taking place, and *disagreed* that over the next 10 years, it will make the world a better place to live.

- 11% *agreed* that global awakening is taking place, but *disagreed* it will make the world a better place to live.

The remaining 19% included:

- 4% were *neutral* regarding global awakening is taking place, but *agreed* it would make the world a better place to live.

- 4% *agreed* that global awakening is taking place, but *were neutral* regarding whether it would make the world a better place to live.

- 3% were *neutral* regarding global awakening is taking place, but *disagree* that it would make the world a better place to live.

- 3% *disagreed* that global awakening is taking place, but were neutral regarding whether it would make the world a better place to live.

- 5% were *neutral* on both of these items.

Global social and spiritual awakening is clearly a meaningful and positive concept to those in the WNL and SCT types. In addition, there is a positive association with those of the PA, CSE, and CC groups.

Global Awakening, Spirituality, and Involvement in Creating a Better World

These three other factors, are basic to a more universal spirituality throughout society:

A Global Awakening is Taking Place

- Americans who most agree that, *"a global awakening to higher consciousness is taking place these days"* are High PFCI/High SMS (89%) and High PFCI/Low SMS (81%). Those who least agree are Low PFCI/Low SMS (28%).

Social and Spiritual Awakening Will Make the World Better

- Americans who most agree that, *"over the next 10 years, social and spiritual awakening will make the world a better place to live"* are High PFCI/High SMS (88%) and High PFCI/Low SMS (85%). Those who least agree are Low PFCI/Low SMS (26%).

Spirituality Index

- Americans who most frequently scored high on a *Spirituality Index* were High PFCI/Low SMS (85%) and High PFCI/High SMS (80%). Those who least frequently scored high were Low PFCI/Low SMS (20%) and Low PFCI/High SMS (34%).

Americans who strongly express the PFCI trait (the upper two quadrants) scored significantly higher on the item that read, *"I would like to be involved more personally in creating a better world at whatever local or global level I can,"* than those who do not strongly express this trait.

Involvement in Creating a Better World

- Of the five different quadrant types, those who are Low PFCI/Low SMS and those who are Low PFCI/High SMS least agreed (only 38%) that they *"would like to be more personally involved in creating a better world at whatever local or global level I can."*

- Those who are in the "middle" section of the quadrant agreed with this question at a significantly higher level.

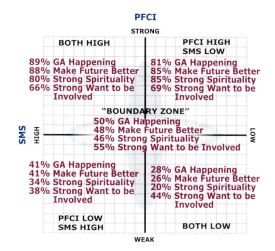

An integral perspective:

"Global awakening" is a general term and concept that has not, until very recently, come into use. Today, Islamic, Christian, Judaic, Hindu, and New Thought religious groups – as well as the non-religious – are beginning to use the expression "awakening" to refer to connecting to cosmic consciousness, Heaven, God, Creator, or other concepts describing more enlightened human evolution that is based on personal and collective connection to higher consciousness. Global awakening naturally takes in an integral perspective of our entire social and natural ecology.

What goes around comes around...

Essentially, Americans who are experiencing higher social material stress endorse the expression, "what goes around, comes around" much more strongly. This could be interpreted in a number of ways. One way might be that these people (who are very stressed socially and materially) envision a time in their lives when "all boats will be raised" (e.g., a time when social and material improvements happen to everybody).

A second way might be that they hold to the adage "do unto others as you would have them do unto you" and thus are more thoughtful overall about their actions and those of others. A third way could imply a more cynical perspective on life – whereby they believe that those who are not currently experiencing as much social material stress (as they do) will eventually come to feel it someday as well.

Spirituality and higher consciousness:

83% agreed that whether we recognize it or not, we all just want to connect to God or a higher spiritual consciousness and 49% strongly agreed.

– IOOW-2000 Research

• Finally, those who are High PFCI/High SMS and those who are High PFCI/Low SMS agreed at a significantly higher level (69% and 66% respectively) than the other three PFCI quadrant types.

What Goes Around

• Americans who most strongly agreed that the statement, *"what goes around, comes around is how the universe really works"* were High PFCI/High SMS (82%) and Low PFCI/High SMS (70%).

• Those who least strongly agreed were High PFCI/Low SMS (59%) and Low PFCI/Low SMS (44%).

It is revealing that so many people identify with and aspire to a global awakening – something that is not in our common language. Global awakening crosses party tendencies and voting likelihood, religious divisions, and most demographic factors. It is clearly an important part of our highest common denominator and represents a powerful attractor bridging those who are less engaged in society as a whole with those who are more engaged.

• The upper two quadrants of the PFCI-SMS model represent a higher common ground for America and include most of the PA, WNL, SCT, and SCE types, as well as significant portions of the CC, ETV, and CMW types. Those people of all the types who are in the upper right quarter represent natural bridges to others of their type who are not yet in this region of values and beliefs.

• The upper right quadrant includes large numbers of people who are already connected with creating more positive future, social, cultural, and political structures and processes. This includes most of the SCT and CSE types, a significant portion of the WNL and PA types from the upper left region, as well as the CMW and ETV types from the lower right, and very slight portions of the DSC and CC types. "Social material stress" that is relatively low contributes toward their ability to act to effect positive change.

Even among those types who express the least concern with spirituality, a need for spiritual growth is acknowledged. Greater movement in the upper right quadrant toward a more compassionate and integral society and leadership will provide meaningful reasons and avenues for action by greater numbers of people, particularly from the upper left portion and middle zone. They, in turn, will be in a position to bridge to others of their type.

This last graphic shows the overlap, across the PFCI-SMS quadrant, of all people who were in agreement with *both* global awakening questions, present and future. The colored circular area marks an approximate "center of gravity" based on the concentration of people. The lighter shading represents those people who are leaning positive and darker shading for those strongly positive. Here also, we can see how global awakening is a unifying theme bridging various tendencies in our society.

Naturally, identification with global awakening is most prevalent in the upper half of the PFCI-STRC quadrant. Those in the upper right are stronger on both future and present term social and spiritual global awakening. *Global awakening is one of the common bridges crossing the social, traditional, and religious continuum.*

As a synthesis of spirituality and personal involvement in creating a better world, social and spiritual awakening embraces a hugely significant social basis for profound change at a personal, community, national, and global level.

Will we answer its call?

GLOBAL AWAKING OCCURING NOW AND WILL MAKE THE WORK A BETTER PLACE

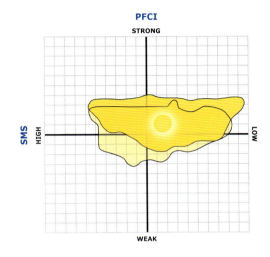

"Global awakening is the worldwide experience of individuals emerging into their higher nature that radiates from the depths of their souls. – Awakening requires remembering who and what we are beyond ordinary considerations of self and experiencing extraordinary dimensions of being. – The vastness of this destiny is such that it can only be known as it creates itself."

– FFGA Vision Statement

GLOBAL AWAKENING OCCURRING NOW

Percentage within each type

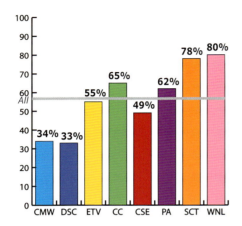

GLOBAL AWAKENING IN TEN YEARS

Percentage within each type

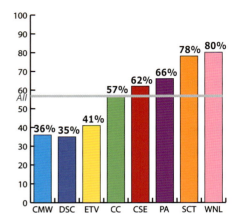

Global Awakening Taking Place Now and The 8 American Types

- Four types most agreeing that a global awakening to higher consciousness is taking place now are: Working for a New Life of Wholeness (WNL – 80%), Seeking Community Transformation (SCT – 78%), Cautious and Conservative (CC – 65%), and Persisting against Adversity (PA - 62%).

- Three types least agreeing that a global awakening to higher consciousness is taking place now are: Connecting through Self-Exploration (CSE – 49%), Centered in a Material World (CMW – 34%), and Disengaged from Social Concerns (DSC – 33%).

- The ETV group is closest to the average for everyone.

Global Awakening in Ten Years and The 8 American Types

- Four types most agreeing that over the next ten years social and spiritual awakening will make the world a better place are: Working for a New Life of Wholeness (WNL – 80%), Seeking Community Transformation (SCT – 78%), Persisting against Adversity (PA - 66%), and Connecting through Self-Exploration (CSE – 62%).

- Three types least agreeing that over the next ten years social and spiritual awakening will make the world a better place are: Embracing Traditional Values (ETV – 41%), Disengaged from Social Concerns (DSC – 35%), and Centered in a Material World (CMW – 36%).

- The CC group is closest to the average for everyone.

Waking Up from Our Sleep

Today, a majority of people identify with the importance of connecting and awakening to the bigger questions about spirituality, existence, and life. There is a growing awareness that everyone – humanity as a whole – must find new ways to function. The alternative is war and conflict over dwindling resources and a rapidly changing ecosystem.

There are also more people than ever before actively trying to get the rest of their fellow humans to "wake up," and offer inspiring ideas, messages, projects, books, media, and whatever else they have to offer.

And yes, with all of this underway, a noticeable minority of people are still going through their lives in a dream-like state, one in which they think they are really "awake" as they agreeably consume the material and emotional distractions our culture so willingly provides. In this state, a person aware that they must wake up, seemingly cannot find a way to do so.

Our lives are so inundated with things vying for our attention – things that are deemed important and meaningful: What path will support my career trajectory, who should I know, where should I live, what should I wear, what image and accoutrements project success and achievement, who do I vote for, should I have children, what are the best schools, who do I follow and emulate, what should I believe in the media, how do I program my VCR/DVD player?

Despite all this, deep down inside nearly everyone feels there must be more to life and their current state of consciousness. Spirituality represents one of the most important gateways to finding true meaning and joy in life.

The process or action of "awakening" – expanding to a greater level of awareness and consciousness – can also be described as a process of remembering who we truly are: A daily progression through myriad challenges on the journey of self-discovery. Along the way, we have innumerable distractions that fall into two categories: Those involved with ensuring our day-to-day survival no matter what venue or environment we're in, and those designed to literally turn our heads and divert us from or blind us to our reality.

"A spiritual perspective recognizes in humanity an evolving biological vehicle for consciousness, part form and part formless, yet something new. Perhaps there has been an innate "governor" that we have not been much aware of, much like an attractor from our future, calling to us."

– IOOW-2000 director comments

As we ask the deeper questions of our existence and meaning in life, as we open to and welcome experiences that uplift and expand our awareness, we automatically arrive at the front door of our own awakening to a greater level of being and consciousness.

Once we begin to welcome in guidance and inspiration from our higher selves, from God, from the Great Spirit of creation, our outlook on life changes almost instantly. We are better able to take a step back from our busy lives to gain a greater and more dispassionate perspective of what we're about, what we're focused on, what we've become. It helps us determine if we are living our lives for ourselves or others, for our ideals and principles or the bottom line-oriented systems of our social institutions. These questions help us look at who we intrinsically are, what our gifts and abilities are, and to discover the things that feed our soul and ultimately lift all of humanity through our daily expression of congruency and authenticity of self-awareness. The very process of discovering what feeds our soul, ultimately provides us with enlightened solutions to the perceived problems at hand.

What we can awaken to is the reverse of intransigence and polarization: the expansive cosmos of our being. Operating in that realm of possibilities, we have the opportunity to activate cooperative processes that honor and respect the uniqueness, values, and beliefs of all peoples so that each of us can give service to and avail ourselves of the best humanity has to offer.

We then discover not only our identity, but also our purpose in life: To know ourselves on a level that far surpasses the limitations of our five senses and ego-driven need for basic survival – to become multi-dimensionally conscious of our interconnectedness with all humanity and the greater cosmos. We gain the ability to see that our fears lead to nothing but resistance, divisiveness, conflict, and pain. This is where the concepts of choice, new patterns, free-will, and discernment with compassion become the activating mechanisms with which we can ascend the spiral of consciousness to a greater quality of life.

What's Next?

It may be possible, sooner than one may think, to develop and implement national level strategies capable of embracing the vast majority of

Americans while involving people – who find little motivation under our current approach to social governance – in voting or more directly participating in society.

Carried out in one of the most resourceful and materially advanced nations, bold new initiatives based on discernment with compassion, and the well being and upliftment of everyone, could provide a beacon of encouragement and inspiration for the rest of humanity, including those who find themselves marginalized or in basic disagreement or conflict with America or its allies.

Nearly continuous migration of people from all countries and continents has created a racial-ethnic-cultural basis for a society in the United States transcending the common lines currently separating other countries and cultures. The potential exists to effectively put an end to a major source of global conflict and create healthier economic relations internally, as well as internationally.

In its opening pages, *A New America* introduced the phrase "discernment with compassion" which, at the very least, assumes our underlying interconnection with one another through the material world of nature and society. Applying discernment with compassion, we can see that the old structures and norms of our society naturally evolved to serve the interests of personal and collective survival and emergence from the feudalism of financial and industrial commerce. Our history and culture emerged from this, thus it is a part of all of us and so it serves little good to complain and always fight these old structures – after all they helped get us to where we are now.

We can use a new type of discernment to decide now what practices of our personal or societal behavior are most harmful and thus should be stopped or redirected. The outcome will be to have determined how best to use our energy for creating new structures and ways of conducting ourselves as individuals and as a society.

If social and spiritual awakening involves changing the ways we think and feel, then one pathway for such change involves sharing information and communication. Let's see what a new social movement would be like.

What if...

As a nation we were no longer guided by the global projection of power in pursuit of material profit, but were instead guided by a higher common denominator and purpose?

What if...

The essentially spiritual values and ethics that America was founded on were extended further to recognize the fundamental interconnectedness of all?

What if...

This could be a way for our society to be mobilized to set an example for itself and the world.

CHAPTER 9

Movement for a Positive Future

"It is our thinking that it is absolutely essential to our vitality and well being that we act only upon our truest and highest aspirations as spiritual beings, as nations, as cultural groups, and as individuals."

P artly relying on the *IOOW-2000* study findings, *A New America* helps us "step out of the box" of our current social structures and institutions that are rooted in control, fear, and conflict. They help to illuminate beliefs and values aligned with a new paradigm for a positive future.

It is only by recognizing a greater positive context in which we can truly embrace everyone that we will reach beyond suffering and conflict.

Might we have a forgotten destiny?

"Our wise forefathers established Union and Amity between the Five Nations. This has made us formidable; this has given us great Weight and Authority with our neighboring Nations. We are a powerful Confederacy; and by your observing the same methods, our wise forefathers have taken, you will acquire such Strength and power. Therefore, whatever befalls you, never fall out with one another."

– Canassatego, the great Iroquois chief, advising the assembled colonial governors on Iroquois concepts of unity in Lancaster, Pennsylvania, 1744.
Exemplar of Liberty

What We May Have Forgotten as a Country

In the establishment of America in the "New World," its founders tried to develop both charter and operating rules for a participatory democracy, as well as reference America's spiritual heritage and destiny for future generations.

In researching a constitution and models of governance for their new society of American colonies, our founders examined historical information on Western civilization and found it lacking, to say the least. Fortunately, they had the benefit of counsel from leaders of the Iroquois Confederacy and *The Great Law of Peace*, a constitution whose origins predate the arrival of white European settlers in America by hundreds of years. The Iroquois Confederacy was the oldest living participatory democracy. Their democratic constitution addressed governmental structure, process, civil rights, international relations, religious freedom, and much more, including equality of women and prohibition of chattel slavery – two points the medieval European mind could not reconcile.

Despite these and other differences, the U.S. Constitution and its definition of Executive, Judicial, and Legislative branches has many close parallels in the Iroquois Confederation. Indeed, the American colonists freely mixed with the indigenous Native American people, meeting formally and informally with their respective leaders. It was through these close relations that an American nation was eventually developed.

Throughout the twentieth century and accelerating in this decade, government in America has been focused on overseeing and administering whatever would facilitate production of wealth, prestige, image, and global power for the nation. To a lesser extent they have made sure that enough of the population had enough material wealth to keep those who didn't have enough from complaining too loudly and upsetting the social order.

Though America came perilously close in its history, it never formally became a plutocratic and/or religious state. Yet today, we are alarmingly close to realizing this scenario. A relatively small number of people, with dangerous intent, have insinuated themselves at key levers of power throughout the central government, communications media, and numerous key institutions for social policy, education, foreign policy, environmental protection, etc. They are now attempting to carry out an agenda combining an insatiable drive for global domination with religious fundamentalism – all without the active consent of the populace.

Approximately 300 years later, in the midst of an extraordinary accumulation of material wealth, we still have an educational system designed not to enlighten and serve an awakened future, but to reinforce old paradigm social norms and prepare young people for specific strata of employment opportunities (or lack thereof). Even the pursuit of "pure" scientific exploration is neglected in favor of developing technologies and products for commercial and military use.

Our materialistic worldview encourages us to identify with material and practical achievement. This has been an important psychological and social driver of our society. Today, it seems that 300 years of pragmatism, opportunism, and materialism has obscured such a high vision from our society's memory. It is as if we are still asleep.

We chose the subtitle "An Awakened Future on Our Horizon," as the word "awakened" is pivotal. The state of being in which we find ourselves today is but temporary: An apparent fog of apathy, self-serving affluence, and agendas based on beliefs and values derived from old socio-cultural paradigms and mythic-religious imperatives. Our subtitle implies that a social and spiritual awakening is indeed within the field of possibility. Like ripples moving outward from a pebble dropped in water, evidence of this awakening is becoming more apparent. That it is recognizable in familiar language and that so many people respond so positively, offers great hope to everyone.

Awakening may appear suddenly at first, like a light coming on in a darkened room. Yet even so, it takes time to notice all the details of the room and appreciate what may be there. The process requires that each of us create our own reality as based on the principles of honesty, sincerity, interconnectedness, service, integrity, responsibility, discipline, and unconditional love.

"They grasped not only the whole race of man then living, but they reached forward and seized upon the farthest posterity. They erected a beacon to guide their children and their children's children, and the countless myriads who should inhabit the earth in other ages."

– Abraham Lincoln, commenting on the founders of America

A type of fatigue can set in that is closely connected with a sense of powerlessness. While people are still receptive to new perspectives and solutions, those people who are offering avenues for positive change simply do not have access to large numbers of people through the various mass media and influential circles, and lack a coherent and coordinated approach. That doesn't mean that this cannot change, it is simply how things are right now.

When we seek answers "outside of the box," things begin to look very different. When we run out of ordinary options to keep the old game going, for many, our inner drive begins to engage in seeking the answers to life and consciousness, solving the riddles of the self-imposed prison, and becoming free once and for all. This is much more than a drive for physical survival, even if it seems to start that way in light of the global threats that face humanity today.

While our society seems to conceal this possibility with endless distractions and tension, it is something that anyone and everyone can welcome into their lives. The mere act of intending to welcome it starts one on the path.

How can we re-discover our spiritual "heroic courage" to thoughtfully and boldly create a new society serving as a shining example to all humanity – a shining society whose future-present does not rest on material production, economic-political-military power, or forced conformity to a religious doctrine – but a society based on a cooperative relationship with nature and the planet, care and conscious evolution of all humanity, the exploration of higher consciousness, and the conscious realization of the very purpose and potential of our being?

The famous expression "we are spiritual beings having a human experience" can suddenly take on new meaning for many more people for the first time perhaps. The question then becomes: How to access a higher state of awareness and create a more enlightened society that will benefit everyone?

It is our thinking that it is essential to our vitality and well being that we act upon our truest and highest aspirations as a species, as nations, as cultural groups, and as individuals. These aspirations and new way of being go beyond the ordinary trappings of life and must now be placed front and center of our personal and global attention.

Awakening to Spiritual Social Action

Unlike the highly visible counter cultural movement or political and social justice coalitions of the 1960s and 1970s, a spiritually inspired "positive future movement" has yet to come into recognizable form, one that can be made visible to large numbers of people. At present, it is dispersed across thousands of groups and inspired individuals throughout the world. Many of those who initiated these groups did so out of personal exploration and their own awakening experiences; others came to it as they sought to create meaningful solutions to social or environmental problems. As a potentially coordinated movement to speak with a coherent voice, they have yet to adopt a common set of unifying principles and strategies. Humanity is "waiting" to be made aware of viable future-present alternatives to conflict, suffering, and corruption – including viable leaders at all levels of society. Such alternatives, to be truly viable, will also have to embrace and encourage a large and encompassing spirituality as well.

Just as during the "First Great Awakening" in America where spiritual seekers mainly left the population centers to focus on their exploration of connecting to higher consciousness and forming new types of community, the spiritual seekers from the 1960s and 1970s were also more inclined to avoid the distractions of the chaotic milieu of society. Even when spiritual groups were represented in coalition meetings, their counsel was often subordinated to the understandable outrage people felt about the injustices in American society and the war in Southeast Asia.

Many of the individuals who were the early seekers of the essence of Christian spirituality during the 1960s and 1970s also had to form their own support enclaves by leaving the cities for rural communalism or by forming support groups within population centers. Some of these later became formalized into strict religious communities with hierarchies and rigid doctrinal interpretations of the Bible. Many of these in turn formed the basis for a number of the Christian fundamentalist organizations today. This is not unlike what happened to many of the experimental communities formed during the 1700s in America. Those people, who were more focused on the injustices in American society, also tended to be non-religious and often anti-religious. Any form of spiritual expression that bore a similarity to a western religion was generally rejected. Eastern

The "First Great Awakening" in America

From 1720 to about 1750 is considered the "First Great Awakening" in America and was not surprisingly related to similar trends in Europe at that time. Despite the problems associated with any "self-elevated" church hierarchy setting itself above the greater church membership, there was, nevertheless, a strong presence of people who followed an inner urge to directly experience and live in a spiritually inspired state of consciousness.

They were visionaries who founded new communities, away from the town centers, living close to nature, and perhaps among or near local Native Americans. Many communities throughout the growing U.S. territory were formed, sometimes spontaneously and sometimes deliberately, by individuals wanting to create a new life based on a spiritual communion. These social-spiritual experiments included various aspects of monastic community and utopian communalism. Often, the central theme was to connect with the original point of Christianity, to connect with a higher consciousness in one's daily life.

Why is this not better known today? Simply put, these were not the people who wrote the official history books. Furthermore, the ideaframe or mindset of the people who do write the history books does not have room for anything not supporting the dominant paradigm and agenda. Historians willing to present alterative viewpoints and evidence are indeed rare.

– *IOOW-2000* research notes

"At present mankind is undergoing an evolutionary crisis in which is concealed a choice of its destiny; for a stage has been reached in which the human mind has achieved in certain directions an enormous development while in others it stands arrested and bewildered and can no longer find its way...."

"A total spiritual direction given to the whole life and the whole nature can alone lift humanity beyond itself...."

"What is necessary is that there should be a turn in humanity felt by some or many towards the vision of this change, a feeling of its imperative need, the sense of its possibility, the will to make it possible in themselves and to find the way. That trend is not absent and it must increase with the tension of the crisis in the human world-destiny...."

– Sri Aurobindo, *The Life Divine*

religions, especially mysticism, provided an alternative to western religions for spiritual exploration. The use of psychoactive substances provided yet another avenue through which to explore mysticism and spirituality.

People who are more spiritually inclined, regardless of their religious identification, have a tendency to not be actively engaged in worldly matters. This is only natural since their focus on spiritual practice is often aided in its early stages by a relative withdrawal from familiar distractions. This is fine and understandable in the early phases of one's exploration into those intimate and expanded spaces of consciousness. However, there comes a time when a decision is required: to remain disengaged from worldly matters no matter what is going on, or to become engaged and utilize a spiritually informed discipline of discernment with compassion.

People who are less spiritually inclined and more oriented toward social-justice have a strong tendency to embrace an "us versus them" mode of judgment, seeking culpability and redress. The effect is a mixed message. Just as human rights, social justice and environmental justice are advocated, there is an implicit advocacy that the human species is at fault and is damaging the planet by its very nature. One could then argue this occupies one side of the same coin as those who advocate human domination over nature: nature should dominate over humans. Even "peace" becomes a questionable issue since the unspoken question is always: Peace, but for and to what end?

The *IOOW-2000* study reveals that most Americans want to address spiritual growth and to be more aware of their personal connection to higher consciousness. For example:

- Over 80% of respondents who acknowledge the Earth as a whole is a living system carries profound implications for humanity's practical relationship with the biosphere. Fifty percent of people strongly agree with this.

- Almost two-thirds of all U.S. households want elected leaders to have moral and ethical values at a higher level than their own, and prefer to support businesses and media that support global awakening.

People are ready to engage in new dialogue and embrace innovative societal structures founded on tolerance, compassion, universal connectedness, and a belief in working toward the greater common good. All that is needed are people and institutions to prominently promote these values and beliefs, instead of holding back or deliberately distorting them.

We are all in this together. How can we move the greatest number of people forward to a more awakened state of being? How can we instill universal spiritual principles, such as compassion and forgiveness, as the supportive framework guiding how we make individual and collective choices?

Such principles can then take a greater role in healing society and freeing up enormous personal and collective energies to co-create a global society based on these greater unifying principles underlying all our great diversity.

Coordinated social expression and actions will need to be grounded in communities, both virtual, as well as geographic ones. In addition to this, we will need to consciously develop new types of leaders, elected and non-elected. New types of leaders must meet very high standards of personal integrity, ethics, and intelligence; be in close alignment with spiritual ideals but not advocates of any one religion; demonstrate a solid commitment to participatory democracy; and support economic, political, and social policy that is in accord with new paradigm, positive future principles.

The choice is ours: work to create a positive, compassionate, and enlightened future, or not – and suffer the consequences.

So let's take a closer look at where there is a social basis for this in our population so that we can gain a broader perspective and more in-depth exposition of some strategies for change.

"As people strive to bring social, environmental, and financial capital into a more positive and meaningful relationship for society and our environment, all our relationships at all levels can be brought into a coherent harmony with one another."

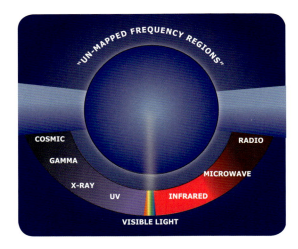

Perception, Science, and Consciousness

By way of analogy, it might be helpful to consider that for a long time, astronomers focused on what they could "see" with optical telescopes. For centuries, it was assumed there were heavenly bodies surrounded by empty space, influenced by hidden forces such as gravity. Today, it is widely recognized that "empty space" is an illusion and that there is more tangible matter and energy in what appears to be empty space than what is indicated by the narrow range of electromagnetic energy we can see with our eyes.

If a few scientists had not been open to looking at material reality in new ways, with "different eyes" and more open minds, we would still believe that space is mainly an empty vacuum. Only recently has our ordinary sight been extended to see that what we thought was empty is immensely full of what some call "dark matter."

By way of analogy, if our perceptions of ourselves are limited by an illusion of conflict and competition with each other (and with the natural world) – then we cannot help but give our attention and energy to that paradigm. It's as if we wind up being personally involved in keeping ourselves imprisoned in a reality governed by conflict and limitation – rather than living in a reality governed by love and freedom to create a new world.

Those plutocratic individuals who have placed themselves at "the helm" of society are aware of the power of perception, the role of deception, and the significance of manipulation through fear. The history of the entire twentieth century America is replete with social engineering, one aim of which has been to make sure that the are enough "opinion leaders" (scientists, historians, governmental executives, media, etc.) in the right places to maintain the necessary collective illusions, from generation to generation – leading society as a whole to participate in their own imprisonment. In the 1960s and 1970s this "barrier" was challenged and broken in places by small but significant numbers of people who constitute the post World War II baby boom generations.

However, if we can at least acknowledge the possibility and begin to perceive that we are interconnected in ways too vast to list here, and if we can learn to "see" with our hearts and higher awareness, it is then possible to *see beyond the limitations of the past and its influence on the present.* The *IOOW-2000* research is one tool to help us do just that – *to see the future-present.*

It is significant news that the *IOOW-2000* research describes in compelling terms that there are overwhelming numbers of people identifying with what can only be called a spiritual and material desire to connect, live, and create in news ways! These are our aspirations – as individuals and as a society.

That...

- ...so many people identify so strongly with such a common set of spiritual values and beliefs that transcend religious doctrines;

- ...so many people of diverse persuasions acknowledge the presence of a sacred connection and a common aspiration to connect with higher consciousness;

- ...so many people want to be personally involved in creating a better world at whatever level they can

...hints at our power if we choose to act.

That we do not behave more positively and compassionately is partly due to the dominance of social, cultural, economic, and political institutions that on a tradition of encouraging, supporting, and sustaining material growth and production – at any cost. Projected globally, its logical extension is the use of military power to dominate others – at any cost. Projected internally, its logical extension is to manipulate public opinion and divert attention away from those influential forces that seek hegemony for their own agendas, even the destruction of democracy – at any cost.

Important as it is to be aware of the true dynamics that dominate our national centers and policies, it is not the time to exclusively condemn social institutions that may have served a useful purpose in years past. If the way we define ourselves as individuals, as societies, as religious groups, etc., continues to be based on past experience, then naturally

"When something is harmful, it should be stopped if possible – but if most of our available energy is expended opposing or attacking something, then we only reinforce that which we don't want and new energy cannot be used toward what will serve a positive future."

Plutarchs – persons of power or influence due to wealth

Plutarchy – government by the wealthy; rule or dominion of wealth or the rich; a controlling or influential class of rich men.

Plutodemocracy – a democracy held to be controlled by people of wealth rather than common man.

Plutogogue – "a person who favors the wealthy or their interests or attempts to present them to the public [ed.: sell them] in a favorable light."

there is little room for forward-looking innovation and choices. That humanity seems to needlessly cling to its past in order to define itself in the present can be understood in the context in which it developed over many generations as *choices* were made – or not made.

Spirituality that relates directly to our individual and collective connection to higher consciousness by whatever name it is known – Christ consciousness, creation consciousness, cosmic consciousness – is a large enough context to help humanity cease its destructive activities and find ways to forgive itself as an immature species. A large spiritual context transcends the arguments among the religious doctrines and can provide inspiration and guidance to everyone who chooses to participate in creating a better world for all of humanity.

This is the time to create new structures and processes that encourage, support, and sustain spiritual growth and an awakened future in which people grow up in an abundance of love, compassion, and trust in a new future of wondrous possibilities.

There is an impulse, a drive, to connect with something greater than what the ordinary or egoic self may know. What if there were no more antagonists? What if there were only protagonists for an awakened society motivated by a desire to explore the frontiers of existence with a reverence and awe for the vastness and beauty of creation? This is a far more exciting dynamic of potential than that produced by fear and conflict. It is the idea of expanding wonder and awe.

"The intelligence capable of orchestrating the diversity of all the cells in the human body is equally capable of orchestrating the diversity of the human family. You do not find the adrenals conceiving of themselves as some kind of ethnic minority, infringed upon by the larger and adjacent kidneys. You do not find the blood cells imagining that they are an aloof commercial civilization.

The spiritual essence of each nation exists in a state of harmony with the spiritual essence of every other nation. The historical conflict between nations has never been between the essences of nations, only between the images of nations. Governmental structures can accept the challenge of truly representing the collective spirit of their people. Or they can accept the false images of themselves cast by commercial greed, rooted in fear. Fear has distorted international relationships. It has done so by first distorting individual perception. Nations are healed because people are healed.

The nations of the Earth are not asked to accept the imposition of any external authority, but to turn instead to their own forgotten spiritual heritage, to examine more closely their own roots, their national passions and interests, to begin intelligently working with their own forgotten spiritual purposes."

– from Ken Carey, *Vision – A Personal Call to Create a New World*

New Conversations for New Actions

To begin with, it is very important that we take a compassionate view of ourselves as a species rather than one of shame or blame over what has happened to the environment and to our societies.

Imagine if you will, our higher selves as parental figures overseeing their children (the "children" in this case being our individuated personality selves that tend to get a little self-important). To continue with this analogy, if the children are running around making a ruckus, making a mess of their house, threatening the neighborhood and paying no attention to their parents, then the parents will need to step in. But in so doing, they cannot blame the children who may not know what they are doing, and the parents will need to place some restrictions on the children while they learn. But wise parents also know it is important for children to learn as much as they can for themselves, as long as the danger to themselves and to others is not too great. In this process, some of the children begin to realize that things are getting out of hand and seek parental intervention.

That is an approximation of what we have today in the world. Only the "children" are "adults" with the ability to inflict great harm on many people, as well as the planetary environment/neighborhood. In response, some people will try to stop them by confronting those who are most active in causing trouble (political action). Of course, confrontation usually causes further polarization. Some may pray that enough of the other children will see the error of their ways and cease participating in the troublesome activities. Others may pray for a cosmic event or natural disaster to intercede. Yet others may pray to be "lifted out" of what may become a most unfortunate situation. And lastly, there are those who believe it best to encourage mass suicidal destruction – justifying it by their religious doctrines and dogma – since that will most certainly put an end to things as we know it, firmly placing matters back into the hands of the "parents," which to their thinking is usually a paternal God.

In addition to praying for forgiveness and guidance for humanity, an extraordinary opportunity exists that requires enough members of humanity to form coherent centers of attention and action from which to reach the hearts and minds of their fellow humans who can be reached.

"A spiritual perspective recognizes in humanity an evolving biological vehicle for consciousness, part form and part formless, yet something new. Perhaps there has been an innate 'governor' that we have not been much aware of, much like an attractor from our future, calling to us."

– IOOW-2000 Director Comments

We need to find ways to help more and more people actively shift their attention to creating a different world – a parallel world in effect – one that can emerge out of the disintegration of the old world and serve as a viable transition for enough people. Their message will emphasize different facets of a whole, depending on who they are trying to reach, for some combinations of these will be necessary in gaining a positive resonance:

- Service to others will be important in bridging to some who are very relationship-oriented, be it individual, community, or global.

- Service to the planet and environment in cleaning up the extensive environmental damage humanity's childhood has inflicted upon its earthly home.

- Connection and community will be an important step toward healing for those people who have felt cut off and disconnected from self and others. This can lead to their engaging in some form of spiritual exploration, service, or both.

- Spirituality and connection to higher consciousness are already important for many. Those people who have shied away from religion know that spirituality is important for their own growth but do not know where to begin. Others who have long sought something more expansive and enlightening than the familiar religious doctrines would welcome spiritual perspectives that do not directly threaten their religious traditions. And there are those who are spiritual seekers who would welcome being part of a larger community of others and engaged in service to the world.

- Forgiveness and reconciliation will be important factors in bridging to many people's situations, irrespective of their personal belief systems. Truth-telling, forgiveness, and reconciliation can allow organizations, societies and individuals to, in effect, "come clean" and acknowledge what needs to be acknowledged without being in a position of blame and retribution. Reconciliation can take place where there is enough mutual recognition and desire to move ahead, comparable to putting society and its organizations and institutions on a "twelve-step program."

These factors help broaden the opening for social and spiritual awakening, a powerful positive future theme, that includes most all religious and non-religious beliefs sharing common elements that have been described in *A New America*.

They can provide an important foundation for national and global dialogue. That in turn could encourage a new type of leadership to emerge.

Where there is resonance, there are those people who can bridge to others in the communities of people with whom they naturally associate. In this way, even individuals who may feel limited or contracted in their views can be touched in some direct and positive way by people whom they trust.

It is the contention of *A New America* that U.S. society is ready for such a conversation for action. However, the opportunity must be well presented if it is to be realized. If established institutions are focused on fear and disinformation, then new institutions and leaders are needed to make present new opportunities for people.

A New Language…of the Awakened Heart

There is now a strong basis for new social initiatives that can embrace everyone with an essentially spiritual worldview transcending doctrines of the past. It embraces nearly all of humanity with the value and significance of service to others and to our planet; and that brings compassion and forgiveness to nearly everyone based on the profound interconnectedness of all life. This spiritual worldview exists outside of the confines of any one belief system or institution.

While in the short term we may lack a common language allowing us to hear what our hearts most deeply desire for ourselves, our children and this planet, humanity nevertheless shares a common dream: to reach beyond the narrow confines of beliefs and practices of our past based more on fear, conflict, and survival than on love and compassion.

- While we may presently lack coherent, visionary leadership that can effectively help us to act accordingly in ways leading to a positive future, the social basis is nevertheless very present and very great and a new type of leadership will emerge eventually.

- While organized religions tend to compete among themselves over who holds the best version of "truth," there are very large numbers of people who do not identify with any organized religion yet are very spiritually inclined and aware. There are also many people who enjoy their social contacts that attendance at weekly religious services provides and who have a level of spiritual awareness that goes beyond their social house of worship.

- While our political laws may require separation of church and state, there is no law prohibiting the integration of civil society leadership with the wide embrace of spirituality.

The time is before us to encourage a new kind of leadership, as well as independent, grassroots, social movements bringing a new conversation to Americans and to the world – a conversation about our actions as individuals, communities, nations, and as a species. A conversation that challenges us to rise to the occasion of creating an awakened world nurturing our spirit and our life based on common core values and beliefs. This is the first step toward living in an awakened world. To accomplish this requires understanding where there is resonance for this in our society.

For a Higher Ground, Some Strategies

This chapter has attempted to frame key elements for a new social movement, one not tied to electoral politics. In Chapter 10, we attempt to frame elements of new political strategies. In addition, two strategies and action plans that are global in scope are presented in Part Three.

- "Decade of the Heart" is a broad-based global initiative aimed at mobilizing large numbers of people around a wide range of activities to create a positive future at whatever level possible. It could provide a level of resonance and support to people regardless of their status, political party or religious affiliation, and introduce a "civil spirituality" back into our daily life as individuals and as a country.

- "The Global Interchange" would be a global Internet presence dedicated solely to facilitating the emergence of positive future innovations in *all spheres of human activity* by bringing together human, financial, informational, and technical resources that are presently unavailable or highly dispersed.

"The expression, 'As a man thinketh in his heart so is he,' not only embraces the whole of a man's being, but is so comprehensive as to reach out to every condition and circumstance of his life."

– James Allen

"This call is like a homing beacon guiding us to our higher selves and higher nature. It seeks to graduate ourselves from adolescence as a species to a more mature position that co-creates a positive future out of greater awareness of our interconnectedness with one another and our natural environment."

– IOOW-2000 Director Comments

To maintain the flow of the story line, Part Four is reserved for additional statistical and interpretive analysis of the U.S. 2000 election that compares traditional analysis of voters based mainly on superficial demographics with a new typological analysis based on values and beliefs.

In looking at either social or political strategies, we are most concerned that new lines *not* be drawn that polarize people in yet more ways. Instead, we prefer to find the greatest possible way to embrace all people. Unlike typical moderate or centrist approaches seeking to find a middle ground of compromise, we are advocating the need for a third, higher ground to be established, strengthened, and extended to all. It must embody self-referencing principles of such clarity that anyone can use these principles to measure validity and truth.

This will take a very high level of discernment and commitment, especially among those who first succeed in establishing these new structures and processes for a positive future. They will be the ones who will initially have the responsibility to set the new operating patterns in place.

A New Type of Social Leadership

A social movement of the heart calls forth separate but related initiatives in all sectors of society including business, the independent sector, government, etc. Electoral strategies will be needed, as well as new social initiatives involving all people who want to make a difference in the world. These social initiatives must be independent of and not led by electoral initiatives.

- As more people question whether an environment of fear, disinformation and conflict is really the best thing, they naturally ask for truth. This in turn encourages people to listen more to each other and to exchange concerns and perspectives.

- America can serve as an extraordinary example of what a modern society can do when it chooses to begin awakening from the deep sleep of force of habit to a higher calling that serves to elevate everyone's awareness and actions and create a positive future for humanity.

- Even in the business world, there is an increased acceptance of socially responsible values, behavior, and spirituality in the workplace and in defining the company mission and ethos.

The greater the effect of grassroots initiatives, the greater the basis for new types of leaders to move into positions of effectiveness, the more new types of leaders succeed in their various positions, the greater the effect of the grassroots social initiatives. Thus, the rate of acceleration of this process can increase.

By any measure, there are a large number of people in America (and the world for that matter) who resonate with positive values for change. However, A New America does not see any single, cohesive group or individual – in any country – in a position to be leading positive change.

Most of those people involved in positive change and integral culture do not cooperate with one another enough nor share access to resources to bring everyone's work to a new stage. The social-environmental justice groups do cooperate, tactically at least, to oppose something or to promote legislation, but this is still ultimately an "us versus them" approach and rarely reaches people outside of the mailing lists of various organizations. While it is important to minimize further degradation of our environmental and social-political environment, the main issue remains: How do we gather and utilize the greatest amount of resources, not to oppose the old, but to create something new and wonderful.

There are people everywhere already in leadership or influential positions (whether they emerged from an old or a new paradigm), as well as large numbers of people who would rise to the occasion and come forward to be involved in positive change – if given the opportunity.

What is missing are the elements of a coordinated, coherent leadership and corresponding material and structural resources to help move the process to a new level.

This is where an initiative such as The Global Interchange can play a pivotal role by bringing together people and groups that are highly dispersed and relatively isolated and achieve greater coherence and focus. In turn, this will become more visible to more people and provide tangible examples of new approaches to life and society.

New structures and processes are most urgently needed to facilitate cooperation, coherency, and coordination. The very forms that served the

BASIC SYSTEM RELATIONSHIPS

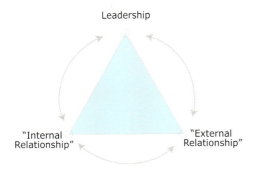

This simple model illustrates the balanced interrelatedness required to create, through cooperative and integrative approaches, a more positive future.

needs of emerging pioneers of new paradigm thought and action were suited to their individual needs and presently do not lend themselves to synergy in action. Those pioneers of a new paradigm presently lack structures and capacity at all levels to implement the very work they are so profoundly called to carry out. Their small, fluid organizations and informal networks that best served early stages of pioneering are not capable of supporting something of global scope and impact. Producing something consistently and at a level great enough for large numbers requires something of a different nature and scale than books, workshops, and lecture circuits.

The time is before us to have in place functional new structures and processes relative to public communications, Internet networking, political leadership circles, business leadership circles, as well as large-scale financial and related resources. Operating at a global level, this cannot be about any one personage, specific teaching, or path.

Rather, it must embrace the totality of what global social and spiritual awakening could mean, and help manifest it in social and material reality.

THREE TIMES THREE

The heart is humanity's most universal connection with each other, as well as with spirit.

The awakening of our heart to our own higher consciousness offers access to solutions and opportunities the everyday self may be unaware of.

The awakened heart-mind is capable of bridging suffering with awakening.

What is it that is wanting to be expressed (that is new and of the highest order of service to humanity's conscious evolution)?

How does it want to be expressed?

How does it want to best be received and connected with?

What is the work's intrinsic value as actual service?

How is this a bridge through which the expression of the new can invite and interface with others (individuals, organizations, countries, etc.?

Where is there synergy with other work (synergy among the parts and synergy with higher consciousness)?

CHAPTER 10
Politics of a Positive Future

"In our ways, spiritual consciousness is the highest form of politics.
We must live in harmony with the natural world and recognize that excessive
exploitation can only lead to our own destruction."

– Chief Leon Shenandoah

As our elections continue to demonstrate, large numbers of Americans do not find sufficient value in voting in the national elections. What if there was a more compelling reason to participate?

America has achieved much in numerous arenas of endeavor, yet as we continue to expand our wealth and influence, we've seemingly left behind the fundamental principles that engender health, well being, and the uplifting of all humankind. Change is in the air, though. Structures and paradigms that have brought us to our current juncture are now in need of a major overhaul. We need a new framework, one that ensures civil and human rights for everyone across the board, high levels of integrity within our governing institutions and from our leaders, and a re-languaging of our intents and strategies. Can our society shift its attention to setting a more positive example for ourselves and the world?

What is before us is how to create new conditions now – a positive future in the present – in which the multiple polarities and violence of social class, race, political, and religious differences can no longer thrive. To create these new conditions now, we must encourage ourselves to live our lives in ways that expand the potential of humanity in a larger spiritual context – by upholding the rewards of service, honoring the interconnectedness of life, and by acknowledging and embracing our unique differences.

Society's Need for a New Framework

How do we affect change in terms of how society behaves and conducts itself within its own borders and in the community of nations? How do we go about affecting a new national dialogue?

This chapter focuses on politics and voting in general: our current state of governance and the need to embrace the new perspectives and wisdom of what lies on our horizon. The potential is there for America to openly address and recognize our common spiritual values and ethics, and make "walking-the-talk" our first priority as individuals and as a country. We are not there yet.

Politics are about society, not power. Power is the corruption of social politics. While politics are a part of our society, they cannot be ignored, nor are politics something to fight against. They have become, though, an intrinsic and undeniably conspicuous presence in our daily lives.

In response to this, there are those most concerned about positive future values who are focused on influencing specific policies and regulations. The challenge here is that we have "tricked" ourselves into "playing" by rules that are essentially stacked against anything truly innovative or that may threaten various powerful and concealed interests.

We need to masterfully use only those existing institutional structures that can be used. More importantly though, we must introduce new "playing rules" that will truly guide our actions in favor of a positive future in the present.

Applied to the two main national parties, this translates to building a "progressive" political movement within either or both of those parties. However, given the enormous stakes involved, it is not likely that any serious challenge can succeed at a national level within either of the two principal parties. And as long as the basic voting rules remain as they are, it will be nearly impossible for anyone not sanctioned by the hidden power circles to win office or gain significant entré – especially to the levers of power in central government, particularly the Executive Branch.

Others who are more focused on developing alternative or third parties find it very difficult to assemble a credible and powerful alternative party to the two dominant ones. How can this be remedied? What is needed to make America a truly participatory democracy?

Currently, the national public voting rules work against such a possibility and succeed in directly reinforcing the two main parties. This has been the case for roughly one hundred years; the state and national voting rules were altered to favor only established powerful interests and to discourage various progressive or alternative third parties. Additionally, the way legislation and voting are controlled in the Legislative Branch makes it nearly impossible for truly positive legislation to be introduced by anyone outside the inner power circles.

While changing the national election rules is not likely to occur any time soon, it is an important goal, one that is feasible mainly at local levels and in a small number of states. Much depends on the level of grass root support for "positive future" candidates, organizations, and policies.

The key element that would facilitate bringing this about is a genuinely new kind of leadership and social movement representing a coherent set of positive future values and practical, innovative programs. This would pave the way for society to discover a new means of functioning and way of identifying itself.

People really do care about their personal well being and the many issues facing America, but they are not voting. It's not that they don't want to vote, it's just that they are not seeing meaningful and valuable choices in terms of national leadership. Neither do they feel that their vote influences political maneuverings. In contrast, industrial and commercial groups do have specific influence over government. To to a more limited extent, a very small number of well-funded non-governmental/non-commercial organizations have access to government processes, but very little genuine influence.

The majority of people who do vote in national elections do so partly out of a sense of duty as citizens and to minimize harm as they may see it – choosing "the lesser of two evils." However, at town, county and national district levels, there is often greater opportunity for local voter

"In our ways, spiritual consciousness is the highest form of politics. We must live in harmony with the natural world and recognize that excessive exploitation can only lead to our own destruction. We cannot trade the welfare of our future generations for profit…. We are instructed to carry love for one another, and to show great respect for all beings of the earth. …Our energy is the combined will of all people with the spirit of the natural world, to be of one body, one heart, and one mind."

– Chief Leon Shenandoah
Fire Keeper of the Central Fire for the
Haudenosaunee (Iroquois) Confederacy

"Our world is on the brink of a new social consciousness, one more acutely aware of our underlying commonality in beliefs, attitudes, values, and widely encompassing spirituality. Circumstances compel humanity to search for a more vibrant, ethical, and heartfelt foundation of supportive enterprise and community, one that emphasizes the interconnectedness of all."

"Imagine a worldwide community exchange of shared, positive values, information, and resources; a nexus of common vision and support; a meta-crossroads of compelling purpose and heart; a portal to practical innovation, remarkable ideas, and new visions in the making; a global, digital arena for staging constructive, social change and strategic partnerships; a source of new philanthropy and investments to ensure a more positive future."

participation in mounting a successful innovative campaign, especially in areas outside of major population and economic centers. Typically, though, with a larger population concentration, the greater the chances of there being hidden power groups controlling what is presented to the public, and thus less likelihood for new alternatives brought to public attention through institutional channels. Therefore, the greatest opportunities for alternative political parties lie in rural or semi-rural areas and neighborhoods and districts in cities.

Knowing all this, what will it take?

- We believe that a grassroots social-spiritual movement, one that is independent of political parties, is vital for waking people from their long sleep and to rejuvenating their lives.

- New political organization and new leadership is urgently needed. This, too, will need to be developed at a grassroots level.

- Where possible, alliances need to be formed with current office-holders and other leaders based upon principles of new paradigm values for a positive future.

- Organization and coordination will be needed to achieve breakthroughs that further benefit the growth of new thinking and new actions.

- New communication media needs to be developed that can reach larger numbers of people with coherent messaging and newsworthy information.

- New sources of funding for communications, leadership development, policy development, and public involvement will be vital.

In short, a major new framework for society and government will be needed that will at times parallel many of the old paradigm structures. These new structures will not be an end unto themselves, but be transitional in nature, helping to give birth to a new way of life. Accordingly, new electoral and procedural rules will need to be created to aid in the widest possible involvement of all people.

For this to begin in earnest, there will need to be courageous individuals ready to step forward to serve the greater good of all. This will require a level of cooperation and dedication to higher principles and action among pioneering people who are accustomed to being the center of attention.

In addition, civil, non-denominational spirituality is vital to all facets of society, and politics is no exception. Individuals want to know their connection to God or higher consciousness, their higher purpose and potential as beings. In the process of seeking and the finding, a naturally greater context enters into people's awareness that helps them to overcome the challenges and embrace the graces to be encountered in life. For an entire society to deny this, leads to great imbalances between individuals and society as a whole. This is like denying life to oneself and one's family. Imagine society proclaiming its goals in terms of connecting to one another through heart and love-centered consciousness, connecting to higher consciousness, and in living and acting in harmony with nature and one another.

Well over a thousand years ago, during a period of war and conflict, a spiritual teacher arrived and helped Native American tribes and nations to form the "Great Law of Peace" and constitution. This in turn influenced the creation of the United States and its founding documents. In our current circumstances, a new "council of councils" – of "elders" and "youngers" – is needed in America and worldwide for a new "Great Law of Peace" to help usher in a new era for all of humanity.

America has a vital role to play as a country in the world. Will the positive future visionaries demonstrate their potential to bring forth new leaders for a new era of compassion and healing that extends itself to all of humanity?

No one says any of this will be easy. And it will take concentrated work, but can we afford not to? It is a matter of our choosing.

Voting Values

As we stated earlier in this chapter, national voting rules would need to be changed in order for America to truly become a participatory democracy. That is not likely to happen in the short term as there are too many individuals and groups with a vested interest in keeping things as they are. Their ability to manipulate votes is extraordinary.

Manipulation of public votes takes place at three levels: the basic election rules, the ballot/polling district, and in the minds and hearts of voters. It is this last area that concerns us most. The "selling of the candidate" is more than clever advertising and market research. It is the very education and preparation of the public as a whole. This includes heavy emphasis on superficial labels such as "conservative," "liberal," "family values," "tough on…" and "soft on…," etc. With the level of central control over the bulk of mass media, these labels and sound bites have very little real meaning. What historical roots they may have has been mostly lost. They do have great value as convenient icons or handles with which to push or pull people with survey research and helping to close the feedback loop back to the campaign. (Obviously, this cannot totally compensate for a badly run campaign.)

While much thought and verbiage exists on liberalism versus conservatism, so called "family values," and all the other political slogans and catchwords, it is our contention that these are anachronisms used as pejoratives or banner slogans – either polarizing or attracting followers by skilled propagandists who know how to use the mass media. Their intent has nothing to do with higher aspirations and the greater good of our country and the world. These terms and code words are used to manipulate public feelings, and have become the sum and substance of the majority of national-level political campaigns over recent decades.

These terms (and the social-cultural values for which they are markers) are long overdue to be replaced by the values and beliefs that are integral to "unity within diversity," "discernment with compassion," and other positive future concepts that can touch people in meaningful ways to evoke our higher sensibilities and higher selves. This is in marked contrast to the fear-based emotional reactions common in political-media parlance.

Why do the two American parties appear so different at election time but not so different afterward?

"The National parties and their presidential candidates, with the Eastern Establishment assiduously fostering the process behind the scenes, moved closer together and nearly met in the center with almost identical candidates and platforms, although the process was concealed as much as possible, by the revival of obsolescent or meaningless war cries and slogans (often going back to the Civil War). … The argument that the two parties should represent opposed ideals and policies, one, perhaps, of the Right and the other of the Left, is a foolish idea acceptable only to the doctrinaire and academic thinkers. Instead, the two parties should be almost identical, so that the American people can "throw the rascals out" at any election without leading to any profound or extreme shifts in policy. … Either party in office becomes in time corrupt, tired, unenterprising, and vigorless. Then it should be possible to replace it, every four years if necessary, by the other party, which will be none of these things but will still pursue, with new vigor, approximately the same basic policies."

– from Carroll Quigley, Tragedy and Hope: *A History of the World in Our Time*

In developing genuinely new leadership that serves to bring forth a positive future – either elected or otherwise – there can be no room for superficial formulations (such as appealing to "faith," "traditional family" values, or "fighting" whatever alleged menace is appearing in the headlines) to garner votes and manipulate the public. Not only are these formulations crass, they are based on implicit or explicit fear-based agendas. And they are not relegated to one particular party or group. Americans are barraged with this political marketing blitz from all sides and angles. It is the nature of the beast as it has evolved.

Today, for example, the various "progressive" and "environmental" tendencies remain relatively isolated and polarized from the majority of the population mostly due to a basic lack of listening and willingness to seek common "language." Positive future values that bring environmental and social concerns into an integral way of life are too important to fall prey to endless "us versus them" thinking and policy debates. Yet that is how much of the progressive and environmental opposition expresses itself.

Quite clearly, anyone claiming to represent truly new solutions cannot clothe themselves in the language and gestures of the old paradigm. They will need to represent new paradigm values and beliefs.

It falls mainly on the shoulders of those people who are most inspired and compelled to act on behalf of a positive future – one in which conflict within humanity and between humanity and natural creation is no longer the case. If they can overcome their own self-righteousness and cooperate through common principles, then a common language of the heart can come into being. This can help people use their free-will to choose and act on behalf of their higher aspirations as spiritual beings and their own connection to higher consciousness. For some, it will be a focus on serving humanity out of love. For others, it will be a focus on planetary stewardship out of love.

This would mark the end to exploitation of people and the planet by small groups of hidden and powerful interests, and the emergence of an awakened society.

"There is no such thing, at this date of the world's history, in America, as an independent press. The business of the journalists is to destroy the truth, to lie outright, to pervert, to vilify, to fawn at the feet of mammon, and to sell his country and his race for his daily bread. We are the tools and vassals of rich men behind the scenes. We are the jumping jacks, they pull the strings and we dance. Our talents, our possibilities and our lives are all the property of other men. We are intellectual prostitutes."

– John Swinton, Chief of Staff New York Times at New York Press Club, 1953

THE THREE PRINCIPLES OF THE GREAT LAW OF PEACE

The Great Law brings together three interrelated concepts, that if properly implemented would assure peace among the member nations of the Confederacy. Together these principles make up the underlying beliefs that will unite humans.

RIGHTEOUSNESS – First is the Concept of Righteousness:

In order to keep violence from interfering in the stability of the community, the people, clans, Chiefs, Clan Mothers and the entire nation must treat each other fairly. Such conduct will assure that political and social justice is maintained. Each individual must have a strong sense of justice, must treat people as equals and must enjoy equal protection under the Great Law. People must be willing to enforce a civil government to oversee that righteousness is enjoyed by all; must shape their own personal conduct so as not to foster resentment or hatred; and must be willing to use the power of reasonable thinking to overcome problems and arrive at a mutually beneficial resolution.

HEALTH – The Second Concept is Health:

Health means that the soundness of mind, body, and spirit will create a strong individual. Health is also the peacefulness that results when a strong mind uses its rational power to promote well-being between peoples, between nations.

POWER – The Third is the Concept of Power:

The laws of the Great Law provide authority, tradition, and stability if properly respected in thought and action. Power comes from the united actions of the people operating under one law, with one mind, one heart, and one body. Such power can assure that justice and healthfulness continue. People and nations need to exercise just enough power to maintain the peace and well being of the members of the Confederacy.

– from the Haudenosaunee Home Page, the official source of news and information from the Haudenosaunee, comprised of the traditional leadership of the Seneca, Cayuga, Onondaga, Oneida, Mohawk, and Tuscarora Nations. (Haudenosaunee means People Building a Long House. That Long House is a way of life where the many native nations live in peace under one common law. We are the first United Nations in this land and operate under the oldest, continually-operating form of government, called the Grand Council of the Haudenosaunee.)

In the chapters contained in Part Four, statistical comparisons and projections are made between "traditional" political demographic concepts and those based on new paradigm and positive future values and beliefs. These comparisons directly lead to identifying the bridges needed to enliven society around new thought and action for a positive future. The insight from these early analytical comparisons will be of value to future research as well.

Discernment with compassion is a future-present concept that can be applied by those people who have a broadness of mind to reach those people who seem more contracted and conflicted in their intimate and larger worldview. It is then a matter of extending the hand of compassion and understanding. The result will be something so empowering that those who seek to gain by manipulating differences in society will find it difficult to maintain a foothold.

An Emerging New Political Force?

Following the controversies over the 2000 election, there have been renewed calls for a new political party, as well as campaign reform. The portion of voters registering for parties other than Democratic or Republican has continued to increase reaching 17% of the total registered in 2002. This suggests that a new party founded on "higher ground" principles, grounded in "positive future" values, and communicating corresponding platforms, could receive substantial support in the U.S.

A new political party, or amalgamations of compatible alternative parties, can succeed by embracing and communicating positive future values and corresponding strategies and platforms. Guided by clearly stated values and principles, a positive future party will facilitate flexibility and broadmindedness in working with people from all parties. At a national level, especially, this can provide visibility needed for public exposure to new "positive future" thoughts, values, and programs. It can aid corresponding local and state-level initiatives. And there always remains the possibility that some practical good can come of it at a national level as well. A key point in contemplating this is to have no illusions as to what it will take to alter national-level policies and actions. It is important to have visible, visionary, and spiritually aligned progressive leadership that can be respected by people of many different persuasions.

Value factors favoring a new political force in the U.S.:

- Spirituality that is non-religious, non-sectarian; the concept of an awakened or enlightened society
- Service to people in the U.S.
- Service to people globally
- Service to the planet
- Connection at personal, local community, state, regional, national, and global levels
- Truth, forgiveness, and reconciliation process
- Special to various generational-specific needs and concerns
- Ethical, truthful, and honest communications

"At some point, society must begin to recognize the emergence of a third, higher position that does not reside in the idea and action 'space' of the old paradigm."

Walter Cronkite on the Department of Peace:

"…wouldn't it be an advantage to have a peer of the secretaries of defense and state whose primary responsibility it was to develop the methods and means of peaceful conflict resolution and to offer peaceful alternatives in the councils of war?"

"…there is an urgency to its adoption. In this dangerous world, where the strength of the United States is needed to keep the peace, we need a visible manifestation of our intention to play that role, without the arrogance that cost us friends and allies among the nations and peoples of the world."

– Walter Cronkite August 2004
King Features Syndicate

Appearances can be deceiving:

In 1776, John Hancock, President of the Continental Congress, was noted for his elegant and aristocratic dress. Yet, it was he (along with other leaders such as Benjamin Franklin) who the Iroquois and other Native American leaders trusted. He was one of the founders of the United States who sought to learn from the native elders and supported their formal representation in Congress as a fourteenth state. In dramatic contrast were those people such as John Adams from Massachusetts who thought nothing but ill of the Native Americans and could barely tolerate alliances with them, even against the British. He, like other English colonists, looked forward to their elimination from proximity to white European society.

In addition, a parallel, politically independent, social movement can aid in shifting national priorities through its endorsement (or non-endorsement) of candidates and programs, regardless of party affiliations. As these strategies gain ground and succeed at various local or state levels, more open and representative elections could also be made possible.

Will an influential third alternative party "subtract" from votes that would go to the two dominant parties? As long as the election rules do not change, then yes, that is likely to be the case. However, more so than ever before, the key question remains: What substantive difference is there between the two main parties in terms of the worldview paradigm they each represent?

At some point society must begin to recognize the emergence of a third, and higher position that does not reside in the idea and action "space" of the old paradigm.

This must be acknowledged and made visible. Without it, powerful minority interests, such as those who deliberately want to precipitate a global conflagration in the name of their religious dogma, will continue to hold sway at all levels of society.

A New Type of Political Leadership

The main issue is how to encourage and facilitate the emergence of courageous and visionary leadership at the highest level of personal integrity. Leadership, elected or non-elected, is needed that will help our society "homestead a new promised land" based on the virtues of a new type of "emancipation proclamation" for an awakening humanity.

Nearly two-thirds (64%) of Americans "prefer that the politicians [they] vote for hold higher and more evolved moral and ethical values than [their] own. This sentiment is strong among those people who scored higher on both the PFCI and SMS scales. Of the 8 Types, WNL and SCT were especially keen on leaders with higher and more evolved values than their own and to a lesser extent was a significant portion of the ETV type. Overall, those who score high on the Spirituality Index prefer leaders with higher and more evolved values.

These new types of leaders *represent* and can *galvanize* our highest aspirations – principles of a whole system of interconnectedness, and the recognition and exploration of the unifying field of consciousness: "underneath it all, we are all connected as one."

From this perspective, it may be that forming a new political party is not the primary issue, but rather what is the most important and pressing matter is the development of a broad social movement with a new type of leadership based on new paradigm principles and higher consciousness – our future-present. In this context, a national campaign could succeed in both launching a new type of political party, as well as winning the hearts of and minds of America – yes, even a majority.

So what might this new leadership look like? We must develop leaders of a new type who will help usher in a positive future. Some of those who emerge may already be in positions of relative influence. Some may already hold elected office, lead commercial businesses, be educators or health professionals, or lead non-profit or non-governmental organizations. Others may be people who have tried to make a difference but found the structural limitations of our society an overwhelming challenge requiring greater resources than they were able to marshal. And others may be "ordinary" people stepping forward for the first time.

There are already elected officials from various states supporting "positive future" values and actions. One example is the initiative for a Cabinet-level Department of Peace that, as of 2004, has been supported by over 50 elected representatives. Of course making this a reality is another matter since it will need to be brought to a vote by elected representatives who currently operate under tightly controlled rules and behind the scenes agendas that generally preclude true innovation for a positive future.

What is most needed at this time are new structures and processes that are entirely dedicated to helping support what is new and vibrant of our positive future, in the present time.

Social Spheres of Leadership

Each of the areas listed require new leadership based not on the moribund parameters and ideologies of our current systems and processes, but on a much larger context of higher values and aspirations focused on the greater good of all humanity.

- Spiritual
- Community/civic
- Economic and financial
- Environmental
- Agricultural
- Industrial
- Social/cultural
- Religious
- Education
- News and Cultural Media
- Social/historical research
- International relations
- Political

PREFER POLITICIANS I VOTE FOR TO HOLD HIGHER AND MORE EVOLVED MORAL AND ETHICAL VALUES THAN MY OWN

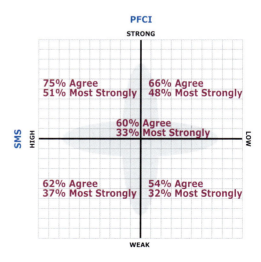

PFCI
STRONG

75% Agree
51% Most Strongly

66% Agree
48% Most Strongly

60% Agree
33% Most Strongly

SMS HIGH / LOW

62% Agree
37% Most Strongly

54% Agree
32% Most Strongly

WEAK

**Ten Key Value Concepts
of the Green Parties**

- Ecological Wisdom
- Social Justice
- Grassroots Democracy
- Nonviolence
- Decentralization
- Community-based Economics
- Equality and Honoring the Feminine
- Respect for Diversity
- Personal and Global Responsibility
- Future Focus/Sustainability

(Each country's Green Party has its own variations of these themes in addition to unique platforms.)

"The political terms 'liberal' and 'conservative' have their most immediate roots in British politics of the nineteenth and early twentieth centuries, as those were the two dominant parties."

Political Labels – What Is the Point?

What does "liberal" really mean? Virtually no one today is aware of its political-economic roots or its theoretical analysis. In common parlance, "liberal" is generally identified with having an interest in open-minded, new, and innovative ideas for society and personal conduct.

Over the past 20 years, "liberal" has also been identified with government spending for social benefit. The people who know the historical meaning are usually the political intelligentsia focused on social policy and political-economic strategy and for whom these designations can be manipulated to support their agendas. There is no operating definition of liberal that is recognized throughout society. Webster's dictionary also describes liberal in reference to freedom and being open and not restricted.

"Conservative" is another term whose political-economic roots are even more obscure. To most people, conservative in the context of elections usually means not wanting innovative change to take place and to encourage traditional policies that may have worked in an earlier era in the hopes of making "living in the past" a more successful experience today. Webster's dictionary also says conservative means strong resistance to innovation and strong support of business interests. A biologically-inspired definition reads "narrowly adapted to a particular environment." (It is ironic that "conservationists" are identified with preservation of the natural environment and "conservatives" tend to be identified with policies that are pro-business, pro-military, and anti-environmental.)

Lastly, we have what is termed a "moderate." Webster's dictionary describes this as not of any extreme, tending to the mean or average. Today, this may also mean "nowhere" since it is so vague as to be meaningless in terms of social or political change.

A "new" term being introduced into "third party" political circles is "progressive." Its roots are found in the populist labor movement in the decades around the year 1920. In the period following the 1950s, "progress" usually was of the economic or technological type, something that has increasingly lost its luster since the 1960s as more people began to become more environmentally and health conscious. Today, only 37% of U.S. households believe that technology ("progress") will solve our current environmental problems. Despite these connotations, its definition means to move forward as if on a journey, to advance.

Much of what remains today of the practical or theoretical application of the term "progressive" is a revision of the earlier farm and labor movement and the U.S. Progressive party, officially formed in 1924. The issues of the time had to do with social and economic rights for small farmers and factory workers, and opposition to the big corporations and militarism. This movement became intertwined with the issues of isolationism and neutrality by the U.S. from wars between the European powers and the fact that the U.S. Congress didn't want to appear "unpatriotic" by debating the issues or informing the public of the true dynamics at stake. This national drama unfolded against a backdrop of U.S.-based oil and financial interests trying to move in on older, established European-based interests – particularly with regard to control of global oil. Nearly a century later, many of these dynamics seem to be re-playing themselves – *with even higher stakes*.

Another new term is "green." Its roots come from both Europe and North America and stem from the various movements for positive change during the '60s, '70s, and '80s. Today, there are "Green" parties in many countries. While the Green Party is fairly new and relatively inexperienced in the U.S., there were over 400 candidates running for elected office in the 2004 elections and more than 200 holding elected office, mostly at local levels.

Although a few organizations have statements of principles that come close to a transition to a new paradigm, the alternative "progressive" parties have been unable to make the bridge from their own forms of "righteousness" to a civil spirituality and key principles that can truly embrace large numbers of people. Much if of this is due to the backgrounds of leading members and of the linkage between religion and spirituality.

A movement on the transformational values of Connection, Service, and Spirituality can bridge diverse communities who may identify more with a positive future than anything else. Analysis of the *IOOW-2000* research data, specifically in regard to voting, further supports this and is discussed more in Chapter 11.

A recent political inquisition:

Later on during the 1950s and into the early 1960s a new type of inquisition was started within the government, and supported by reactionary news media. The target was anyone in America who was sympathetic to any left-leaning philosophy or any progressive cause that in any way challenged the American post-WWII dominator mentality of "might is right" and the "American century." Anyone who didn't unquestioningly support the dangerous military buildup by the U.S. against Russia was branded a heretic and publicly vilified, their means of earning a living deliberately destroyed.

Now, in the new millennium, we have secret laws and regulations that are so secret, that until someone is charged with them, it is illegal to reveal their content. In addition, under various "Patriot Acts," basic constitutional rights – such as legal representation and right to not be imprisoned without being charged – and centralization of military and police powers have in effect created a national security state of unprecedented power and control.

Longest living participatory democracy

It was from such difficult times that The Great Law of Peace emerged and helped establish the longest living participatory democracy in the world. [Editor]

"Native societies became a counterpoint to the European order, in the view of the transplanted Europeans, including some of the United State's most influential founders, as they became more dissatisfied with the status quo. They found in existing native polities, the values that the seminal European documents of the time celebrated in theoretical abstraction – life, liberty, happiness, and a model of government by consensus, under natural rights, with relative equality of property.

The two narratives, *Oresteia* and the *Kaianeraserakowa (The Great Law of Peace),* represent two distinct cultures, and they illustrate how each society goes from unbridled passions to control and order through the creation of law.

The Oresteia is a trilogy of Greek dramas. In the first two narratives, "Agamemnon" and "The Liberation Bearers," there is war, murder, vengeance, guilt, and jealousy that perpetuate a vicious cycle of violence and lawlessness. *The Great Law of Peace* narrative begins in a similar way, for there is much unrest and violence before the Peacemaker unifies the people under the Great Law of Peace.

The Peacemaker, who was sent by the Creator, carries with him a message from the Creator. The Peacemaker came to the people carrying the message of the Great Law of Peace during a time when the people were warring amongst themselves. The people, like those in the Oresteia seek revenge and were filled with hate, greed, revenge, and jealousy."

(Continued to next page)

Whatever your position of leadership or influence, basic to all of this is what we intend for ourselves, our children, and our planet. A new mode of language is needed to assist such a shift.

The Language of Intent

From the classical Greek of Euripides' mythic dramas to the spare resonances of Japanese Haiku to the highly punctuated rhyming verse of today's rap music, language has always been a means by which humanity can express the thoughts, feelings, and aspirations of its existence. Language is also used to persuade, cajole, manipulate, incite, defend, imbue, deride, assuage, misinform, delineate, sanctify, rationalize, inspire, and elucidate. At its most basic, it is simply a tool with which to communicate and organize the mundane exigencies of life. At it's its most profound, it reaches into the hearts of mankind to lift us toward higher realms of consciousness, authentic being, and our collective humanity.

Language has the power to evoke ecstatic visions or boil one's blood, polarize us into static morbidity or reveal expansive new possibilities, incite us to righteous destructiveness or create inclusive cooperatives of service and common purpose. Its multi-faceted shadings and nuances allow us to express the gross and profane, and likewise, the subtle and sublime. Language involves both reflection, as well as formation of new thought patterns – so much like "genetic codes" of thought they are also called "memes." From earliest spiritual teachings comes the expression: "in the beginning, there was the Word." Words can carry powerful energy. They can heal and they can damage, they can bring together and they can tear apart.

As eras and millennia recede into history, language is a constant, changing and evolving as mankind extends it reach over the planet and peers into the inky night of the cosmos. Words that in one generation meant one thing can now mean something quite different, its connotations switching from positive to negative and vice versa. Yet, the intent of language remains the same: to make that which is within us understood by at least one other person. Whether we are using verbal or written language, sign language or body language, music or visual art – each of us is on some level striving to let the external world in on our private, interior universe.

Our intention works hand-in-hand with the use of language. As stated earlier, language can move people to act or respond in innumerable ways, both positively and negatively. Even a single word can evoke powerful emotional responses depending on one's background and life experience. For instance, the word spirituality.

- For some people, the words "spirituality" and "religion" are synonymous. Religion encapsulates the theology and formal organization of a specific following. Spirituality would pertain to the focusing on of principles, and emulating the traits and characteristics of specific deities or personages. Neither exists without the other and are therefore one and the same.

- For others, the word "spirituality" is still synonymous with "religion" but produces an opposing response of repugnance, a desire to withdraw from those using either word for fear of being proselytized or made to feel excluded because they themselves don't subscribe to a specific organized system of religious belief. They are considered one and the same and to be avoided.

- There are others who perceive a distinction between "religion" and "spirituality." For them, being spiritual has nothing to do with the institutions of religion. Their understanding of spirituality can bring an immediate change to a person's interior rhythms, creating a gentling attitude and a sense of expansiveness, one's heart opens, and levels of consciousness can be contemplated and explored.

- And still for others, "spirituality" is considered too unconventional, amorphous, and downright absurd. "Religion," on the other hand, is found to be too narrow, limited, and rigidly dogmatic. Both are to be avoided or handled with kid gloves as each can carry a negative stigma, and aligning with either can bring about rejection or compartmentalization from either camp.

The "art of language" has been pronounced on its dying legs by every generation as it views its evolution with succeeding generations. Older forms of grammar and syntax fall away as new uses and purposes are brought to bear. Words are invented to encapsulate new concepts and nuances, yet the intent remains pretty much on target: understanding.

"...these warring people had great energies and powers that when controlled under the Great Law of Peace would set a stronger foundation for the law to take root.

...We have tied ourselves together in one head, body, one spirit and one soul to settle all matters as one. We shall work, counsel and confirm together for the future of coming generations."

Basic concepts found within *The Great Law of Peace* possess multiple layered meanings. For example, Peace to the non-*Haudenosaunee* might mean absence of war, or an inner tranquillity and power may mean something acquired that sets one above another. However, when the Peacemaker spoke of the concepts of Peace and Power, he meant that when man understands that his life is delicately woven into the Great Web of Life, this strength and unity creates a spiritual peace and power. Peace also means law and Power also refers to energies that are generated when the chiefs, clan mothers, faith keepers, the people, and the natural world unite in harmony.

Health refers to the balance and harmony that is created when man realizes that he is just one strand in the delicate Web of Life. The Haudenosaunee believe that human beings are not the most important things on earth. Instead, they are just mere caretakers whose duty it is to protect Mother Earth and all her inhabitants for the generations yet born.

Righteousness is a hard concept to put into English, for it represents being of the good mind and of having respect, love, generosity, and compassion for all the natural world. Righteousness also represents the political and spiritual authority and duty of the chiefs, clan mothers, faith keepers, and other societies that comprise the infrastructure of the Great Law of Peace. It is these philosophical concepts that the Peacemaker brought to the warring people."

– Kanatiyosh, a legal scholar who is Onondaga/ Mohawk from Akwesasne (land of the drumming partridge) also known as St. Regis Mohawk Indian Reservation located in New York and Canada

"Righteousness is a hard concept to put into English, for it represents being of the good mind and of having respect, love, generosity, and compassion for all the natural world. Righteousness also represents the political and spiritual authority and duty of the chiefs, clan mothers, faith keepers, and other societies that comprise the infrastructure of the Great Law of Peace. It is these philosophical concepts that the Peacemaker brought to the warring people."

– Kanatiyosh, legal scholar for the Onondaga/Mohawk from Akwesasne (land of the drumming partridge) also known as St. Regis Mohawk Indian Reservation located in New York and Canada.

From the *IOOW-2000* research findings, it is abundantly clear that language is one construct requiring close attention. Not in the sense of correcting one's grammar and spelling, but more in the sense of reframing purpose and outcome. Is what we're conveying about bringing together or exclusivity, about private agendas or the highest good of all, about maintaining old systems of conflict and divisive polarization or cooperation and an encompassing inclusiveness?

As we've seen with the word "spirituality," a new language is required, one that brings together and celebrates our extraordinary diversity through commonalities and unity of purpose toward a more positive future. As we explore new structures, processes and constructs, we need a new language to support this progression.

- The dominant parties' national rhetoric is heavily laced with words and expression that are all about power, domination, success, control, and strength (us versus them).

- The alternative progressive/green organizations reference interconnectedness of life and the environment, as well as conflict in the context of social and economic justice (us versus them).

Are they not two sides of the same coin enabling and espousing the same values, rules, and verbiage of the old paradigm? The most significant understanding is that the language of a new political movement is not about disingenuous platitudes and rhetoric. It's not about propaganda and manipulation. It is not the institutionalized or legislated truth of one group over another.

Instead, it is a language allowing each person their own truth so that they may experience a life journey of authenticity and breathtaking richness. It is a language of honesty and clarity – the power of being present, of speaking a language with which one can "walk their talk," and discovering and taking part in the brilliant and inspired intersecting connections of all humanity.

Helen Keller reflecting in her book, The Story of My Life, recounted the discovery of a new language that opened her to a whole new universe for not only herself, but for untold millions around the world. "The mystery of language was revealed to me. I knew then that 'w-a-t-e-r' meant the wonderful cool something that was flowing over my hand. That living word awakened my soul, gave it light, joy, set it free!"

The intersection of language – and that which can be brought forth in creative innovation beyond the boundaries of our current systems – is to truly experience freedom. It can find voice in new conversations, new choices, new strategies, and new leadership. It is a fundamental building block of Connection, Service, and Spirituality as we seek to integrate the greater whole and awaken to a more positive future. Let us welcome in our own "New Mind" as individuals and as societies.

"The Peacemaker told him: The words we bring constitute the New Mind, which is the will of Tarachiawagon, the Holder of the Heavens [Creator]. There shall be Righteousness when men desire justice, Health when men obey reason, Power when men accept the Great Law."

– Kanatiyosh, legal scholar for the Onondaga/ Mohawk from Akwesasne (land of the drumming partridge) also known as St. Regis Mohawk Indian Reservation located in New York and Canada.

CHAPTER 11

Integrating the Greater Whole: A New Paradigm

"A new current is flowing, one that emanates from our future-self. It carries the waves upon which we can shift to a higher and more evolved state of being."

ow to bring enough people into a higher awareness and active participation in a greater whole? How to reach the majority of people who have goodness in their hearts and are open to hearing of genuinely new possibilities? What if it were possible to connect 84% of Americans into a more unified and positive field of consciousness and action?

At present, there is no coordinated or coherent transformational movement for a positive future. There are many large and small groups focused on various material issues: health, civil rights, race, women's rights, environment, war, peace, population, hunger, etc. Others are focused on religious dogma, survivalism, militarism, and the usual panoply of commercial interests, etc. Those who do share and cooperate are mainly found in commerce and business, the defense industry, religious fundamentalism, and, of course, the two dominant political parties in the U.S.

Yet, an opposing intention for a positive future is blossoming and energizing around principles of a non-sectarian spirituality, connection with all life, and service to humanity and the planet. Are these the principles that will create the wave upon which humanity will ascend to higher and more evolved states of consciousness and being?

Within the beautiful spectrum of leading positive future visionaries, there is little to no coordination and resource sharing among those who most present ideals of caring for the environment, caring for all people, and creating a new future in which exploitation, conflict, and domination are the exception, not the rule. Much of this is due to their relative newness, lack of collective maturity, and the enormity of the task. Regardless of the contributing factors, *the time is now* for new and old leaders and visionaries to rapidly *"come of age"* and show the world what could be possible.

What if the spiritual principles of fundamental interconnectedness and compassion are applied? Suddenly there is no one ultimately to blame.

What if humanity, regardless of social class, could see itself as a young species growing up, possibly with the potential to give birth to something extraordinary, wonderful, and expansive?

Suddenly, forgiveness and reconciliation could become more possible than ever before, and individuals who were formerly in conflict would be able to find ways to work for the common good of all, instead of their own respective agendas. Much depends on whether enough people choose a bright new future for themselves and future generations, or allow the world to continue along an increasingly dangerous course.

As we look at ways to draw people's attention to bring a new world into being, the *IOOW-2000* research once again provides a grounding reference for us.

Chapter 11 At A Glance

Integrating the Greater Whole: A New Paradigm

- Universal Bridges: Connection, Service, and Spirituality
- Connection
- Service
- Spirituality
- A Higher Common Denominator
- Natural Linkages
- A New Dynamic with a Higher Common Denominator
- Integrating the Greater Whole

"Nothing in the universe can resist the converging ardor of a great enough number of united and organized intelligences."

– Pierre Teilhard de Chardin

Universal Bridges: Connection, Service, and Spirituality

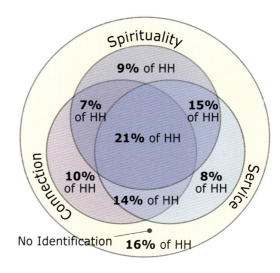

Having presented The 8 American Types, the Positive Future - Cooperative Integrative types in conjunction with Social Material Stress and with Social Traditional - Religious Conservative factors, this is a good opportunity to take a step back and look at ways to consolidate these insights by simplifying everything down to three commonsense, yet fundamental, factors.

The *IOOW-2000* research found three common elements representing nearly universal bridges that could address the vast majority of Americans. Each of these can also be seen in combination, and taken together, represent a set of core aspirations embracing 84 % of American households:

- Connection Index – represents a range of values and beliefs from the personal connection to one another, connection with creation and nature, and a sense of sacred connection.

- Service Index – represents a range of values and beliefs from helping one another, making a difference in the world, and nations helping nations.

- Spirituality Index – represents a range of values and beliefs from traditional and alternative churches, sense of the sacred in all life, and connection to higher consciousness or God.

Connection

Applied to the PFCI-SMS typology, as well as The 8 American Types, "connection" (or lack thereof) is one of the most basic: connection to self, connection to human community, and connection to the sacredness of life. With a sense of connectedness, people can reach out to aid others and the planet – hence, "connection" with service to others. For those people lacking in connection, offering new types of connection can provide an important avenue for healing. Non-whites more than whites tended to score lower on the connection index and women tended to place in the top quartile.

Eighty-five percent of Americans agree that, "the bottom line is that we are all just looking to be loved and accepted as human beings."

Since the 1960s, "connection" and "alienation" have become mainstream concepts. Though the previous world wars had been a decidedly cooperative effort that expanded the envelope of many people on countless levels, the idea of connection to self and others on a more intrinsic basis, not just one of survival, made its way into the public consciousness. The Aquarian Age focus of the '60s and '70s shook many people out of their comfortable mental and emotional constructs and asked the questions: "Who are we to each other?" and "What is the purpose of our being?" Connection opens the door to one's own relationship with self, with others, nature, the cosmos, higher consciousness, and with God.

In the ensuing decades, the questions haven't changed. Young people today continue to search for answers through their own expressions, while alternately heightening generational angst and disengaging from old paradigms or joining the fast track to pop culture vacuity and intellectual oblivion. Either path brings about disconnection from self, others, and the greater community. As the following shows, each generation has dealt with life, death and disconnection issues, always coming back to one of our basic needs: Connection to self and to society as a whole.

- 1960s: Questioning of authority, the Vietnam War, the draft, justice and equality among all people, purpose in life, spirituality, and community.

- 1970s: The prospect of complete world annihilation through the threat of nuclear war as the world's two super powers faced off. Global environmental concerns, including food and hunger.

- 1980s: Renewed threat of nuclear war. Death in the form of a virus transmitted via one of our most basics acts of humanness: sex.

- 1990s: aimless and generic anger acted out through aggressive acts from gang violence to overt sexuality to new drugs of escapism to hyper-stimulation via our media and modes of recreation.

- 2000s: Greed and corruption rampant throughout society. Heightened threat of world war, decline of democracy, and weapons of mass destruction being wielded by many military-political powers in the world. Violent global power struggles often masquerading as religious strife. Millennial prophecies receive greater attention by more people.

Four years into the new millennium, we are *still* seeking the ways and means to overcome and resolve these same issues, as the ability to develop weapons of mass destruction becomes ever more prevalent globally, and "legal" and "illegal" acts of terrorism escalate throughout the world.

These factors all impinge on an individual's ability to stay centered in themselves, in their relationships with others, and ultimately with the world. In the midst of these extreme pressures, spirituality offers more than a refuge of peace for people, it also provides a source of meaning and comprehension and context within a greater whole that is beyond humankind's difficulties.

Without a functional connection within self and with others, many people resort to cynicism, withdrawal from society to religious sects, drugs or material distractions, as well as acting out one's anger and hate. Profound alienation leads to an accelerating downward spiral for individuals, as well as society.

Those people who maintain a healthy sense of self and connection can play an important role in reaching people who are most in need of healing through connection. From healthy "connection" can emerge new possibilities in life, including service to others or the planet; spiritual connection to higher consciousness, nature, and God; and creative personal and social expression for a positive future.

Without "connection" – to society or self – there is less impetus to be involved, to be of "service," or to even vote.

Service

"Service" represents another layer to connection of self with society. *A New America* shows where there are segments of our population who may not be inclined to vote but who do, nonetheless, donate money and time as they can. Donating and volunteering are two of the basic indicators of serving others for a greater good. Service for the highest good of all and the enlightenment of humanity is yet another layer beyond these. More non-whites than whites placed higher on the service index. Men and women placed nearly equally on this measurement. The "service" factor on its own has no strong relationship with likelihood to vote.

Too many people feel overwhelmed by all that they discern is wrong about the world and discouraged about how ineffective current efforts seem to be in correcting these ills. It is challenging to address world hunger and disease when constant warfare produces new refugees and western industry destroys the land and agriculture. Offering new ways for individuals, communities, and nations to be of service to one another will revolutionize how all society functions.

Ninety-one percent of Americans "would like to be involved more personally in creating a better world at whatever local or global level" they can be.

"Service" is a word with a vaguely enigmatic sense to it. It is, again, one of those words in our language requiring somewhat of a reframing as to its intention. Historically, service has been the province of religious groups, a spiritual philosophy and principle concerning action and benevolence. Since the advent of the industrial revolution, though, "service" organizations have sprung up in every arena of contemporary society expanding its intent with a more generic usage. As the U.S. government withdrew from supporting social benefit programs, it became more the province of the philanthropic and charitable sector. Their focus has been on providing aid and sponsorship to individuals and groups seeking financial support, legal redress, or even expiation to those requiring a helping hand out of poverty, emotional succor, or community representation.

This particular form of service has even stretched around the globe through programs such as the Peace Corps, Amnesty International, the International Red Cross, The Floating Hospital, Habitat for Humanity, and countless other organizations addressing every frailty and foible of humankind.

A reframing of "service" would include the idea of not only helping individuals and groups in need, but the maintaining of cultural uniqueness and diversity without the need of imposing one's own cultural and societal conventions, processes, and structures.

It is also not just about the individual or group we're focusing on, but about seeing that the good we do in service to others forever uplifts all of humanity. It is the expansive perspective that includes all of us as a team working toward a future wherein all benefit positively. It is knowing that we are taking care of each other, that all our endeavors support the astonishing matrix of humanity striving for greater consciousness so that none shall know the despair of disenfranchisement.

Being of service – whether it be one-on-one or as an entire organization, community, or nation – also provides a model for others who can then see the rewards of establishing ever-deeper levels of connection and compassion. Each of us has the capacity to experience the greater rapport and relationship of connection when giving of ourselves through being of service. Combined with spirituality, they create a triumvirate of solidarity, resilience, and spaciousness.

Spirituality

"Spirituality" is about connecting with God and higher consciousness. It recognizes the presence of consciousness and spirit in all forms of creation and, as such, gives us the capacity for a wholistic world-view that takes into account more than our physical and social environment.

Spirituality also leads to "awakening" to higher awareness and higher potential. It embraces the elements of connection and service, a very large context that helps us nurture our diverse connections with one another and to be of higher service to one another and our planet.

Spirituality holds the promise of a new way of being and connection. Offering a new type of social expression that embraces all forms of religious and spiritual beliefs can help heal religious conflict and provide a larger context in which differences can be worked out peacefully. To those people who suspect that we are, after all, spiritual beings having a human experience, it is possible to see more of the greater context in which the human drama unfolds. This perspective also makes it possible for forgiveness and reconciliation among people. In a measurement index of non-religious spirituality values, the *IOOW-2000* research showed no discernable difference between whites and non-whites, but it did show a marked difference between women and men, with women placing higher on this index.

Spirituality has no strong relationship to voting on its own. However, spirituality is of such paramount importance – at all imaginable levels – that it is crucial to the success of any type of progressive, positive future-oriented initiative.

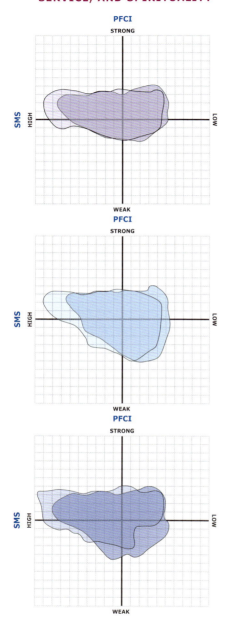

These three graphs show how connection, service, and spirituality are truly basic bridges across diverse aspects of our society. Lighter shaded areas indicate extension to weak voters.

– *IOOW-2000* Research

We would like to make the case that, based on our experienced opinions and research, there is a social basis for embracing a new civil spirituality that can include and engage people of traditional and non-traditional beliefs – a basis that does not need to argue the merits of one religious doctrine over another. We all live in a grand context of a vast web of interconnection of all life and creation.

A Higher Common Denominator

Taken together, *Connection, Service,* and *Spirituality* provide a strong basis for engaging the vast majority of Americans around a higher common denominator than we have ever had, one transcending individual belief systems, dogma, and doctrines. We are already "primed" to engage in a national dialogue and embrace innovative societal structures founded on tolerance, compassion, a universal connectedness, and a belief in working toward the greater good.

Large numbers of people, though, are influenced by many levels of "disconnection" – from self, others, community, nation, humanity, nature, or spirituality. Lack of connection to self or others contributes very strongly to "negative social ballast," which pulls everyone to a lower *common denominator.* Without meaningful connection at one or more of these levels, it is hard to have a motivated and active population creating a positive future. Community-based initiatives can provide "connection" and community for people for whom this is an important ingredient. In turn, this can reduce feelings of social disenfranchisement and provide avenues through which people can connect to others outside of their type.

The three fundamental factors of Connection, Service, and Spirituality can serve as bridges for those people who may still be struggling with the stresses of daily life. This also leads to a more universal *higher common denominator* – the emergence of an awakened and enlightened society.

Our evolution into a new way of being emphasizes our higher potential and it encourages our growing more spiritually aware and evolved as individuals and as a species. It follows then, that our social and political institutions must be very different than they are now. New social, cultural and institutional constructs will need to be based on an entirely different set of assumptions and intentions than those upon which our current ones are based.

Natural Linkages

To further demonstrate potential strategies based upon interconnecting values and beliefs in our diverse society, we've created a simple "recipe" using the elements of Connection, Service, and Spirituality and applied this formulaic approach to The 8 American Types. As this chapter points out, these three concepts are innate within each of us. They are not dependent on social conventions, religious ideology, or moral imperatives. They are core facets of our human makeup, no matter how modestly hidden or overtly expressed. As we continue to see, no one type stands alone and the possibilities for forward movement toward a more positive future are striking.

The first thing you may have noticed is that the SCT, CSE, and to a lesser extent, WNL types appear to share much in common making them the most natural intermediaries to bridge all the other types in helping move Americans toward greater interconnectedness and higher potential. These are also three of the types that share a strong positive identification with the PFCI scale that measures wholistic and spiritual factors.

These types represent social anchors that can bridge to PA and CC types based on shared spirituality, and in so doing, could offer a context in which the PA and CC types could gain a greater sense of connection to self, society, and creation. Likewise, the SCT and CSE types have a basic common denominator with ETV and CMW types based on their sense of connection. In an appropriate context, connection can be expanded to recognition of a greater interconnectedness.

As you read through this section, notice how these linkages could become additive and eventually embrace large numbers of people – potentially a substantial majority. As we have shown earlier, the three-ring Connection-Service-Spirituality model embraces 84 % of the population.

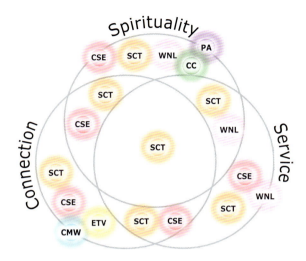

Connection, Service, and Spirituality and the 8 Types

- SCT (strongly bridges all three factors)
- SCT + CSE + WNL (Service is strong commonality)
- SCT + CSE + ETV (Connection is strong commonality, + CMW moderately strong)
- SCT + WNL (Spirituality is strong commonality, + PA + CC + CSE also moderately strong on this)
- SCT + CSE (Strongly share combination of Spirituality with Connection)
- SCT + WNL (Strongly share combination of Spirituality with Service)
- SCT + CSE (strongly share combination of Service with Connection, + WNL moderately strong)

THE 8 TYPES RELATIVE TO PFCI, SMS, STRC QUADRANTS

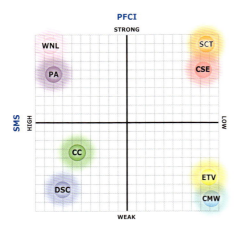

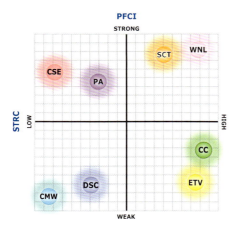

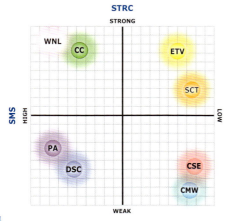

In the sequence of three graphics to the right, on the next page, we can see the 8 Types and their relationship between Spirituality combined with Service; Spirituality combined with Connection; and Connection combined with Service. Those in the upper right have the strongest relationship with these pairs of factors.

The only way in which to initiate and maintain a movement of more enlightened consciousness in society is through the acknowledgement and support of the values and beliefs that can bring us together. Connection, Service, and Spirituality are universal social principles that appeal to the core of our being. Is it any wonder that when envisioning the center of our being, we use the words "at heart" to express our deepest longings? The potential is there, we just need to chose and do so without fear.

The next section shows where these connections can become dynamic and new movement in our society can be found.

A New Dynamic with a Higher Common Denominator

The PFCI scale reflects beliefs and values embracing optimism and a nascent spirituality – what is most needed at this time for humanity to move into an era based on a new paradigm. The SMS scale reflects more the effects of society and material life. Together, these two measurements have a dynamic tension. As we look through a lens that further magnifies and differentiates, we can see that there are generational and other factors that can be used to further identify new social strategies.

To gain some insight into some general ways of connecting various types in our society, let's first look again at the PFCI-SMS model with the 8 Types overlaid and aligned with the CSS factors.

To the right we have repeated the three combinations of PFCI-SMS-STRC models with The 8 Types identified in each quadrant. Applying insights from the CSS models and other analysis, we can see that:

- The WNL, PA, CSE, and SCT types share a powerful commonality with one another as being highest on the PFCI scale. The values of the PFCI scale can also help overcome the pressures and stressors

(SMS) of modern life and thus offer one way to engage the WNL and PA types with the SCT and CSE types.

- The WNL and SCT groups are also strongest on the spirituality index, followed by the PA and CC types.

- Global awakening is one of the concepts included in the Spirituality index and is a point of future optimism especially shared between WNL and SCT types, as well as with the PA and SCE types to a somewhat lesser extent. In addition, global awakening is also a source of inspiration in the present for the WNL and SCT types, as well with the PA and CC types to a somewhat lesser extent.

- The SCT, CSE, and WNL types are also strong on service and with the Spirituality component can provide an avenue of commonality through which to engage the PA and CC types. Spirituality and Service may also provide an important context in which to enliven or heal these groups' sense of connection to self and society. This may also be a way to bridge the generational difference between SCT, WNL, and PA types.

- The SCT, CMW, ETV, and CSE types are strong on Connection, thus providing another avenue for engagement. Expanding connection from a simple social level to a larger level of interconnectedness can be a way to engage with these types. The SCT and ETV share some commonalities with regard to their age, as well as traditional social values. The CSE and CMW share commonalities in terms of less traditional social and political orientation.

Overall, we can see how the connection and service factors can be joined to the spirituality bridge. There are those in the CC type who are positive on the spirituality index and the PFCI scale, thus providing one more bridge to reaching a portion of CC types. Since the CSE and SCT groups express relatively low social material stress, they have a high potential to move forward.

These generalized vectors can also produce a "tailwind" effect that can bring along those people who are more influenced by factors of "disconnection," such as the CC and DSC types.

As the two graphics on the next page show, The 8 American Types are not simply found in one small circle, they are actually found spread

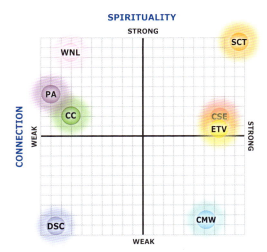

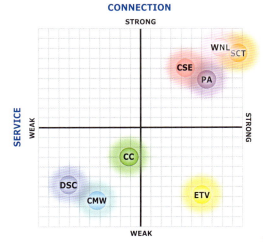

THE 8 TYPES: BRIDGES OF CONNECTION TO A POSITIVE FUTURE

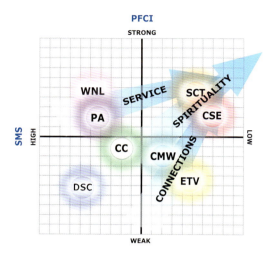

across portions of our PFCI-SMS map, representing American society. The circles merely indicate where the relative "center of gravity" is for each type.

This graphically shows that within a group such as ETV that is generally socially and politically traditional or conservative, there are elements that are more identified with spirituality that is not tied to religious doctrine, who don't all vote for Republican conservative candidates, and who do share values in common with those more concentrated in the upper right PFCI-SMS quadrant. In a similar vein, not all CC types are low on the PFCI scale, thus a portion of those who are most open to PFCI values and perspectives can in turn act as bridges within their own group, as well as DSC people who share a similar sense of values.

The point here is to show ways of reaching and bridging to people with new hope for a positive future and a higher common denominator than what society currently has before it. Strategic social and political initiatives embodying key messages and actions for a positive future are core essentials to our survival and conscious evolution as a species. Positive actions joined and supported with our highest intentions and prayers for healing and our highest realization, can lead to a brighter future for all humanity.

Integrating the Greater Whole

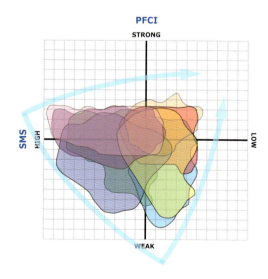

Globally or within our own country, a basic lack of integration of spirituality and social counterparts of ethical values and conduct provides a basis for old paradigm themes that substitute a false sense of control and power over our entire environment and obscures our vision of what is possible.

In dramatic contrast, awareness of our fundamental interconnectedness and natural compassion encourages only the best to emerge from all levels, from the individual to all humanity. It is this over – arching basis for a greater unity-of-the-whole that represents a way forward into a more enlightened and awakened state of being. It is this basic approach and its simple operating principles that can provide long – lasting solutions at personal and collective levels. It facilitates solutions allowing everyone to think and act in ways they may have only imagined being possible.

Humankind has had its moments of peace (such as when a major war ended or people saw the Earth from space for the first time) when a profound sense of connection, gratitude, awe, and the beauty of creation was felt by so many. We cannot afford *not* to choose a new way. As a species, we have stubbornly tried to "do it our way," as separate from a greater whole. We are a young species and have much to learn.

As a species, humanity is still very young and has much to learn. Our higher nature calls to us, inviting us home. As the graphics on this page illustrate, we are an amalgam of diverse interests, beliefs, yearnings, and hopes. Collectively, we have unattained potentials that are inviting us to explore, to reach beyond our fears. We need but make a choice to open our hearts and minds to acknowledge and create a forward movement toward a more positive future. As a whole, our innate capacity to embrace deeper levels of connection, to encourage a more inclusive and compassionate sense of service, and our instinctive desire to understand ourselves as spiritual beings can ultimately move us into the realms of our higher destiny. At last, we can envision an awakened future on our horizon.

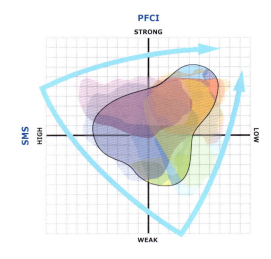

In The Future of Man, de Chardin referred to "...the moment of affective attraction." He was discussing the likelihood that one day we would all together move into a closer union, where our human nature would change for the better, and there would result a "human totalisation." This totalisation would take place within a field of affective attraction sufficiently intense to influence the human mass as a whole and at the same time.

– Pierre Teilhard de Chardin

The "Turquoise Meme" – Insights from Spiral Dynamics

In Spiral Dynamics: Mastering Values, Leadership, and Change, Don Beck and Christopher Cowan describe the development of a newly emergent meme (gene-like structures based on thought and that influence society and individuals) that is coded "Turquoise values" meme. They characterize it as being delicately balanced with interlocking forces, and seeking ways to re-order chaos. [Need an explanation of what "spiral dynamics" means.]

This meme has a global and wholisitc view:

- Blending and harmonizing a strong collective of individuals

- Focus on good of all living entities as integrated systems

- Expanded use of human brain/mind tools and competencies

- Self is part of a larger conscious, a spiritual whole that also serves self

- Routine global (and whole-Spiral) networking

- Acts for minimalist living, so that less is actually more

- Everything flows with everything else in living systems

- Embraces a global communitarian sense without attacking individuals' rights to be

- Discovers a new version of spirituality

- Macro-view perspective translates into action on behalf of the whole spiral and all its parts

This emerging meme-type integrates some of the most evolutionary aspects and capacities of humanity.

This meme has the potential to succeed in using whatever structures and process that it finds usable. Certain qualities of the Turquoise meme can be useful in avoiding unnecessary conflict with old systems and focusing on development of the new ones that will serve our future evolution.

It is also transitional in form – not a stage to strive for – but rather needs to recognize itself as a transitional stage that is vitally needed by humanity at this time. If those people who most identify with this stage see it as an end unto itself, a life to achieve and rest in, then it is likely to fail in helping humanity. If those people who most identify with the Turquoise value meme can recognize the pivotal role they can play – that this meme can play – then there is a better chance of succeeding at laying a solid basis for a newly-evolved system that might well be barely imaginable for the Turquoise meme.

A proposed mission-goal for the Turquoise value meme is: Find ways to bring along the largest numbers of humanity into its future meme, rather than to consolidate the Turquoise meme as "the" new stage of evolution. The better the agents of change can apply the principles of the merging of spiritual (heaven) energies and consciousness with those of physical (biological) consciousness energies and non-physical consciousness, the more effective and accelerated will be humanity's overall evolution in connecting with our destiny as inter-dimensional beings – part of the greater All that Is – and discover what there may be in the greater play of creation.

– Adapted from *Spiral Dynamics: Mastering Values, Leadership, and Change,* Don Beck and Christopher Cowan

A SUMMARY OF THE WORLD

If we could shrink the Earth's population to a village of precisely 100 people with all the existing human ratios remaining the same, it would look like this:

There would be 57 Asians, 21 Europeans, 14 from North and South America, and 8 Africans.

51 would be female; 49 would be male.

70 would be non-white, 30 would be white.

70 would be non-Christian; 30 would be Christian.

50% of the world's wealth would be in the hands of only 6 people, and all 6 people would be from the U.S.

80 would live in substandard housing.

70 would be unable to read.

50 would suffer from malnutrition.

One would be near death; one would be near birth.

Only one would have a college education.

No one would own a computer.

When one considers our world from such an incredibly compressed perspective, the need for both tolerance and understanding becomes glaringly apparent.

Imagine our species as a village of 100 families.

Then, 65 families in our village are illiterate, and 90 do not speak English.

70 have no drinking water at home.

80 have no members who have ever flown in an airplane.

Seven families own 60 percent of the land and consume 80% of all the available energy. They have all the luxuries.

Sixty families are crowded onto ten percent of the land.

Only one family has any member with a university education.

And the air and the water, the climate and the blistering sunlight, are all getting worse.

What is our common responsibility?

(Source: Carl Sagan: Billions and Billions - Thoughts on Life and Death at the Brink of the Millennium, 1997)

What matters most...

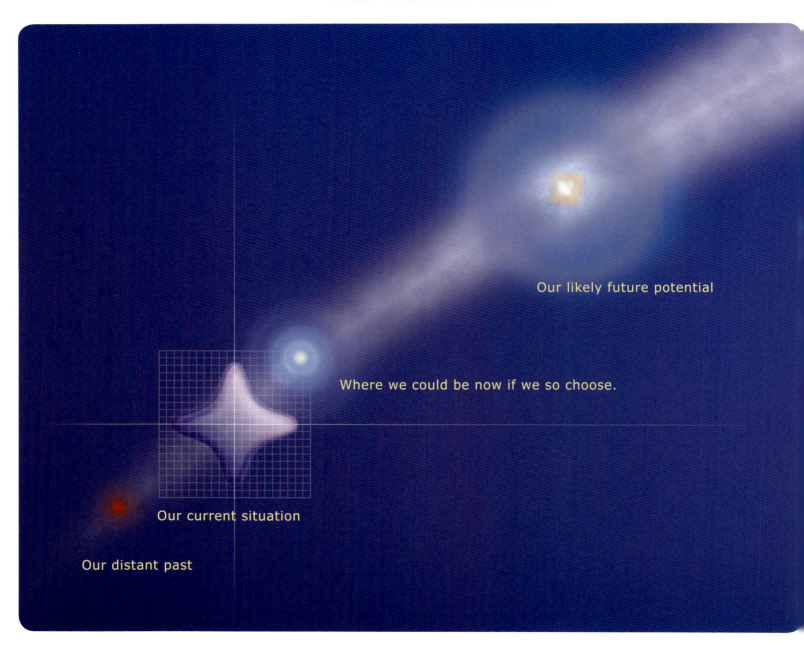

Our likely future potential

Where we could be now if we so choose.

Our current situation

Our distant past

Our higher potential awaits us – as we graduate from the conditions of human suffering and conflict – an awakening to our true nature as spiritual beings. The adventure has barely begun.

It is also a launching point to new dimensions of consciousness and being, as more people welcome it for themselves.

Still in the quadrant grid, but moving into the upper right area is where a majority of people could be living now – the dawn of an enlightened civil society.

Just like a snapshot, the quadrant grid represents our current situation and current value systems.

In our journey through existence, what matters most are our intentions and actions.

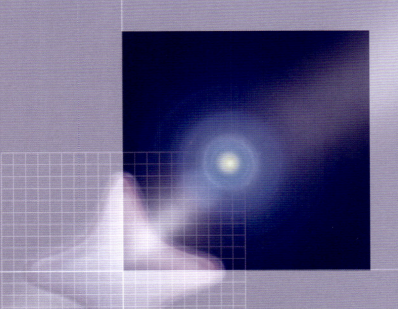

PART THREE

*Strategic Initiatives
of Connection and
Movement*

PART THREE:
Strategic Initiatives Of Connection and Movement

This is an important time for humanity, perhaps a most pivotal one. There are more people than ever before identifying with positive, spiritually aligned and integral choices to heal themselves and the planet. Yet, there are virtually no structures and processes in national or global society to encourage and nourish this new consciousness in an organized and demonstrable way.

Recent research in America demonstrates that a sense of the sacred, while not directly linked to the observance of a recognized faith, is experienced as ever-present in daily life. It is true that many people and organizations are making contributions to various facets of global awakening, but *there is yet to emerge a coherent and stable nexus of leadership or coordination.*

A new type of social movement is needed to help give voice and material expression to a new generation of social movement like the earlier spiritually-based, peaceful, non-violent approach to addressing and reconciling differences championed by Rev. Martin Luther King, Jr., in America in the 1960s and Mahatma K. Gandhi decades earlier in India.

A new set of spiritually aligned leaders – young and old – need to be encouraged and assisted in every way. A refashioned fabric for human society – a new infrastructure purely intended to facilitate in every way possible an emerging new consciousness and to materially aid the manifestation of a more positive and compassionate future – is most needed now.

Even a modest number of spiritually aware leaders, when working in a more balanced and unifying alignment and with a coherent and focused purpose, has the potential to produce some very powerful results – results that could catalyze many more who are truly looking for a new way forward.

To sustain a world for the highest good of all, one must first acknowledge the truth and wisdom connecting us all. This is the time for humanity to see itself in a greater light, to search out new strategies and initiatives aiding in creating something new that is more closely aligned with our highest aspirations. Two such initiatives – Decade of the Heart and The Global Interchange – encapsulate this future-present intention of which both are thoroughly supported by the findings and insights of the *IOOW-2000* research.

CHAPTER 12

For A Decade of the Heart

*"The compassion we hold in our hearts for our families and
communities is growing ever larger, encompassing the world, and reaching
out into the universe."*

There is a calling, a gentle and powerful calling, in all of us – an urging from our hearts to care and to give, providing us with the courage to embrace our future with compassion and joy.

Decade of the Heart encourages this call to rise within the hearts and minds of every individual. It comprises our diverse humanity, and inspires through acts of service a renewed sense of connection to one another and the cosmos.

Decade of the Heart offers possibilities for all of society to connect with one another through a larger context of unconditional love, as well as discernment with compassion. Such a context can help us find the capacity to embrace differences without engendering conflict, to heal, and to evolve in positive directions as individuals, families, communities, and nations.

Will we allow ourselves to listen?

A new spiritually aligned movement needs to be encouraged and assisted in every way. A new fabric for human society – a new infrastructure, one purely intended to facilitate in every way possible an emerging new consciousness and to materially aid the manifesting of a more positive and compassionate future – is most needed now.

It is our hope that this initiative can be embraced and supported by one and all – from ordinary people from all walks of life to the leaders of our highest social institutions, with a special emphasis on the co-equal participation of young people. It unites both the religious and the secular in a consciousness of the heart and in so doing energizes people to rise to the occasion of spiritually aligned leadership, and social and spiritual awakening.

An Urgent Call

This is an important time for humanity, perhaps the single most pivotal. There are now more people than ever before identifying with spiritually aligned and integral choices for themselves and the planet. Yet, there are virtually no structures and processes in national or global society to encourage and nourish this new consciousness for everyone. It is certainly not going to come from the mass media, government, or business. How then?

A new type of social movement will help give voice and material expression to a new generation of social involvement like the earlier spiritually-based movement for non-violence begun with Mahatma Gandhi, Martin Luther King, Jr., and others during the early and mid 1900s. Unlike earlier movements *against* oppression, Decade of the Heart is intended to be a movement *in support of* compassion, truth, reconciliation, healing, and growth. This is a crucial necessity, especially now in such challenging times that call forth the most righteous indignation and opposition from a multitude of seemingly disparate groups. A new way is needed for humanity to evolve into a more enlightened society.

A new social movement such as this will be able to place the awakening of our hearts in the forefront of every person, community, and nation – as a gift for all humanity.

- It will involve people of all cultures and beliefs and from every strata of society in acts of service for others and to the planet.

- Organizations and individuals will become inspired and encouraged to create a culture of forgiveness, creativity, and compassion.

- It can establish a framework uniting people who already are taking some type of lead in global awakening with yet larger numbers of people who resonate with this.

- It will demonstrate diverse practical and social expression of our greater consciousness in ways that have not previously been widely experienced.

This is what we mean by setting in motion a context large enough to successfully embrace the wide spectrum of expression that can be aligned with higher heart consciousness. Such a context can embrace and help reconcile the main polarities in our world and involve people at all levels of society – from the highest levels of political and social institutions to ordinary individuals. It must connect rich, middle class, poor, educators, politicians, religious leaders, the non-religious, environmentalists, businesses, and especially young people in co-equal leadership. Decade of the Heart will involve young people for their own sake, as well as to provide a meaningful context for their collective voice to be heard by all. It is thus that meaningful values based on connection, service, and spirituality can be encouraged and actively developed by newer and older generations.

For a New Social Initiative

The awakening of our hearts immediately provides tangible alternatives to conflict, anger, and competitive interaction. It allows everyone and anyone the necessary personal and cultural permissions needed to experience their own truth from a universal connection of the heart.

Over thousands of years, many teachers have spoken of humankind's higher destiny, the connection to all of creation that is engrained in our beings. Connecting with this higher power requires the honest reconciling of our individual everyday sense of being in the world to a deeper wisdom. In America, whose strength is based in part on its potential for fulfilling the highest aspirations of humanity, this "promise" remains unfulfilled and largely neglected.

In what is widely regarded as the most diverse spiritual and religious society on Earth, spirituality seems to have lost its place in civil society. Whenever spirituality is equated with religion, and in turn spirituality is relegated to the "department of religion," attempts at public discourse on spiritual matters become stifled. In the U.S., as well as in many other countries, a challenging illusion has been institutionalized: The belief that our basic laws require the separation of church and state. With modern society equating *spirituality* with *religion* and therefore institutions of religion, our society as a whole has been unable to find a place for a civil-wide spirituality. As various religious factions use political power to

Humankind is at a crossroads:

- How can humankind overcome thousands of years of conflict and heal itself?

- Can we transcend the constraints of our various individual selves, cultures, faiths, nations, and personalities?

- Can we evolve beyond the inherent limitations of collective ego that have led to a long history of cultural, political, and religious conflict, by appealing to the deeper wisdom that resides in each of our hearts?

- Is there a way to appeal to the collective higher nature of the human race?

- Given the current world situation, how can humanity not afford to invest in an enlightened future?

"...a Frenchmen who came to America in 1759, described an American, 'this new man,' as 'one who leaves behind all ancient prejudices and manners to become a new person who acts upon new principles....'"

"...the civil religion that once united America is dead. ...instead, [we have] an increasing conflict over fundamental conceptions of moral authority; conflicts over different ideas and beliefs about truths, the good, obligations to one another, the nature of community and so on."

– from James Joseph, former President of the U.S. Council of Foundations in his 1995 book, *Remaking America*

impose their own doctrines on our entire society, it is not difficult to understand why a civil spirituality might not enjoy the renaissance it deserves. Add to this a growing portion of the U.S. population that does not embrace traditional religious institutions, but is nonetheless concerned with spiritual matters, that are being effectively excluded from the public dialogue. Religions are simply forms of social organization whose earliest roots were fundamentally about ways for people to be reminded of their own innate spirituality and connection to higher consciousness.

Over thousands of years, religions have become so codified and static that the living, evolving message of spiritual growth has been sidelined in favor of institutionalization. This development necessitates a fixation with maintaining "what was" while cutting itself off from the potentials inherent in the exploration of consciousness that move us upward in the spiral of spiritual unfoldment. Without this forward movement, human beliefs and values become calcified, which can only lead to divisiveness as individuals and groups entrench and polarize.

Decade of the Heart is an experiment in participatory and spiritualized democracy that starts at a grassroots level and builds and maintains a network of people and communities around the world.

Decade of the Heart will be an important vehicle to introduce a non-denominational, non-sectarian, civil spirituality. The positive effects this will have on all facets of society are tremendous.

As Iroquois leader Leon Shenandoah expressed, "...spiritual consciousness is the highest form of politics" – a sort of global spiritual civics. The greatest virtue and strength of a pluralistic society is not relativism, but the universal practice of tolerance and compassion.

Creating a positive future requires no special skills or pedigrees. It all starts from a simple and powerful desire and intent to give from the heart. Our simple actions – all actions – create change in the world. Intentionality is a form of action of the mind and spirit. The external manifestation of our actions in society is an extension of this. Through the process of linking our efforts, we can create an embrace of love and kindness encompassing the entire world. We are the change that we seek.

How might this vision come about?

How?

A project with the potential impact of Decade of the Heart cannot be simply announced with the hopes that a spontaneous response will occur. A spontaneous response will occur, but only once it has been well anchored in the world. It is thus that some deliberation and preparation will be necessary, as will be material resources to start the process moving forward.

As we presented in the first two parts of this book, there are various common elements explored by the *IOOW-2000* research findings that represent nearly universal bridges, ones that could be used to address and connect the vast majority of Americans. These elements range from the simplest, such as "wanting to be involved in creating a better world" to more sophisticated indicators of shared values such as connection, service, spirituality, and the core drivers of The 8 American Types.

As a social expression, Decade of the Heart presents us with an opportunity to forgive, suspend judgment, and embrace the awakening heart of humanity. It is also proposed that "forgiveness and reconciliation" for a global awakening be part of its initial focus to help humanity begin moving beyond social and interpersonal polarities to a context of larger consciousness that can embrace diversity.

Support from cultural and institutional leaders at the highest levels is one facet. It is anticipated that the Decade of the Heart campaign will generate endorsements at all levels, and identify and secure sources of material support to implement a wide range of specific project initiatives. As a coordinated cross-sectional spectrum, it is essential that Decade of the Heart not represent any one organization, personage, or teaching path. All types of organizations, communities, and individuals are invited to participate in a distributed yet coordinated network to further this worldwide connection.

Through the use of mass media, websites, model initiatives and co-creative partnerships, this network will assist communities of individuals at all levels of society in building their own heart-centered networks and activities. Various new models of social and economic cooperation already exist that can be learned from and better applied. There will no doubt

"If we…wish to reach the mind and heart of Mankind…then we – seekers, ourselves, for the Truth – must bring to those who are seeking, the news of a greater work to be accomplished that calls for the whole entire body of their effort."

– Pierre Teilhard de Chardin

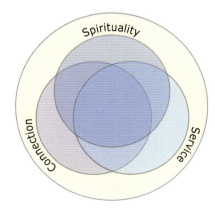

An Unprecedented Movement

"The widespread flourishing of spirituality appears to have a number of defining characteristics, the primary one being that the motivating power behind it is not originating in mainstream institutionalized science, religion, or education. Rather, we are witnessing a popular phenomenon of epic proportions that is at once profoundly personal, experiential, and transcendent.

On this point hangs an important distinction between religion and spirituality that also characterizes this apparently new movement. The denominational churches are not the ones leading the current awakening. This is not the elevation of one catechism over another or the rise of some new organized religion that everyone must follow. Instead, the revolution is occurring in the minds and hearts of million of individual people whose biographies cut across all categories of type and culture."

– from Eugene Taylor, *Shadow Culture*

be many new models and initiatives that will emerge as more people are encouraged to live and act by their higher heart consciousness. A coherent and coordinated network could give millions of people all over the world a new reason and new way to live that honors life and spirit and our planet.

From the beginning, this project has also been about learning new patterns of self-governance, self-referencing, and self-empowerment. This is one of the ideals of the early experiment called "American Democracy" – to experience the benefits of self-governing and self-referencing of something beyond what one person, one vote could ever achieve. This is yet another aspect of the many paths leading to unity within our diversity. Practically, this can be seen as a more developed form of consensus – not a consensus of 100 percent agreement, but a consensus representing a group "self-sense" that can embrace diversity and difference, yet not give rise to conflict.

- With the aid of information and communications technology, a growing global network of people could communicate and coordinate with one another in near real time.

- Diverse models of self-governance and organization could be explored and results shared across the network.

- Various thematic focus centers could be developed to cross over purely geographically focused communities of people. The combination of grassroots efforts and virtual communities would be positively tremendous.

- Gatherings of all types would be organized and resources made available to begin action on what is prioritized.

Decade of the Heart could usher in a highly evolved and ever-evolving type of democratic social organization that would help empower people all over the world around positive future principles. Rather than be in conflict with elected and non-elected governmental bodies, this type of infrastructure and network of people would serve as an inspiring example to people everywhere, helping to gradually transform old processes and structures for the benefit of all people and the planet.

A Pilot Project

A general strategy for launching Decade of the Heart may well include a combination of efforts, including invitational conferences and a *scalable pilot project* involving a number of communities, possibly in the range of 10 to 50 that would roughly approximate the population diversity of various regions. The campaign might begin by introducing the theme of forgiveness and reconciliation and asking localities to identify what this may encompass conceptually and through initiatives for them. An example of a related theme would be discernment with compassion.

The combination of forgiveness and reconciliation, and all that they imply, is a theme that has rarely been addressed in modern culture in a widespread public discourse or forum. It is being put forth as one of the cornerstones associated with Decade of the Heart. The pilot campaign is guided by the understanding that forgiveness is a portal to not only individual but global awakening. By freeing us to connect with our higher selves, forgiveness opens us to broader conflict resolution throughout all levels of our current society. This in turn allows for the walls of separation and disconnection to be dissolved, which then facilitates the uplifting theme of discernment with compassion, interconnectedness, unity within diversity, and civil spirituality, to name a few.

The potentials are unlimited and extraordinarily encompassing. They delve deep into the heart of our being as we seek to address the challenges facing humanity and the Earth today. At heart, we all desire a more positive future. The question is: How to initiate and sustain a movement toward a more positive future?

Positive Future Principles

In each locale, young people would be deliberately involved as co-equals in these early stages. The pilot project would seek to identify natural leaders within communities and not rely solely upon existing organizations. An initial pilot project could be centered around the school term and by the end of the term, outcomes will have been realized. This is quite realistic as there are projects already existing that have accomplished outcomes in three to four months. (Necessarily, other aspects of a pilot project would have longer cycles.)

Given that such a projects would involve young people, it would be realistic to structure the timing of the project to coincide with typical school semesters. The project would occur in school and outside of school. Realistically, it's easier to bring about school participation by having an in-school component. In addition, parents can be more involved if the initial pilot project takes into account school year calendars.

Elements of a Campaign

It is hoped that the Decade of the Heart campaign will provide a framework supported by diverse peoples and organizations, particularly youth, embracing a consciousness of the heart that facilitates rising to positions of leadership in all levels of society.

- One of the challenges is to achieve greater personal and material cooperation among leading proponents of positive future concepts and initiatives. Collective sharing of resources will "raise all boats." The roles played by various levels of deliberate process and project facilitation will likely prove crucial to the success of Decade of the Heart.

- An invitational call for an initial "leadership and advisory group" needs to be made to individuals who are leading social-spiritual innovation and whose voices would be listened to by others in more established positions of social influence.

Support from cultural and institutional leaders at the highest levels will be important. Decade of the Heart will reach out to all people and all levels of society, and in so doing, generate endorsements and participation at all levels, as well as secure necessary resources to implement a range of specific project initiatives. Representing a greater oneness within diversity, it is essential that Decade of the Heart not represent any one organization, personage, or teaching path.

- Community-based pilot projects fostering a community of communities to help raise up spiritually aware citizens and to help spiritualize those in positions of leadership. This project would involve totally fresh, grassroots approaches and serve as a model in much the same way early spiritually inspired movements for nonviolence and peace throughout the twentieth century served as models in their day.

- It will be useful to identify any existing media initiatives that can be brought to bear to reach large numbers of people around the world. Media and general awareness campaigns will need to be implemented to spread the message and value of forgiveness. A media campaign pilot "Messages: Awakening the Heart of

Humanity" has already been created as one example. A television series on American society and spirituality is also in the early planning stages.

All participants will be "seeing" each other on the Internet becoming easily familiar and knowledgeable about each other and project themes. Eventually, the wider public will be connected. As greater connection occurs involving larger numbers of people, the value of the Internet will play a greater role in helping to bridge large numbers of people, thereby making it convenient to meet in a "virtual town meeting" amongst all of them. This is where technology partners can play a role in helping to make this part of the pilot more easily implemented. In addition to facilitation and coordination, the pilot project phase will require budgeting for communication technology.

Facilitation and Coordination

For any pilot project such as Decade of the Heart to successfully embrace 10 to 50 or more communities, a coordinating team and network is necessary. More so it will require facilitation of its very process. To bring together strong-minded leaders will require facilitation of the highest order, as will the assemblage of ordinary people who step forward from their locales. It is crucial that such an experiment in participatory and spiritualized democracy be supported to the fullest measure possible from its inception.

It is essential that initial pilot communities be well chosen to make it easier for people to see the extraordinary nature and potential inherent in each of the pilot communities' efforts, as well as Decade of the Heart as a whole. They will all be like the first gems in a new crown for humanity setting an example for others.

The projects must specifically identify how they are in alignment with heart-centered awakening and connection to our greater potential as spirit, our greater consciousness, and our connection to all of creation and each other as part of the whole of creation. Each locale must achieve a positive impact in their community.

The criteria will also include identifying existing or anticipated support from projected immediate spheres of influence and constituencies so that from the beginning as much public support as possible can be encouraged. This is preferable to one-sided support through the pilot phase funding. It's important to encourage additional energies to be brought to bear on these special projects, even if it's initially a small fraction.

As the focus of each locale and pilot project focus begins to move past the pilot phase, there will be a spiritually aligned facilitative leadership team resident in each community who will maintain connection with other leadership teams.

- As the local and coordinating center teams become more intimately acquainted with their work and personally involved on a daily/ weekly basis with each other and those people in each community project, new people are naturally going to be identified in each community project center. This process will occur through their support structures and all facets involved with each Community Pilot.

- The facilitators need a context to reference, so as to not get caught off balance and driven solely by peoples' trauma, suffering, issues, apparent limitations, or the particular strengths of any given pilot member. Hence, there is a need for the Guiding/Governing Body, of which the Chief or Master Facilitators are going to be an essential part. But, it includes others helping to guide the structure, process, and communications of this project.

Each locale and project focus will receive facilitation in better understanding and expressing how their work may offer humanity heart connection and heal suffering through awakening to higher consciousness. In every way possible, Decade of the Heart will help people access solutions and opportunities of which the everyday self may be unaware. Numerous benefits will be derived, including:

- The attention paid to developing a facilitative leadership style at local and regional levels will directly benefit a community's quality of life as people learn new ways to govern themselves as individuals and as communities.

- In each locale, as well as for the pilot project group as a whole, facilitation can help to "push the envelope" by taking on something even more advanced than what may be initially proposed.

- When they've become a community of communities, they have a model with the capacity for something even larger.

Each participating locale would be informed of available resources. As the project moves past the pilot phase and takes on a more permanent life of its own, developing a local and regional base of support will become more important.

"COUNCIL OF COUNCILS"

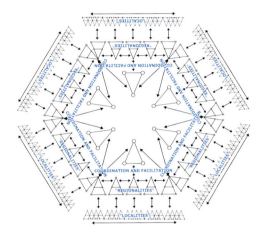

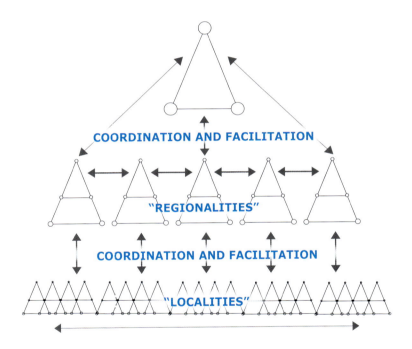

Numerous individuals and groups around the world are already working to improve the lives of others and the conditions in which they live, from emotional to physical environments. One essential reminder for all of us is that we are inherently linked by our humanness, that what we do in action and word impacts all of humanity. Therefore, it is vitally important that no one feel left out as we seek to implement processes and initiatives supporting the greater heart of humanity.

We must appeal to and work with individuals, cultures and communities of all ages, ethnicities, perspectives, talents, and consciousness so that we may all move forward together – as much as possible – on an upward spiral of awakening. Each must sincerely feel that he or she is an integral member of each pilot program and community, and that his or her voice is heard.

One school-based example is the Language of the Awakened Heart classroom program that encourages young people to find new ways of contemplating and expressing values and beliefs leading to a more compassionate perspective in life. This project was designed to awaken children to their natural wisdom, present exciting tools with which to improve their language skills, and provide an opportunity for children to express their highest visions through the creative medium of poetry. Lesson plans were developed based on themes of generosity, wisdom, joy, forgiveness, and envisioning a new future. From that, a guidebook based on successful pilot programs was published for teachers and others who work with young people.

Another national and global-level project is A Season for Nonviolence. Its focus over the past ten years has been a campaign conducted at the beginning of each year dedicated to demonstrating that nonviolence is a powerful way to heal, transform, and empower our lives and our communities. Inspired by the 30th and 50th memorial anniversaries of Dr. Martin Luther King, Jr., and Mahatma Gandhi, this international event honors their vision for an empowered, nonviolent world.

An Invitation

The needs of a growing spiritual awakening require structures and processes optimally designed to conduct and amplify a new energy and consciousness in the world. The structures of the old energy cannot be expected to serve this function. This is not unlike having a high electrical potential and non-existent or poor conductors. The result is the same – the potential energy cannot do useful work and therefore remains only that: potential. In other words, we cannot expect governments or social institutions such as private corporations, which are organized to maximize profit and accumulate and concentrate wealth, to do this sort of work. Something new is needed.

Even a modest number of ethical and enlightened people, when working in an alignment of higher consciousness and with a coherent and focused purpose, has the potential to produce some very powerful results – results that could catalyze many more who are truly looking for a new way forward.

A new spiritually aligned movement needs to be encouraged and assisted in every way – and it is most needed now. While Decade of the Heart does not presume to be the answer to everything that ails humanity, it is intended to be a powerful catalyst and practical vehicle for compassionate and enlightened change for a positive future.

It is our hope that this initiative can be embraced and supported by everyone – from ordinary people from all walks of life to the leaders of our highest social institutions – with a special emphasis on the co-equal participation of young people. It unites both the religious and the secular in a consciousness of the heart and in so doing energizes people to rise to the occasion of spiritually aligned leadership, and social and spiritual awakening.

Decade of the Heart will help clarify how the two worlds represented by the heart and mind, so long perceived as separate, are actually connected through their shared foundation of consciousness and common source of spirit.

"There are rare moments in the life of every nation, when opportunities arise that enable the entire population to transcend the limitations of the past, allowing them to express self-determination as they discover true freedom."

"Decade of the Heart can help form a new fabric for humanity, one purely intended to facilitate in every way possible an emerging new consciousness and to materially facilitate a more positive, compassionate, and enlightened future for ourselves and for generations to come."

"It is only with the heart that one can see rightly' what is essential is invisible to the eye."

– from *The Little Prince* by Antoine de Saint-Exupéry

America was founded on a promise of freedom and equality – a freedom that provides the opportunity for a full exploration of spirituality, and equality that allows a deeper experience of community to exist.

Decade of the Heart will assist humanity in finding a way to allow the presence of *grace* to replenish our divinity, which will restore our true humanity as it heals and awakens each human heart.

There are rare moments in the life of every nation when opportunities arise that enable the entire population to transcend the limitations of the past, allowing them to express self-determination as they discover true freedom. Striking a tone as uplifting and resonant as the Liberty Bell, Decade of the Heart is a clarion call to soar beyond the accumulation of confusion, seeking a future resolving the disagreements of the past, while restoring the full distinction of our destiny.

Decade of the Heart can help form a new fabric for humanity, one purely intended to facilitate an emerging new consciousness and to materially facilitate a more positive, compassionate, and enlightened future for ourselves and for generations to come.

If we listen carefully, we can hear the sweet, clear sound of a new voice, speaking above the cacophony of the modern world. It speaks of a deeper purpose for life than we have yet imagined and invites each of us to explore the possibilities of that purpose.

Let us explore together those possibilities!

Universal Connection:

- Belief that "What goes around comes around" (and thus do no harm) helps provide a basis for people to recognize another facet of our mutual interconnectedness.

- Our earth is a unique kind of living organism, and as a whole system is fundamentally alive.

- Underneath it all, we're all connected as one.

Tolerance and Reconciliation:

- Interacting with others broadens our horizons.

- To have a successful community, we do not all have to agree.

- Tolerance of lifestyles and groups is essential in a society composed of such diversity.

- Forgiveness and reconciliation helps us all accomplish much more.

- We are all looking to be loved and accepted as human beings.

Spirituality:

- We need to be more conscious of and connected to all aspects of our own selves.

- Whether we recognize it or not, we all want to connect to God or a higher spiritual consciousness.

- Acknowledge the importance of and need for spiritual growth.

- Social and spiritual awakening can make the world a better place in which to live.

- Experience a sense of sacred in everything or see everything as spiritually connected.

Service:

- Be more personally involved in creating a better world. Helping those in need is one of the most important things nations can do within the global community.

CHAPTER 13
The Global Interchange

"Imagine a very large-scale network of communities of individuals and communities of communities who, over time, come to own and manage a new form of cooperative social enterprise that is entirely dedicated to assisting humanity's positive evolution as a social and biological species."

Imagine an Internet-based service organization that is a practical bridge for anyone, anywhere, who is interested in positive future change in the world. Imagine a full spectrum of advanced information and communications technologies, professional level staffing, public outreach, and more – all devoted to optimizing user experiences in favor of a positive future. Imagine that such an initiative also embraces new funding relationships, as well as content. Imagine also that there are regional headquarter facilities encouraging participation and governance at local and global levels, with new forms of participatory democracy emerging for the benefit the world.

Imagine feeling and being part of a diverse, global community of individuals who share basic values and beliefs about compassion and the interconnectedness of life, the importance of service and helping others, and a sense of purpose in support of a better future for new generations that does not include war, conflict, and scarcity. Imagine, new structures, processes, resources, and personal facilitation that can be used cooperatively by the growing community of organizations and individuals throughout the world who are working toward a more positive future.

Now, imagine this could all be true.

The Vision

In addition to the *IOOW-2000* research, the Fund For Global Awakening's second (and largest) project has been the planning and development of a strategic initiative called The Global Interchange (GIC). Utilizing the best practices of both business and the independent sector, it introduces new structures and processes to allow for the emergence of a global funding and communications hub aligned with positive future values and actions. The GIC is a synthesis of commercial and philanthropic models.

The Global Interchange: a worldwide community exchange of shared, positive values, information, and resources; a nexus of common vision and support; a meta-crossroads of compelling purpose and heart; a portal to practical innovation, remarkable ideas, and new visions in the making; a global, digital arena for staging constructive, social change and strategic partnerships; a source of new philanthropy and investments to ensure a more positive future.

Our world is on the brink of a new social consciousness, one more acutely aware of our underlying commonality in beliefs, attitudes, values, and widely encompassing spirituality. Circumstances compel humanity to search for a more vibrant, ethical, and heartfelt foundation of supportive enterprise and community, one that emphasizes the interconnectedness of all.

A Strategic Hub Focusing the Internet's Full Potential

More so than at any other time in history, we have the ability to break through the barriers of our currently limited, conventional systems to clearly envision the possibilities of our true nature and capacity as human beings.

The Global Interchange is positioned to play a pivotal role in the emerging world community through a growing recognition and alignment of the basic interconnectedness underlying humanity's extraordinary diversity. A primary goal of the GIC is to facilitate the growing need for informational, technical, human, and financial resources that serve practical innovations for a more enlightened approach to the global environment and all facets of human society.

The rapid expansion of Internet usage within the past several years in America and the world is nothing short of staggering. We see great value in the Internet to help focus attention and energy toward creating a positive and more enlightened future for everyone.

- In place of an overflow of incoherent and unverifiable information moving across the World Wide Web, the GIC introduces new patterns of reliability and coherency. It uses artificial intelligence to help bridge barriers of specialization and language, especially to identify new trends and elements of a positive future as they emerge.

- The GIC brings together inspired projects for a positive future with large-scale financial, technical, and human resources. Together, these early participants will help establish new patterns for cooperation and resource-sharing aligned to assist humanity's positive evolution.

- Instead of competition and commercialism, the GIC encourages the growth of cooperative, transnational initiatives, and coordination of human and material resources to address planetary and social ecology in ways formerly thought to be impossible.

The processes devised to manage and implement the GIC from its inception will lead to a very large-scale network of people who, over time, will come to own and manage the future of the GIC as a new form of cooperative social enterprise.

"There is so much inspiring innovation coming forth in the world today, but it has no framework, it has no common hub, it does not have a place to be seen in a coherent whole by the whole world."

"The Global Interchange is based on a phased implementation of 8 Core Elements into a strategic hub, bringing together infrastructure, facilitated processes, and resources to connect a culturally diverse mix of communities."

Overview of The Global Interchange

Core values of the GIC embrace compassion and service. It exists to bring together people who are engaged in making a positive difference in the world. The GIC makes available new structures, processes, resources, research, and facilitation to be used in cooperative exchange for new projects that benefit all humanity.

Through analysis of the *IOOW-2000* research, unique typologies provided startling new insight into our society by identifying segments of the adult population who have different attitudes and behaviors, as well as distinctive decision-making patterns. The insights gained through our extensive experience and formal research will be used to develop special applications for the GIC.

We are exploring and forming strategic alliances with private and organizational funding centers, leading to the eventual engagement of the broadest possible public involvement.

The current model for a rationally phased implementation is projected to lead to social enterprise with revenue in the range of one billion dollars. An encompassing business plan and scaled financial models have been prepared, as has been much legal groundwork to facilitate the funding process.

If some of the description of the GIC sounds very business-like, it is simply that the GIC will be using very large sums of money to develop itself fairly quickly and that technology business has evolved certain efficient modalities that can be used advantageously in the start-up of something as innovative as the GIC. Furthermore, investment and donor funds must be used in an appropriate and cost-efficient manner. As the GIC evolves, the people involved will develop new ways of conducting themselves within their collective affairs, just like any evolving community.

WHAT IS THE GIC?

The Global Interchange is:

- *a portal*
- *a portal of portals*
- *a community of communities*
- *a global community of the most forward-looking and practical action people*
- *a solid resource for manifesting a positive and functional world now*
- *a place where anyone can see an awakened future emerging*
- *a means by which anyone can support this awakening process*
- *a means by which anyone can be involved at any level*
- *an alternative philanthropic funding and banking center*
- *an incubator of new and economically sustainable products/services*
- *a source for product and services information*
- *emphasis on products and services with high green environmental and social responsibility*
- *a solid set of human, technical, financial, and informational resources*
- *a powerful synergy of eight core elements*
- *an initiative dedicated to a positive future in the present*

Comprehensive Content Coverage

- arts, creative culture
- environment, infrastructure
- health, wellness
- relationship, empowerment
- energy, food, water
- economics, business
- science, technology
- communications, media
- governance, law
- spirituality, religion
- social justice, security
- learning, education
- ...and nearly anything else imaginable

The Global Interchange fulfills the vision of its founders, who have decades of experience with positive social innovations, economic development, research, information technology, and planning. Seeing the need, they have put the GIC together with key differentiators:

- It creates a transnational, online network where people can access, participate, and contribute to a wide range of human, technical, informational, and financial resources.

- It builds tangible relationships and provides beneficial exposure at all levels toward making a positive difference in the world.

- It serves as an important source of new philanthropic and venture funding to partners and members.

Unique synergies of the GIC will yield new applications and systems, intellectual property, and products and services that will contribute to a substantial portion of the revenue by year five.

It represents a logical and potentially synergistic addition to existing telecommunication, Internet, and other information industry activities. The GIC anticipates developing and utilizing the latest information technology and knowledge synthesis applications to facilitate user relationships, as well as its own operations.

The GIC fulfills a coherent set of needs and interests that are not being met and uses the new generation of technology in ways that emphasize human values and needs. The GIC addresses these requirements through a financial and operational model that includes both individual and organizational accounts. Throughout all aspects of this enterprise, the value of human, technical, informational, and financial resources is continuously amplified. This is accomplished through unique processes and structures, as well as informational and financial strategies, and by connecting individual and organizational wealth for the highest good.

Utilizing the best practices of both the business world and the independent sector, the GIC introduces new structures and processes to allow for the emergence of a global funding and communications hub.

Thoughtfully structured and properly used and facilitated, the GIC can serve as a powerful catalyst to bridge geographic distances, encouraging large numbers of people to see the connection between many wonderful acts of innovation and service currently being expressed throughout the world.

The GIC can facilitate the emergence of a coherent community of diversity, aligned with the larger context of a positive and more enlightened future. It will be a means by which people can explore and learn, where they will find community with like-minded individuals, and where they will find financial and other resources to accomplish their worthy efforts toward creating a more positive future.

The Global Interchange is based on a phased implementation of 8 Core Elements into a strategic hub, bringing together infrastructure, facilitated processes, and resources to connect a culturally diverse mix of communities. (These are not to be confused with The 8 American Types of the *IOOW-2000* research.)

Examples of what GIC includes:

- text and image systems
- streaming and static news feeds
- video and audio downloads
- Internet radio
- group facilitation
- learning
- sharing
- forums
- live, in-person conferences and events
- involves young people in a respectful and meaningful way
- source of highly reliable information
- traditional and non-traditional publishing of all kinds
- new media, new content, and new values
- involves people in many ways, not just as paid staff or contractors
- no commercial advertisements
- …and more

Eight Core User Elements of the GIC

The Global Interchange will be a means by which people can explore and learn, where they will find community with like-minded individuals, and where they will find financial and other resources. Our focus is to create a vibrant, ethical, and productive online community of social responsibility and positive change. To do this, the GIC has developed 8 Core User Elements that offer compelling reasons for users to become subscribers.

These 8 Core User Elements offer infinite interconnectivity, attracting users of diverse background, perspective, talent, and insight who desire to share and invest in an extraordinary synthesis of purpose. Each of the 8 Core User Elements is a hub in its own right, providing ever-expanding levels of information and connection rich in content, free of advertising, and offering sophisticated features and capabilities.

1. NETWORKING AND INTERCONNECTIVITY

Intelligent software, content analysis, and human facilitation to utilize Internet communications and knowledge synthesis tools to ensure optimal interconnectivity between resources and between individual, nonprofit, educational, non-governmental, business, and government members. This nexus is the interchange of all communities of individuals and organizations participating in the GIC and includes subscribers, as well as casual Internet users.

2. FACILITATION AND PROJECT COMMUNITIES

A community of individuals, organizations, and businesses at the leading edge of social-cultural, economic, and techno-scientific innovation for a positive future; increased effectiveness of individual and group innovation with access to exemplars, interlinking forums, and project incubators representing the world's best instances of positive innovation.

3. INFORMATION AND RESEARCH SUPPORT

Key informational attractors, information application development, and strategic resources focused on acquiring, validating, creating, and publishing both free and fee-based knowledge and custom research.

7 Learning Communities
2 Facilitation and Project Communities
6 New Content Media Center
1 Networking and Interconnectivity
3 Information and Research Support
5 Global News Network
4 Funding and Communities of Support
User Services and E-Store
8

Provides strategic information support throughout the GIC and manages a major portion of the GIC's public information and search function resources.

4. FUNDING AND COMMUNITIES OF SUPPORT

Collecting, assembling, and transferring individual, entrepreneurial, and organizational resources in ways that bridge charitable giving, venture philanthropy, commercial funding, ethical investment funds, and visionary wealth.

5. GIC NEWS NETWORK

Gathering, validating, shaping, and delivering existing and alternative news, geographic and topical interests, and project announcements through electronic, broadcast, and print channels designed to connect participants on one-to-one, one-to-many, and many-to-many levels. The GIC is also an alternative to traditional media outlets for localized and worldwide information.

6. NEW CONTENT MEDIA CENTER

Gathering, developing, and producing creative, original, and inspiring, factual and imaginative material aligned with positive social-cultural innovation delivered through print, electronic, live, and all other media channels. As such, it is not limited to the opportunities presented by the Internet for delivery and interactivity.

7. LEARNING COMMUNITIES

Innovative variety of transformational and traditional core curricula and learning programs made available through online, broadcast, and traditional channels. Leading educational innovators will be brought together to develop a core set of offerings from the best of the best.

8. USER SERVICES AND E-STORE

A gateway to services geared toward maintaining a large subscriber base, such as membership services, interconnectivity, expanding communications and networking, online conferences, event calendar and registration services, member directory, e-mail, storage, transcription, tools, help desk and technical support, and interlinking business and

Basic Operational Units of the Global Interchange

- Web Portals, User Interface, Search Systems, Desktop
- e-Commerce Portal
- Media: Print Publishing, Online, TV, Video, Audio, Radio
- Events and Event Planning and Services
- Internet Service Provider, Data Center, Hosting
- Consulting and Information Research Services
- Information and Research Products, Applications
- Philanthropic and Charitable Fund Group
- Investment and Financial Services
- Research and Development
- Organization-wide Overlay Functions

nonprofit organization directories. The online store will also offer goods and services from GIC constituents, as well as the larger universe of commercial providers.

While the GIC does not plan to become a product distribution business, it will be in a position to receive pass-through fees and commissions. In addition, various unique commercial opportunities have been identified in the preliminary planning of the GIC that could quickly lead to a new source of commercial revenue from the development of this core element.

Operational Units and Implementation

This section summarizes the initial GIC units that will emerge during the first year from launch and is intended to provide more insight into how the GIC analyzes its various revenue streams. Some of these business units will receive greater attention and investment than others. Those receiving less attention are anticipated to grow more organically or in a deliberately controlled manner. Each of these operates somewhat uniquely, and each is matched to mature technologies currently in the marketplace. Not all the business units are expected to be directly profitable centers in their own right, such as overlay functions.

Success and Risk Factors

The key to the GIC's potential, success, and reduction of risk rests largely on its ability to address sets of needs and wants that are virtually ignored or vastly underserved. The GIC does so with an organizational model that melds the best of collaborative and cooperative structures with proven mission-project-focused approaches. We believe this model will lead to the development of a stable organization that has depth and longevity while, at the same time, taking advantage of market and economic opportunities that few are currently positioned to address in the world.

Why will it succeed in ways that well-known and large-scale commercial businesses cannot?

The GIC:

- Taps a market they cannot understand given their paradigm
- Builds loyalty based on community and trusting relationships
- Is immune to most ordinary market forces
- Has no on-line advertising
- Has no commercial agenda (such as sales of products or advertising)
- Uses a profound management matrix leading to long-term stability

To support this business and economic model, we have highlighted several areas that, through diligence, insight and astute implementation, the GIC can become an Internet hub of and for innovation, expertise, flexibility, interconnectivity, and informed communities worldwide

- User interface strategy
- Marketing strategy
- Intellectual property
- Business and economic model
- Organizational development and corporate culture strategy
- Technology, distribution, and support infrastructure
- Socially and environmentally responsible values, ethics, practices

The Global Interchange builds a solid community of people and customers who will strongly identify with the GIC, increasingly so over time as more and more sharing of technical, financial, informational and other resources occurs.

Technology, Research, and Development

The GIC's research and development efforts will include a new type of visual language user interface, search engine, browser, and desktop management functions. Through the use of artificial intelligence applications and simple human attention to user needs, the GIC can offer a user experience that will be highly appreciated by both novice and experienced users. The GIC will emphasize the use of proven technology and applications to support an early commercial launch parallel to its own proprietary research and development efforts.

Partly based on a proprietary typology and research database, and partly based on unique statistical algorithms, The Global Interchange includes a unique system comparing actual user behavior including search engine activities, product interests, and other online actions with professed behavior based on statistical, survey-based indicators. This creates a set of sophisticated tools for predicting behavior and for developing and tracking strategic positioning and communications campaigns. The typology and analytical systems are equally applicable to internal management, employee assessment, customer profiling, and other marketing applications.

Examples of GIC technology include:

- a unique search engine with value-based typologies and artificial intelligence
- a user-customizable desktop and browser interface
- pioneering uses and markets for voice over the Internet
- a professional information expert for the general public
- software application services for personal and commercial use
- a web interface
- an e-mail and instant messaging service for individuals and organizations
- an audio and video conferencing center
- Internet telephony
- …and much more

Who Will Use GIC Technology?

The primary value of the Internet to people is its interconnectivity and potential for interactivity. All other forms of media only push messages to their constituents, with little or no means of gathering quality feedback on constituent reactions as they occur. Websites and organizations that capitalize upon frequent highly tailored and customized content delivery, as well as the facilitation of communication among their users, have a much greater chance to succeed in this arena.

Private and public companies, nonprofit organizations, government agencies, and educational institutions spend billions of dollars every year seeking the answers to soft questions (customer satisfaction, consumer demands, and employee performance) they need in order to drive their respective missions forward. A basic advantage for non-commercial ventures and large corporations is in understanding barriers to success and/or how to fulfill clearly stated needs of constituents. The Global Interchange utilizes both proprietary analysis and knowledge management software as a very powerful toolset to address many of these needs.

Over time, unique technological, scientific, informational, and entertainment content will emerge from the GIC that will represent additional sources for intellectual property of strategic and economic value. There can be many "spin-offs" emerging from the GIC that would be commercially viable with little negative impact on the advantageous position of the GIC as an enterprise.

Market Opportunity and Value Proposition

The Global Interchange fulfills a need that has been identified through a sophisticated, landmark research study of American households conducted at the turn of the millennium (*IOOW-2000*). The first phase of the research has identified millions of U.S. households with online access that are willing to subscribe to a low-cost, non-commercial, Internet service dedicated to personal and global transformation.

The Global Interchange is designed to be a financially self-sustaining, strategic hub focused entirely on enriching people's lives. It will leverage the Internet's full potential to interconnect millions of individuals, philanthropic and educational organizations, government agencies, non-governmental organizations, and businesses around an earnest desire to invest and participate in a positive future for humanity.

It will do this by integrating four key resources:

- Human
- Technical
- Financial
- Informational

This high level of integration and facilitation is enhanced through proprietary knowledge synthesis software, content validation and resource management, all of which will foster synergy between users' needs, information engineering expertise, and constructive resources.

Captured in a compelling model, the GIC integrates leading edge, philanthropic principles with the strength of business processes, bringing together an extensive range of human and material resources to aid and facilitate the emergence of an awakened world.

Some investors tend to separate their interests between social-environmental ethics and "hard business economics." Those who are primarily focused on the "hard business" approach can rest assured that The Global Interchange has identified and defined markets and strategies that are most distinctive and potent to yield a highly successful enterprise. We take advantage of unique analytical insights and statistically projectable typologies of core values and beliefs underlying people's interests, aspirations, and behaviors. This data draws from various research sources, including our own proprietary market study of over 1,600 U.S. households. This, plus the availability of mature information technologies, makes it possible to realize the enormous potential of the GIC. The key assumptions behind the GIC lead to straight and clear marketing strategies and corporate implementation.

In addition to being founded on highly marketable values and business assumptions, the GIC embodies positive social values and ethics in its internal and external business affairs. This added enhancement is something everyone can feel good about. We also believe that what may be an enhancement today will become an important business element tomorrow. Thus, for those people who do emphasize positive values and ethics in their investments, The Global Interchange is an ideal vehicle that can exceed most expectations.

The GIC is positioned primarily as a for-profit entity with a strong secondary philanthropic and charitable component, this emphasis can be readily inverted. In whatever way it is primarily financed, the GIC will have both for-profit and charitable and philanthropic aspects to it.

While we would prefer altruist philanthropic support, we are aware that most people and organizations want to know how they will benefit financially in the short term. It is for this reason our planning has emphasized for-profit relationships. Whether it be through fees, returns on investment in the project, or direct professional involvement – or any combination of these – the GIC will be in a position to enhance the situation of individuals and partner organizations in many ways. Technology partners will also find new outlets for their commercial offerings and derive tremendous benefit from sophisticated social-science research and related data-mining applications. Six years after being launched, the GIC could grow to a one billion dollar plus enterprise with multiple technology and other intellectual property spin-offs. The Global Interchange will demonstrate the promise of information technologies to improve people's lives in very tangible ways.

"Our world is on the brink of a new social consciousness, one more acutely aware of our underlying commonality in beliefs, attitudes, values, and widely encompassing spirituality. Circumstances compel humanity to search for a more vibrant, ethical, and heartfelt foundation of supportive enterprise and community, one that emphasizes the interconnectedness of all."

IMAGINE…

- A fresh, new user interface – unique and customizable to your changing needs – that combines browser, file manager, and portal navigation functions, that operates across nearly all common platforms and devices, and all without advertising messages.

- Easy-to-use, state-of-the-art information search retrieval, and relevancy systems at your fingertips with tools that meet the needs of experienced professionals, as well as first-time users.

- Natural language search and retrieval capability for your desktop, LAN/WAN, and GIC system, as well as Internet-wide.

- Unlimited access to global information sources – instantly and in all forms as well as through information research professionals.

- An extensive content provider of original and redistributed materials across all media and delivery mechanisms.

- A wealth of intellectual property covering content, technology, applications, and approach.

- An infrastructure of new technology, distribution, and support – initially emphasizing proven technology and applications while developing innovations for the long term, many of which may be commercially valuable unto themselves.

- An extraordinary marketing strategy with a unique, dual-track approach to organizational constituencies and users at-large.

- A socially responsible and sustainable business and economic model that bridges and builds upon the strengths of both for-profit and not-for-profit models.

- Access to financial, technical, and human resources dedicated to making a positive difference in the world while serving your personal needs.

- An organizational development and corporate culture strategy that can be applied to internal development for long-term stability and provides a marketable set of consulting services.

- Socially and environmentally responsible values, ethics, and practices applied throughout a large and vibrant organization that truly "walks its talk."

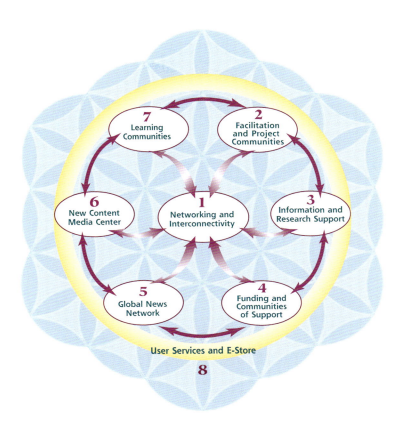

THE GLOBAL INTERCHANGE

INCORPORATED IN 2002 IN CALIFORNIA, THE GIC IS
NOT LIMITED OR INFLUENCED BY ANY POLITICAL,
ECONOMIC, OR RELIGIOUS INTERESTS.

P.O. Box 1179 Point Reyes Station, California
94956-1179 USA

E-mail: info@gic-one.com

PART FOUR

*A New Look at
the American
Electorate*

PART FOUR:
A New Look at the American Electorate

A *New America* identifies ways to elicit and facilitate new patterns of behavior in our society for creating an awakened, positive future based on values such as compassion and the interconnectedness of all life. Our concern remains with the social and spiritual forward movement and leadership for a positive future – elected or otherwise. Watchwords of concern influencing recent national election cycles are: religiosity, gender differences, Gen-X and Gen-Y, values-voting, and election fraud. The deeper questions for our present and future regrettably are entangled in superficial rationalizations and are either obfuscated or omitted by a mass media generally unwilling to truthfully present the real issues of the day to the public. What has become ever more apparent is that there is less and less difference between the two national political parties that have long dominated U.S. elections.

So much information was collected and analyzed from the *IOOW-2000* research that it is difficult to refrain from presenting the reader with too much content such that the bigger picture isn't jeopardized. We have therefore focused the chapters that comprise Part Four to presenting the factors unique to the voting and non-voting publics; values, typologies, and voting behaviors are described and overlaid with traditional demographics; select demographic and psychographic variables, and other factors from the *IOOW-2000* study in the context of voting for the period leading up to the 2000 election. In these three chapters, you will also find information concerning gender, urbanization, geography, generational differences, and religious-spiritual factors.

Statistical research has the power to reveal an accurate representation of core values, beliefs, attitudes, and preferences of our population and thus has the potential to shape public opinion and inform key influencers in society. Part Four summarizes, for the first time, key findings relative to U.S. elections and socio-political patterns. The analysis is of the early period before the actual election of 2000 and compares traditional approaches to voting tendencies to more meaningful and useful typological approaches.

Much of our current political system tends to write off people who generally don't vote and, as such, helps perpetuate "structural voter discouragement." Occasionally, intensive voter registration drives and get-out-the-vote campaigns are used where elections have high stakes and the share of voters between the leading candidates is close.

Just because someone doesn't vote doesn't mean they are "hopelessly apathetic" or part of some "middle morass" as some researchers believe. Models such as The 8 American Types and the PFCI-SMS quadrants show that there are "discouraged voters" present throughout our society. As part of a new set of social strategies, it is important to address this differently than the ways the two national political parties usually do. There is, however, a group of people whose values and outlook constitute a type of "social ballast" as we discussed in Chapter Six. In developing new strategies for a positive future, it will be important to bear in mind this existence of "social ballast" and the way in which its strength and influence is deliberately exaggerated to suit the interests of a powerful elite in maintaining social control.

There are several good indicators that weak or non-voters do care to make a positive difference and in helping others – and in fact do so. It is also worth noting that 62 % of weak or non-voters also strongly prefer elected leaders that have *higher and more evolved* moral and ethical values than they do themselves. While this may be in line with the 64 % average for everyone, it is another important *positive* factor to bear in mind, especially given the generally poor quality of leadership that has risen to national office in recent decades.

Overall, it is not just about whether people vote or not. The chief concern should be whether we are to have a participatory democracy or a plutocracy – and secondarily, whether America can lead the way toward anchoring a positive and enlightened future for all humanity.

CHAPTER 14

Elections as a Reflection and Projection of Society

"A new type of politics is needed – one that serves to promote enlightened society and humanity's highest potential. It requires enlightened social and economic leaders who operate under the highest and most evolved ethical values and principles."

J ust because people do not vote does not mean they are apathetic or do not care about the health of our planet or humanity. As a simple example, 72 % of non-voters donate to charitable causes compared to nearly 86 % of voters who donate money. Forty-four percent of non-voters volunteer their time compared to 66 % of voters who volunteer.

An understanding of current voting trends is typically developed through demographics, yet traditional demographic analysis falls short of revealing the needs and desires of the populace as our society evolves. Conventional methods of distinguishing sections of our population require more detailed, discriminating consideration in order to understand the decline in voting participation and the extreme impact of language, marketing, and packaging that have become the hallmark of our elections and policy-making from local to national levels.

To break out of the confining and controlling parameters set by mass media and traditional campaign rhetoric, it is necessary to understand the extent to which traditional political polling and demographic concepts are used to box-in people's awareness and deliberately divide society into pockets of disconnection and disenfranchisement. Through the analysis of the *IOOW-2000* survey data, we empirically demonstrate that we can move in a new direction, one that supports the deep resonances of our hearts and minds rather than keeping us reliant on the external accoutrements of civilization.

IMPORTANT NOTE

Please keep in mind that this data was collected in early 2000. Its greatest value is in providing a set of real data from which to compare core values and beliefs of Americans relative to their voting inclinations. It is not intended to be a retrospective predictor of the 2000 election.

Elections and Society: Destabilization and Opportunities for Change

The U.S. national elections and declared candidates help to illuminate, as well as obfuscate, the shadow side of our society. In the U.S. today, we have a situation wherein:

- A significant portion of the potential electorate that would likely support positive change has been historically disaffected or discouraged

- The portion closer to being "change-agents" for a positive future paradigm are fragmented philosophically and organizationally

- One portion identifies more with maintaining an old way of life they have grown accustomed to

- Another portion is generally disengaged from society, and may fear positive change simply for lack of a higher vision

The social impact of the destruction the World Trade Center in 2001, the wars the U.S. has been waging against Iraq and other countries, the security state paranoia, loss of a free and independent mass media, and a generalized atmosphere of uncertainty among Americans has destabilized U.S. society and facilitated the loss of democratic rights without public discourse.

What this has created is a state of flux that allows those with a strong agenda (and the means to project and implement it) to set the "landscape" and the limits for national discussion and public awareness. The limits thus set allow only the narrowest of choices to be made, so narrow as to almost entirely remove awareness of our innate freedom to choose widely and wisely. However, this same state of flux can also permit new alternatives and strategies to be put forward by those who have only the most positive interests for humanity and our planet at heart.

The formal U.S. national election rules, laws, and established practices are designed to maintain control over political process and public discourse under the two nationally dominant political parties. Currently, national voting for a positive alternative to either of the two dominate parties, in effect, becomes a vote for that which you most oppose. Consequently, supporting positive future candidates for presidential and certain state-level races can appear to be self-defeating and at best a "protest vote." Naturally, many people want to change the voting rules to improve the chances of new alternatives. However, these rules serve to maintain the dominance the two main parties hold over national and most state elections. Therefore, it would be surprising if either would permit a change that could favor the rise of an independent challenge to their control over society. Here again, we see the importance of developing grass roots and other localized power. It is mainly at local and certain state levels that voting rules can be used to aid in the emergence of new alternatives for a positive future.

An estimated 59% of *eligible* voters actually voted in the 2004 election. With the presidential vote split roughly in half, that means approximately 30% of the potential voters decided the national elections for 70% of the population. In 2000, only 25% of potential voters helped decide the presidential election. These statistics are important to bear in mind, especially for those people who are most discouraged with the process, choices, and outcome of recent U.S. elections.

Of the 25% to 30% whose votes are used to decide the presidency, it is reasonable to assume that those who voted for the winning party's administration were not all motivated to the same extent ideologically. Many were concerned with their own personal material interests or swayed by fear-based propaganda that was carefully scripted to create an Orwellian sense of fear from a "threat of terrorism" or an equally Orwellian "war on terrorism." Additional considerations included a number of conservative religious and psycho-social factors specifically designed to manipulate socially traditional people who have often been more concerned with their religious and spiritual practices and community than with voting, regardless of who was running for office.

An important issue that needs to be raised is the current processes involving politics, elections, voting, and the purposeful segmenting of society to support the private agendas of an economic/political elite. An extraordinarily sophisticated propaganda machine has been unleashed upon a seemingly unwitting populace. Its tools are language, money and profit, and media monopolies. What we have been fed in recent elections is the idea that we are more segmented – and therefore less connected – than we actually are.

"Regardless of what position you may hold, important opportunities still exist in many States for alternative candidates and parties to make headway. Even greater opportunities for positive future-minded initiatives and leaders exist at county and other local levels."

"Voter Apathy?" Look Again

IOOW-2000 provides an original yet significant overview of U.S. election dynamics just prior to the 2000 election and, for the first time, makes sense of what has been obscured by disputes over voting irregularities and simple party affiliations. It points out the discrepancy between the dysfunctional paradigm of traditional voting patterns (defining and analyzing the population strictly for mass media-oriented campaigns) and that to which people truly aspire – not in terms of materialism but the intrinsic values that engender significance and meaning in one's life, in one's community, and on a global level.

By analyzing these election dynamics, a shift in perspective is possible that would allow society to explore a new paradigm that elevates and unifies American society and provides a beacon of encouragement and inspiration for all of humanity at all levels of being.

For example, those voters stigmatized in some circles as "the religious right" (corresponding somewhat to our own Social Traditional – Religious Conservative index) *do not all fall under that label.* We've been led to believe that people of the religious right are all about old-time religiosity and "might makes right." Granted, there is a large majority who fall under that description, but there are still many within that grouping that are very spiritually-oriented without being confined to old religious paradigms. How they comport themselves in society and how they vote are not necessarily what we might call "along party lines." For the purposes of those who wish to manipulate voting outcomes, a strict black/white, either/or barrage of propaganda is put forth. This manipulates not only what is termed "the liberal left," but *also* the religious right – the proverbial two birds with one stone scenario.

The propaganda geared toward the religious right is so carefully designed and implemented that seemingly intelligent people are easily and willingly used to propagate issues and platforms among these pre-defined constituencies and congregations – and pit them against others. This approach is based on the narrowest of perspectives: fear of the potential loss of home, family, and religious/moral values. In the black and white world of leaders of certain constituencies, divisiveness becomes the only outcome available: "You're either for me or against me."

As discord and fear are sown, various segments of the population feel more acutely the cold shoulder of being segmented, unsupported, and ignored. Such is the world of current politics and economic forces vying for positions of control, authority, and dominance.

The level of social disconnection and political disenfranchisement felt by so many people further plays into a downward spiral. (This shows up in such rationalizations as: "If you do not think the system can work, then why bother to participate?" or "If you don't participate, then doesn't this become a self-fulfilling scenario?")

To be sure, the current electoral zeitgeist is one of complexity and confusion. Therefore, in order to establish some common baseline concerning voting tendencies, let's first look at voting from a historical perspective and then, in Chapter 15, voting and how it was qualified in the *IOOW-2000* research.

An Historical Look at Elections

The roots of demographic analysis are found in the situational practicalities of polling methods. They have been used to identify differences within a population that can best be exploited to position a candidate in order to gain votes. This very process – powerfully reinforced by our mass media – tends to perpetuate itself by reinforcing superficial demographic variables. Traditional demographic factors, such as age, race, gender, ethnicity, income, education, political affiliations, etc., offer very little insight into what people identify with, aspire to, or hold as deeply important – all key factors influencing future behavior.

Historically, demographics have been a convenient and objective way to distinguish sections of the population having corresponding counterparts in society. Organizations and causes emerged clearly associated with certain segments of the population, civil rights, movements for economic and workplace improvement, women's right to vote, etc. Over time, these affiliations and demographic associations could be quickly identified and negotiated with to manipulate voting blocs. The more reliable these organizations proved to be in maintaining social order by providing a "reasonable" conduit between their constituencies and those who held power, promises of greater influence were made to these organizations' leaders.

The result was social and economic improvements that paradoxically reinforced differences. One example of this can be seen in the history of trade unions not supporting civil rights. Another example would be the false conflicts that arose between those championing environmental quality and those who feared loss of job security and material well being.

On one hand, it could be argued that this is a way for people to make their voices heard. As a convenient channel through which to negotiate votes, it also works in reverse. It reinforces the divisions of society to the extent the process is successful in manipulating voting behavior.

2000 Presidential Election

- Voting age population: 211 million
- Voting eligible population: 194 million
- Votes for president   105 million
- Voting age turnout: 50%
- Turnout eligible voters: 54%

2004 Presidential Election (preliminary)

- Voting age population: 218 million
- Voting eligible population: 204 million
- Votes for president   121 million
- Voting age turnout: 55%
- Turnout eligible voters: 59%

– Source: U.S. Federal Election Commission, U.S. Census, Infoplease, Brookings Institution

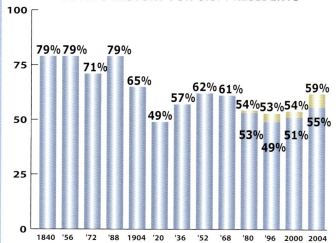

Important note concerning voting turnout:

Over the past 30 years, the difference in voter turnout has grown between what is officially reported as voting age population versus eligible voting population. Additionally, the percentage of people who are ineligible to vote – non-citizens, prison population, etc. – has increased dramatically. Depending on how turnout is calculated, it can be shown that the apparent decline in voting participation is much less than official statistics suggest. Nevertheless, over the last 30 years, voting participation has continued to be low by longer historical standards.

We have shown in the above bar graph the approximate percentage point spread between these two ways of calculating voter turnout for the presidential election.

In the year 2000 and more so in 2004, many questions have yet to be answered as to voting "irregularities" that could affect the total votes cast, as well as which candidate won the popular election.

Decline in Voting Participation

Historically, between Presidents William Henry Harrison (elected in 1840) and William McKinley (elected in 1900), approximately 70% to 80% of eligible adults participated in the presidential elections, or 77% on average. (The Emancipation Proclamation was issued January 1, 1863.) From the election of President Theodore Roosevelt in 1904 to President John F. Kennedy in 1960, this rate declined fairly steadily to 63%. As a point of reference relative to "social discouragement," voter turnout dropped to 34% in 1930 at the beginning of the Great Depression. The 2000 U.S. elections resulted in a near-equally split House and Senate and the election of a U.S. president *with less than 25% of the eligible vote.*

Political analysts generally accept recent historical voting patterns and look for ways to provide marginal changes in voting. In the absence of a truly aware and involved electorate, a majority of national-level political campaigns are generally guided by a combination of personal egos, key financial supporters, political-economic architects, and research and media strategists.

The dominance of "power brokering," as a way to shift policy and leadership votes, also tends to marginalize those citizens who do not have high social-economic standing. Thus, those who are less likely to vote continue to be discouraged from voting – in terms of personal perception of feeling "disenfranchised," as well as by the persistent and systemic, top-down influence favoring citizens who are materially better off.

Election Packaging and Marketing

The general pattern in U.S. elections over recent decades has increasingly relied on a heavy product-marketing approach – in effect the packaging and selling of a candidate to special interests and then to the voters, and vice versa. The influence of political research strategists usually means that, based on recent historic voting patterns, enormous portions of the American public are nearly "written off" as "soft votes" or "non-voters." Sophisticated candidates and campaigns have become clever at spinning or omitting information – as well as *appearing* to embrace whatever values research shows will best manipulate voters.

For example, in the 2000 election campaign, if a candidate needed to convey more appeal to religious (mistakenly equated with spiritual) voters, he, a spokesperson, running mate, or other suitable stand-in was brought before the news media and public gatherings to deliver speeches referencing God, spirit, and other key words representing themes that polling groups had identified could strengthen their position. If new polling tested this new theme and determined it was sufficiently successful, then more of it would be used in like manner. Conversely, if polling determined these new "themes" failed to contribute to positive public or media perception – and eventually votes – they would be dropped or modified.

Guided by the weight of past history and by crassly marketing themselves like so many consumer products, it is not surprising that most candidates and their campaigns help perpetuate a situation whereby a small majority of the population votes and those who attain elected office do so with a small minority of public support. This is one of the by-products of a culture and society so heavily dominated by a social and economic paradigm that reduces nearly everything to a commodity.

If an entire society has established that progress is measured by growth of revenues and profits, and how a nation measures its well being is indicated by gross national production and economic data, then is it any wonder that nearly half of our eligible population does not see fit to participate in presidential elections? Given a structurally imbedded system designed to discourage genuine alternatives, is it possible to encourage a new social movement and develop new types of leaders possessing high moral and intellectual integrity – and who stand for a positive future?

We believe it is both essential and possible.

CHAPTER 15

IOOW-2000 Research and Political Demographics

"A New America presents sophisticated social science research and analysis that makes this an extraordinary treasure-trove of insight into American society circa 2000."

To help orient you to the *IOOW-2000* values-related analysis, let us first present a selection of voting related data from that research. Necessarily, this chapter is comprised mostly of demographic data. This is the common language of the mainstream voting discussion, so we address it in its "native language," demographics.

While any number of topics from the *IOOW-2000* can be compared to voting information, for the sake of brevity, we chose to present only a small portion of common topics and themes.

Why do we have a chapter on traditional political demographics? Simply put, it is prerequisite to less traditional approaches such as value-based typologies. If you like, skip ahead to the next chapter on Values-based Typologies and Voting, then come back to this chapter for a little more detail.

Chapter 15 At A Glance

IOOW-2000 Research and Political Demographics

- Voting Patterns in America
- Candidate
- Party
- "Ideology"
- Complexity in Combinations
- Candidate by Party
- Party by Ideology
- Candidate by Ideology
- Candidate by Ideology and Party
- Preferring No Candidate or Not Voting
- Volunteering, Donating, and Not Voting
- Generation and Gender
- Religiousness, Spirituality, and Voting

Why is this data relevant now? First, the *IOOW-2000* research focuses on values and beliefs that are more stable than temporary opinions. Second, the candidates involved are still very much in circulation today. Third, these dynamics will continue to drive Americans, no matter how much the public is manipulated and misdirected. Lastly, the data was collected early on in the election cycle before most of the media and campaign "spin" took place.

Our purpose here is not to predict election outcomes, rather to provide useable and valuable insight into American values and voting. Again, please remember that most of our election data was collected in the early part of 2000, at the early primary period, many months before the actual election.

Voting Patterns in America

In taking a more traditional look at voting patterns, party or ideology identification, it is important to separate likely voters from those who are not likely to vote. As the example to the right shows, by eliminating those people who did not support any candidate and selecting those people who said they were highly likely to vote, a more accurate representation of future "likely behavior" can be made. The purpose of the exercise is not to demonstrate retrospective predictive accuracy, but rather to provide a clearer contrast in analyzing weak voters from strong voters with regard to core values.

Considering recent history, 84% saying "highly or somewhat likely" to vote over-estimates actual voting behavior (given that only 51.2% of eligible Americans actually voted in 2000). Inflation of an indicator can be attributed to pro-social responses bias to a given question. Essentially, when you ask somebody if he or she *intends* to do something "good," there is a very strong bias to answer in the affirmative. As we can see, one single question measuring intent (and one that also has pro-social bias) does not make a very useful indicator.

We next examined choice of candidate as an indicator of voting. Removing those who said they were only "somewhat likely" would give us 73% respondents more likely to actually vote. However, this is still too far removed from the actual voting turnout.

In examining the candidate choice question, 78% of respondents selected a candidate. It was also found that 22% who said they were *highly likely* to vote had no answer when asked for which presidential candidate they would vote. While some portion of these people may eventually prefer a candidate as voting day draws closer, experience with political polling data indicates most of these people are likely to be soft voters or non-voters. Because our purposes were to examine values and beliefs, not to predict election results, it was important to find a way to provide a useful contrast between strong voters and those who are considered "soft," unlikely, or non-voters.

By combining the responses of those people who were less than "highly likely" to vote with those people who did not provide a candidate response, a practical, reliable criterion was created to provide contrast between likely and unlikely voters.

By examining answers to *"Which presidential candidate would you vote for?"* one could infer that if a person had preferred a candidate, he or she would also actually vote for that choice on Election Day. However, this question was asked in a hypothetical format *"If the election were held tomorrow, which presidential candidate would you vote for?"* People may change their minds over time, and simply choosing a candidate says nothing about how strongly a person endorses their choice. Choosing a candidate, but *weakly* endorsing that choice, is not as indicative of a vote as choosing a candidate and *strongly* endorsing that choice. A more useful indicator of voting behavior would include a *combination* of making *a clear choice of candidate* combined with a *strong intention to vote.*

Since a more reasonable indicator of voting behavior would include *both* preferring a candidate *and* being likely to vote, we created a combined factor in which respondents who preferred an actual candidate, *and* who said they were "Highly Likely" to vote were coded as being "Likely" voters – while all others (those who preferred "None" and who were not "Highly Likely" to vote) were coded as being "Not Likely" voters.

With this more accurate combination (of preferring a real candidate and being highly likely to vote), only 55% of Americans were likely voters. *(This percentage more closely matches the actual popular vote turnout of 51.2%.)*

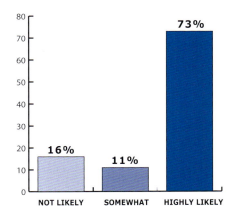

HOW LIKELY ARE YOU TO VOTE?
Percent of all respondents

Overall, 84% of the *IOOW-2000* respondents indicated they were "highly or somewhat likely" to vote in the 2000 presidential election, 11% were somewhat likely, and 16% said they were not likely to vote.

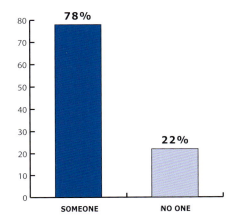

CHOOSE A CANDIDATE?
Percent of all respondents

78% of all respondents chose a candidate while 22% did not.

CHOOSING A CANDIDATE AND LIKELY TO VOTE

Percent of all respondents

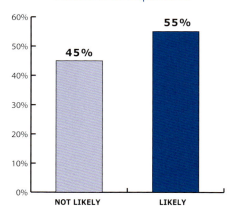

Combined Factor as Indication of Likelihood to Vote:

- Highly Likely to Vote: 73%

- Chose a Candidate: 78%

- Highly likely to Vote combined with Choosing a Candidate = > 55% "Most Likely to Vote"

As such, we employed this indicator in examining how "likelihood to vote" related to various demographic variables, core values, and personal traits. In more sophisticated political models intended to analyze and predict specific election outcomes, a number of factors, including precinct-level and other geographic-demographic data are used to adjust survey data to achieve a more accurate projection.

It is this combination of candidate choice and likelihood to vote that is used here throughout, unless otherwise noted, to distinguish strong voters from weak or soft voters.

We ask the reader to bear in mind that the *IOOW-2000* election data was collected several months prior to voting day. It is important to emphasize again that the goal of the *IOOW-2000* research was *not* to predict the election outcome. To make more accurate estimates of likely election outcomes requires interviewing over longer time periods and statistical adjustments for telephone access, geographical differences, historic patterns, exit polls, and other factors. Nevertheless, the *IOOW-2000* research succeeded in comparing voters impressions of candidates, estimating voting likelihood, and comparing traditional political identification with radically new values-based typologies. That this information can be related to a wide range of socio-cultural categories of lifestyles, media habits, and much more makes this an extraordinary treasure-trove of insight into American society circa 2000.

While there are many seemingly unique reasons people may have for not voting, what it usually comes down to is that they are simply not motivated enough. Familiar themes among non-voters include:

- Lack of relevant meaningful choices in candidates
- Lack of relevant or meaningful information
- Feeling their vote won't matter
- Belief that the "system" cannot be changed or is rigged, no matter who is elected
- Personal concerns overshadow social concerns
- Philosophical, ideological, religious, or other principles preclude participation

It is our hope that enough people, voters and non-voters alike, will find not only clarity but the impetus to participate as voting citizens – engaged in finding avenues of connection and commonality that inspire Americans and the global family – in evolving toward a more positive future.

As you study the data breakdowns in the following sections, you'll not be surprised at the figures – the outcome of the 2000 elections is a moot point. It is in Chapters 16 and 17 that the "heart" of our electoral process is revealed: our shared values that dispel the notion that we are living in separate realities with nothing in common to connect and unify us.

But, let's begin with a traditional analysis of the *IOOW-2000* research data.

Candidate

"If the election were held tomorrow, which one of the following presidential candidates would you vote for?"

To show the contrast between general sentiments among the population as a whole, the first graphic shows candidate preference for all respondents and the second graph shows candidate preference only for those most likely to vote.

For those least likely to vote, 72% preferred None of the possible 2000 presidential candidates, followed by Bush (12%), Gore (9%), McCain (3%), and finally, Others (4%).

In contrast, those respondents who were both highly likely to vote and who chose a candidate, the ranking was: Bush (41% of likely voters), Gore (25% of likely voters), McCain (18% of likely voters), and Others (16% of likely voters).

The odds of voting (simply by choice of candidate) were fairly evenly split: Bush supporters (89% likely), Gore supporters (86% likely), McCain supporters (92% likely), and supporters for Other candidates (90% likely).

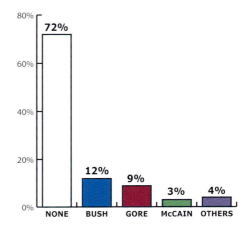

CANDIDATE PREFERENCE

Percent of respondents least likely to vote

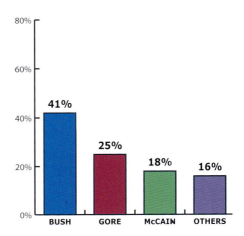

CANDIDATE PREFERENCE

Percent of respondents most likely to vote

PARTY PREFERENCE

Least likely to vote

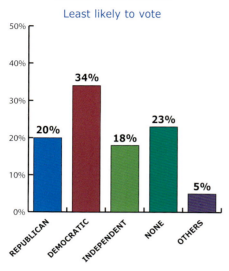

Party

"Regardless of your actual voter registration, how would you describe your political orientation?" (Democrat, Republican, Independent, Libertarian, Green Party, None, or Other)

To provide the greatest contrast, the first graphic shows party preference for those least likely to vote and the second graph shows those most likely to vote and choose a candidate.

In examining those least likely to vote, 34% were Democrats, 23% did not identify with any party (None), 20% were Republicans, 18% were Independents, and 5% were of some other party.

For those most likely to vote, the ranking was: Republicans (43% of likely voters), Democrats (33% of likely voters), Independents (15% of likely voters), None (6% of likely voters), and Others (3% of likely voters).

Republicans showed higher odds of voting (75% likely) than did Democrats (57% likely), Independents (53% likely), or Other/None (32% likely).

"Ideology"

"Which of the following best describes your political ideology?" (Most Conservative, Conservative, Moderate, Liberal, or Most Liberal)

For those least likely to vote, 5% placed themselves as Most Conservative, 32% as Conservative, 38% as Moderate, 22% as Liberal, and 4% as Most Liberal. In contrast, of those most likely to vote, 12% were Most Conservative, 40% were Conservative, 34% were were Moderate, 13% were Liberal, and 2% were Most Liberal.

Conservatives showed higher odds of voting (68% likely) than did Moderates (58% likely) or Liberals (46% likely). (The term "ideology" has lost most of its historical meaning with the mass marketing of candidates and sound bites for public consumption.)

PARTY PREFERENCE

Most likely to vote

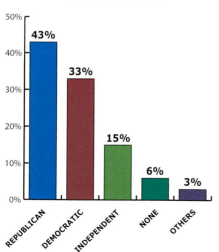

Complexity in Combinations

At this point, we have only examined three typical Political Demographic variables – Candidate, Party, and Ideology – against likelihood to vote.

As you can imagine, the complexity of trying to derive anything useful from ordinary demographic analyses becomes quite daunting when looking at them *in combination* (i.e., Candidate by Party by Ideology) with other population characteristics such as age, gender, geography, socio-economic status, etc. For example, four candidate choices (Bush, Gore, McCain, and Others) by three Parties by three Ideologies results in a statistical "pie" with 36 slices.

For readers who enjoy looking at complex patterns, at the end of Chapter 16 we present a visual overlay on the PFCI-SMS quadrant of Candidate, Party, and Ideology.

It is important to note that the analysis you'll be reviewing throughout the rest of this chapter is seen through the view scope of traditional demographic analysis. This analysis points out is two clear insights:

- not everyone votes the same way and how they vote is dependent on a number of variables that traditional demographic surveys cannot hope to illuminate;

- the American populace can be easily manipulated and exploited by the agendas of others when, as As a society, we maintain allegiances to self-identifying concepts such as "traditional," "conservative," and "family/social values" – all of which have been defined by a small but virulent segment of American society.

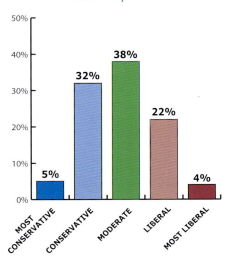

POLITICAL "IDEOLOGY"
Least likely to vote

POLITICAL "IDEOLOGY"
Most likely to vote

REPUBLICANS

Most likely to vote

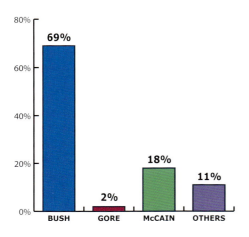

What this leads to is a state of protective-reactive behavior, a lack of high level discernment, discouragement of independent thinking, and communities held hostage to a perceived chaotic world of fear and distrust.

Chapter 16 provides us with data analysis through the view scope of the values-based typology of The 8 American Types – a much more significant and descriptive understanding of Americans. As shown in Parts One and Two, it is through our heart-centered values and principles that America has the potential to create a more positive future.

As you read these data-oriented chapters, be aware that there may be slight variations due to multiple variables producing results slightly different than reported with single variables.

DEMOCRATS

Most likely to vote

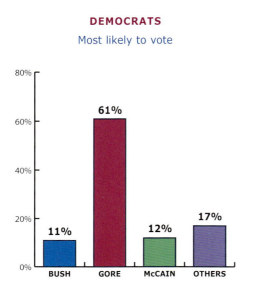

INDEPENDENT

Most likely to vote

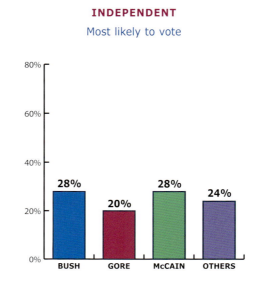

OTHER OR NO PARTY

Most likely to vote

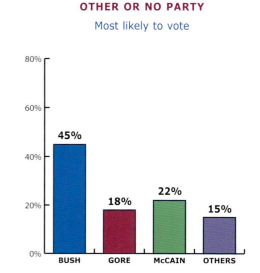

Candidate by Party

For those respondents who were most likely to vote, we have separated these candidate preference by party identification.

- 69% of Republicans preferred Bush, 2% preferred Gore, 18% preferred McCain, and 11% preferred someone else for president.

- 11% of Democrats preferred Bush, 61% preferred Gore, 12% preferred McCain, and 17% preferred someone else.

- 28% of Independents preferred Bush, 20% preferred Gore, 28% preferred McCain, and 24% preferred someone else for president.

- For those who identified with some other or no party, 45% preferred Bush, 18% preferred Gore, 22% preferred McCain, and 15% preferred someone else.

Party by Ideology

In looking at the total population of those least likely to vote,

- 13% placed themselves as Republican/Conservative, 6% as Republican/Moderate, and 1% as Republican/Liberal

- 9% placed themselves as Democrat/Conservative, 16% as Democrat/Moderate, and 12% as Democrat/Liberal

- 15% placed themselves as Other or Non-affiliated/Conservative, 16% as Other/Moderate, and 13% as Other/Liberal.

For those most likely to vote,

- 33% placed themselves as Republican/Conservative, 10% as Republican/Moderate, and 1% as Republican/Liberal

- 9% placed themselves as Democrat/Conservative, 13% as Democrat/Moderate, and 10% as Democrat/Liberal

- 9% placed themselves as Other or Non-affiliated/Conservative, 11% as Other/Moderate, and 4% as Other/Liberal.

Overall, Republicans were predominantly Conservative, Democrats were Moderate or Liberal, Independents were Conservative or Moderate, Libertarians tended more toward Moderate, and those who chose "Other" tended to be Conservative or Moderate.

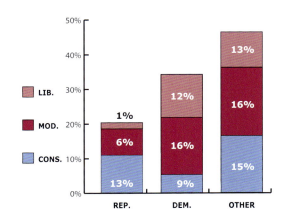

PARTY BY "IDEOLOGY"
Least likely to vote

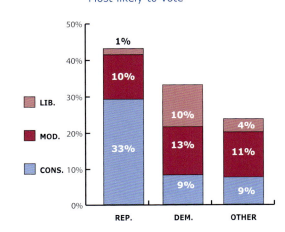

PARTY BY "IDEOLOGY"
Most likely to vote

Overall, Republicans placing themselves as Most Conservative or Conservative were especially likely to vote, as were Moderate Democrats, Moderate Independents, Moderate or Liberal Libertarians, and Moderate Non-affiliated. Weakest in terms of likelihood to vote were Moderate or Liberal Republicans, and Conservative or Liberal Democrats. Interestingly, Moderate Democrats and Conservative Republicans were also likely to be non-voters, as well as voters.

Democrats and Others most chose None as a candidate, with little variation across Ideology. This suggests that Conservative Republicans collectively liked what they saw in Bush and his party platform, while others did not have any one clear candidate or platform to attract their votes.

Candidate by Ideology

In examining candidate by "ideology" for those respondents who were most likely to vote, the following breakdown was obtained for the main candidates:

Bush: 19% Most Conservative, 55% Conservative, 23% Moderate, 3% Liberal

Gore: 3% most Conservative, 22% Conservative, 42% Moderate, 28% Liberal, and 5% Most Liberal

McCain: 6% Most Conservative, 35% Conservative, 47% Moderate, 11% Liberal, and 1% Most Liberal

Other candidates: 13% Most Conservative, 32% Conservative, 35% Moderate, 17% Liberal, and 3% Most Liberal.

In examining those people who were most likely to vote and who chose a candidate, 60% who placed themselves as some type of Conservative supported Bush, 12% supported Gore, 15% supported McCain, and 14% supported some other candidate. Among Moderates, 31% supported Gore, 29% supported Bush, 25% supported McCain, and 16% supported some other candidate. Of Liberals 56% supported Gore, 9% supported Bush, 14% supported McCain, and 21% supported some other candidate.

In examining those people least likely to vote, there was no discernible difference for Party and Ideology.

CANDIDATE BY "IDEOLOGY"

Most likely to vote

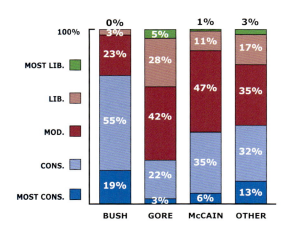

Candidate by Ideology and Party

For respondents who identified themselves as Conservative Democrats predominantly chose Gore (37%), followed by Bush (23%), None (22%), Other (11%) and McCain (7%). Conservative Republicans chose Bush (65%) followed by McCain (13%), None (11%), and Other (9%). Conservative Independents chose Bush (27%), followed by None (26%), McCain (20%), Others (18%), and Gore (10%). Those people who placed themselves as Conservative Other party mostly chose None (41%), followed by Bush (33%), Gore (9%), McCain (7%), and Other candidate (9%).

Respondents who identified themselves as Moderate Democrats predominantly chose Gore (48%), followed by None (22%), McCain (11%), Bush (9%), and Other candidate (11%). Moderate Republicans chose Bush (46%), followed by McCain (26%), None (16%), Other candidates (12%). Moderate Independents mostly chose no candidate (28%), followed by Bush (22%), McCain (21%), Gore (16%), and Other candidate (14%). Moderates of Other mostly chose McCain (33%) followed by Bush (22%), None (22%), Gore (11%), and Other candidates (11%).

Respondents who identified themselves as Liberal Democrats predominantly chose Gore (58%), followed by Other candidates (16%), None (15%), McCain (7%), and Bush (4%). Of the 6% who were Liberal Republicans, most chose Bush (67%). Liberal Independents mostly chose None (32%), followed by Gore (27%), and Other candidates (24%). Those who placed as Liberal Other party, most preferred no candidate (46%), followed by McCain (31%), Gore (15%), and Bush (8%).

When the likelihood to vote was compared to party-ideology-candidate, there were a few situations where it made no difference to candidate, party, or ideology whether someone was likely to vote or not. Those included Democrats and those people who preferred "Other parties."

LEAST LIKELY TO VOTE BY PARTY

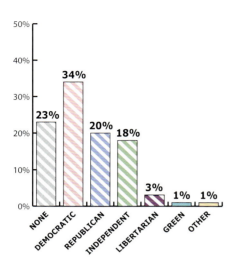

Preferring No Candidate or Not Voting

Now, what about the 22 % of people who in the first half of 2000 did not like any of the candidates – or the 16 % who stated that they were not likely to vote?

As common sense suggests, those respondents who actually chose a candidate (as opposed to None) would seem more likely to vote. When examining traditional political demographics (candidate, party, and ideology) Conservative Republicans were most likely to vote, and they most preferred Bush as their candidate. Those least likely to vote were Moderate Others, Moderate Democrats, Conservative Others, and Liberal Others. At this level of analysis, we simply see the effects of one strongly aligned cohort (Conservative Republicans) out-weighing all the other various combinations – whose voting was lower (in terms of overall likelihood), and whose choices of candidates were more diverse. This choice frequently included None.

Gender was not a significant factor in terms of strong likelihood to vote. Social-economic ranking was one of a number of significant factors – in that people with higher income and/or higher educational backgrounds were most likely to vote. Age also was a strong factor with older generations most likely to vote and the younger generations least likely to vote.

A values-based typology provides more useful insight. First and foremost was the dramatic relationship between likelihood to vote and the Social Material Stress (SMS) scale. If you placed high on this measure, chances were you would not vote. If you placed low, chances were you would vote.

LEAST LIKELY TO VOTE BY "IDEOLOGY"

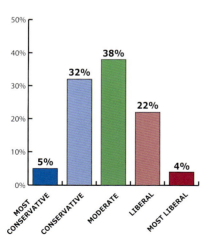

The more a respondent was involved in traditional religious activities, the more likely they were to vote. Of those who closely identified with the *older* Christian religions, 61 % were most likely to vote. Of those who identified with the *newer* Christian religions, only 50 % were most likely to vote. (Going to religious services is often closely associated with other traditional values and beliefs, such as a civic duty to vote.)

Democrats who chose None as a candidate showed a higher incidence of being either Liberal (42 %) or Conservative (35 %). Republicans who chose None showed a higher incidence of being Conservative (66%). Others who chose None showed a higher incidence of being Liberal (33%). Democrats who chose Somebody as a candidate showed a higher incidence of being either Moderate (43%) or Liberal (29%). Republicans who chose Somebody showed a higher incidence of being Conservative (74%). Others who chose Somebody showed a higher incidence of being Moderate (46%).

Once again, Conservative Republicans showed a much higher likelihood of choosing a candidate than did any other Party/Ideology. Democrats and Others most chose None as a candidate, with little variation across Ideology. This suggests that Conservative Republicans liked what they saw in Bush and his party platform, while others did not have any one clear candidate or platform to attract their votes.

Volunteering, Donating, and Not Voting

Are people *not likely to vote* completely uninvolved? One simple indicator is the reported extent of volunteering or donating of money. Another would be the strength of responses to the question of wanting to be involved in making a better world.

As we might expect, those who are more likely to vote are also more likely to volunteer and donate.

However, the fact that 72% of those people who were less likely to vote do donate, and 44% do volunteer, and that 90% of those who were not likely to vote do want to be involved in making a difference in the world tells us that eligible voters who are discouraged from voting or have a low interest in voting should not to be written off as hopelessly apathetic.

Americans who engaged in volunteer activities and who made charitable donations were also more likely to vote. These tendencies both increased as income increased. Volunteering and donating were also related to wanting to be more personally involved in creating a better world at local and global levels. (Americans who were likely to vote – but who did less volunteering and donating – were less likely to agree that they wanted to be more personally involved in creating a better world).

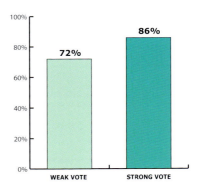

DONATE MONEY TO CHARITABLE CAUSES AND VOTING LIKELIHOOD

Percentage of all respondents

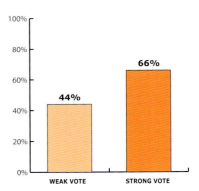

VOLUNTEER TIME TO CAUSES AND VOTING LIKELIHOOD

Percentage of all respondents

GENERATION AND GENDER COMPARISON

Generation by likely to vote

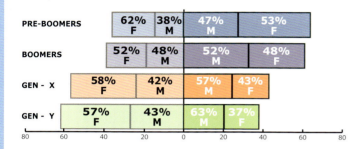

PRE-BOOMERS	62% F	38% M	47% M	53% F
BOOMERS	52% F	48% M	52% M	48% F
GEN - X	58% F	42% M	57% M	43% F
GEN - Y	57% F	43% M	63% M	37% F

80 60 40 20 0 20 40 60 80

LEAST LIKELY TO VOTE   **MOST LIKELY TO VOTE**

Generations

The *IOOW-2000* research collected age data in such a way as to permit analysis by various age groups, including generational. In our usage, the following age compositions were used:

- "Generation-Y" (born after 1978) 7.9% of respondents

- "Generation-X" (born 1965 - 1977) 25.4% of respondents

- "Baby boomers" (born 1946 - 1964) 37.3% of respondents

- "Pre-boomers" (born before 1946) 29.4% of respondents

In conducting most analyses, those 9.6% of unknown age due to refusals were excluded.

Generation and Gender

Demographers have divided the U.S. population into the following generations:

- Pre-Boomers - born before 1946 (55 + yrs)

- Baby Boomers - born 1946 - 1964 (36 to 55 yrs)

- Generation X - born 1965 - 1977 (23 to 36)

- Generation Y - born 1978 and later (18 to 23)

When looking at generation breakdown among The 8 American Types,

- SCT and WNL types have the most noticeable concentration of Pre-Boomers and are the least likely to include Gen-X or Gen-Y individuals.

- ETV has the most noticeable concentration of baby boomers and are also among those least likely to include Gen-X or Gen-Y individuals.

- DSC, and PA have noticeable concentrations of those in the 18-36 age range and are joined by those CSE types who to a lesser extent include those of younger generations. DSC and PA types are least likely to include older individuals of the pre-boomer generation.

- CC and CMW types had no outstanding generational differences whatsoever.

Women are generally less likely to vote than men and remain undecided about who their candidate choice for a longer period. Younger women of Gen-X and Gen-Y ages are conspicuously least likely to vote (twice as likely to not vote in those respective age groups). The older a person is, the more likely is they will vote (baby boomer and pre-boomer groups are almost twice as likely to vote as Gen-X and Gen-Y).

In comparing the "single women" vote, it was found that this demographic was more likely than expected to vote for Gore (57%) and less likely than expected to vote for Bush (39%). None and Others were holding at the 48% level. Once women who were least likely to vote were removed, the only significant difference was between Bush (men) and Gore (women). Single females are more likely than expected to be affiliated with the Democratic Party (59%) and less likely with the Republican Party (38%).

Whites were more likely to vote than non-whites. The only clear difference in candidate preference, regardless of voting likelihood, was between Bush (white) and Gore (non-white).

On the question of politicians having higher and more evolved moral and ethical values than themselves, older men and women pre-boomers were most likely to strongly agree – and women more so than men. Younger men who are most likely to vote are also most likely to disagree, as well as neither agree nor disagree.

This raises an important point as to why this question does not evoke a more clear response in favor of higher and more evolved moral and ethical values among younger people.

It could be due to a general immaturity that feeds a "child-parent rejection dynamic." The civil protections advocated by previous generations may be seen as "establishment" prerogatives that succeeding generations generally tend to want to resist and break down. It could also be due to a lack of awareness of common sense and Constitutional rights and responsibilities. A recent major study showed that only half of U.S. high school students thought that newspapers should be allowed to publish freely, and over one third thought that newspapers should get government approval before publishing.

One would think the impetus toward a free society is deeply ingrained in our collective psyche. Clearly, it is not as evidenced by the *IOOW-2000* study, as well as recent research on awareness of constitutional rights. This is of even graver concern in the face of our country being presented with various manufactured, as well as real "threats of terrorism" within our own boundaries, Right now, we have an immediate threat to Democracy by a growing state security apparatus. Worse yet is that the younger generations that are eligible to vote do not have anywhere near the same sense of "moral" or "ethical" values as the pre-boomers in their "thought lexicon." A parental/generational dynamic feeds into the disassembling by younger generations of the rules and conventions supported by previous generations. (Pre-boomers are the closest generation to World War II, of which one aspect was to stop fascism.)

"Freedom's just another word for nothin' left to lose."

– Janis Joplin, lyrics from "Me and Bobby McGee"

Constitutional Rights and Future of Democracy

High school students are less likely than adults to think people should be allowed to express unpopular opinions or that newspapers should be allowed to publish freely without government approval of stories.

- While 83% of high school students do agree that people should be allowed to express unpopular opinions, one–third think the First Amendment goes too far with the rights it guarantees.

- 75% of high school students lack basic knowledge of our constitutional rights to freedom of expression.

- Only 51% of high school students agree that "newspapers should be able to publish freely without government approval of a story." Only 24% strongly agreed.

- 52% of students either do not know about the First Amendment rights or have not taken classes in which this was discussed. Of this group, only 68% agree that people should be allowed to express unpopular opinions.

    – from the Future of the First Amendment, John S. and James L. Knight Foundation – Research included 112,000 students from 544 high schools across the country in 2004

The Preamble of the Constitution for the United States of America

"We the People of the United States, in Order to form a more perfect Union, establish Justice, insure domestic Tranquility, provide for the common defense, promote the general Welfare, and secure the Blessings of Liberty to ourselves and our Posterity, do ordain and establish this Constitution for the United States of America."

The First Amendment of the U.S. Constitution on Freedom of Religion, Press, and Expression

"Congress shall make no law respecting an establishment of religion, or prohibiting the free exercise thereof; or abridging the freedom of speech, or of the press; or the right of the people peaceably to assemble, and to petition the Government for a redress of grievances."

Viewed broadly through a large generational lens, one could say that perhaps the pre-boomer generation fought to stop fascism and permit the continued growth of a capitalist form of democracy. Perhaps this was necessary so the boomer generation would live in a free enough society so they could have the experience of the '60s and '70s, which was about challenging old beliefs and values and experimenting with new ways of thinking and living as a next step for society. This often challenged and confronted the "establishment" through cultural forms such as music and social and political protest. At the core of this was a small but significant portion of the boomer generation, most of whom today are most identified with various social, cultural, political, and progressive ideas. As of yet, they have barely tasted the fruits.

Despite this, there could be a new ethos emerging among young people – the Gen-X and Gen-Y who could be part of such an evolutionary generational process – that is still too new to be defined. For those of the boomer generation who participated or somehow shared in the experience of the '60s and '70s, there was a desire for freedom of expression, freedom to explore, and freedom to try something different as expressed and shared through music and other forms.

Given the current crisis on all fronts, it is critically imperative that the members of the pre-boomer and boomer generations who are leading edge "change agents," cooperate and establish bridges with young people now. Out of this needs to emerge a new type of leadership for a positive future.

Religiousness, Spirituality, and Voting

Americans who were more likely to vote were also likely to attend church more frequently. Moreover, those who attend church weekly or more often preferred Bush. As discussed in earlier chapters, religion and spirituality are not the same. A worldview that embraces God or higher consciousness and also embraces diversity, tolerance, forgiveness and a sense of the sacred in our surroundings is not the same worldview held by those who score high on the Social Traditional – Religious Conservative index.

When we combine the measures of Social Material Stress (SMS) with Social Traditional – Religious Conservative (STRC), we find that the largest portion of people who voted for Bush were *low* SMS and *high* STRC, with a smaller, secondary portion who were *high* SMS and *high* STRC. Those who preferred Gore were *low* on both of these measures, with a smaller secondary component who were *low* STRC and *high* SMS. Those who were low on both measures also preferred some other candidate. McCain was somewhat preferred by those in the *middle* SMS-STRC zone.

Those who didn't want any candidate were high SMS, regardless of their placement on the STRC measure. It is worth making an important generalization here: people who tend to be "low" on the SMS scale are people who derive *material* benefit from their lifestyle. One could say they believe that their reality of American society "works" for them.

It was only among those people of the older Christian traditions that Bush scored higher, and only by a few percentage points. Overall, all Christian affiliations responded closely in line with national averages – suggesting that the "religious-conservative" vote in 2000 was not as strong on the Republican-Bush "flavor "as their campaign machine would have everyone believe. This further reinforces why such crass and negative sentiments were employed by the Republican-Bush campaign in 2004 to stimulate religious-traditionalists to vote.

It is significant, however, that those people of the newer traditions preferred no candidate, something that carried forward to the 2004 elections, as well as when they were targeted by Republican agitation campaigns that emphasized reactionary and negative morality factors and relied heavily on church hierarchies to get out the vote for Bush.

Furthermore, for all the talk about the "religious" vote for Bush – a distortion in its own right – it was only McCain who attracted voters, those who rank in the upper quartile of the Spirituality Index, a measurement that does not exclude key factors measuring traditional religious expression. However, in widening the criteria of the Spirituality Index to a simple median, both McCain and Gore attracted comparable proportions of very spiritually-oriented people.

The research data did not acquire large over-sampling of non-Christians, therefore very little analysis can be made concerning them. However, the majority of others, including those who simply didn't identify with

---

IOOW-2000 Categories of Religious Expression

- "Christian I" includes Baptist and other mainline Protestants such as Methodist, Episcopalian, Church of England (Anglican), Presbyterian, Lutheran, AME, Roman and Orthodox Catholics, Greek Orthodox, Eastern Orthodox, Church of God in Christ, Disciples of Christ.

- "Christian II" religions include Mormons, Jehovah's Witnesses, Seventh Day Adventists, Quakers, Unitarians, Pentecostals, Assembly of God, Church of Nazarene, Christian Science, Molokans, Anabaptists, Mennonites, and Non-denominational Christian.

- "Middle Eastern/Asian" includes Buddhism, Hinduism, Islam, Sufism, and Baha'i.

- "New Thought" includes Native American Church, Wicca, New Age, Spiritualism, Free Thinker, etc.

- "Judaism"

- "Non-Believers"

– from *IOOW-2000* Research

The Religious Landscape – 2004 Election Survey

	Percent Population	Voter turnout
ALL	100.0%	60.8%
Evangelical Protestant	26.3	63%
Traditionalist Evangelical	12.6	69%
Centrist Evangelical	10.8	52%
Modernist Evangelical	2.9	65%
Mainline Protestant	16.0	69%
Traditionalist Mainline	4.3	78%
Centrist Mainline	7.0	68%
Modernist Mainline	4.7	71%
Latino Protestants	2.8	49%
Black Protestants	9.6	50%
Catholic	17.5	67%
Traditionalist Catholic	4.4	77%
Centrist Catholic	8.1	58%
Modernist Catholic	5.0	70%
Latino Catholic	4.5	43%
Other Christian	2.7	60%
Other Faiths	2.7	62%
Jewish	1.9	87%
Unaffiliated	16.0	52%
Unaffiliated Believers	5.3	39%
Secular	7.5	55%
Atheist, Agnostic	3.2	61%

Source: The American Religious Landscape and the 2004 Presidential Vote: Increased Polarization - Fourth National Survey of Religion and Politics, conducted November-December 2004 at the University of Akron.It had 2,730 re-interviews of surveys conducted in the spring of 2004 (a margin of error) For additional background refer to the Appendix.

any religion or who simply refused to answer, placed in the lower range of the Spirituality Index. Those people of older Christian traditions are distributed in a fairly average manner across the Spirituality Index. Those of the newer Christian tendencies tended to place in the upper range of the Spirituality Index.

Clearly, we have shown in this chapter that basic political demographic information is useful but only to a limited extent. Hopefully we have provided some background data that will be useful in its own right, as well as helpful in moving on to the next chapter, which covers values and voting. Once again it is important to bear in mind that this data is more important for its ability to allow us to select tendencies in the population. For example, it is not so important that we fully address factors that predict or influence whether someone actually goes to the polls to vote.

As stated in Chapter 3, while surveys based on simple demographics and opinions can reflect some basic trends and differences in our society, they also fail to detect and explain the deeper drivers of our conscious and unconscious behaviors.

What is important is that we are able to compare larger patterns of likelihood to vote, or not to vote, against a wide spectrum of other concerns, ranging from simple demographics to complex typologies.

Let's now take a look at voting and typologies where we can see how simple "pigeon-holing" of people breaks down in the context of more encompassing patterns.

CHAPTER 16
Values-based Typologies and Voting

"These typologies offer a unique synthesis of the whole of society – and lead to practical strategies that can unify and elevate the whole to be greater than the sum of its parts."

The *values and beliefs* Americans employ to make voting decisions are at the heart of *A New America*. The 8 Types typology present an entirely new perspective as we look at the potential for a more positive and integrated future.

In this chapter, we continue to examine how Americans express themselves in terms of values and their voting choices, and the extent to which these choices reflect their core values and related "mind space." Measurements of personal *condition* such as the Social Material Stress scale relate closely to voting likelihood, since it is an indicator of overall connection and comfort within society. However, measurements of personal *values and beliefs*, such as PFCI or STRC, are differentiators of important choices (candidate, voting, etc.).

This chapter further highlights commonalities between what has been historically viewed as disparate segments within American society that don't communicate or find meaningful ways in which to come together. What is a key influence is the extent that wholistic and spiritually oriented values shift or override STRC values.

It is entirely possible for us to create new social and political movements that have the greater good of our country, humankind, and our planet as their central focus and agenda.

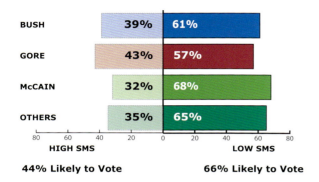

SMS SCALE:
Likelihood to vote and choose a candidate

BUSH	39%	61%
GORE	43%	57%
McCAIN	32%	68%
OTHERS	35%	65%

HIGH SMS   LOW SMS

44% Likely to Vote   **66% Likely to Vote**

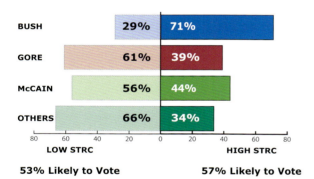

STRC INDEX:
Likelihood to vote and choose a candidate

BUSH	29%	71%
GORE	61%	39%
McCAIN	56%	44%
OTHERS	66%	34%

LOW STRC   HIGH STRC

53% Likely to Vote   **57% Likely to Vote**

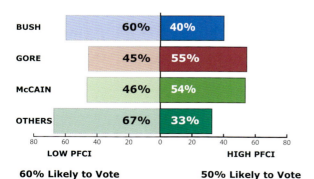

PFCI SCALE:
Likelihood to vote and choose a candidate

BUSH	60%	40%
GORE	45%	55%
McCAIN	46%	54%
OTHERS	67%	33%

LOW PFCI   HIGH PFCI

60% Likely to Vote   **50% Likely to Vote**

Expansion or Constriction? A Comparison of Indicators

As we reintroduce the quadrants models from earlier, we first want to emphasize crucial differences between these general models relative to candidate and voting likelihood. PFCI-SMS is used most extensively because it is a differentiator of voting and because it relates to positive values that bridge many social and personal value sets.

Social Material Stress (SMS) scale

The SMS scale emphasizes personal and social condition more than values and belies and thus is very complimentary with other measurements of values and beliefs, such as PFCI or STRC. Here we see that low SMS relates to greater "ease" in terms of functioning in our society. The lower social, psychological or material stress, the more likely they are to vote and choose a candidate for president. The higher on the SMS scale, the less likely. When applied to candidate choice, regardless of likelihood of voting, there is no discernible difference in candidate choice.

Social Traditional Religious Conservative (STRC) index

The STRC index emphasizes two closely related sets of values: social traditionalism and religiousness with conservatism and lack of tolerance. It is a differentiator of voting likelihood to the extent that "traditional" social values include a sense of responsibility to vote. Over recent decades, the Republican party has allied itself with "God and country" themes as well as conservative personal and family issues, thus engineering a dynamic for itself using STRC values.

Positive Future Integrative Cooperative (PFCI) scale

The PFCI scale emphasizes closely related sets of values of a different sort: Desire for a positive, life-affirming future, cooperation and a recognition of the interconnectedness of life with spirituality that is not tied to any religion. This scale demonstrates a set of values that have powerful bridging qualities. It too differentiates between candidate and other choices.

Revisiting the 5 PFCI-SMS Types

Before going into voting and values, let's first take a quick look at the Positive Future – Cooperative Integrative and Social Material Stress (PFCI-SMS) model presented in earlier chapters. We will be examining how this quadrant model can provide greater clarity and deeper understanding of Americans' voting preferences. As you may recall, the two scales are used to define a quadrant model, which has some very interesting characteristics. To help in reframing this general quadrant model, we have given each of the main divisions a name:

"Acting on New Ways"

- 15% of Americans identify with a more positive and integrated future, and they do *not* express feeling social material stress.

"Open to New Ways"

- 22% of Americans identify with a more positive and integrated future, and they express feeling social material stress.

"Boundary Zone"

- 21% of Americans are "boundary zone" or "middle-of-the-road" in that they are very close to the boundary between two or more quadrants, and as such cannot be reliably identified as belonging to any one quadrant.

"Wanting to Improve Old Ways"

- 18% of Americans do not identify with a more positive and integrated future, and they do not express feeling social material stress.

"Disengaged but Getting By"

- 25% of Americans do not identify with a more positive and integrated future, and they express feeling social material stress.

While this model only reflects generalized patterns of attitudes and behaviors, it does identify some broad patterns of values and beliefs among Americans.

Looking at the typology defined by the PFCI-SMS model and then more closely through the magnifying "lens" of The 8 American Types, we gain a closer look at some important commonalities, as well as some interesting differences.

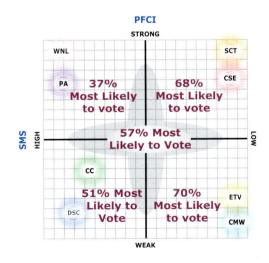

305

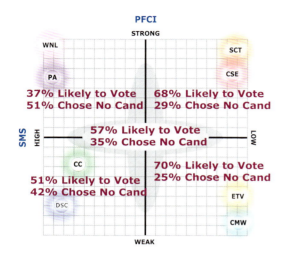

PFCI

STRONG

WNL

SCT

PA

CSE

37% Likely to Vote
51% Chose No Cand

68% Likely to Vote
29% Chose No Cand

57% Likely to Vote
35% Chose No Cand

SMS HIGH

LOW

CC

70% Likely to Vote
25% Chose No Cand

51% Likely to Vote
42% Chose No Cand

ETV

DSC

CMW

WEAK

VOTING LIKELIHOOD

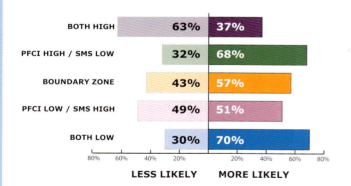

BOTH HIGH	63%	37%
PFCI HIGH / SMS LOW	32%	68%
BOUNDARY ZONE	43%	57%
PFCI LOW / SMS HIGH	49%	51%
BOTH LOW	30%	70%

80% 60% 40% 20%   20% 40% 60% 80%

LESS LIKELY   MORE LIKELY

Voting Likelihood: 5 PFCI-SMS Types and The 8 American Types

Overall, Americans who are *low* PFCI and low SMS are most likely to vote (69.7%), as are Americans who are high PFCI and *low* SMS (68.4%). Those least likely to vote are *high* PFCI and *high* SMS (37.4%).

5 PFCI-SMS Types:

"Acting on New Ways" Upper Right – (High PFCI/Low SMS) – Stronger Voters (15% of Households (HH))

- Those Americans in the upper right quadrant (High PFCI and Low SMS) are also very involved politically (68% likely to vote). Like the "Traditional" voting Americans, this group does not strongly feel social material stress, but unlike them, they identify with a more positive and integrated future.

"Open to New Ways" Upper Left – (High Both) – Weaker Voters (22% of HH)

- Those Americans in the upper left quadrant (High PFCI and High SMS) are not very involved politically (37% likely to vote). These Americans strongly identify with a more positive and integrated future, and also strongly feel social material stress.

"Boundary Zone" Center Region – Average Voters (21% of HH)

- Those Americans who cannot be reliably identified as belonging to just one quadrant are slightly more involved politically than the average American (57% vote). These Americans have moderately mixed levels of social material stress and somewhat identify with a more positive and integrated future.

"Wanting to Improve Old Ways" – Lower Left – (Low PFCI/High SMS) – Weaker Voters (25% of HH)

- Those Americans in the lower left quadrant (Low PFCI and High SMS) are "typically" involved politically (51% vote). These Americans do not identify with a more positive and integrated future, and strongly feel social material stress.

"Disengaged but Getting By" Lower Right – (Low Both) – Stronger Voters (18% of HH)

- Those Americans in the lower right quadrant (Low PFCI and Low SMS) are very involved politically (70% vote).

The 8 American Types

While the three basic traits revealed striking differences across groups who preferred different candidates, not all of the American population has a type comprised of just one predominant trait. There are five other types of Americans (who have types comprised of different *combinations* of scores on the three basic traits).

When examining the 8 Types, those who were less likely to want any candidate were in the CMW, PA, or SCT groups.

Strong Likelihood to Vote (60% of HH)

- Americans who were more likely to vote are Embracing Traditional Values (78% likely), Connecting through Self-Exploration (69% likely), Seeking Community Transformation (60% likely), Centered in the Material World (58% likely), and Conservative and Cautious (56% likely).

Weak Likelihood to Vote (40% of HH)

- Americans who were less likely to vote are Persisting through Adversity (37% likely), Disengaged from Social Concerns (43% likely), and Working for a New Life of Wholeness (43% likely).

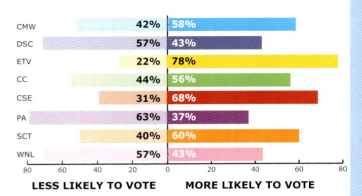

LIKELIHOOD TO VOTE BY THE 8 TYPES
Percentage within each type

LESS LIKELY TO VOTE   MORE LIKELY TO VOTE

THE AMERICAN 8 TYPES
Percentage of U.S. households

14.4% (CMW) Centered in a Material World

14.2% (DSC) Disengaged from Social Concerns

12.1% (ETV) Embracing Traditional Values

10.0% (CC) Cautious and Conservative

11.9% (CSE) Connecting through Self-Exploration

9.4% (PA) Persisting through Adversity

11.6% (SCT) Seeking Community Transformation

16.4% (WNL) Working for a New Life of Wholeness

CANDIDATE CHOICE BY PFCI-SMS

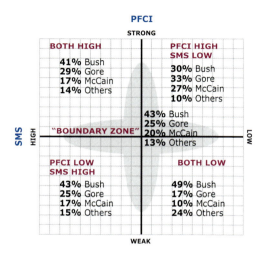

PFCI
STRONG

BOTH HIGH	PFCI HIGH SMS LOW
41% Bush	**30%** Bush
29% Gore	**33%** Gore
17% McCain	**27%** McCain
14% Others	**10%** Others

43% Bush
25% Gore
"BOUNDARY ZONE" **20%** McCain
13% Others

PFCI LOW SMS HIGH	BOTH LOW
43% Bush	**49%** Bush
25% Gore	**17%** Gore
17% McCain	**10%** McCain
15% Others	**24%** Others

WEAK

VOTING LIKELIHOOD BY PFCI-SMS

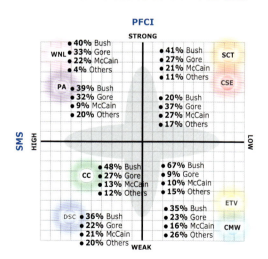

PFCI
STRONG

WNL ● **40%** Bush
● **33%** Gore
● **22%** McCain
● **4%** Others

SCT ● **41%** Bush
● **27%** Gore
● **21%** McCain
● **11%** Others

CSE

PA ● **39%** Bush
● **32%** Gore
● **9%** McCain
● **20%** Others

● **20%** Bush
● **37%** Gore
● **27%** McCain
● **17%** Others

CC ● **48%** Bush
● **27%** Gore
● **13%** McCain
● **12%** Others

● **67%** Bush
● **9%** Gore
● **10%** McCain
● **15%** Others

ETV

DSC ● **36%** Bush
● **22%** Gore
● **21%** McCain
● **20%** Others

● **35%** Bush
● **23%** Gore
● **16%** McCain
● **26%** Others

CMW

WEAK

Candidate Choice: 5 PFCI-SMS Types and the 8 Types

In this section we will be taking a look at few selected factors relative to the PFCI quadrant model. (Americans who are "Both High" were least likely to vote, while Americans who are "Both Low" and "High PFCI/Low SMS" were most likely to vote.) Percentages reported are only for likely voters, not all respondents.

5 PFCI-SMS Types:

- Bush supporters were most likely to fall into the Low PFCI/Low SMS category in the lower right quarter.

- Others, meaning some candidate other than those in the running, were most likely to fall into the Low PFCI/Low SMS category in the lower right.

- McCain supporters were most likely to fall into the High PFCI/Low SMS category in the upper right.

- Gore supporters were most likely to fall into the High PFCI/Low SMS category in the upper right.

The 8 American Types:

- Bush supporters were most likely to be Embracing Traditional Values (ETV), Conservative and Cautious (CC), or Seeking Community Transformation (SCT) types.

- Gore supporters were most likely to be Connecting through Self-Exploration (CSE), Working for a New Life of Wholeness (WNL), or Persisting through Adversity (PA) types.

- McCain supporters were most likely to be Connecting through Self-Exploration (CSE), Working for a New Life of Wholeness (WNL), Seeking Community Transformation (SCT), or Disengaged from Social Concerns (DSC) types.

- Others, meaning some candidate other than those in the running, were most likely to be supported by Centered in a Material World (CMW), Persisting through Adversity (PA), or Disengaged from Social Concerns (DSC) types.

The 8 American Types, Candidate Choice, and Gender

When we look at candidate choice for each of the 8 Types, certain choices stood out:

- Three types didn't like any of the candidates: Centered in a Material World (CMW), Persisting through Adversity (PA) and Seeking Community Transformation (SCT).

- Two types were most likely to prefer Bush: Embracing Traditional Values (ETV) and Cautious and Conservative (CC).

- Connecting through Self-Exploration (CSE) was the only type that preferred McCain.

- Gore was most strongly preferred by Connecting through Self-Exploration (CSE), followed by Working for a New Life of Wholeness (WNL), and Persisting through Adversity (PA).

- Centered in a Material World (CMW) and Disengaged from Social Concerns (DSC) were the most likely types to prefer a candidate other than Bush, Gore, or McCain.

As we look at candidate preferences within each type by gender, the most notable gender differences by type are apparent:

- Gore, overall, had the strongest support among men of the CSE and WNL types. He also had more support from women than men within the PA, CC, CMW, DSC, and SCT types.

- Bush, overall, had the strongest support from men and women of the ETV type. He also had more support from men than from women within the DSC, CC, CSE, PA, and SCT types.

- McCain, overall had the strongest support from men and women of the CSE type. He also had more support from men than from women within the CMW, DSC, CC, and WNL types.

- Other candidates had the strongest support from men of the CMW type. They also had more support from men than from women within the CMW and PA types, as well as more support from women than from men within the CSE and DSC types.

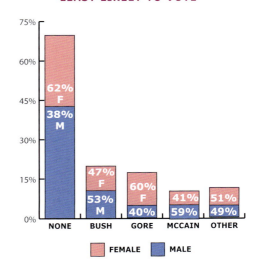

GENDER BY CANDIDATE LEAST LIKELY TO VOTE

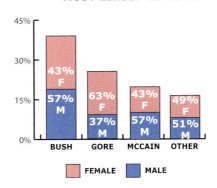

GENDER BY CANDIDATE MOST LIKELY TO VOTE

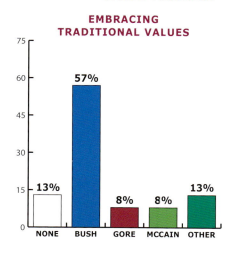

CENTERED IN
A MATERIAL WORLD

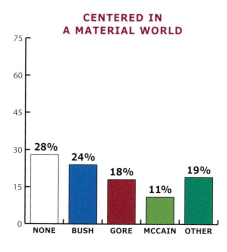

DISENGAGED
FROM SOCIAL CONCERNS

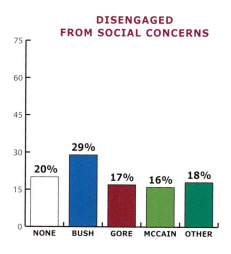

EMBRACING
TRADITIONAL VALUES

CAUTIOUS
AND CONSERVATIVE

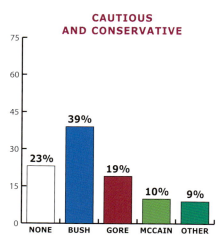

CONNECTING THROUGH
SELF-EXPLORATION

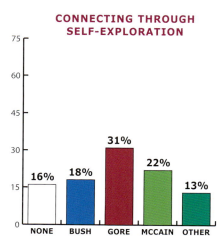

PERSISTING AGAINST
ADVERSITY

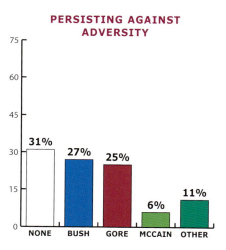

SEEKING COMMUNITY
TRANSFORMATION

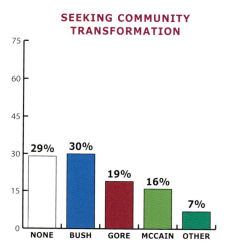

WORKING FOR A NEW LIFE
OF WHOLENESS

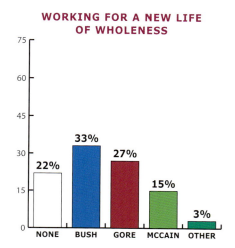

The Three Core Traits and Candidate

As this section is devoted to voting and social typologies, it is worthwhile to also take a look at the three core statistical traits, introduced in Chapter 4, that were used to define The 8 American Types. A clear trend emerged from the data in examining scores on these three trait scales that were used to develop The 8 American Types for respondents who preferred Bush, Gore, McCain, or None as candidates.

Likelihood to Vote:

- High scores on the *Following Tradition* core trait are associated with a 58% likelihood of voting, whereas low scores on this core trait are associated with a 52% likelihood of voting.

- High scores on the *Coming From Within* core trait are associated with a 52% likelihood of voting, whereas low scores on this core trait are associated with a 58% likelihood of voting.

- High scores on the *Disengaged* core trait are associated with a 44% likelihood of voting, whereas low scores on this core trait are associated with a 66% likelihood of voting.

Bush Supporters and the Following Tradition Trait:

- Analysis of variance indicated that those who preferred Bush scored significantly higher on the Following Tradition trait scale.

Gore Supporters and the Coming From Within Trait:

- Analysis of variance indicated that those who preferred Gore scored significantly higher on the Coming From Within trait scale.

Those Who Preferred "None" and the Disengaged Trait:

- Analysis of variance indicated that those who preferred "None" as a candidate scored significantly higher on the Disengaged trait scale.

McCain Supporters:

- Those who preferred McCain scored second highest on the Following Tradition scale (only Bush supporters scored higher), and scored second highest on the Coming From Within scale. (Only Gore supporters scored higher.)

Those Who Preferred "Others":

- Those who preferred "Others" consistently scored the lowest of all groups on all three scales (Following Tradition, Coming From Within, and Disengaged).

THREE CORE TRAITS VOTING LIKELIHOOD

TRAIT IS WEAK	TRAIT IS STRONG

FOLLOWING TRADITION

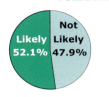

COMING FROM WITHIN

DISENGAGED

In the above graphic, each of the three core traits shows as a pair of pie charts with percentage likely to vote. For example, in the bottom pair of pie charts, we see a dramatic difference in voting likelihood. The column on the right where the "Disengaged" trait is strongest and people have the *least* sense of connection to self or society, voting is *least* likely. On the bottom left pie chart, connection to self or society is *strongest* and voting likelihood is *strongest*.

Summary Table of the 8 Types

	THE 8 AMERICAN TYPES															
	CMW Centered in a Material World		DSC Disengaged from Social Concerns		ETV Embracing Traditional Values		CC Cautious and Conservative		CSE Connecting Through Self-Exploration		PA Persisting through Adversity		SCT Seeking Community Transformation		WN Working New Life of Wh
Group Size	14%	of Pop.	14%	of Pop.	12%	of Pop.	10%	of Pop.	12%	of Pop.	9%	of Pop.	12%	of Pop.	16%	o
Gender	56% 44%	M F	58% 42%	M F	57% 43%	M F	54% 46%	M F	37% 63%	M F	44% 56%	M F	25% 75%	M F	48% 52%	M F
Voting - highly likely	58%	Likely	43%	Likely	78%	Likely	56%	Likely	69%	Likely	37%	Likely	60%	Likely	43%	L
Gender Voting - highly likely	54% 46%	M F	63% 37%	M F	60% 40%	M F	64% 36%	M F	41% 59%	M F	52% 48%	M F	25% 75%	M F	53% 47%	M F
Candidate preference overall (without tight voting filter)	28% 24% 18% 19% 11%	None Bush Gore Others McCain	29% 20% 18% 17% 16%	Bush None Others Gore McCain	57% 13% 13% 8% 8%	Bush None Others Gore McCain	39% 23% 19% 10% 9%	Bush None Gore McCain Others	31% 22% 18% 16% 13%	Gore McCain Bush None Others	31% 27% 25% 11% 6%	None Bush Gore Others McCain	30% 29% 19% 15% 7%	Bush None Gore McCain Others	33% 27% 22% 15% 3%	B G N M O
Candidate (with tight voting filter applied)	35% 26% 23% 16%	Bush Others Gore McCain	36% 22% 21% 20%	Bush Gore McCain Others	67% 14% 10% 9%	Bush Others McCain Gore	48% 27% 13% 12%	Bush Gore McCain Others	37% 27% 20% 16%	Gore McCain Bush Others	39% 32% 20% 9%	Bush Gore Others McCain	41% 27% 21% 11%	Bush Gore McCain Others	40% 33% 22% 4%	B G M O
Ideology (without voting filter)	41% 34% 24%	Con Mod Lib	33% 44% 22%	Con Mod Lib	76% 22% 3%	Con Mod Lib	65% 28% 7%	Con Mod Lib	29% 41% 30%	Con Mod Lib	27% 45% 28%	Con Mod Lib	53% 36% 11%	Con Mod Lib	42% 33% 25%	C M L
Party (without voting filter)	30% 35% 19% 16%	Dem Rep Ind Othr	32% 24% 20% 24%	Dem Rep Ind Othr	13% 66% 12% 9%	Dem Rep Ind Othr	28% 40% 11% 22%	Dem Rep Ind Othr	37% 27% 22% 15%	Dem Rep Ind Othr	36% 15% 17% 32%	Dem Rep Ind Othr	36% 38% 17% 9%	Dem Rep Ind Othr	50% 21% 14% 14%	D R Ir O
Global Awakening Taking Place Now	34%	Agree	33%	Agree	55%	Agree	65%	Agree	49%	Agree	62%	Agree	78%	Agree	80%	A
Global Awakening Make World Better in Ten Years	36%	Agree	35%	Agree	41%	Agree	57%	Agree	62%	Agree	66%	Agree	78%	Agree	80%	A
Spirituality Index	24%	Strong	21%	Strong	47%	Strong	59%	Strong	51%	Strong	61%	Strong	85%	Strong	75%	S

Illustrated Synthesis of Voting Demographics and Typology

Before moving on, we want to share with the reader a graphical glimpse into the overlaying of traditional voting demographics with the PFCI-SMS model. In conducting future research, it will no doubt be of value to find ways to bridge old paradigm approaches to voting campaigns toward a new values-based typology.

The quadrant-circle graph below the PFCI-SMS graph also includes all U.S. households and accounts for strong and weak voters, while distinguishing candidate, party, and ideology preferences. We have enlarged this to a full size on the next page.

The outer-most ring shows those people least likely to vote by a combination of two factors: self-placement on a scale from conservative to liberal and their political party identification, if any.

The next ring shows those people *most likely to vote* by candidate preference.

The next ring in shows those people *most likely to vote* by a combination of two factors: self-placement on a scale from conservative to liberal and their political party identification, if any.

The ring closest to the center shows those people *least likely to vote* by candidate preference.

The two pie charts show the breakdown of the center or boundary zone area for candidate and for party and ideology, since it was not possible to include this detail in the main wheel graphic.

The rings are arranged so that differences between strong and weak voters can be readily compared.

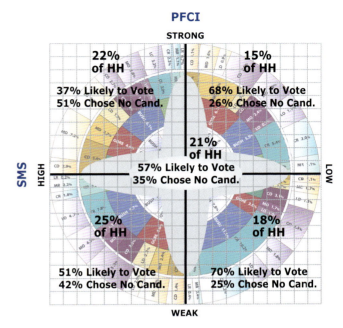

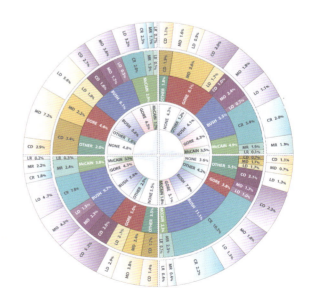

Summary of Typologies and Voting

In our voting analysis, we examined patterns of behavior and intent first from a traditional political-demographic perspective, then analyzed voting patterns by various typological scales. To help summarize and to compare similarities and differences, we then presented a color-wheel model showing some of the traditional perspectives on voting overlaid on the PFCI quadrant model.

As we have just seen, the traditional political-demographic approach is inherently limited in its ability to identify significant patterns that can be translated into meaningful strategies and positions. Hopefully, these can be represented by a more evolved leadership in terms of a more spiritually conscious world view, ethics, and other qualities. Vote manipulation aside, this failure contributes further to the inability of traditional political-demographics to accurately predict voter inclinations.

- Multiple demographics are unreliable (single item-based) measurements and in combination with one another produce too many sub-groups to be useful.

- Multiple demographics are unreliable (single item-based) measurements and in combination with one another produce too many sub-groups to be useful.

- Through the use of statistically reliable multi-item "scales," the PFCI-SMS model captures two major societal trends that can be applied to help lead us into either an ascending evolution or a descending devolution into darkness.

- Different types of people are identified with each quadrant based on their core values and attitudes.

- Shared core values will allow us to "build bridges" between quadrants – as opposed to building "walls" between them.

- The "tension" or "fusion" between the quadrants will play a critical role in our overall social trajectory.

The *IOOW-2000* research demonstrates there are very few gender or age differences relating to voting per se. However, we find some noticeable demographic patterns within The 8 American Types, such as gender, age, U.S. birthplace, income, etc. As the voting analyses show however, results based exclusively on such surface characteristics are less than illuminating when compared to a typological approach based on consciousness, values, and beliefs.

These typologies provide insight into ways to develop meaningful strategies that can help elevate and unify the whole so that for American society, the whole can truly be much greater than the sum of any individuated parts. They show that it is possible to identify strategies that could bring an overwhelming majority of Americans into a new form of social and voting participation.

We may be closer than most people think toward choosing to create a positive future – instead of a devolving one.

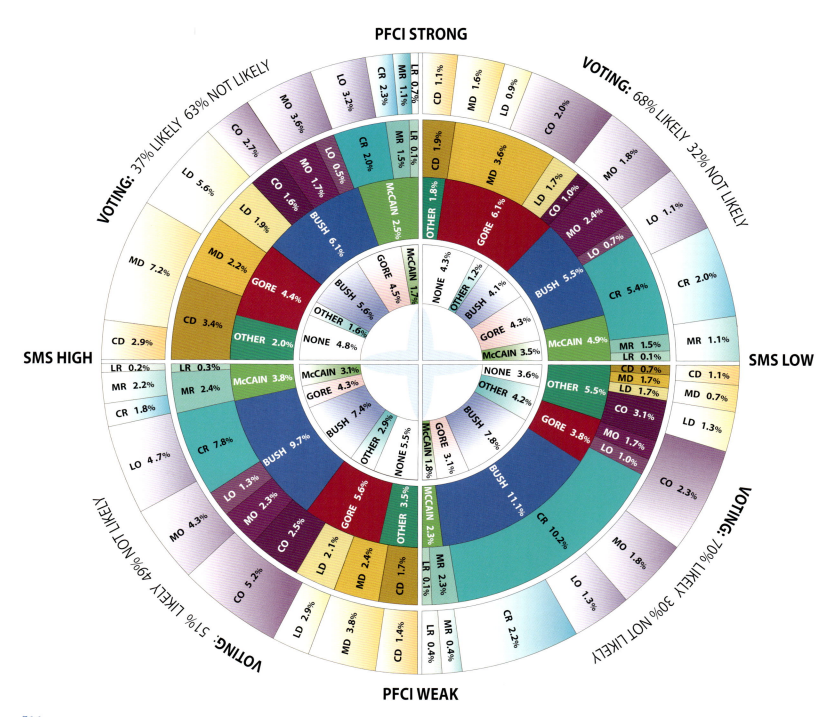

Further Explanation of Wheel Graphics

To help in using this graphic display of typology and voting, let's use as examples the upper right quadrant where PFCI is high and SMS is low, and the upper left quadrant where both PFCI and SMS are high.

The two inner rings present candidate preference by voting likelihood. The innermost ring uses a lighter shade and includes both strong and weak voters. The next ring with stronger color shading includes only those people most likely to vote and choose a candidate.

The portion of voters supporting McCain changed little as we compare the two inner rings in this quadrant. This suggests that McCain support was composed of stronger voters. Alternately it could mean that he was an attractive alternative. Due to a mixed influence of social traditionalism with new paradigm values, there was a roughly even change in voting support as non-voters are filtered out with Gore, with Gore seemingly gaining slightly more.

By contrast, in the upper right quadrant, the influence of voting and values is more apparent. Those people who were strong voters who had a more conservative orientation gave Bush a stronger proportion of votes than did those people who favored Gore. McCain showed strong appeal as an alternative to either leading candidate.

Similar comparison can be made in the outer two rings showing how likelihood of voting is affected by values and beliefs.

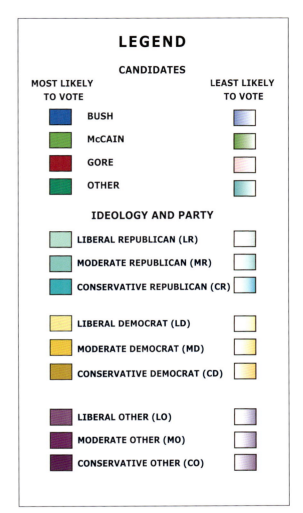

LEGEND

CANDIDATES

MOST LIKELY TO VOTE — LEAST LIKELY TO VOTE

BUSH
McCAIN
GORE
OTHER

IDEOLOGY AND PARTY

LIBERAL REPUBLICAN (LR)
MODERATE REPUBLICAN (MR)
CONSERVATIVE REPUBLICAN (CR)

LIBERAL DEMOCRAT (LD)
MODERATE DEMOCRAT (MD)
CONSERVATIVE DEMOCRAT (CD)

LIBERAL OTHER (LO)
MODERATE OTHER (MO)
CONSERVATIVE OTHER (CO)

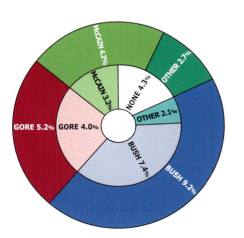

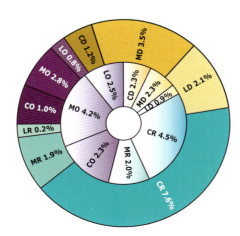

CHAPTER 17

Healing and Evolution: Beyond Voting

"Connection, service, and spirituality provide a useful model for a higher common denominator for society that is very removed from the worn out traditional conservative paradigm that is continually pushed to divide (and conquer) society by the powers that be."

This concluding chapter brings into clearer focus the need for America and its citizens to consciously (and with as little pre-judgment as possible) do more than just entertain the idea of finding avenues of commonality and resonance. The competing societal forces and civil upset we see at work today serve as significant clues as we search for clear direction and a higher vision for the attainment of just governance, equitable livelihood, and peaceful co-existence.

We are undoubtedly in the transitional throes of evolving our society and all civilization. As in all transitions, confusion is the embodiment of our process. *A New America* offers new prospects, as a light at the end of a tunnel offers welcomed release from the unseen.

The three operating principles of Connection, Service, and Spirituality are all-encompassing in their ability to break down old paradigms and systems that no longer serve us. We can create positive change if we so choose. Global awakening is possible if we so choose. It is entirely up to us.

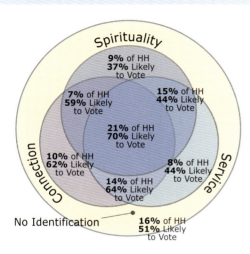

Voting and the Connection, Service, and Spirituality Indexes

This illustrates the relationship between the presence of connection, service, spirituality and voting likelihood in the 2000 election. Those who are most oriented to "spirituality" and who have little relationship with "connection" or "service," are not strong voters. This is not surprising as their primary focus naturally tends to be less "worldly." It is where we see a balance between strong spirituality, service, and connection that there is the greatest participation. Overall, it is the presence of "connection" that most closely relates to voting participation. The outlying group least identifying with any of these three factors is one of two groups discussed in Chapter Six as "social inertial ballast."

– IOOW-2000 Research

Positive Change

What is perhaps most obvious given all of the *IOOW-2000* data is that it highlights many of the challenges before us. Clearly we need a coherent strategy that develops a plurality of public interest and voting involvement. No amount of traditional public policy analysis can find sufficient common ground here either. The sheer complexity and cost of running research of this type is beyond most socially and spiritually progressive political campaigns.

Those people who preferred another candidate (or none) over Bush, show that they are at least thinking along some other line of thought than what has come to publicly dominate our society. Clearly half of the electorate did not support the current regime and what it has come to represent. Additionally, nearly half of potential voters do not support the overall system (whatever that may mean, is of course, unique to each person). Many of the non-voters have been what is superficially known as traditional religious or spiritually-oriented – a concept that does *not* always equate to conservative and reactionary.

To those people who oppose the Bush administration, it is easy to make the mistaken conclusion that the Democratic candidates must therefore represent the hopes and aspirations of those people who voted Democratic. Not so. What we see here in the two dominant party's candidates is merely a *reflection* of woefully inadequate choices – framed by a voting system that is fundamentally flawed or worse.

In contrast, we are saying that it is possible to create a new social movement based on some of the most evolved initiatives *and* create a new political movement.

While it is obvious that cooperation and coordination must exist between a broad social movement and a political organization, it is essential they be given "separate lives." Without well-defined and appropriate boundaries between them, the danger remains that political factions will naturally want to control a social movement to support electoral and legislative initiatives – and a social movement would allow itself to become subsumed by political personalities and policies. The social factors must have their own energy to build strong roots at local and regional levels, as well as to develop strong ties across all communities of interest and do so across the planet.

We do not pretend to have all the answers, but offer this as part of our contribution toward developing workable social and political strategies that operate at a higher common denominator, one sufficiently above society's "background noise," but not too far removed so that it can engage with large numbers of people.

Chapter 11 introduced a conceptual and statistical model that could allow a majority of Americans to move up and beyond a decaying old paradigm that threatens to take everyone down with it. Graphics from that chapter are again provided here.

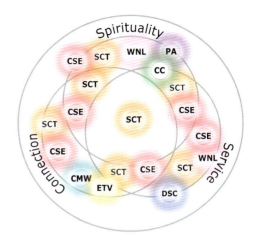

We keep returning to this simple model of Connection, Service, and Spirituality (CSS) as a way to embrace a larger whole and to seek possible vectors that can connect people broadly. Within that context, people can be communicated with and connected to in ways more specific to their unique makeup. This model offers insight into practical strategies that can address and potentially involve 84% of society in a positive way.

It is important to emphasize that voting, while it is important, is not all there is to healing and evolving America to its real potential as an enlightened society. In the context of this section, voting is more important as an *indicator* and a *reflection* of social tendencies. To put it more plainly, this is not about mobilizing voting blocks according to typology. The CSS model provides us with a new model of societal connection that is very removed from the worn out traditional conservative paradigm that is continually pushed to divide (and conquer) society by the powers that be.

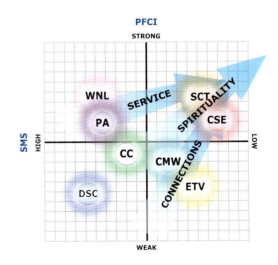

It is worth noting that Gore and McCain registered more strongly among those people who placed in the group that is the intersection of all three of these factors – Connection, Service, and Spirituality – a group that is by far the most likely to vote. As we might expect, the SCT type tended to prefer McCain and Gore in the 2000 election. This group also includes a high component of pre-boomer-aged Americans – especially women.

In contrast, the younger X and Y generations who were least interested in any of the candidates or voting are a large component of those outside the boundaries of the entire CSS model. While it is *not in the least* appropriate to conclude that the pre-boomers are to be written off, *it is appropriate* to raise the alarm at this disparity between those people in our society who generally may well be the most mature and evolved, and the gulf that apparently exists between them and younger people with whom they should most be working.

Simply speaking, as a generational matter, building strong ties with those who are youngest may well provide the greatest influence on those in the middle: the baby boomers. Despite small but keenly dedicated segments of the baby boomer generation, generally speaking, this is one of the most self-centered and irresponsible generational groups in our history. (Only a substantial but small portion of boomers were involved and aware of the times. In particular, for women early on, it was difficult because the political side of things were male dominated.)

Those people in the centrally overlapping group, as well as those in the Spirituality and Service group, include the highest components in agreement with global awakening and its potential for extraordinary change. This central group also includes an interesting mix of Social Traditional – Religious Conservatives and those who clearly are more open and expansive in their worldview. In contrast to most social traditional – religious conservatives, the SCT type is generally opposed to the death penalty.

When viewed through the "lens" of The 8 American Types, we find an interesting mixture of SCT, CSE, and ETV in the central nexus of the CSS model. The more traditional social perspectives of the SCT group lend it the greatest potential to bridge to many of the ETV who remain open to new ideas and are genuinely concerned about the future of humanity – particularly those ETV who are high PFCI. While most ETV types are naturally strong on the STRC index, there are those who are not and more than a quarter are in the middle zone.

In addition, there are many shared values and beliefs between this central nexus group and their closest allies – the Connection-Spirituality and Service-Spirituality groups – thus including the upper left portion of the PFCI-SMS quadrant with elements found in the lower right portion. Consequently, five of the 8 Types are bridged: SCT, CSE, ETV, WNL, and

PA. Significantly, it is through the PA and CSE types that younger people in the Gen-X and Gen-Y ages can be reached. Global awakening will play an important role in providing one of a few broad contextual umbrellas. It can be an important attractor to "wake up" many of those in the CC type as well, given their religious-spiritual tendencies.

The next likely allies would be those in the CMW type who are genuinely interested in positive change and positive values and who are not attracted to division and polarization.

As was extensively highlighted in Chapter 11, Connection, Service, and Spirituality are the motivating keystones that can help all of us move toward the enactment of a higher vision for humanity. Connection is achieved through unconditional positive regard for all living things, including our planet. Service affords each of us the ability to do for others that which they may not be able to do for themselves – and considers each person worthy of our investment on all levels of consciousness. Spirituality is *trans-religious* in that it is an innate imperative within all of us and is not the exclusive province of a few self-chosen leaders who use religion as a commodity for social control.

As we have discussed before, Religion and Spirituality are *not* the same. This is true both in the minds of the American public as well as demonstrated by important differences between people who ranked very high in a composite of spirituality factors and those who ranked very high on measures of traditional religious factors.

While Bush attracted a majority of traditionally religious people, McCain and Gore attracted a majority of spiritually-oriented people who also cared about the state of the world and wanted to work toward a positive future. Now this doesn't mean that these candidates' and their campaigns made this difference. Clearly they did not: These values and beliefs were already in place in our society. These candidates represented an alternative to what the Bush campaign *represented* to people relative to what they valued most.

Since this section has a focus on politics, it is should be obvious from the foregoing, that it is quite feasible for a national campaign to succeed that clearly distinguishes itself with the qualities of love and compassion, cooperation and interconnectedness, caring for the health and well being of ordinary people and the planet, and genuinely embrace a spiritually-elevated world view without pandering to superficial religiosity. Such a campaign could not afford accept support from the mega-corporations and the power elite. In turn, a majority of Americans would respond with their ballots and those who have lost interest in the "system" would find a reason to vote. Perhaps today, American society would be far different and the rest of the world could find better reasons to look to America for a more positive future.

As we have expressed earlier in this book, *"America is a society whose strength is based in part on the hopes and aspirations that arise from a longing for enlightenment and compassion. ...What choices will Americans make to tap this enormous potential?"*

Global Awakening

Global awakening is relatively free of religious dogma and religious institutional association. It is also something that is embedded in nearly all the main religions. Additionally, it can be a way to bridge many religious, as well as non-religious, people. When considering the questions focused on global awakening, *"...global awakening is taking place"* and *"...that a social/spiritual awakening will make the world a better place to live in ten years,"* 71.5% of U.S households agreed with either or both of these.

It is revealing that so many people identify with and aspire to a global awakening – something that is not in our common language. Global awakening crosses party lines and voting likelihood, religious divisions, and most demographic factors. It is clearly an important part of our highest common denominator and represents a powerful attractor bridging those who are less engaged in society as a whole to those who are more engaged.

Of the 8 Types, four – WNL, SCT, PA, CC – all agree with both questions – that *"...global awakening is taking place"* and *"...that a social/spiritual awakening will make the world a better place to live in ten years."* These four types make up 47.4% of U.S. households – ones that are most likely to support alternatives representing an awakened society for a positive future. These four types also account for over half (54%) of all those people not likely to vote. In addition, the CSE group has a positive association with global awakening when looking out over ten years, thus five of the 8 Types support global awakening in some fashion.

This suggests that global awakening, properly presented as a national concept, perhaps in conjunction with a social initiative such as Decade of the Heart, can be used to attract many concerned people who currently do not see much reason to be involved in national-level matters, including voting in presidential elections. One of the strong relationships to non-voting is a singular focus on spirituality without the balance of connection and service. Given its implicit and explicit ability to connect people and to encourage people serving others' needs, global awakening is an important bridge in reaching less likely voters, as well as likely voters

Focus on awakening to higher consciousness, with its positive social and spiritual connotations, represents an important factor in any positive future-oriented social movement or political campaign.

Voting in elections at all levels of governance has been a struggle for many groups who at some time in our history have felt the coldness of disenfranchisement. It has become one of the most basic mechanisms by which we can enact change, institute organizational support and restraint, and activate initiatives in the service of greater humanity. What has not been focused on or supported by prior elections are the true values and beliefs upon which Americans make their decisions. Emotional harpstrings have been plucked with skillful drama to sway various segments of our society to vote one way or another. Short term and superficially, it may appear to work. However, this method of influence and control fails to feed the people's deeper, higher, and truer values.

Everything that has been put forth in *A New America* points to the fact that our current election process and demographic polling systems do not reflect or meet the true needs of American society. This means that what we currently have in place has become one-dimensional and therefore, outmoded. We cannot expect to create something new and viable utilizing the same old apparatus.

Our current voting system and its accompanying structures cannot possibly meet the needs of the movement toward our higher potential. Now is the time for Americans to reassess the efficacy of our voting system – before it is too late. Now is the time for us to reactivate our innate drive toward something greater – something more expansive – a positive future in the present.

As Chapter 11 and Part Four show, the 8 Types comprising American society demonstrate the unity within our diversity. By understanding this core facet of our society, we have the option of connecting in ways previously unacknowledged. This opens the door of opportunity for individuals, communities, our nation, and the global community to break through our fears and biases to see that we are connected via an extraordinary matrix. We are, after all, spiritual beings having a human experience.

The act of voting is but one mechanism by which we can express ourselves. For those who don't vote for whatever reason, *A New America* profers new information to invigorate our entire election process. Each vote is one voice heard. Every voice is integral to a highly functioning society wherein the highest aspirations of humankind are at the heart of every thought and action. Global awakening is our providence if we so desire.

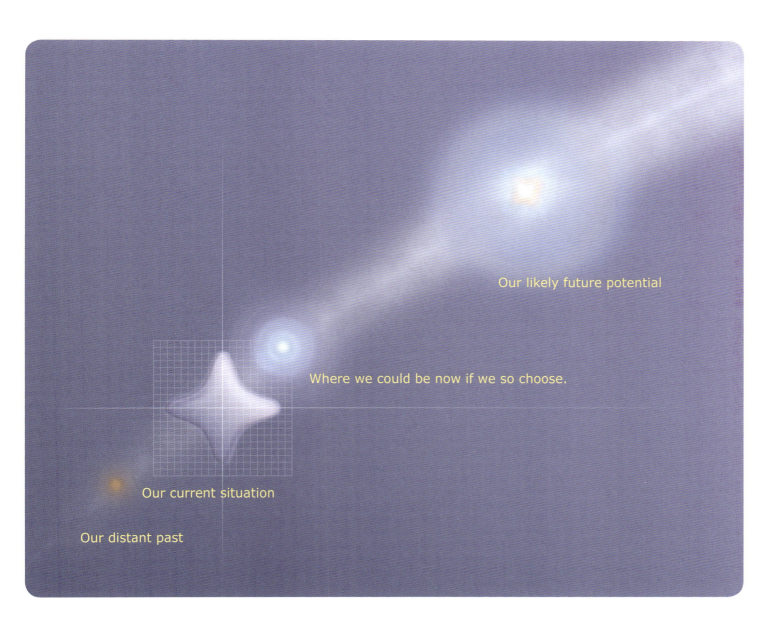

Our likely future potential

Where we could be now if we so choose.

Our current situation

Our distant past

PART FIVE
Epilogue

Epilogue

Humanity is closer than ever before to activating the most extreme consciousness and reality-shifting possibilities. As of this writing, the level of tension between catastrophic change by human or natural origins and the influx of higher consciousness has grown to a truly unprecedented magnitude.

We have before us a very simple proposition: *If a sufficient portion of* humanity *as a whole* proves unable to voluntarily make *new* choices based on a *greater level* of discernment on behalf of a spiritually-based and life-affirming future, then events will rapidly catalyze this process for us. However, there is no principle that says we must allow ourselves to fall into a catastrophic abyss first before deciding it is not in our best interests as human and spiritual beings.

Our ultimate destiny is that of spiritual beings occupying a unique medium between the solid physical matter of planets and the non-physicality of pure Spirit. This is the purpose of human biology: to provide a distinctive interface between these two aspects of creation. Our destiny is to discover the possibilities available within the magnificence of Creator consciousness.

The human species is a young species by cosmic, as well as human social-psychological measures. We have *so much potentia*l that is far beyond that which seems, from our limited perspective, to be an endless array of material and social failures and successes at personal or global levels. The relationship between consciousness – especially that anchored through human form – and our natural and synthetic environment is truly an intimate one. This is gradually being discovered through many of our physical and biological sciences, and is something that people focused on the spiritual sciences have known for a long time. We are indeed a vital part of an entire planetary organism, whether we see this clearly or only vaguely. By the brief measure of a few thousand years and now by an even briefer measure of decades as we face impending planetary climate change – it would seem that we have lost our way. Not so – *if* we only intend and choose differently – *right now.*

Humanity has reached a point wherein we have devoted our resources toward destructive conflict among ourselves and with our natural world.

This cannot continue unabated. We can and must make new choices and act upon them. It is within in our grasp and capacity to do so. The first step is to wake up to this option. We have so artfully managed to distract ourselves with personal and collective pleasures and power-seeking that we, as a species, seem hopelessly *unconscious* to an impending dramatic crossroad in our reality.

An enlightened future *is not* about polarities. It is not about who we do or do not vote for, democracy or plutocracy, or war or peace. It is not about differences between various religious texts and what various groups of people think about them. It is not about capitalism or the corruption of society by the "commodification" of our personal and social relationships. These are all the short-term choices that we seem to have already made by default and for which we now seek remedies.

An enlightened future *is* about how diversity and contrast can truly function as part of a coherent and unifying whole that is greater than the sum of its parts – and that at the same time benefits each unique part with the perspectives of all parts. Our challenge now is to facilitate ways for the greatest number of people to see this as a choice for themselves and to act accordingly.

What is before us is the emergence of an evolutionary shift in our physical, social, psychological, and spiritual existence. This shift benefits everyone, regardless of their personal circumstances or belief system. All that is needed is to surrender our ordinary personal and societal "ambitions" to welcome the adventure beckoning to us more powerfully every day from our future selves. Thus, we can find resolution to all aspects of ordinary human suffering and our seemingly endless conflict with our natural environment.

Can we open ourselves to the possibility of something wonderful? Can we let go of the old long enough to intend for ourselves an enlightened future?

This is truly the choice before us now. It has always been our choice to make.

What matters is *now*. Always.

"…After mastering winds, waves, tides and gravity, we shall harness the energies of love, and then, for the second time in the history of the world, man will discover fire."

– Pierre Teilhard de Chardin

Three Prayers for Humanity

May we come to know and acknowledge our new selves as our species emerges from its long gestation within our earthly biosphere.

May we recognize and acknowledge all that we have done to each other, to our own self, and to our planetary mother out of ignorance, selfishness, anger, and fear.

May we reconcile the shock of such realizations with that of new intentions and new actions that serve our higher purpose as spiritual beings.

May we come to realize love as a universal principle that allows for this experience of physical reality and out of such realization, learn to apply this principle with a newly-rediscovered will to choose and serve our higher destiny as spiritual beings.

May we come to experience the joy and happiness in the freedom and transformative results of applying ourselves in this new way.

May this be manifest as the dawn of a new reality for all to see and experience in contrast to their experience of the old reality.

May each within humanity so choose for themselves which reality best serves their highest aspirations.

May it be so.

Thank you for this day. I feel truly blessed and loved and cherished, as I treasure this world and all who live upon it.

Thank you for all humankind. May all find some blessed moment today to feel loved.

Today, may all find some moment of solace and help, some sweet inner tear to comfort those in need.

May all know some moment of tenderness today, some moment free from fear, from pain, and from strife.

May today bring forth a tomorrow where there is mending, with a fresh day full of new connections and a new-found awareness of self.

Let there be an experience of awakening to a brighter, higher, and loving life – a place where all may find the home for which they have been longing.

May all be healed and made one with the heavens and the greater power and nature we are all part of.

May tomorrow be our dawn to light a new life.

I think over again my small adventures
My fears,

Those small ones that seemed so big,

For all the vital things

I had to get and to reach.

And yet there is only one great thing,

The only thing,

To live to see the great day that dawns

And the light that fills the world.

– Old Inuit song

PART SIX
Appendices

Strategic Research

The experience, technical background, logistics, complexity, and pure monetary costs associated with research on the scale and scope of the *IOOW-2000* study is typically unavailable to the very people who could best use such information for the greater good of all. It is for this reason we are making the results of this research widely available through *A New America* and the Positive Future Consulting group.

APPENDIX A:
The IOOW-2000 Research

Background on the Research

In Our Own Words 2000 (IOOW-2000) was a three-year landmark research project originally commissioned by the Foundation for Global Awakening and Fund For Global Awakening to explore the state of social and spiritual consciousness of Americans.

At the turn of the millennium, over 1,600 U.S. households were systematically interviewed across America for a representative combination of age and gender selected by each of the twelve Census divisions. The *IOOW-2000* research yielded a wealth of information: rich typologies and valuable conceptual maps showing greater connection than may be apparent among the many diverse tendencies in American society. Most importantly, it identified positive commonalities among Americans that can be used to help stimulate positive social change and greater awareness of our innate spirituality on a societal scale.

- The *IOOW-2000* research examined key values, attitudes, and beliefs concerning forgiveness and tolerance, ethics and leadership, compassion and service, expectations for the next decade, technology, media, healthcare, and other vital contemporary concerns.

- From this, the research presents a set of radically new "typologies" categorizing and differentiating between segments of the adult U.S. population by describing various prevalent traits. Included in the typologies are The 8 American Types, a more fundamental set of three core traits, and various quadrant-type models.

- Presented in a unique context derived not from generic "external" observations, the typologies are instead based on behavioral attitudes, values, and beliefs – a context in which individuals and society can better understand themselves on a more intrinsic basis.

- The results of the survey show that a significant portion of the American population places a high value on spirituality, service, and the interconnectedness of all life – values not yet well-recognized by our leadership or popular culture.

- What was also discovered is that an ever-increasing proportion of the population is embracing a more encompassing understanding of themselves, a deeper spiritual awareness, a universal connectedness, and a belief in working toward a greater common good.

A New America: An awakened future on our horizon underscores this unacknowledged level of connection and commonality, unmistakably affirming the unity within our diversity.

The underlying goal of this research study, and the program of which it was a part, is to document and communicate new perspectives on our society that transcend current social, cultural, and political divisions in order to bring about a more compassionate and positive world.

The analysis of The 8 American Types offers startling insight into our society and indicates new strategies for just such a positive future. The study identifies key areas of strategic importance to all of American society and to individuals in positions of leadership in all sectors. As a major contribution to the study of social research, the innovative typologies of the *IOOW-2000* research provide a valuable tool with which an organization, institutions, businesses, and policy and opinion makers can develop strategies informed by a profound understanding of current American values and aspirations. Such data can also be used to position and target media communications, as well as to assist cultural and political initiatives.

Subsequent phases of this program could include further statistical research, in-depth personal interviews, workshops, and broadcast television programming to heighten awareness of how ordinary people are becoming more spiritually aware of their connection to society, nature, and the cosmos. As part of its overall effort to promote healing and reconciliation, FFGA has developed a media campaign, Messages: Awakening the Heart of Humanity, and a strategic social initiative, Decade of the Heart. Also in the planning is an Internet-based, large-scale portal – The Global Interchange – a new type of social enterprise intended to help foster a more vigorous and visible social-spiritual-economic community of positive future oriented people throughout the world.

Examples of Categories in the *IOOW-2000* Research

Social Beliefs and Attitudes
- Compassion & Service
- Connection & Tolerance
- Forgiveness

Perspectives on Life
- Work & Money
- Future Outlook, World, & Life
- The Next Ten Years

Lifestyle and Media
- Personal Growth
- Leisure Activities
- Media Habits & Attitudes
- Computers & Internet

Health and Well Being
- Current Health & Well Being
- Traumatic Life Experiences
- Health & Wellness Practices

Spirituality, Religion, and Consciousness
- Practices & Beliefs
- Spiritual Self
- Higher Consciousness
- Social & Spiritual Awakening

(Continued on next page)

Politics

- Political Affiliation & Ideology
- Voting
- Ethics & Values of Leaders

Demographics

- Age, Gender, & Children
- Income & Education
- Employment & Occupation
- Housing & Ownership
- Race, Ethnicity, & Birthplace
- Geographic & Related Data

Representing U.S. Society

Because large-scale, statistical research has the capacity to reveal an accurate representation of an entire society, it has the potential to shape public opinion and the perspective of leaders. As we take a new look at the American electorate, key findings of the *IOOW-2000* survey are published for the first time concerning the mindset of the voting and non-voting public leading up to the 2000 U.S. election.

Statistical Research: What Can It Show Us?

How does formal social science research fit in with all this? The *IOOW-2000* study was first intended as a tool for the pure exploration of social consciousness. Once enough data was collected, extensive analysis and review was conducted with a particular focus on the extent to which a shift in consciousness is occurring. Next, we asked ourselves what we could do with these remarkable findings that would be of benefit to others. The result is the first study quantifying, defining, and demonstrating a strategic and powerful direction along which people can move "out of the box" toward their higher aspirations.

The identification of these vitally important factors within our society provided interpretive and strategic insight, insight that will prove much more meaningful and well-grounded than if the information were only based on intuition or opinion.

As for statistical research, analysis based on simple demographics (such as age, gender, income, political party, etc.) confuses matters and provides very little insight into core values and beliefs that inform people's actions, behaviors, and opinions. (For example, knowing statistically that someone is a "white, urban female under 40 years age" tells us very little about what motivates and inspires this individual or what governs her choices.)

Unfortunately, due to cost and expediency, this is what is most commonly used in public opinion and media research. What this also does is help to keep things at a superficial level. When applied to specific strategies and public communications, this approach actually reinforces stereotypes and divisions between people. Since much of advertising research, political campaigns, and media placement rests on such a superficial approach, it is no wonder that our society seems to have self-reinforcing patterns that hold everyone back in a lowest common denominator scenario. Though demographic statistics can describe simple trends and patterns among people, more powerful and sophisticated analyses can describe peoples' traits and types.

A "trait" is a personal characteristic that is relatively persistent and stable across people, places, and time. Traits determine (to a fairly predictable extent) an individual's potential behavior, which can help predict patterns such as voting. From this, a "typology system" can be created that measures multiple traits and determines to what extent they exist (singly or in combination) within the population at large. The *IOOW-2000* typology system, upon which *A New America* is based, is a statistically reliable and valid means of categorizing and differentiating various segments of the U.S. population, each having different combinations of traits.

The rigorous standards observed in data collection and analysis, as well as the extraordinary depth and breadth of the survey instrument, give the *IOOW-2000* research exceptional reliability, validity, and usefulness for a broad range of applications.

Survey Sampling, Methods, and Standards

Conceived in 1993, this groundbreaking *IOOW-2000* study is based on interviews conducted in 2000 and scientifically selected to statistically represent current American society. Each participant answered more than 210 questions covering a broad range of topics. This *IOOW-2000* executive briefing and the multi-volume full report afford a surprising look at American views on politics, leadership, business, ethics, and spirituality – and their important relationship to individuals, society, and the common good.

The *In Our Own Words 2000* research team completed over 1,600 interviews with American householders over 18 years of age. The sample of respondents was closely controlled by age, gender, and geography for each of the 12 standard U.S. Census regions. This is a degree of representativeness seldom achieved in survey research. The overall margin of error is ± 1.5% to ± 2.4% at a 95% confidence level. Each interview took approximately 43 minutes and covered over 210 questions on beliefs, values, and attitudes concerning society, work, spirituality, media, health, and lifestyle.

A team of social scientists and other research professionals was responsible for the design, implementation, analysis, review, and reporting of this major research program. A professional research company employing highly-trained telephone interviewers gathered the data using a computer-aided interviewing system.

What is a Trait?

A "trait" is a personal characteristic that is relatively persistent and stable across people, places, and time. Traits determine (to a fairly predictable extent) an individual's potential behavior.

What is a Typology?

A typology is the analysis of human social groups. It exemplifies an image, impression, or model of a certain set of shared tendencies. Each social group in a typology has unique qualities that are stable, inherent, and essentially defining characteristics as opposed to superficial, impermanent ones. The use of the term "types" then becomes shorthand for variations within a typology.

Technical Note

The psychometric standards and processes for developing a trait-based typology system are beyond the scope of this book. Interested readers may purchase the lengthy *IOOW-2000 Methods and Validity White Paper* for further information.

(Continued on next page)

The proper use of well-constructed and validated assessment instruments is governed by the standards established by The American Psychological Association, The National Council on Measurement in Education, and The American Educational Research Association. These standards arise from traditionally accepted psychometric concepts regarding relevant forms of reliability and validity. The usefulness and credibility of *IOOW-2000* research data and analyses are supported by the project's rigorous adherence to these standards.

Reliability and Psychometrics

When seeking to measure the extent to which people have specific traits, values, attitudes, or beliefs, psychologists typically develop a series of questions that, in combination, give an indication of how a particular group of people think and/or feel about something. Responses to these questions are analyzed using various statistical techniques to determine their reliability and veracity. As used in psychometrics, the term "reliability" means consistency. Cronbach's alpha measures consistency. The higher the alpha, the more reliable the scale.

Any group of questions that has sufficient statistical consistency to be a trustworthy measure is typically called a scale (alpha = .70 or higher). Any group of items that does not have sufficient statistical consistency to be considered a scale (but which may warrant further exploration and improvement) is called an index (alpha = .60 to .70). As such, the Positive Future – Cooperative Integrative (PFCI) questions qualify as a true psychometric scale, while the Social Traditional – Religious Conservative (STRC) questions are only an index requiring further research and refinement in order to provide more reliable assessments. (See Chapter 3 for an introduction to the PFCI scale and STRC index.)

Comparative Research

The *IOOW-2000* Research Program also included comparative summaries and reviews of survey data and other research across many related studies of American values and beliefs concerning ethics, spirituality, and the Internet, which have been conducted by other research foundations, pollsters, academic institutions, and independent researchers. This additional body of work is summarized in the *IOOW-2000* Executive Briefing.

Future Research and Communications

As extensive as the present study may be, there are many future opportunities for cooperative and shared-cost research with other organizations. Additional research and communications work has been anticipated that includes ongoing statistical research, in-depth interviews and group discussions, and television and other communications.

To communicate the insights and creative value of the *IOOW-2000* results, highlights from interviews and group discussions about the 8 Types can be prepared for both popular broadcast television and video-based programming and tailored to specific applications. Showing people speaking in their own words about their awakening to new ways of being – based on compassion and a growing awareness of the connectedness of all life – can offer fresh perspectives that bridge differences within society and can lead to powerful and creative solutions. The needs of young people in their teens and twenties requires special attention in terms of the questions, methods of interviewing, and of course, how this work is to be communicated.

As people speak and share their stories, they become living proof of how individuals and society as a whole can embody a greater capacity to embrace diversity. The outcome is the opening to thresholds of possibility and potential. The trajectory of humanity has the potential to reach beyond its current state of "reality" to something more profoundly engaging and affirming of that which resides deep within us: our true heart's desire.

A Few Technical Notes: Standards for Reliability & Validity (continued)

Content validity

- Each scale represents a set of beliefs, attitudes, or behaviors important to the study (i.e., each scale measures a meaningful area germane to the research).

- Each scale is seen by experts as within the scope of interest (i.e., experts in this field of research agree that each scale is relevant to the study).

Across-item consistency

- Each scale has an alpha coefficient of .70 or higher (i.e., scores on items in a scale are statistically consistent with each other).

The research undertaken by IOOW-2000 highlights how, in many ways, American society appears to be approaching a turning point in its development.

OUR DEEPER CONNECTIONS

"As we look to create a more positive future that emphasizes our common denominators and highest aspirations, new constructs and structures are needed to expand our social and political institutions in support of our higher potential. The three concepts of "connection, service, and spirituality" can help us reach a more inclusive "common ground" that serves our desire for a better world and our awakening to a higher consciousness. Connection, service, and spirituality engage each of us on an individual level which, in turn, embraces the whole of humanity as we look to create a more enlightened future now from our current position in the present. It is the perspective of a "future-present" that enlivens the ideals of our deeper connections, our desire to serve others for a greater good, and an intrinsic spirituality encompassing all of humankind. It is yet another indicator of a social and spiritual awakening on a global scale."

– the Authors

APPENDIX B:
The IOOW-2000 Survey Questions

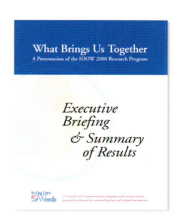

SCALE LEGEND

S1-5	Scale of 1-5
CAT	Categorical Responses
OE	Open Ended Response
YN	Yes/No Response
MR	Multiple Responses

In Our Own Words

Q #	SURVEY QUESTIONS	SCALE

SOCIAL BELIEFS & ATTITUDES

Compassion and Service

A010	I would like to be involved more personally in creating a better world at whatever local or global level I can.	S1-5
A046	I believe that helping those in need is one of the most important things nations can do within the global community.	S1-5
D130	Do you or any members of your household make any charitable contributions?	YN
D135	(If D130 = Y) Which of the following describes a charity to which you or any members of your household make contributions?	CAT
D140	(If D130 = Y) Which of the following amounts best describes your total household contributions over the past year?	CAT
D210	Do you or any members of your household volunteer personal time for purposes outside of the family like charitable causes?	YN

Connection and Tolerance

C030	I have a strong sense of belonging and feeling connected to others in my local community.	S1-5
C035	I sometimes think of moving elsewhere because I feel that I don't belong where I am.	S1-5
A020	People don't seem to connect to each other these days.	S1-5
A225	Interacting with other cultures broadens our horizons.	S1-5
F020	It is important to teach our children to feel a connection to the earth, people, and all life.	S1-5
A075	I often feel lonely and cut off from those around me.	S1-5
A030	Most people cannot be trusted.	S1-5
C010	To have a successful community we don't all have to agree.	S1-5
C040	There is a good balance between the traditional and the modern in my community.	S1-5
C005	We should be tolerant of all lifestyles and groups even if we don't like what they do.	S1-5
C025	My community is too diverse in its beliefs.	S1-5
A080	I feel judged by most others around me.	S1-5

Q #	SURVEY QUESTIONS	SCALE

Forgiveness

A040	I find it easy to let go of emotional hurt inflicted by others.	S1-5
A205	If we could forgive and reconcile all our past hurts and conflicts, we could all accomplish so much more.	S1-5
A195	For me, forgiveness feels like letting go of an uncomfortable burden.	S1-5
A090	I offer forgiveness to those who do me wrong.	S1-5
G800	To what extent do you support having a death penalty in any state of the U.S.?	CAT

WORK AND MONEY

A215	I believe it is important to love the work I do.	S1-5
G045	One of the most important achievements in life is to acquire a higher standard of living.	S1-5
G030	All I want out of life is getting by day-to-day.	S1-5
G010	My main goal in life is to make a lot of money.	S1-5
G005	My main priority is to succeed in my job, business or profession.	S1-5
G055	The things I own aren't all that important to me.	S1-5
G056	Which of the following best describes how important is it for you currently to work hard now to secure your future financial security?	CAT

PERSPECTIVES ON LIFE

A050	I want a world where people live by traditional values.	S1-5
C050	Maintaining law and order is the most important issue today.	S1-5
A025	There is basically only one correct way to live.	S1-5
L010	I take risks that most people don't ever take.	S1-5
A055	I like to have my thinking and beliefs challenged.	S1-5
A085	I believe that good eventually prevails.	S1-5
A175	Greed is one of our greatest problems as a society.	S1-5
A235	I prefer a less complicated way of living with less technology for everyone.	S1-5
F010	I believe that it is possible to see the world around me with the freshness of a child's eyes	S1-5
A100	The statement 'What goes around comes around' is how the universe really works.	S1-5
A130	People have become kinder and more compassionate over the course of history.	S1-5
F015	My family is my most important priority.	S1-5
A065	I believe that most people are genuinely caring.	S1-5
F005	Children and youth are allowed too much freedom today.	S1-5
F030	Family values are the basis for a successful society.	S1-5
G020	I want to accomplish great things in life.	S1-5
A185	Everyone should look at life as a glass half full rather than half empty.	S1-5

Future Outlook on World and Life

A240	No matter what happens in the future, we will adapt to it.	S1-5
S060	Science eventually will be able to explain everything.	S1-5
C055	I am well prepared for natural or man-made disasters such as floods, hurricanes, tornadoes and earthquakes.	S1-5

Q #	SURVEY QUESTIONS	SCALE
C065	Which of the following is the greatest threat to the future of the world?	CAT
F025	I believe that most children are not worried about their future.	S1-5
A160	Technology will help foster trust among people by increasing communication.	S1-5
A140	I believe that the more information and knowledge I have at my fingertips, the better my life will be.	S1-5

The Next Ten Years

C095	During the next 10 years, technological breakthroughs will take care of the environmental problems facing us today.	S1-5
C075	I am concerned that humanity is headed for serious problems and disasters in the next 10 years.	S1-5
C090	Over the next 10 years, I believe that life will go on much the same way as it always has, but with small or minor improvements	S1-5
C100	Over the next 10 years, social and spiritual awakening will make the world a better place to live.	S1-5

LIFESTYLE & MEDIA

Personal Growth

A170	It is important that we each attend to our own personal growth.	S1-5
G025	One of the most important things in my life is expressing my own creativity.	S1-5
L075	Do you read books for inspiration and personal growth?	YN
L080	(If L075 = Y) Which of the following best describes how often you read traditional religious material for inspiration and personal growth?	CAT
L081	(If L075 = Y) Which of the following best describes how often you read metaphysical, New Age or healing books for inspiration and personal growth?	CAT
L082	(If L075 = Y) Which of the following best describes how often you read poetry, novels, or short stories for inspiration and personal growth	CAT
L065	Have you ever attended a New Age cultural event, expo or fair?	
L070	(If L065 = Y) Which of the following best describes how frequently you have attended New Age cultural events, expos or fairs?	L070
L095	Have you ever participated in self-help, personal growth groups or classes?	YN
L100	(L095 = Y) Which of the following best describes how often you participated in self-help, personal growth groups or classes?	CAT
L115	Have you ever made use of psychics, channelers or mediums for personal or business guidance?	YN
L120	(If L115 = Y) Which of the following best describes how often you use psychics, channelers, or mediums for personal or business guidance?	CAT

Leisure Activities

L030	My favorite pastime is reading a good book.	S1-5
L035	I prefer activities that are done around my home.	S1-5
L040	Going for a drive is one of my favorite activities.	S1-5
L045	I enjoy socializing away from home	S1-5
L050	Quiet contemplation is one of my favorite pastimes.	S1-5
L056	Which of the following best describes how often have you traveled outside of the U.S. and Canada for personal reasons or pleasure in the past two years?	CAT
L015	I especially like to spend time in nature.	S1-5
L025	What, if any, physical activities do you enjoy?	OE

Q #	SURVEY QUESTIONS	SCALE

Media Habits

M020	How many days a week do you personally watch television?	OE
M025	Typically, what is the least amount of television you personally watch per day in hours?	OE
M026	Typically, what is the most amount of television you personally watch per day in hours?	OE
M030	How many days a week do you watch local news on television?	OE
M040	How many days a week do you watch national or international news on television?	OE
M050	Do you have cable or satellite television installed at home?	YN
M052	What are the names of your three favorite television channels (broadcast affiliation)?	OE
M070	What are your three favorite television programs?	OE
M080	What are your three favorite movies?	OE
M055	How many days a week do you listen to the radio?	OE
M065	What kind of programming do you primarily listen to on the radio?	MR
L104	Do you purchase books for your own personal use?	YN
M075	What are your three favorite magazines?	OE

Media Beliefs & Attitudes

M005	I wish there were more uplifting news stories.	S1-5
M010	There are too many negative or 'dark' themes on television shows these days.	S1-5
M015	I prefer watching television programs or films that have positive or 'uplifting' themes.	S1-5
A110	Reading or hearing about the hardship of others always touches my heart.	S1-5
M054	Assuming the products and services were what I wanted, I would prefer to purchase from businesses that solidly supported global awakening.	S1-5
M053	When watching television, I would like to see creatively produced 30-second messages which are not connected to any religious institution on themes about spiritual awareness such as forgiveness and connection to all life.	S1-5

Compter and Internet Usage

M095	(If M085 > =1) Do you have access to the Internet at home?	YN
M096	Do you have access to the Internet at work?	YN
M100	(If M095 =Y or M096 =Y) Do you like to browse the Internet?	YN
M105	How much do you use the Internet each week?	CAT
M085	How many computers do you have at home?	OE
M090a	(If M085 = 0) Do you plan to have a home computer in the next six months?	YN
M090b	(If M085 > =1) Do you plan to add another home computer in the next six months?	YN
M110	(If M085 > =1) For what activities do you use your computer at home?	MR
M111	If there were a low-cost online internet service which was entirely dedicated to personal and global transformation for a more compassionate and caring world, was not commercially oriented, and offered a wide range of news and information, interactive discussion services, e-mail, as well as comprehensive Internet access, would you be interested in subscribing?	YN
M112	(If M111 = N) Which of the following best describes why you would not be interested in this service?	CAT

Q #	SURVEY QUESTIONS	SCALE

HEALTH & WELL BEING

Current Health Status

L085	Have you ever participated in professional counseling or psychotherapy sometime in your life?	YN
L090	(If L085 = Y) Which of the following best describes how often you participated in professional counseling or psychotherapy in your life?	CAT
N070	Thinking about your overall health status, are you currently experiencing any serious problems with your health?	YN
N071	(If N070 = Y) Would you say you experience serious health problems:	CAT
N075	In the past 2 years has there been a serious physical or mental health crisis with any member of your immediate family?	YN
N090	Thinking about your overall emotional life, are you currently experiencing any serious problems with your emotional relations?	YN
N095	(If N090 = Y) Would you say you experience serious emotional problems:	CAT
N100	(If D054 = Y) Thinking about your general job history, are you currently experiencing any serious problems with your work life?	YN
N120	At any point in the past four weeks, have you felt so sad and unhappy that nothing could cheer you up?	YN
N125	(If N120 = Y) Would you say you have this experience:	CAT
N130	At any point in the past four weeks, have you felt so anxious and agitated that nothing could calm you down?	YN
N135	(If N130 = Y) Would you say you have this experience:	CAT
G120	Have you ever used tobacco products?	YN
G130	Have you ever used alcohol?	YN
G135	(If G130 = Y) Would you say you drink alcohol:	CAT
G140	Have you ever used marijuana?	YN
G145	(If G140 = Y) Would you say you use marijuana:	CAT
G150	Have you ever used LSD, mescaline or psilocybin?	YN
G160	Have you ever used cocaine, methamphetamines, or ecstasy?	YN

Trauma

N025	As a child or teenager, were you ever been assaulted by a parent, for example being hit or kicked to the point of physical injury such as bruising or cuts?	YN
N030	(If N025 = Y) Would you say you had this experience:	CAT
N055	Have you ever experienced a physical assault from someone who was not a member of your family?	YN
N035	At any time in your life, have you ever lived in a place that was a war zone or armed conflict, or have you been at some point a combatant?	YN
N050	Have you ever been in a major accident like a car crash or plane crash?	YN

Alternative Health Care Practices

L125	Do you currently use vitamins and nutritional supplements as a part of your personal health strategy?	YN
L145	Have you used chiropractic care, massage, Rolfing, or other visceral or skeletal manipulation in the last 2 years?	YN

Q #	SURVEY QUESTIONS	SCALE

L155	Have you used naturopathy, homeopathy, or herbal medicine as an alternative healing method in the last two years?	YN
L160	Have you used acupuncture as an alternative healing method in the past two years?	YN
L170	Have you ever used energy or faith healing as an alternative healing method in the past two years?	YN
L171	(If L170 = Y) Which of the following best describes how frequently you used energy or faith healing in the last 2 years?	CAT

SPIRITUALITY AND RELIGION

Spiritual & Religious Practices

S045	I practice meditation or prayer regularly.	S1-5
S055	I follow the teachings of a specific spiritual or religious teacher.	S1-5
D075	Do you attend church services or other meetings of a religious organization?	Y/N
D080	(If D075 = Y) Which of the following best describes how long you have attended the meetings of your current church or religious organization?	CAT
D085	(If D075 = Y) Which of the following best describes how frequently you attend services or meetings at this church or religious organization?	CAT
D090	Have you ever changed your religion or denomination in your lifetime?	Y/N
D070	Which of the following best describes your religious affiliation?	CAT
S010	Going to church, synagogue, or mosque gives me the opportunity to make and maintain social contacts.	S1-5

Spiritual & Religious Beliefs

S050	I believe that traditional religious literature tells the literal truth.	S1-5
S090	Whether we recognize it or not, we all just want to connect to God or a higher spiritual consciousness.	S1-5
S015	To me religion and spirituality are not the same thing.	S1-5
S080	The best way to connect to God or a higher spiritual consciousness is through yourself.	S1-5
S031	I believe that God or a higher spiritual consciousness is something separate from me.	S1-5
S070	I believe in God or a higher spiritual consciousness	S1-5
S040	I feel that my spiritual needs are not currently being met.	S1-5
S030	Whether I am aware of it or not, I believe that God or a higher spiritual consciousness is present everywhere	S1-5
G085	Do you believe that consciousness or some kind of life-force existed before the universe came into being?	YN

The Spiritual Self

A145	The bottom line is that we are all just looking to be loved and accepted as human beings.	S1-5
A125	I believe that every person has a purpose in life.	S1-5
A150	We all want to experience inner peace.	S1-5
A210	We all need to become more conscious of and connected to all aspects of our own selves.	S1-5
S095	Do you feel the need in your life to experience spiritual growth?	YN

Q #	SURVEY QUESTIONS	SCALE

Global Awakening

A001	Our earth is a unique kind of living organism and as a whole system is fundamentally alive.	S1-5
A115	Underneath it all, we're all connected as one.	S1-5
A180	There is a global awakening to higher consciousness taking place these days.	S1-5
E005	Have you ever been directly aware of or personally influenced by the presence of God or a higher spiritual consciousness?	YN
E010	(If E005 =Y) Would you say you have this experience:	CAT
E035	Have you ever experienced a sense of the sacred in everything around you or perceived everything as being spiritually connected together as one?	YN
E040	(If E035 =Y) Would you say you have this experience:	CAT

EXPANDED CONSCIOUSNESS & NON-ORDINARY EXPERIENCES

E135	Has your child demonstrated wisdom or abilities far beyond his or her life experience or years?	CAT
E050	Have you seen a light without a physical source which seemed to fill the whole space around you but was not due to any kind of medical condition?	YN
E051	(If E050 =Y) Would you say you have this experience:	CAT
E055	While awake, have you ever seen, heard, or felt something which seemed real, but you realized in retrospect was not really there in the same way as ordinary everyday objects?	YN
E056	(If E055 =Y) Would you say you have this experience:	CAT
E095	Have you ever known people's thoughts without being told, known their feelings without having to see or hear them, or known about events before they happen?	YN
E096	(If E095 =Y) Would you say you have this experience:	CAT
E045	Have you ever had a near-death experience, which is an unusual or special conscious experience (while awake) occurring at the time of a major life-threatening event such as a major accident or a medical emergency?	YN
E046	(If E045 =Y) Would you say you have this experience:	CAT
E075	Have you ever had an out-of-body experience, while awake, in which you find yourself floating above your body or seemed to be flying to a place other than where you are physically?	YN
E076	(If E075 =Y) Would you say you have this experience:	CAT
E105	Do you personally know anyone who has encountered extraterrestrial beings?	YN
E115	Have you ever had an experience of being thrust into an alternative reality?	YN
E116	(If E115 =Y) Would you say you have this experience:	CAT
E140	Have you ever felt as though you were receiving the thoughts and inner expressions of your pets or other non-human animals?	YN
E141	(If E140-Y) Would you say you have this experience:	CAT

POLITICAL

D115	Which of the following best describes the likelihood that you will be voting in the year 2000 presidential election?	CAT
D120	If the election were held tomorrow, which one of the following presidential candidates would you vote for?	CAT
A007	I prefer that the politicians I vote for hold higher and more evolved moral and ethical values than my own.	S1-5
A006	I prefer that the politicians I vote for hold the same moral and ethical values I do.	S1-5
D125	Regardless of your actual voter registration, how would you describe your political orientation?	CAT
D129	Which of the following best describes your political ideology?	CAT

Q #	SURVEY QUESTIONS	SCALE

DEMOGRAPHICS

Education, Age, Gender, & Residency

D035	What is the highest grade or year of school you completed?	CAT
D005	When is your birthday? (M/D/Y)	OE
D006	What is your age?	OE
D007	Would you be willing to tell me which of the following best describes your age range?	CAT
Age	Computed age from date of birth and survey date.	--
D010	Gender?	CAT
D031	How long have you lived in the state you currently reside in?	OE

Ethnicity

D015	Which racial or ethnic background best describes you?	CAT
D016	Are you of Spanish or Hispanic origin?	YN
D020	Were you born in the United States?	YN
D030	(If D020 = N) In what country were you born?	OE

Household/Family Size

D040	Which of the following best describes your current marital status?	CAT
D045	How many children reside in your household?	OE
D046	(If D045 = 1) What is the child's age?	OE
D047	(If D045 > 1) What are the children's ages?	OE

Employment, Income and Ownership

D054	Are you currently employed?	YN
D055	(If D054 =Y) Are you currently employed by a private for profit company, a private not-for-profit organization, a governmental agency or department, self-employed in your own business, or working without pay in your family business?	CAT
D056	(If D054 = N) Are you currently retired, out of work for more than 1 year, out of work for less than 1 year, unable to work, a student, or a homemaker?	CAT
D057	(If D054 = N) Are you currently looking for work?	YN
D060	Which of the following best describes your current occupation?	CAT
D061	(If D060 >1) Which of the following best describes the type of industry in which you work?	CAT
D065	Are you a veteran?	YN
D069	Regardless if you are currently employed full-time for someone else or not, are you an owner or co-owner of a business?	YN
D105	Do you have personal ownership in any real estate or property?	YN
D110	Including all possible sources of income, what was the total income for your household last year?	OE
D111	Including all possible sources of income, which of the following ranges best describes the total income for your household last year?	CAT

SCALE LEGEND

S1-5	Scale of 1-5
CAT	Categorical Responses
OE	Open Ended Response
YN	Yes/No Response
MR	Multiple Responses

Partial list of publications and white papers:

Voting Technical Report
Methods and Validity
The Death Penalty in the U.S.

For further information on this research,
please contact us.

APPENDIX C:
Supplemental Research on Religion in the U.S.

The American Religious Landscape

Excerpted from research by John Green, Ph.D., Director: Bliss Institute, University of Akron titled "The American Religious Landscape and the 2004 Presidential Vote: Increased Polarization." The article was published by The Pew Forum on Religion and Public Life.

The American Religious Landscape and the 2004 Presidential Vote: Increased Polarization by John C. Green, Corwin E. Smidt, James L. Guth, and Lyman A. Kellstedt

The American religious landscape was strongly polarized in the 2004 presidential vote and more so than in 2000. Both President Bush and Senator Kerry benefited from strong support among key religious constituencies, with only a few religious groups closely divided.

Increased polarization is the principal finding of the Fourth National Survey of Religion and Politics post-election survey. Other major findings include:

- Mainline Protestants, once a strong Republican constituency, divided their votes evenly between Kerry and Bush, producing the highest level of support for a Democratic presidential candidate in recent times.

- Modernist Mainline Protestants and Catholics strongly supported Kerry, dramatically increasing their Democratic vote and turnout over 2000.

- Kerry gained ground among the Unaffiliated compared to 2000, but turnout remained unchanged.

- Bush's biggest gain came among Latino Protestants, who moved from the Democratic column in 2000 to the Republican column in 2004.

- Non-Latino Catholics, once a bedrock Democratic constituency, gave a majority of their votes to Bush. This gain was largely due to increased support among Traditionalist Catholics, but Bush also won the crucial swing group of Centrist Catholics.

- Black Protestants and Latino Catholics supported Bush at a higher level than in 2000, but were still solidly Democratic.

- Foreign policy and economic priorities were far more important to the overall vote than social issues, such as abortion or same-sex marriage. However, social issue priorities were most important to Bush's religious constituencies. In contrast, economic issues were most important to Kerry's constituencies.

Data and Methods

The Surveys. This report is primarily based on the Fourth National Survey of Religion and Politics, conducted by the Bliss Institute at the University of Akron. The survey was a national random sample of adult Americans (18 years or older), conducted in March, April, and May of 2004. The total number of cases was 4,000 and the margin of error is plus or minus two percent. In November and December of 2004, 2,730 cases were re-interviewed; the margin of error is 2.5 percent. The pre-election report can be found at www.uakron.edu/bliss/research.php. Voter turnout was estimated by weighting reported turnout to match overall national turnout among vote eligible population. Similar surveys were taken in the spring of 1992, 1996, and 2000. All of these surveys were supported by grants from the Pew Charitable Trusts, and in 2004, by the Pew Forum on Religion & Public Life.

Defining the Religious Landscape

The eighteen categories used in this report were derived from measures of religious belonging, believing, and behaving. (For more details on the construction of these measures, contact John Green, the Bliss Institute, green@uakron.edu.)

The first step was to use the detailed denominational affiliation collected in the survey to sort respondents into religious traditions. Ambiguous categories (such as "just a Christian") were sorted with the aid of other religious measures. Latino Protestants and Catholics and Black Protestants were then placed in separate categories because of their religious and political distinctiveness.

The remaining portions of three major traditions were then broken into traditionalists, centrists, and modernists based on three sets of measures. First, six belief measures (belief in God, belief in an afterlife, views of the Bible, the existence of the devil, evolution, and the truth of all the world's religions) were combined into a single scale running from the most traditional beliefs to the most modern. This measure allowed for a great deal of nuance. Second, five measures of religious behavior (worship attendance, financial support of a congregation, private prayer, scripture reading, and participation in small groups) and the salience of religion were combined into a single scale running from the lowest to highest level of religious engagement.

Third, scales measuring identification with religious traditionalist and modernist religious movements were constructed. For evangelical Protestants, traditionalists were those who claimed to be fundamentalist, evangelical, Pentecostal, or charismatic, and those without movement identification who agreed in preserving religious traditions. Modernists were those who claimed to be liberal or progressive, ecumenical or mainline and those without a movement identification who agreed in adopting modern religious beliefs and practices. For mainline Protestants and Catholics, traditionalists were those who claimed to be "traditional or conservative" in the context of movement identification and those without movement identification who agreed in preserving religious traditions. Modernists were those who claimed to be liberal or progressive in the context of movement identification and those without a movement identification who agreed in adopting modern religious beliefs and practices.

For the three largest religious traditions (white evangelical and mainline Protestants and non-Latino Catholic), the belief, behavior and movement scales were combined and then divided into three groups. Although the cut-points were slightly different in each of the major tradition (reflecting their special circumstances), the traditionalists scored high on all three scales – identifying with traditionalist religious movements, having traditional beliefs, and a high level of religious engagement. The modernists identified with modernist religious movements and had a high level of modern beliefs (religious engagement made less difference in defining modernists, but overall modernists had longer levels of religious engagement). Centrists were members of each tradition that did not fall into the traditionalist or modernist groups.

Finally, the respondents who reported no religious affiliation were subdivided on the basis of belief. The Unaffiliated Believers were those with the same level of belief as the Centrists in the three largest traditions. Atheists and Agnostics were defined by self-identification, and the Seculars were the residual category.

While these categories are certainly not definitive, they do capture important regularities across the American religious landscape. Table 7 lists the size of the original categories and the partisanship of the groups; Table 8 illustrates the content of these categories by looking at three important measures of religiosity: worship attendance, views of God, and views of traditional beliefs and practices.

THE RELIGIOUS LANDSCAPE AND SELF-IDENTIFIED PARTISANSHIP, SPRING 2004

	Percent Population	Partisanship*		
		Republican	Independent	Democratic
ALL	100.0%	38%	20	42
Evangelical Protestant	26.3	56%	17	27
Traditionalist Evangelical	12.6	70%	10	20
Centrist Evangelical	10.8	47%	22	31
Modernist Evangelical	2.9	30%	26	44
Mainline Protestant	16.0	44%	18	38
Traditionalist Mainline	4.3	59%	10	31
Centrist Mainline	7.0	46%	21	33
Modernist Mainline	4.7	26%	20	54
Latino Protestants	2.8	37%	20	43
Black Protestants	9.6	11%	18	71
Catholic	17.5	41%	15	44
Traditionalist Catholic	4.4	57%	13	30
Centrist Catholic	8.1	34%	19	47
Modernist Catholic	5.0	38%	11	51
Latino Catholic	4.5	15%	24	61
Other Christian	2.7	42%	36	22
Other Faiths	2.7	12%	33	55
Jewish	1.9	21%	11	68
Unaffiliated	16.0	27%	30	43
Unaffiliated Believers	5.3	28%	37	35
Secular	7.5	29%	27	44
Atheist, Agnostic	3.2	19%	27	54

* Partisan "leaners" included with Republicans and Democrats; minor party affiliation included with independents.Source: Fourth National Survey of Religion and Politics, Bliss Institute University of Akron, March-May 2004 (N=4000).

DEFINING THE RELIGIOUS LANDSCAPE: MEASURES OF RELIGION

	Worship Attendance:			View of God:			View of Tradition:		
	Regular	Often	Rarely	Personal	Impersonal	Unsure	Preserve	Adapt	Adopt
ENTIRE SAMPLE	43%	32	25	40%	41	19	45%	40	15
Evangelical Protestant									
Traditionalist Evangelical	87%	11	2	89%	11	0	78%	18	2
Centrist Evangelical	36%	41	23	60%	37	3	48%	43	9
Modernist Evangelical	23%	46	31	12%	56	32	30%	42	28
Mainline Protestant									
Traditionalist Mainline	59%	33	8	75%	24	1	61%	35	4
Centrist Mainline	33%	45	22	28%	55	17	33%	53	14
Modernist Mainline	19%	46	35	4%	58	38	3%	62	35
Latino Protestants	63%	31	6	57%	33	10	57%	29	14
Black Protestants	57%	33	10	54%	44	2	43%	38	19
Catholic									
Traditionalist Catholic	87%	11	2	56%	44	0	65%	32	3
Centrist Catholic	45%	36	20	34%	59	7	29%	55	16
Modernist Catholic	21%	49	30	4%	56	40	3%	66	31
Latino Catholic	47%	41	12	35%	55	10	44%	31	25
Other Christian	57%	28	15	43%	43	14	63%	28	9
Other Faiths	40%	35	25	12%	62	26	37%	43	20
Jewish	24%	49	27	10%	45	45	37%	46	17
Unaffiliated									
Unaffiliated Believers	9%	33	58	15%	70	15	NA	NA	NA
Secular	1%	20	79	2%	28	70	NA	NA	NA
Atheist, Agnostic	1%	16	83	0%	5	95	NA	NA	NA

Legend: Worship attendance: "regular": weekly or more; "often": 1-2 a month; few times a year; "rarely": seldom or never; View of God: "Personal": God is a person; "Impersonal": God is a spirit or force; "Unsure": not sure or doesn't believe in God; View of Tradition: "Preserve": strive to preserve beliefs/practices; "Adapt": strive to adapt beliefs/practices to new times; "Adopt": strive to adopt new beliefs/practices; NA: Not asked.

APPENDIX D:
Hallmarks of Fascism

Commonalities of Fascist or Proto-fascist Countries

1. Powerful and continuing expressions of nationalism. From the prominent displays of flags and bunting to the ubiquitous lapel pins, the fervor to show patriotic nationalism ... often bordered on xenophobia.

2. Disdain for the importance of human rights. Through clever use of propaganda, the population was brought to accept these human rights abuses by marginalizing, even demonizing, those being targeted. When abuse was egregious, the tactic was to use secrecy, denial, and disinformation.

3. Identification of enemies/scapegoats as a unifying cause. The most significant common thread among these regimes was the use of scapegoating as a means to divert the people's attention from other problems, to shift blame for failures, and to channel frustration in controlled directions. ...relentless propaganda and disinformation were usually effective. Active opponents of these regimes were inevitably labeled as terrorists and dealt with accordingly.

4. The supremacy of the military/avid militarism. Ruling elites always identified closely with the military and the industrial infrastructure that supported it. A disproportionate share of national resources was allocated to the military, even when domestic needs were acute.

5. Rampant sexism. Beyond the simple fact that the political elite and the national culture were male-dominated, these regimes inevitably viewed women as second-class citizens. They were adamantly anti-abortion and also homophobic. These attitudes were usually codified in Draconian laws that enjoyed strong support by the orthodox religion of the country, thus lending the regime cover for its abuses.

6. A controlled mass media. ...mass media were under strict direct control and could be relied upon never to stray from the party line. ... subtle power to ensure media orthodoxy ... control of licensing and access

to resources, economic pressure, appeals to patriotism, and implied threats. The leaders of the mass media were often politically compatible with the power elite.

7. Obsession with national security. Inevitably, a national security apparatus was under direct control of the ruling elite. It was usually an instrument of oppression, operating in secret and beyond any constraints.

8. Religion and ruling elite tied together. ...attached themselves to the predominant religion of the country and chose to portray themselves as militant defenders of that religion. ...opposing the power elite was tantamount to an attack on religion.

9. Power of corporations protected. Although the personal life of ordinary citizens was under strict control, the ability of large corporations to operate in relative freedom was not compromised.

10. Power of labor suppressed or eliminated. Since organized labor was seen as the one power center that could challenge the political hegemony of the ruling elite and its corporate allies, it was inevitably crushed or made powerless.

11. Disdain and suppression of intellectuals and the arts. ...freedom of ideas and expression ...were anathema to. ...Intellectual and academic freedom were considered subversive to national security and the patriotic ideal. ...politically unreliable faculty harassed or eliminated.

12. Obsession with crime and punishment. Most of these regimes maintained Draconian systems of criminal justice with huge prison populations. Fear, and hatred, of criminals or "traitors" was often promoted among the population as an excuse for more police power.

13. Rampant cronyism and corruption. ...business circles and close to the power elite often used their position to enrich themselves. ...worked both ways; the power elite would receive financial gifts and property from the economic elite, who in turn would gain the benefit of government favoritism. ...power elite were in a position to obtain vast wealth.

14. Fraudulent elections. elections with candidates ...would usually be perverted by the power elite to get the desired result. ...methods included control of the election machinery, intimidating and disenfranchising opposition voters, destroying or disallowing legal votes, and, as a last resort, turning to a judiciary beholden to the power elite.

– from Laurence W. Britt, *Free Inquiry Magazine,* Volume 23, Number 2

Does any of this ring alarm bells? Of course not. After all, this is America, officially a democracy with the rule of law, a constitution, a free press, honest elections, and a well-informed public constantly being put on guard against evils. Historical comparisons like these are just exercises in verbal gymnastics. Maybe, maybe not.

– from Laurence W. Britt, *Free Inquiry Magazine,* Volume 23, Number 2

APPENDIX E:
Bibliography and Source Readings

The following books and other sources have been of some value in preparing
A New America, An Awakened Future on Our Horizon.

Although no websites are listed here, we urge the reader to search out the wealth of information available via the Internet and, with an open mind and heart, discern for themselves.

Alcoholics Anonymous. The Big Book. Alcoholics Anonymous World Services, 1976.

Alder, Vera Stanley. The Initiation of the World. Samuel Weiser, 2000

Alder, Vera Stanley. When Humanity Comes of Age. The Initiation of the World. Samuel Weiser, 1974

Alterman, Eric. What Liberal Media? – The Truth About Bias and the News. Basic Books, 2003

Andreev, Daniel. The Rose of the World. Lindisfarne Books, 1997

Armstrong, Karen. Holy War – The Crusades. and Their Impact on Today's World. Anchor Books, 1988

Barna, George. The Index of Leading Spiritual Indicators: A Statistical Report on the State of Religion in America. Nashville: West Publishing Group, 1996

Beaudoin, Tom. Virtual Faith: The Irreverent Quest of Generation X. New York: John Wiley & Sons, 1998.

Beck, Don Edward and Christopher C. Cowan. Spiral Dynamics – Mastering Values, Leadership, and Change. Blackwell Business Press, 1999

Bentov, Itzhak. A Brief Tour of Higher Consciousness – A Cosmic Book on the Mechanics of Creation. Destiny Books, 2000

Borjesson, Kristina. Into the Buzzsaw – Leading Journalists Expose the Myth of a Free Press. Prometheus Books, 2002

Bushby, Tony. The Bible Fraud – An Untold Story of Jesus Christ. The Pacific Blue Group, 2001

Carey, Ken. Flat Rock Journal – A Day in the Ozark Mountains. Harper San Francisco, 194

Chossudovsky, Michael. The Globalization of Poverty and the New World Order. Ontario, Canada: Global Outlook, 2003.

Chossudovsky, Michael. War and Globalization – The Truth Behind September 11. Ontario, Canada: Global Outlook, 2002.

deChardin, Pierre Teilhard. The Future of Man. Harper, 1969

deCrèvecoeur, J. Hector St. John de. Letters from an American Farmer: And Sketches of Eighteenth-Century America. New York: Penguin Group, 1981.

Dalai Lama, His Holiness. Ethics for a New Millennium: His Holiness The Dalai Lama. New York: Penguin Putnam, 1999.

Dalai Lama, His Holiness. The Good Heart – A Buddhist Perspective on the Teachings of Jesus. Wisdom Publications 1996

Eisler, Riane. The Power of Partnership. New World Library, 2002

Ellis, Joseph. Founding Brothers: The Revolutionary Generation. New York: Random House, 2002.

Etzioni, Amitai. The New Golden Rule – Community and Morality in a Democratic Society. Basic Books, 1996.

Florida, Richard. The Rise of the Creative Class: And How It's Transforming Work, Leisure, Community and Everyday Life. New York: Basic Books, 2002.

Gardiner, Laurence. Genesis of the Grail Kings. Element Books, 2000

Griffin David Ray .The New Pearl Harbor – Disturbing Questions about the Bush Administration and 9/11. Olive Branch Press, 2004

Hamburger, Philip. Separation of Church and State. Boston: Harvard University Press, 2004.

Hanh, Thict Nhat. Going Home – Jesus and Buddha as Brothers. Riverhead Books 1990

Hawken, Paul, Amory Lovins, and L. Hunter Lovins. Natural Capitalism: Creating the Next Industrial Revolution. New York: Little, Brown and Company, 1999.

Hibbing, John, and Elizabeth Theiss-Morse. Stealth Democracy: American's Beliefs about How Government Should Work. New York: Cambridge University Press, 2002.

Hubbard, Barbara Marx. The Revelation: Our Crisis is a Birth. Springfield: Nataraj Publishers, 1993.

Hubbard, Barbara Marx. Conscious Evolution: Awakening the Power of Our Social Potential. Novato: New World Library, 1998.

Jaffa, Harry. A New Birth of Freedom: Abraham Lincoln and the Coming of the Civil War. Lanham: Rowman & Littlefield Publishers, 2000.

James, William. Varieties of Religious Experiences. New York: Routledge, 2002.

Jacobson. Leonard. Bridging Heaven and Earth – A Return to the One. Conscious Living Publication 1999.

Joseph, James. Remaking America: How the Benevolent Traditions of Many Cultures Are Transforming Our National Life. Jossey Bass

Judis, John B., and Ruy Teixeira. The Emerging Democratic Majority. New York: Scribner, 2002.

Hartmann, Thom. Unequal protection – The Rise of Corporate Dominance and the Theft of Human Rights. Rodale Press, 2002

Kurzweil, Ray. The Age of Spiritual Machines. New York: Penguin Group, 1999.

LaFollette, Robert. M. La Follette's Autobiography – A Personal Narrative of Political Experiences. University of Wisconsin Press, 1960

Lakoff, George. Moral Politics: How Liberals and Conservatives Think. Chicago: University of Chicago Press, 2002.

McIlhany, William H., II. The Tax-Exempt Foundations. Arlington House, 1980.

McWhorter, John. The Power of Babel. New York: Henry Holt & Co., 2001.

Millegan, Kris et al. Fleshing Out Skull and Bones – Investigations into America's Most Powerful Secret Society. TrineDay, 2003

Morgan, Lewis Henry. Ancient Society. Transaction Publishers 2000

Nace, Ted. Gangs of America – The Rise of Corporate Power and the Disabling of Democracy. Berrett-Kohler, 203

Needleman, Jacob. The American Soul: Rediscovering the Wisdom of the Founders. New York: Penguin Putnam, 2002.

Neihardt, John G. Black Elk Speaks. Pocket Books 1972

O'Neal, David ed. Meister Eckhart – from Whom God Hid Nothing. Shambhala. 1996

Palast, Greg. The Best Democracy Money Can Buy – The Truth about Corporate Cons, Globalization, and High-Finance Fraudsters. Plume Book, 2002

Parker, A.C. The Constitution of the Five Nations or the Iroquois Book of the Great Law. Canada: Iroqrafts, 1984

Quigley, Carroll. Tragedy and Hope: A History of the World in Our Time (New York: Macmillan, 1966

Ravitch, Diane. The Language Police – How Pressure Groups Restrict What Students Learn. Alfred Knopf, 2003

Ring, Kenneth and Evelyn Elsaesser Valarino. Lessons form the Light – What We Can Learn from the Near-Death Experience. Persus Books, 1998.

Robinson, James M. The Nag Hammadi Library. Harper San Francisco 1990.

Roof, Wade Clark. Spiritual Marketplace: Baby Boomers and the Remaking of American Religion. Princeton: Princeton University Press, 1999.

Ruppert, Michael C. Crossing the Rubicon – The Decline of the American Empire at the End of the Age of Oil. New Society, 2004

Scaff, Gregory. Wampum Belts - Peace Trees – George Morgan, Native Americans, and Diplomacy. Fulcrum Publishing, 1990

Schell, Jonathan. The Unconquerable World: Power, Nonviolence, and the Will of the People. New York: Henry Holt and Company, 2003.

Skarin, Annalee. Ye Are Gods. DeVorss, 1992

Snow, Chet. Mass Dreams of the Future. Deep Forest Press, 1989.

Sussman, Linda. The Speech of the Grail – A Journey Toward Speaking that Heals and Transforms. Lindisfarne Press, 1995

Taylor, Eugene. Shadow Culture. Washington, D.C.: Counterpoint, 1999.

Tocqueville, Alexis de. Democracy in America. New York: Penguin Putnam, 2001.

Van Vrekhem, Georges. The Mother - The Story of Her Life. HarperCollins, India, 2000

Van Vrekhem, Georges. Beyond the Human Specieis – The Life and Works of Sri Aurobindo and The Mother. Paragon House, 1998.

Sri Aurobindo, various writings

Walsh, Neale Donald. Conversations with God - Book 1. Putnam 1996

Whitman, Walt. Democratic Vistas and Other Papers. New London: Fredonia Books, 2002.

Whitman, Walt. Preface: Leaves of Grass. : Bandanna Books, 1992.

Wise, Elia. Letter to Earth – Who We Are Becoming…What We Need to Know. New York: Harmony Books, 2000

Zinn, Howard. A People's History of the United States. Harper Colophon Books, 1980.

Articles Cited in the Original *IOOW-2000* Research

Astin, J. A. (1998) Why Patients use Alternative Medicine: Results of a National Study. Journal of the American Medical Association. 279, 19. 1548-53.

Couper, D. (1998). Forgiveness in the community: Views from an Episcopal priest and former chief of police.

In Enright, R. & North, J. (Eds.) Exploring Forgiveness. Madison, WI: University of Wisconsin Press. 121-130.

Eisenberg, D., Davis, R., Ettner, S. Appel, S. Wilkey, S., Van Rompay, M., Kessler, R. (1998). Trends in alternative medicine use in the United States, 1990-1997). Journal Of the American Medical Association. 280, 1569-1575.

Eisenberg, D., Kessler, R., Foster, C., Norlock, R. Calkins, D. & Delbanco, T. (1993). Unconventional medicine in the United States. The New England Journal of Medicine. 246-252.

Enright, R. & North, J. (1998). Introducing forgiveness. In Enright, R. & North, J. (Eds.). Exploring Forgiveness. Madison, WI: University of Wisconsin Press.

Genia, Vicky. The Spiritual Experience Index: Revision and Reformulation. Review of Religious Research, Vol. 38 No. 4 (June, 1997), and pp: 344-61.

Hoffmann, J. (1998). Confidence in Religious Institutions and Secularization: Trends and Implications. Review of Religious Research, Vol.39 No. 4. 321-43.

Inglehart, R., Basanez, M. and Moreno, A. (1998). Human values and beliefs: A cross-cultural sourcebook.. Ann Arbor, MI: University of Michigan Press.

North, J. (1998). The "ideal" of forgiveness: A philosopher's exploration. In Enright, R. & North, J. (Eds.) Exploring Forgiveness. Madison, WI: University of Wisconsin Press. 15-34.

Scott, R. (posted 2.1.99). The Practice of Forgiveness.

Shriver, D. (1998). Is there forgiveness in politics? Germany, Vietnam, and America. In Enright, R. & North, J. (Eds.) Exploring Forgiveness. Madison, WI: University of Wisconsin Press. 131-149.

Tutu, D. Without forgiveness there is no future. Enright, R. & North, J. (Eds.) (1998). Exploring Forgiveness. Madison, WI: University of Wisconsin Press. Xiii-xiv.

Utne Reader (March-April 1999):

Creedon, J. (1999, March-April). To hell and back. Utne Reader, 56-59.

Dowrick, S. (1999, March-April). The art of letting go. Utne Reader, 46-50.

Gelernter, D. (1999, March-April). What do murderers deserve? Utne Reader, 52-53.

Layton, M. (1999, March-April). Apology not accepted. Utne Reader, 45-50.

Mitchell, E. (1999, March-April). The decade of atonement. Utne Reader, 58-59.

Steiner, A. (1999, March-April). Mother knows best. Utne Reader, 51.

Stimpson, C. (1999, March-April). The victim's dilemma. Utne Reader, 54-55.

Van Biema, D. (1999, April 5). Should all be forgiven? Giving up that grudge could be good for your health. Time.

Zinnbauer, B., Pargament, K., Cole, B., Rye, M., Butter, E., Belavich, T. Hippm K., Scott, A., Kadar.J. (1997). Religion and Spirituality: Unfuzzing the Fuzzy. Journal for the Scientific Study of Religion, 549-64.

Reports & Working papers reviewed for the original *IOOW-2000* Research:

Elgin, D. (1997). Collective Consciousness and Cultural Healing. The Fetzer Institute.

Elgin, D. & LeDrew, C. (1997). Global Consciousness Change: Indicators of an Emerging Paradigm. The Simple Living Network.

Fetzer Institute/National Institute on Aging Working Group. (1999, October). Multidimensional measurement of religiousness/spirituality for use in health research. Kalamazoo, MI: 18) Fetzer Institute. General Social Survey (GSS) 1997-1998.

Forman, R., Davison, K., and Jorgensen, S. (1997). Grassroots Spirituality. The Forge Institute and Fetzer Institute.

Hubbard, Barbara Marx. (1998). Conscious evolution: Awakening the power of our social potential. Novato, CA: New World Library.

Kornfield, Jack. (1990). Buddhist Meditation and Consciousness Research. Institute of Noetic Sciences.

Ray, Paul. (1996). The Integral Culture Survey. Sausalito, CA: Institute of Noetic Sciences.

Herman, Willis W. and Quincey, Christian de. The scientific Exploration of Consciousness: Toward an Adequate Epistemology. Research report. Causality Project CP-6. Sausalito, CA: Institute of Noetic Sciences.

Books Referenced in the Original *IOOW-2000* Research

Griffin, David Ray (1997). Parapsychology, philosophy, and spirituality: A postmodern exploration. Albany, NY: SUNY Press.

Harman, Willis (1998). Global Mind Change. San Francisco: Berrett-Koehler Publishers, Inc.

Roof, W.C. (1999). Spiritual Marketplace. Princeton, NJ: Princeton University Press.

Taylor, E. (1999). Shadow Culture: Psychology and spirituality in America. Washington, DC: Counterpoint.

Wuthnow, R. (1998). After heaven: Spirituality in America since the 1950s. Berkeley, CA: University of California Press.

Additional Summary of *IOOW-2000* References:

A Campaign for Forgiveness Research

Astin, J. A. (1998) Why Patients use Alternative Medicine: Results of a National Study. Journal of the American Medical Association. 279, 19. 1548-53.

Barna Research on line April 26, 2000.

Barna, George. (1996). Index of Leading Spiritual Indicators. Dallas, TX: Word Publishing.

Couper, D. (1998). Forgiveness in the community: Views from an Episcopal priest and former chief of police. In Enright, R. & North, J. (Eds.) Exploring Forgiveness. Madison, WI: University of Wisconsin Press. 121-130.

Eisenberg, D., Davis, R., Ettner, S. Appel, S. Wilkey, S., Van Rompay, M., Kessler, R. (1998). Trends in alternative medicine use in the United States, 1990-1997). Journal of the American Medical Association. 280, 1569-1575.

Eisenberg, D., Kessler, R., Foster, C., Norlock, R. Calkins, D. & Delbanco, T. (1993). Unconventional medicine in the United States. The New England Journal of Medicine. 246-252.

Elgin, D. (1997). Collective Consciousness and Cultural Healing. The Fetzer Institute.

Elgin, D. & LeDrew, C. (1997). Global Consciousness Change: Indicators of an Emerging Paradigm. The Simple Living Network.

Enright, R. & North, J. (1998). Introducing forgiveness. In Enright, R. & North, J. (Eds.). Exploring Forgiveness. Madison, WI: University of Wisconsin Press.

Fetzer Institute/National Institute on Aging Working Group. (1999, October). Multidimensional measurement of religiousness/spirituality for use in health research. Kalamazoo, MI: Fetzer Institute. General Social Survey (GSS) 1997-1998.

Forman, R., Davison, K., and Jorgensen, S. (1997). Grassroots Spirituality. The Forge Institute and Fetzer Institute.

Gallup, G., Jr. & Lindsay, D.M. (1999). Surveying the religious landscape. Harrisburg, PA: Morehouse Publishing.

Genia, Vicky. The Spiritual Experience Index: Revision and Reformulation. Review of Religious Research, Vol. 38 No. 4 (June, 1997), and pp: 344-61.

Griffin, David Ray (1997). Parapsychology, philosophy, and spirituality: A postmodern exploration. Albany, NY: SUNY Press.

Harman, Willis (1998). Global Mind Change. San Francisco: Berrett-Koehler Publishers, Inc.

Hoffmann, J. (1998). Confidence in Religious Institutions and Secularization: Trends and Implications. Review of Religious Research, Vol.39 No.4. 321-43.

Hubbard, Barbara Marx. (1998). Conscious evolution: Awakening the power of our social potential. Novato, CA: New World Library.

Inglehart, R., Basanez, M. and Moreno, A. (1998). Human values and beliefs: A cross-cultural sourcebook. Ann Arbor, MI: University of Michigan Press.

International Forgiveness Day

International Forgiveness Institute

Kornfield, J. (1990). Buddhist Meditation and Consciousness Research. Institute of Noetic Sciences.

Lenhart, A. (2000, September). Who's not online: 57% of those without Internet access say they do not plan to log on. Pew Internet and American Life Project. www.pewinternet.org/

North, J. (1998). The "ideal" of forgiveness: A philosopher's exploration. In Enright, R. & North, J. (Eds.) Exploring Forgiveness. Madison, WI: University of Wisconsin Press. 15-34

National Public Radio – Internet Technology Survey

Pew 1999 Millennium Survey – July 3, 1999.

Pew Center for Civic Journalism – Straight Talk from American 2000.

Pew Media Consumption - June 8, 1998.

Pew New Internet Users: What do they do online, what they

don't, and implications for the "Net" future. 2000.

Pew Religion and Politics – June 25, 1996.

Pew Value Updates - April 20, 1998.

Rainie, L. (2000, May). Tracking online life: How women use the Internet to cultivate relationships with family and friends. Pew Internet and American Life Project. www.pewinternet.org/

Ray, P. (1996). The Integral Culture Survey. Sausalito, CA: Institute of Noetic Sciences.

Roof, W.C. (1999). Spiritual Marketplace. Princeton, NJ: Princeton University Press.

Scott, R. (posted 2.1.99). The Practice of Forgiveness.

Shriver, D. (1998). Is there forgiveness in politics? Germany, Vietnam, and America. In Enright, R. & North, J. (Eds.) Exploring Forgiveness. Madison, WI: University of Wisconsin Press. 131-149.

Taylor, E. (1999). Shadow Culture: Psychology and spirituality in America. Washington, DC: Counterpoint.

The scientific Exploration of Consciousness: Toward and Adequate Epistemology. Herman Willis W. and Quincey, Christian de. Research report Causality Project CP-6. Institute of Noetic Sciences.

The UCLA Internet Report: Surveying the digital Future. October 2000.

Tutu, D. Without forgiveness there is no future. Enright, R. & North, J. (Eds.) (1998). Exploring Forgiveness. Madison, WI: University of Wisconsin Press. Xiii-xiv.

U.S. Department of Commerce. (2000). Falling through the Net: Toward digital inclusion.

Utne Reader (March-April 1999):

Creedon, J. (1999, March-April). "To hell and back." Utne Reader, 56-59

Dowrick, S. (1999, March-April). "The art of letting go." Utne Reader, 46-50

Gelernter, D. (1999, March-April). "What do murderers deserve?" Utne Reader, 52-53.

Layton, M. (1999, March-April). "Apology not accepted." Utne Reader, 45-50

Mitchell, E. (1999, March-April). "The decade of atonement." Utne Reader, 58-59.

Steiner, A. (1999, March-April). "Mother knows best." Utne Reader, 51.

Stimpson, C. (1999, March-April). "The victim's dilemma." Utne Reader, 54-55.

Van Biema, D. (1999, April 5). "Should all be forgiven? Giving up that grudge could be good for your health." Time.

Wuthnow, R. (1998). After Heaven: Spirituality in America since the 1950s. Berkeley, CA: University of California Press.

Zinnbauer, B., Pargament, K., Cole, B., Rye, M., Butter, E., Belavich, T. Hippm K., Scott, A., Kadar.J. (1997). Religion and Spirituality: Unfuzzing the Fuzzy. Journal for the Scientific Study of Religion, 549-64.

APPENDIX F:
Background on Principal Authors and Contributors

Alexander S. Kochkin - Project Director

In 1993 Alex Kochkin wrote of a research study that would inform, enlighten, heal, and inspire all people. It was named, at the time, In Our Own Words and included a mass media component that would help communicate the greater commonality of values and higher aspirations all people have. It was not until 1998 and the founding of Fund For Global Awakening with Tish Van Camp, his wife and spiritual partner, that the first phase of this dream would come into being and eventually lead to this book.

Alex is also a founder of The Global Interchange, a new type of social enterprise designed to utilize the latest in information technology for the highest good. He is also a director of Foundation for Global Awakening, a private foundation, and of Fund For Global Awakening, a public benefit corporation. It was through Fund For Global Awakening that various leading-edge projects were begun, including a large-scale social science research project (In Our Own Words 2000); research and planning into an advanced Internet-based social enterprise (eventually leading to the founding of The Global Interchange); social and educational initiatives including a television and print campaign on forgiveness ("Messages: Awakening the Heart of Humanity"); a successful school program for young people (Language of the Awakened Heart); a television documentary and book series on social and personal transformation; and more.

He has a 20-year professional background that includes employment and consulting in advanced optics, control, and measurement systems for scientific and industrial uses as well as experience with natural resources and international trade. Assignments included an emphasis on product development, marketing management and planning; qualitative and quantitative research; and strategic information and data services for scores of commercial, governmental, and non-profit clients. He has been an expert user of dedicated on-line and Internet-based information systems for more than 25 years. His facility for effectively working in a fluid environment with complex sets of information and synergistic relationships remains one of his operating strengths.

His background includes extensive knowledge of many spiritual traditions, experience with many scientific and technical disciplines, as well as historical and cultural research. He has carried a passion for a global spiritual and social awakening most of his life. Since a very early age, Alex has been aware of the vastness of consciousness and has been concerned with human evolution and consciousness. This also served to develop an early and ongoing interest in the natural and physical sciences. Various transformative experiences led to further emphasis on spiritual awakening and exploring the potential for the spiritual and bio-physical transformation of humanity.

Other personal background includes: studied music and visual arts, extensive experience in precision mechanical design and manufacture, helped to found a non-graded alternative high school in New York, progressive social activism, natural and mineral sciences, equestrian training, scuba diving, and avid gardening.

Patricia M. Van Camp – Project Director

Tish Van Camp is president of Foundation for Global Awakening (formerly the Van Camp Foundation), co-founder and vice-president of Fund For Global Awakening (formerly Institute for Social Trauma), and director and co-founder of The Global Interchange. Compelled by her commitment to social transformation, she started the Institute for Social Trauma in 1993 to find effective ways for large-scale social interventions to aid in global healing and awakening. She has been an active philanthropist through the Van Camp Foundation since 1990, a key participant at various private invitational conferences, and was an invited presenter at the U.S. Council on Foundations.

She comes to her work with a broad perspective gained from an in-depth background in conservationism, art, commercial albacore fishing, ballet, photography, archeology, world travel, philanthropy, and spiritual, psychological, and physical healing. Her experience includes an intense study of art, experience in archeological fieldwork in Europe and the Middle East, and the founding of a Tai-Chi center in Western Canada.

A social visionary from an early age, as a young child she experienced a clear vision about the need to heal the world. A diverse life journey eventually provided the clarity and the skills for her to realize her original dream, culminating initially through her philanthropic work at funding innovative programs for the healing and prevention of child sexual abuse and family violence in the U.S. and Eastern Europe. And later, through her ground-breaking work at FFGA, addressing the awakening of individuals to their full consciousness and potential.

As a young woman, her work as a field archeologist in Israel, Cyprus, and the Occupied Territories had a profound effect on her life. Transcending cultural, racial and religious boundaries, and viewing different sets of beliefs, she gained a broad perspective of nations, countries, and peoples and the importance of eliminating pre-conceptions. Witnessing the challenges and struggles of living in a potentially volatile environment, she learned the value of not focusing on the polarity between the Arabs and the Israelis, and the importance of employing heart-centered diplomacy.

Reflected in her life and her work is the importance of eliminating pre-judgments and the value of approaching all conflict with an open mind and heart, while looking for a higher path of healing that transcends sides. She seeks the healing vector – the higher ground between pairs of opposites.

This insight and understanding, along with her fortuitous meeting with Alex Kochkin, developed an expanded awareness that led IST to be renamed and reborn as Fund For Global Awakening in 1997. Her meeting with Alex resulted in a partnership and synthesis of her work in recognizing very deeply the suffering of the world. His large and comprehensive understanding of how to bring new energy and insight into the healing of suffering was pivotal in giving Tish the framework and structure for what she had dreamed of as a small child. She had finally come home.

David Christel – Senior Editor and Special Contributor

Bitten by the theatre bug at age 10, David eventually moved to New York City at age 21 to pursue a career in dance. He worked with numerous luminaries in the dance field, as well as in opera, music, television and theatre, appeared on PBS Great Performances twice, taught at many well-known schools, and traveled extensively throughout Europe and Central, South, and North America.

Upon retiring from dance in 1986, he was hired by a computer-based training company and either worked on or led projects for clients ranging from American Airlines to Halliburton Oil Company, NASA/Lockheed, Northern Telecom, NYNEX, Fireman's Fund, Boeing/McDonald-Douglas, and the Top Gun School when it was still located in San Diego. David also taught offices in Canada and throughout the U.S. in computer-based training methodology, design, technical writing, and on-line course authoring.

In 1982, he began working with Persons With AIDS (PWAs) in New York and upon moving to San Diego, founded the AIDS Response Wholistic Health Program at a major Community Center. He returned to school to attain a Master's in Counseling Psychology continuing to work with PWAs and their families, and facilitating numerous support and therapy groups.

Currently, David is an editor, ghost writes books for well-known individuals, is involved in several book collaborations, is working on five books of his own, teaches yoga, and devotes numerous hours to community service.

Dr. John J. Hudy – Research Director

John Hudy served as research director for the In Our Own Words 2000 research program for three years. He has 20 years of experience as an Industrial/Organizational psychologist. His clients included many of the Fortune 500, as well as major corporations in Japan, Great Britain, France, and Sweden. His expertise has been applied to projects involving: Organizational Development, Coaching and Facilitation, Performance

Management, Organizational Culture Surveys, Psychometric Assessment, and Computerized Assessment & Feedback Tools.

Dr. Hudy was on the ad-hoc Editorial Review Board for The Academy of Management REVIEW, was published in professional journals, and served as an invited speaker at various Human Resource-oriented conventions. He was a member of the Academy of Management, the American Psychological Society, and the University of South Florida Psychology Foundation.

John enjoyed his music enormously and often played with a group of other musicians. He had a lifelong passion for identifying patterns for social and personal transformation. Thank you, John, for everything!

Contact Information

Contact us for more information about our work, to explore new ideas and approaches to life or the world situation, or just to let us know what you think!

www.pfcn.net/newamerica.html

POSITIVE FUTURE CONSULTING
A division of The Global Interchange

P.O. Box 1179, Point Reyes Station, CA
94956-1179 USA • info@pfcn.net